S0-BRQ-620

POLITICS IN SRI LANKA 1947–1973

By the same author

ELECTORAL POLITICS IN AN EMERGENT STATE: THE CEYLON GENERAL ELECTION OF MAY 1970

Politics in Sri Lanka 1947–1973

A. JEYARATNAM WILSON

Professor and Chairman, Department of Political Science
University of New Brunswick
formerly Professor of Political Science and Head,
Department of Economics and Political Science
University of Sri Lanka

ST. MARTIN'S PRESS NEW YORK

St. Martin's Press, Inc., 175 Fifth Avenue, New York, N.Y. 10010
Printed in Great Britain
Library of Congress Catalog Card Number: 73–90319
First published in the United States of America in 1974

AFFILIATED PUBLISHERS:
Machillan Limited, London –
also at Bombay, Calcutta, Madras and Melbourne

For Süsili and Malliha, Maithili and Kümanan

Contents

List of Maps and Tables

Acknowledgements

This work is the result of many many years of research on and first-hand observation of political developments in Sri Lanka since 1947.

The many hundreds of students I taught at the University of Sri Lanka during 1952–72 helped me tremendously in the formulation of my views, theories and interpretations by their immediate and critical responses in classroom discussions, and to them I owe special thanks.

There are close friends in Peradeniya from whose criticisms and observations I benefited greatly. I should like to make particular mention of Professor K. M. de Silva for his unfailing generosity and helpful advice. Professors W. J. F. Labrooy, H. A. de S. Gunasekere, Mr H. A. I. Goonetilleke, Professor Stanley Kalpagè, Drs B. Hewavitharana and W. A. Wiswa Warnapala also had long conversations with me on various aspects of this work. Outside Sri Lanka, Professor Dennis Austin of the Victoria University of Manchester, Professor George Lerski of the University of San Francisco, Professor Ferdinand Hermens, formerly of the University of Cologne and presently Fellow of the Woodrow Wilson International Center for Scholars, Washington, and Dr Calvin Woodward of the University of New Brunswick were helpful. I am grateful to the latter and to Brown University Press for permission to base my two maps on the map in Woodward's *The Growth of a Party System in Ceylon.* Needless to say the responsibility for any errors are mine.

I am specially grateful to Mrs N. M. Hettiaratchi of Peradeniya for patiently typing several drafts of this book. Many thanks are also due to Mrs Rheta MacElwain of the University of New Brunswick for making an accurate typescript of the final draft.

My wife Süsili and my children Malliha, Maithili and Kümanan showed forbearance and patience while I was on this project through the years. To my younger brother, Mr R. K. Wilson, I owe a debt for supplying me with essential documents almost at a moment's notice.

I owe much to Mr Tim Farmiloe of Macmillan for his patience whilst awaiting the completed manuscript and for the encouragement he gave me in this endeavour. Mr H. W. Bawden of the same firm did everything possible to bring out this publication in good time, and I am grateful to him for all his efforts.

A.J.W.

Fredericton
April 1973

List of Abbreviations

Note, Ceylon and Sri Lanka, as used in this book, are interchangeable.

B.B.P.	Bosath Bandaranaike Peramuna (The Bodhisattva S.W.R.D. Bandaranaike Front). Note a bodhisattva is a being destined to be a Buddha
B.J.B.	Bauddha Jathika Balavegaya (National Front for the Protection of Buddhism)
B.L.P.I.	Bolshevik Leninist Party of India
B.R.P.	Buddhist Republican Party
B.S.P.	Bolshevik Samasamaja Party (the Bolshevik Equal Society Party)
C.P.	Communist Party (Moscow)
C.I.C.	Ceylon Indian Congress
C.W.C.	(Indian) Ceylon Workers' Congress
D.M.K.	(Ceylon) Dravida Munnethra Kazhagam (Dravidian Progressive Front)
D.P.	Dharma Samaja Party (Social Justice Party)
D.W.C.	(Indian) Democratic Workers' Congress
E.B.P.	Eksath Bhikku Peramuna (United Front of Buddhist Monks)
F.P.	(Tamil) Federal Party
I.B.R.D.	International Bank for Reconstruction and Development

I.M.F.	International Monetary Fund
I.S.F.	Islamic Socialist Front
J.V.P.	Jathika Vimukthi Peramuna (Sinhalese) National Liberation Front
L.P.	Labour Party
L.P.P.	Lanka Prajathanthrawadi Party (Ceylon Democratic Party)
L.S.S.P.	Lanka Sama Samaja Party (Ceylon Equal Society Party)
M.E.P.	Mahajana Eksath Peramuna (People's United Front)
P.L.F.	People's Liberation Front
R.P.	Republican Party
S.L.F.P.	Sri Lanka Freedom Party
S.L.F.S.P.	Sri Lanka Freedom Socialist Party
S.L.J.P.	Sri Lanka Jathika Peramuna (the Sri Lanka National Front)
S.M.P. (R. G. Senanayake)	Sinhala Mahajana Peramuna (Sinhalese People's Front)
S.M.P. (I.M.R.A. Iriyagolle)	Samajawadi Mahajana Peramuna (Socialist People's Front)
S.M.S.	Sinhala Maha Sabha (the Great Council of the Sinhalese)
S.P.	Swaraj Party
T.C.	Tamil Congress
T.R.P.	Tamil Resistance Party
T.S.R.P.	Tamil Self Rule Party
T.U.F.	Tamil United Front
U.F.	United Front (Samagi Peramuna)
U.L.C.	United Lanka Congress
U.L.F.	United Left Front
U.N.P.	United National Party
V.L.S.S.P.	Viplavakari (Revolutionary) Lanka Sama Samaja Party

Introduction

Sri Lanka was the model British crown colony that made the transition from dependence to sovereign status without rancour or violence. Transfer of power was in stages and the island's political elites were, unlike in the case of other volatile societies in Asia and Africa, voluntarily put through a gradual process of political education and experience which taught them to exercise power with moderation and democratic fervour. It was the same with the electors, the island being the first among colonial territories to have universal franchise, years before independence, as early as in 1931. The Buddhist ethos and a continuing process of modernisation even up to present times have, through the years, contributed in no small measure to generate that tolerance and accommodation which are so necessary for the satisfactory functioning of parliamentary government. Our chapter dealing with the problems of Ceylonese society spells out in detail this process of give and take, of compromise and middle-path solutions which have in fact been the guidelines of Sri Lanka's political development since the beginning of the twentieth century. Whereas in other societies, communal and religious strife have become endemic and more the rule, in Sri Lanka these have, with one or two exceptions (the Sinhalese Buddhist-Muslim disturbances of 1915 and the Sinhalese–Tamil riots of 1958), been kept within the bounds of constitutional agitation, and on occasion extra-parliamentary but non-violent protests.

The principle of buying off social discontent in order to stabilise political authority started by the British but taken over with more eagerness and less hesitation by Sri Lanka's political elites anxious to maintain themselves in the seats of power is today the insoluble problem of governments in office. The state as the supreme almsgiver is not very different from the Buddhistic view of gaining merit through the performance of good deeds. The system worked well as long as population remained at optimum levels and primary products brought good prices despite the vagaries of a fluctuating international market. But it has reached the utmost limits with the expansion of population and the instability of export prices. Achieving a balance between economic development and the maintenance of welfare services is today the unanswerable political question. That is why we have detailed at some length the nature and mechanisms of economic and social progress in Chapter 3. In Sri Lanka, as in most political societies, but somewhat more so, politics is a question of economic well-being which in terms of governmental survival means nothing more than providing as many social services as possible to the vast majority of underprivileged people. In this way violence and revolution was postponed until only the other year (the 'che guevara' rebellion of April 1971), but the price has been, in terms of arrested balanced economic growth, almost disastrous. The fact is that the problems of Sri Lanka's multi-communal society are linked with her social and economic progress and these in turn underpin constitution and government as well as patterns of political conduct and behaviour.

The question today is how long will the system last? Have we reached the limits of tolerance? Can democratic institutions survive in the context of rapid economic contraction? Political leaders pose a centralised state system of socialist democracy and a private-enterprise oriented democratic socialism as the possible alternatives. But survival is linked with increasingly pathetic dependence on assistance from the rival power blocs and international credit agencies. Nonalignment in foreign policy may suit a big nation such as India where the stakes are considerable, but will it pay much dividends to a strategic speck on the Indian Ocean? There is an unwillingness to face up to the realities due to a variety of considerations, chiefly economic and political. In the meanwhile the tendency is for governments especially of the post-1956 phase to lean on one side or the other while protesting to tread the middle path. Our chapter on foreign policy and defence arrangements seeks to describe this frustrating exercise which at times has tended towards self-stultification.

In effect democracy and parliamentary institutions in Sri Lanka today can survive only as long as artificial economic respiration can be rendered by the nations of both power groups. But will either be satisfied with a 'non-commitment' that does not go far enough to support its interests on issues that could be vital to it?

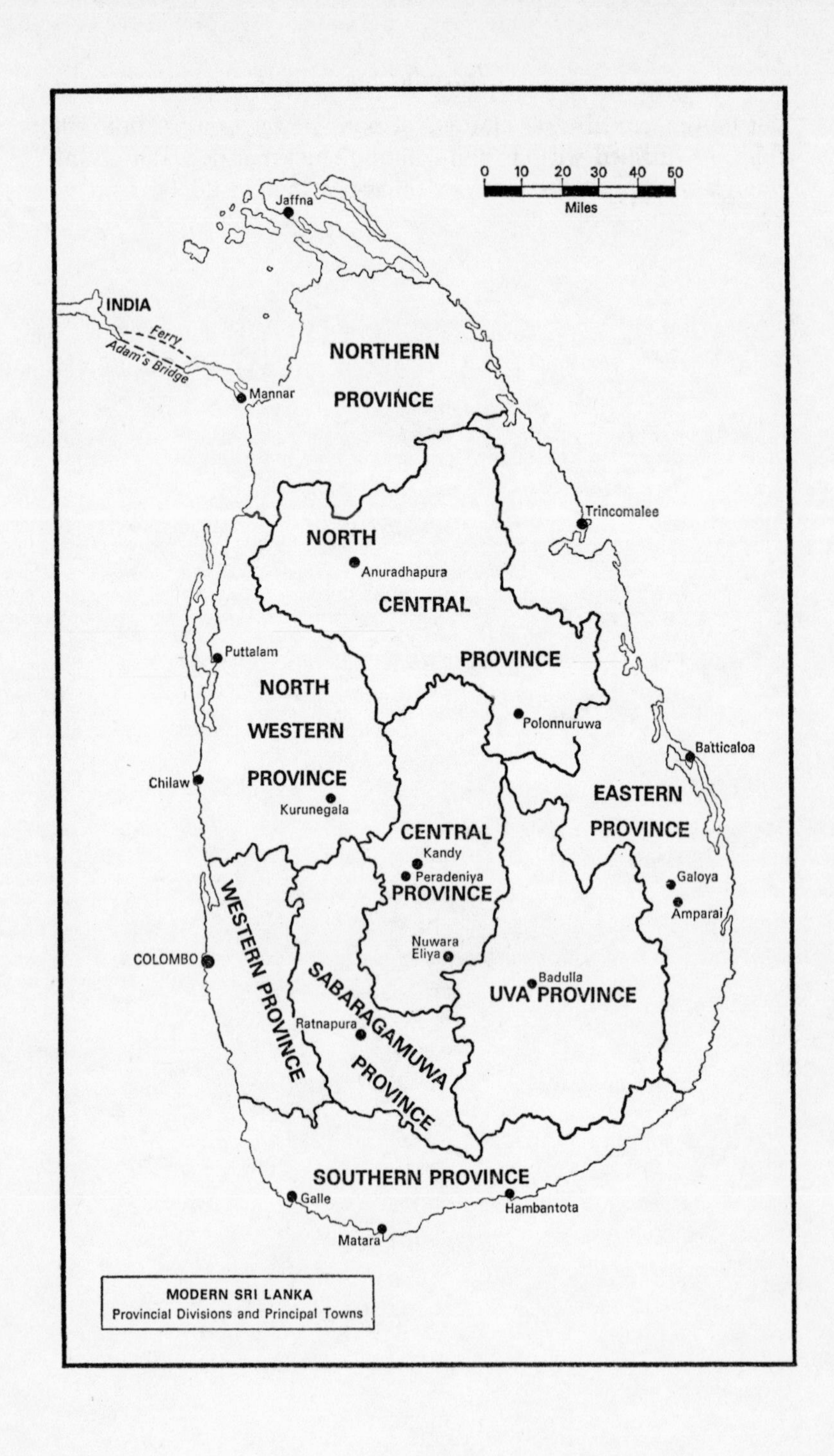

MODERN SRI LANKA

Provincial Divisions and Principal Towns

1 The Land and its History

GEOGRAPHY

Sri Lanka is some 25,332 square miles in area, almost the size of Greece, or of the Low Countries combined, or about one-half the area of England and Wales. It is 270 miles at its longest from north to south and 140 miles at its broadest from west to east. The population at the last census (1971) stood at 12,711,143 and the density per square mile in mid-1965 was 444.

The principal towns are Colombo, the metropolis and chief port, Galle, the southern capital, also an important port, Kandy, the hill capital, the seat of the last kings of Kandy where the Dalada Maligawa (the temple of the Sacred Tooth Relic of the Buddha) is located, Jaffna which is the centre of the indigenous Tamils in north Ceylon, and Batticaloa and Trincomalee on the east coast, the latter possessing one of the world's finest natural harbours.

The natural relief of the island is not very complicated. The south-central portion is a mountain mass with an elevation range of 3,000 to 7,000 feet surrounded in turn by a belt of lower elevation of 1,000 to 3,000 feet. The rest of the island is comparatively flat land, narrower on the west, east and south but containing a vast expanse of dry area towards the north.

Temperatures are comparatively high, 80° to 82°F in the plains because of the islands proximity to the equator, its situation being within the latitudes of 6° to 10°N. But this severity is to a considerable extent modified by oceanic winds, the island at its broadest being only 140 miles. On the average the temperature in the hilly zones falls 10°F for every 300 feet of elevation. Thus the temperature in Nuwara Eliya, the chief hill station which is 6,200 feet above sea level, is 60°F while at its minimum, usually in February, it is 45°F but occasionally falling to below freezing point. The areas north or north-west of the hill country and the plains in the east and north-east have the highest temperatures, usually from March to June, but these seldom exceed the blood heat (98.4°F).

The wet seasons are during the south-west (May–September) and north-east (December to February) monsoons. There are afternoon and evening conventional showers as well as depressional rains during the inter-monsoonal periods. In the dry zones of the north-west and south-east the annual average rainfall is below 40 inches while in certain places in the south-west on the slopes of the hill country, the rainfall averages to as much as over 200 inches.

THE ANCIENT CIVILISATION

Before the arrival of Vijaya, the legendary founder of the Sinhalese race, with his band of seven hundred men, at Tambapanni on the north-west coast of Sri Lanka, some time in the sixth or fifth century B.C. (no exact date as to when the exact landing took place is available), tradition has it that a human species of obscure origins referred to as *Nagas* and *Yakkhas* inhabited the island.[1] There are, however, scholars who hold to the view that a people of Dravidian stock were the earliest settlers. Basham, for example, opines that 'Dravidian infiltration into Ceylon must have been going on from the earliest historical times and probably before'.[2] It is however a proven fact that a pre-Aryan aboriginal tribe of hunters called *vaddas* lived in certain parts of the island before the arrival of the Vijayan band. These *vaddas*, according to the doyen of Sri Lanka's historians, G. C. Mendis, probably lived in southern India and walked across before the island got separated from the mainland by a stretch of sea.[3] The question of who were the original settlers, Sinhalese or Tamils, is a point of controversy between politicians and scholars of both communities.

From Vijayan times and shortly thereafter, Sri Lanka was colonised by successive bands of invaders and settlers who probably arrived from both the east and west coasts of north and central India. These people spoke an Indo-Aryan language. They settled by the shores of rivers in the northern, south-eastern and western parts of the island. They were originally engaged in pastoral occupations but in course of time they took to agriculture and spread into the interior where they developed Anuradhapura in the north, and Magama in the south, into great cities.

At first the agricultural activities of the ancient Sinhalese depended on the periodic outbursts of the monsoon, but being in the dry zone, it became evident that if success was to be guaranteed, other methods had to be found to provide the necessary supply of water. It is out of this necessity for water that the ancient Sinhalese perfected their skill in irrigation engineering. They cut channels from rivers and constructed huge tanks which were storage reservoirs, and in undertaking these displayed an amazing knowledge of hydraulic principles as well as trigonometry. These activities proceeded apace from at least the first century A.D. till about the thirteenth century.[4]

The building of great religious edifices dedicated to the promotion of Buddhism, the construction of irrigation facilites to ensure a regular supply of water, and the guarding or freeing of the country from south Indian invaders as occasion demanded were the main preoccupation of Sinhalese kings in ancient times.

Buddhism was first introduced to the island from India by Mahinda the emissary of the great Buddhist emperor, Asoka, during the reign of Devanampiya Tissa (247–207 B.C.), a king renowned for his piety and good deeds. Previously the religious beliefs of the islanders were by and large of a primitive and animistic kind. There were besides small groups practising various forms of Brahmanism, Jainism and Saivism. Most of these practices were absorbed into Buddhism, and over the years Sri Lanka evolved a kind of *theravada* Buddhism for which it has acquired a reputation among the Buddhist countries of south and south-east Asia.[5]

The Tamil invaders generated national solidarity among the Sinhalese. The first real occasion was when Elara, a prince from the Chola kingdom in south India, seized the northern Sinhalese kingdom, ruled it for forty-four years and was ultimately dislodged by the Sinhalese warrior from the southern sector of the island, Dutthagamani, who succeeded in bringing the entire island under his sway.[6] The idea of an all-island sovereignty with the northern capital, Anuradhapura, as the central seat of government, and the notion that Sri Lanka is for the Sinhalese and is the home of the Sinhalese Buddhists, can be traced back to the reign of Dutthagamani (*circa* 161–137 B.C.).

South Indian invasions reached their peak when the Cholas conquered most of the island in A.D. 1017 in pursuance of their objective of making the Bay of Bengal a Chola lake, and of monopolising the trade to Malaysia and China.

During the long years of Chola occupation (1017–70) Buddhism and the Sinhalese suffered a great deal from neglect and oppression. With it also came to an end, Anuradhapura, the centre of Sinhalese civilisation in northern Sri Lanka for well over a thousand years. The Sinhalese capital was shifted to Polonnaruva and then to other places further south. Thereafter Sinhalese history followed a chequered course. It reached, for the last time, its zenith in the reign of Parakrama Bahu the Great (1153–86).[7] After him, save for a brief decade of peace and stability, confusion reared its head in Polonnaruva and the signs of the end of a great and ancient civilisation became quite evident. It was felt that the costly wars that Parakramabahu had engaged in and his over-centralised administration contributed substantially to this decline and decadence. In course of time, in about the early years of the thirteenth century, a separate kingdom of the Tamils in the north, Jaffna, established itself.[8] It continued, except for a period of seventeen years (1450–67), when it was seized by a Sinhalese prince, Sapumal, until its subjugation by the Portuguese in 1618.

THE WESTERNERS

At the time of the Portuguese arrival in 1505, the island comprised three kingdoms, Jaffna in the north, Maha Nuwara or Kandy in the central highlands, and Kotte in the south-west maritime districts. By 1594 the Portuguese had secured undisturbed possession of these south-western districts and in 1619 they annexed Jaffna. But they met with disaster in their attempts to gain control of the central kingdom of Kandy.

The wars with Kandy led the Sinhalese kings there to seek the assistance of Portugal's rivals, the Dutch, who by war, dubious diplomacy and deceitful transactions which made the ruling Sinhalese king, Rajasinha II, legitimately feel that he had been defrauded in all of the negotiations, became rulers of the maritime districts of Ceylon in 1638.[9]

The record of Portuguese rule was not altogether sterile, for interspersed are some enduring monuments. Their brand of

Christianity, Roman Catholicism, found lasting adherents and they left behind a well-ordered educational system of churches, convents and schools. Their language survived them as did the mixed community arising from Portuguese–Sinhalese unions. They adapted the native systems of administration to their own uses and a lasting benefit was their painstaking compilation of registers of all the landholdings in their territories which they did to utilize for their purposes, as best as possible, the Sinhalese system of land tenures.

The entire period of Dutch rule in Sri Lanka could be said to have been run on a profit-and-loss basis by their Vereenigde Oost-indische Campagnie (the United East India Company). In one good year a fantastic dividend of 132·5 per cent was paid out in three instalments.[10] In another, it was 50 per cent, often it was 40 per cent, but eventually the company settled down to paying an average of 24 per cent over a period of ninety-six years.[11] The company avoided getting embroiled with Kandy save for one punitive expedition there. After an initial success, it met with the usual disasters of all foreign incursions into the central high-lands.

For obtaining the best possible revenue from local sources, the Dutch prepared most meticulously a record of registers of lands and persons, called *tombos*, subject to *rajakariya*, a system under which Sinhalese kings gave grants of land to their subjects in return for services of various kinds. They further codified the laws and customs of the Tamils of Jaffna, a compendium which came to be referred to as the *Tesavalmai*, as well as those of the Muslim faith. Since the Sinhalese of the lowlands did not have a single coherent system, they superimposed on them their Roman-Dutch laws, a legal system which continues to this day. In their efforts to spread Dutch Protestantism, however, they failed to obtain many adherents.

Dissatisfaction with the Dutch finally made Kandy deal with the English East India Company which in 1795 entered into a treaty very favourable to the reigning monarch of the time, the Malabari, Rajadi Rajasinha (1780–98). In the following year, Dutch power in Ceylon passed into the hands of the English company.

The English company administered the maritime districts on a commercial basis during 1796–8. This caused a revolt among the natives in late 1796 leading to the intervention of the home government which in 1798 imposed a dual administration comprising itself and the company. The arrangements did not work well and on 1 January 1802, the maritime provinces were transferred to the sole control of the British crown. In the years that followed the British, like their predecessors, got involved in the affairs of Kandy. Their first expedition ended in complete failure in 1803 but in 1815 they succeeded in capturing the kingdom with the assistance of the majority of its chiefs who were incensed by the tyranny of the Malabar ruler, Sri Vikrama Rajasinha. Under the Kandyan Convention of 2 March 1815, signed between the British and the chiefs of the kingdom, the latter were guaranteed their 'right, privileges and power'; Britain undertook to uphold the ancient laws and customs 'according to the established forms and by the ordinary authorities', to declare inviolable the religion of the Buddha and to maintain and protect 'its rites, ministers and places of worship'.[12] These were onerous obligations which ultimately ended in each side accusing the other of backsliding. The formidable Kandyan rebellion of 1817–18 which followed was put down ruthlessly and Britain, in consequence, opted out of the terms of the Convention. An aftermath of the rebellion was the colonial administration's decision to bring the entire island under a single unified set-up with an adequate network of communications especially into the central highlands as an insurance against similar uprisings in the future. Kandy made one more such attempt in 1848 but on this occasion the military authorities put down the disturbances with ease and a use of force not warranted by the circumstances.[13]

The first steps towards unified administration were taken when the Colebrooke–Cameron Royal Commission of Inquiry made its recommendations in 1831.[14] Legislative and executive councils were established, an exclusive civil service organised and the Kandyan provinces which had hitherto been governed separately integrated with the rest of the island.

The years that followed saw the island go through long periods of prosperity interspersed with occasional economic recesses. For over sixty years, till 1886, king coffee ruled the roost under conditions made most favourable to British investors by the colonial government's land policies. The crown lands encroachment ordinance of 1840 which stipulated that 'all forest, waste, unocuppied or uncultivated lands shall be presumed to be the property of the crown until the contrary be proved' was the most glaring example of this policy of taking over lands and alienating them to speculators and investors at ridiculously low prices. By the 1880s, however, coffee was on its way out.[15] The fell coffee disease, *hemileia vastatrix*, coupled with competition from the cheaper Brazilian coffee, put an end to the coffee boom but it was soon replaced by other rewarding commercial products, primarily tea, and rubber too.[16] Compared with tea, there was greater Ceylonese investment in rubber while coconut remained the major industry of local smallholders.

The fairly buoyant economic conditions that prevailed in the second half of the nineteenth century produced an English-educated Ceylonese middle class which was western-oriented in its political outlook. They gradually replaced the Britishers and Burghers who were actively involved in the movement for constitutional reform in the earlier years. These Britishers had sought change as a method of expediting the development of a network of communications that would benefit the plantation industry. The Ceylonese middle class on the other hand desired constitutional advancement mainly to secure, progressively, positions in the middle and higher rungs of the country's administrative set up.

By the closing years of the nineteenth century and the first decade of the twentieth, many associations and societies had been formed by local men of property and the professional classes for addressing memorials, petitions and prayers to the secretary of state for the colonies towards this end. These reached coalescence with the formation of a Ceylonese National Congress in December 1919. Alongside this reforms movement which embraced the westernised middle and upper layers of Ceylon's plural society, there flourished a Sinhalese nationalism wholly devoted to the promotion of the Buddhist cause to the exclusion of all others.[17]

The imperial response was reform in stages. Changes effected in the composition of the Legislative Council in 1909 and 1920, however, did not go far enough to satisfy the Ceylonese reformers despite the introduction of the elective principle on a very limited scale.[18] In 1923, the Legislative Council was expanded so as to have a majority of Ceylonese unofficial members with a large elective element.[19] But the franchise was restrictive, extending to only 4 per cent of the island's population. Representation through the years and even after 1923 continued to be largely communal in character. At this stage a cleavage occurred between the Sinhalese and the Ceylon Tamils. While the latter, with support from other minority groups, namely Indians, Muslims, Burghers and Europeans, wished communal representation to be maintained, the Sinhalese reformers asked for the introduction of the territorial principle. This they obtained in 1931 under the Donoughmore reforms but with universal adult franchise. On the latter, however, they were not altogether enthusiastic.

The *raison d'être* for the appointment of a royal commission under the Earl of Donoughmore in 1927 was to investigate the failure of the 1923 experiment in representative government. It was felt that the Ceylonese unofficial majority in the Legislative Council had exercised 'power without responsibility' to the utmost discomfiture of a British-dominated minority executive as well as British officialdom in Ceylon.[20]

The core of the Donoughmore system was government by executive committees. It was based on the organisation of the London County Council. The legislature, the State Council, after a general election divided itself into seven executive committees each of which was placed in charge of a group of government departments and each of which elected its own chairman who became the minister in charge of the various departments in its control. There were besides three officers of state, all Englishmen, responsible for (1) the administration of the public services, defence and external affairs (the chief secretary); (2) legal and judicial matters (the legal secretary); and (3) finance (the financial secretary).[21] The three officers of state and the seven chairmen formed a board of ministers. The board, however, was not in the overall charge of a chief minister nor did it adhere to any principles of collective responsibility save in respect of the annual budget.[22]

The executive committee system provided an invaluable training in administrative matters to the Ceylonese members of the State Council. It permitted members of minority groups, political, economic, social, racial and religious, a voice in the decision-making process. But the private member gained undue importance, the growth of a healthy party system was inhibited, and, as a perspicacious governor correctly remarked, the system prevented 'the fixation and concentration either of policy or of responsibility'.[23]

Communal tensions were exacerbated during the period of the Donoughmore constitution (1931–47) because the Sinhalese desired further change and utilised the power they had obtained to improve the conditions of the Sinhalese electorates, while the minority groups, especially the Ceylon Tamils, felt neglected and 'dominated' and at every stage demanded safeguards which, however, were construed by the Sinhalese reformers as impedimental to the path of self-government. The pan-Sinhalese board of ministers elected by the State Council after the general election of 1936 was the Sinhalese answer to this growing minority 'perverseness'. However, it served only to further worsen inter-group relationships and the situation reached its nadir with the formation of the Sinhala Maha Sabha (the Great Council of the Sinhalese) by S. W. R. D. Bandaranaike in 1937 and the All Ceylon Tamil Congress in 1944. Other communal organisations such as the All Ceylon Moors' Association (1935), the Burgher Political Association (1938) and the Ceylon Indian Congress (1939) also made their appearance, while the European Association (1918), the All Ceylon Malay Association (1922) and the Ceylon Muslim League (1924) formed in the previous decade continued to thrive. There was one man who tried to stand above all this communal conflict and function as a conciliator amidst all the rival claims and counter-claims of the various ethnic-oriented organisations. He was D. S. Senanayake, the leading conservative Sinhalese statesman from the mid-1930s to his death in March 1952. It was to him that the British ultimately transferred power in February 1948.[24]

In recognition of Sri Lanka's contribution to the war effort, the imperial government had in 1943 given the board of ministers the assurance of further advancement towards responsible government. In furtherance of this, the board was required to draft a constitution providing for internal self-government which should find acceptance among 75 per cent of the full membership of the State Council. The draft was ultimately the result of the endeavours of D. S. Senanayake and his constitutional adviser, Ivor Jennings, at this time Principal of the Ceylon University College. The Senanayake–Jennings draft provided for minority safeguards, a territorial system of representation weighted in favour of the backward as well as the rural districts of Ceylon which at the same time benefited the areas where the principal indigenous minority groups, the Ceylon Tamils and the Muslims, mainly resided, and most importantly, the cabinet system of government. It came to be referred to as the ministers' *Draft Scheme* of 1944.[25]

Fears expressed by minority groups as to the efficacy of these safeguards persuaded the imperial government to appoint a royal commission of enquiry headed by Lord Soulbury. The commission visited Ceylon during 1944–5 and eventually recommended a constitution very similar to the minister's *Draft Scheme* with a few modifications – added safeguards for the minorities and a second chamber.[26] The ministers had left this latter question for decision by their proposed unicameral legislature.

The Soulbury Report and the imperial government's proposals on it were embodied in a White Paper and presented to the State Council for debate and decision. D. S. Senanayake recommended its acceptance and it passed through the State Council with only two dissentients. The general election which followed in August-September 1947 under the Soulbury constitution gave D. S. Senanayake's newly formed political grouping, the U.N.P., the largest number of seats, though not a majority, in the House of Representatives. He was appointed prime minister by the British governor, Sir Henry Monck-Mason Moore. In the months that followed, Senanayake, ably assisted by his wily lieutenant, Oliver Goonetilleke, conducted negotiations with His Majesty's government resulting in the conclusion in November 1947 of three agreements relating to defence, external affairs and public officers.[27] In December of that year, the British Parliament adopted the Ceylon Independence Act and with the consent of the Senanayake government had 4 February 1948 as the appointed date on which Sri Lanka was to pass into sovereign statehood.

2 Problems in a Plural Society

ECONOMIC RIVALRIES

Sri Lanka is a mosaic of ethnic, religious and social groups in which the Sinhalese Buddhists (Low Country and Kandyan) form the sizeable majority.* This majority had been neglected during the long years of western rule. Nor were their grievances looked into with sympathy by post-independence governments of the 1948–56 phase.

Further, these Buddhists, in particular their indigenous-oriented elites, entertain fears in respect of two important minority groupings.

They complain that the Ceylon Tamils have a disproportionate share of jobs in the public and private sectors, and when taken with the one million odd Indian Tamils they tend to regard the total Tamil population as a threat to the existence of the Sinhalese race especially when viewed in the context of neighbouring south India's Dravidian millions.

The Christians (the majority of whom are Sinhalese and the rest Tamils and Burghers) pose as big a problem. Their efficient organisation and their superior resources, the Sinhalese Buddhists opine, are a menace to the stability of their social and religious structures.

* The census of population of 1971 gives the distribution of population as follows: Low Country Sinhalese 5,445,706 (42.8 per cent), Kandyan Sinhalese 3,700,973 (29.1 per cent), Ceylon Tamils 1,415,567 (11.1 per cent), Indian Tamils 1,195,368 (9.4 per cent), Ceylon Moors 824,291 (6.4 per cent), Indian Moors 29,416 (0.2 per cent), Burghers 44,250 (0.3 per cent), Malays 41,615 (0.3 per cent) and others (mainly Britishers and other foreigners) 13,957 (0.1 per cent).

Religionwise the Sinhalese Buddhists are 8,567,570 (67.4 per cent), Hindus (Ceylon and Indian Tamils) 2,239,310 (17.6 per cent), Muslims (Ceylon Moors, Indian Moors and Malays) 909,941 (7.1 per cent), Roman Catholics (Sinhalese and Tamils) (6.9 per cent), and other Christians (Sinhalese and Tamils) 103,576 (0.8 per cent).

Political styles and patterns of governmental conduct are therefore influenced by pressures from the Sinhalese Buddhists. Populism affords a short cut to electoral success but in the implementation of the solutions advocated, governments have encountered stiff opposition from the minority groups affected. Consequently 'middle-path' compromises result, claimed to be in keeping with the Sinhalese Buddhist ethos which avoids extremes, and these obtain approval from the majority of people who do not want trouble during their lifetime.

Two Surveys conducted by the Central Bank of Ceylon in 1953 and 1963 provide evidence of prevailing discontent.[1] The Survey of 1963 indicated that more than half the total Indian Tamil population (51·4 per cent) was employed, compared to a little less than a quarter of the total Kandyan Sinhalese population.

A comparison of the Surveys of 1953 and 1963 show that the income gain (arithmetic mean, before taxation) of the Kandyan Sinhalese and Low Country Sinhalese was 20 per cent and 26 per cent respectively, whereas that of the Ceylon Tamils was 31 per cent. The Ceylon Tamils also had a larger increase in per capita income while the Indian Tamils enjoyed a higher per capita income than the Sinhalese (Kandyan and Low Country) in 1953 and higher than that of the Kandyan Sinhalese in 1963.

The employment figures reveal an all-round improvement in respect of all other groups, as between the years 1953 and 1963, except the Ceylon Tamils. The latter showed a rise in unemployment. Partly this was due to increasing Sinhalese Buddhist ethnocentricity in the years after 1954 and consequent discrimination against Ceylon Tamils in public sector jobs.

Figures in the field of higher education provide more evidence of the reasons for continuing rivalry and antagonism between the groups concerned. A study conducted by a member of the University of Ceylon's sociology department reveals that disproportionate numbers of Ceylon Tamils obtained places in the science, engineering and medical faculties (employment for graduates from these faculties being more certain) compared to Sinhalese, while larger numbers of Christians entered the university than their population warranted.[2]

More pertinent than all these considerations, however, is the fact that in Sri Lanka's society as a whole, a wide social and economic gulf separates the English-educated from the Sinhalese- and Tamil-educated. This is to some extent being narrowed with the English-language medium in primary, secondary, and university education being progressively if not altogether eliminated. The English-educated social class, however, is self-perpetuating in that it transmits the benefits and values of its orientation not only to its immediate dependants but to those with whom it communicates educationally and politically. The books in history, geography, civics and economics used in schools and universities are Sinhalese and Tamil translations of English texts, or have been specially written for schools and universities by persons who have had some or all of their education in English. Modern, if not western concepts are transmitted in this way.

Political leadership still comes from this English-speaking class. Though the indigenous intelligentsia is now a powerful force, it has not yet thrown up an articulate leadership with a style of its own. The English-educated political elites therefore play a complex role. They are split into rightists, conservative-minded democratic socialists, centrists, left wingers, and ethnic and religious oriented protagonists of the Sinhalese, Tamil or Roman Catholic positions. Generally, however, the English-speaking elites have succeeded in preventing Sri Lanka from going in the direction of a theocratic or a Sinhalese Buddhist oriented polity.

ECONOMIC INEQUALITIES

The occupational distribution of the island's population indicates that a majority is engaged in agriculture. The 1963 Survey estimated that 51.8 per cent were involved in agriculture and forestry while the wholesale and retail trade employed 7.9 per cent, industries and crafts 7.3, transport and communications 4.6, and government services 2.3. In terms of employment status, the 1963 figures indicated that 60.41 per cent of the estimated workforce of 3,077,568 were paid employees while 28.85 per cent were self-employed and the rest belonged to the category of employers (2.44 per cent) and unpaid family workers (8.20 per cent).[3]

Employment in government departments and semi-government institutions (public corporations, universities, research institutes, boards etc.) still remains the highest aspiration of most people who have some kind of educational qualification. The majority of those in these sectors belong to the category of subordinate, minor and casual employees while a relatively small proportion is in the administrative, technical and professional staff grades. There was a total number of 303,674 employees in the public service in 1970. The average all inclusive salary per month was Rs 273, but there were as many as 178,129 drawing less than this amount.[4]

Employment in government departments is prestigious and provides security of service besides other benefits such as pensions, holiday travel warrants, better leave facilities, more public holidays than for those employed in the private sector and greater promotional prospects. Further, wage scales of government employees in the lower and middle categories are much better than in most private sector establishments.

In the private sector, especially in a large number of establishments which come under the Shop and Office Employees Act of 1954 including banks, and in wages boards trades and allied trades, schemes of wage scales are fixed from time to time by negotiation. Since 1959 the majority of workers in these sectors is assured of superannuation benefits under the terms of the Employees Provident Fund Act. At the end of 1968 there were 1.7 million employees registered under the Act.

Income distribution according to the 1963 Survey showed wide disparities.

The overwhelming majority of income receivers, 84.14 per cent, received salaries of between Rs 25 and Rs 200 a month and as many as 45.9 per cent of income receivers got salaries of between Rs 25 and Rs 75 a month. Income was defined as 'receipts from work and property, transfers and other receipts that added to the spending power of an individual'.[5]

There was besides a big disparity between incomes earned in the urban and rural sectors. Average income per month inclusive of income in kind (such as goods produced and consumed at home, goods received free as for example meals, lodging, and purchases of goods from the workplace at discount rates) was a little more than double (Rs 255.09) in the urban sector than in the rural (Rs 127.01).[6]

A preliminary report of a socio-economic survey conducted by the Department of Census and Statistics and released in April 1972 showed even more alarming disparities in income.[7] Over nine million people or nearly three-quarters of the total population received no income at all. Of the remaining 3.5 million, about half received monthly incomes ranging from Rs 100 to Rs 400 while the other half received less than Rs 100. There were only 175,000 in the island's entire population who received incomes exceeding Rs 400 per month.

The scale of indebtedness is considerable. The 1963 Survey showed that 95.67 per cent of income receivers in the island with average income levels of Rs 800 per two months were net dis-savers.[8] The socio-economic survey, April 1972, showed no improvement in the situation. The average household comprising six persons, it stated, received an average monthly income of Rs 298 but spent as much as Rs 325.65 on consumption alone. Loans were mainly obtained from friends and relatives revealing the extent to which society is closely knit.[9]

ETHNIC AND RELIGIOUS RIVALRIES

Sinhalese Buddhist Grievances

Broadly there are three aspects to the Sinhalese Buddhist problem: (1) education and employment; (2) religion and the national culture, which in effect means Sinhalese culture; and (3) language. All of these are in fact interconnected. It is the Sinhalese Buddhist view that these are urgent questions which must engage the immediate attention of the state.

Until the advent of S. W. R. D. Bandaranaike's S.L.F.P. in 1951, no political party was willing to involve itself in what was thought at that time to be sectarian politics. The U.N.P., owing to its inter-group character, was unwilling to create discord among its constituent elements, while the Marxist parties insisted on maintaining their secularism, focusing their attention on the economic and social problems of the day.

On education, the Sinhalese Buddhists began by asking that religious instruction be imparted to Buddhist children attending schools run by the Roman Catholic and Protestant missionary organisations. The Buddhist demand arose from the anxiety that these Christian institutions were being utilised as vehicles for proselytisation and conversion. The Christian response was one of outright refusal.

There were other legitimate grievances as well. The best schools were owned by the Christians. The alumni of these schools had better opportunities of securing employment in the public and private sectors.

Christian intransigence only resulted in an escalation of the Buddhist demands – that the schools themselves should be taken over by the state. But this did not gain momentum till the mid-1950s. In the meanwhile the Christians were able to hold their ground, especially the Roman Catholic Church, in return for the political support they gave the U.N.P. Neither the S.L.F.P. nor the left-wing parties wished to nationalise the schools until the matter became a strong political issue.

Parallel to the demand for better educational facilities for Buddhist children was the view that the latter were denied the employment that was due to them in proportion to their population in the country, a view reinforced by the fact that a number of important positions in the public services and the armed forces was held by Christians (particularly Roman Catholics) and Ceylon Tamils.

The Buddhist militants and activists launched virulent attacks on what they alleged were the insidious workings of 'Catholic Action' and Ceylon Tamil communalism. They accused the English-educated Sinhalese political elites of the time of not taking 'corrective action'.

From the Sinhalese Buddhist angle there were three ways of dealing with this situation.

First, make the mother tongue the compulsory medium of instruction at all levels in the educational system – in effect from the kindergarten to the university. This became accepted state policy. Once the mother tongue principle was adopted, it was hoped that admissions to the institutes of higher learning, especially to the faculties of science, medicine and engineering in the universities could be regulated on a proportionate basis in relation to religion and race.

Secondly, declare Sinhalese the sole official language throughout the country. This, it was hoped, would throw out most of the English-educated Sinhalese and the Ceylon Tamils from the positions they held in the public services. It would also, it was expected, make it difficult in the future for the Ceylon Tamils to enter the public services. However, the acceptance of the principle by all Sinhalese political parties (at various times) did not bring about *all* the results that were anticipated, because the policy of having Sinhalese as the only official language was qualified by provisions for 'the reasonable use of the Tamil language' in education, and in certain administrative spheres.

The demand for employment on the basis of religion and race and for key appointments to be reserved for Sinhalese Buddhists was not conceded even by the pro-Buddhist Bandaranaike governments of 1956 or 1960.

Thirdly, nationalise the schools which in turn would, it was thought, right the balance in the public services.

The principal instrument of Buddhist pressure politics at the time, the Unofficial Buddhist Committee of Inquiry appointed by the All Ceylon Buddhist Congress in 1953 to go into all aspects of the Buddhist question in Sri Lanka, in its Report of 1955, condemned Section 29(2) of the Ceylon constitution which prohibited legislative discrimination on racial or religious grounds.[10] The Committee asked that all denominational schools be taken over by the state by 1 January 1958. The substance of this demand was met when Mrs Bandaranaike's S.L.F.P. government nationalised the majority of schools in 1960–1.

The Roman Catholic laity at first resisted the nationalisation by occupying the schools, but later withdrew after the intervention of the head of the Catholic hierarchy in India, Cardinal Gracias. It was reported that Mrs Bandaranaike's government gave the assurance that those schools which opted to remain as privately run institutions would not be taken over, provided they conformed to requirements laid down by the state.

The M.E.P. of S. W. R. D. Bandaranaike had given vague undertakings to the All Ceylon Buddhist Congress on the schools question at the general election of 1956. But in office it was beset with the problems resulting from the official language question and stalled on this matter.

The second aspect of the Buddhist problem related to fears of religon and culture being undermined by the process of deracination that had set in from westernisation and the activities of Christian proselytising agencies. Protests went unheeded until

1956 when the vehicle of Buddhist nationalism, the M.E.P., rode to power.

The U.N.P. governments of the post-independence phase (1948–56) extended a measure of patronage to Buddhism but were unwilling to move against Christian agencies. D. S. Senanayake's government officially participated in the religious celebrations connected with the arrival of the Buddha relics from Sanchi in India and in 1951 provided a sizeable financial subsidy for specific Buddhist activities to the government of Burma. But at the general election of 1952, the U.N.P. under Dudley Senanayake's leadership, in countering the S.L.F.P.'s call for the state to provide greater facilities for the propagation of Buddhism declared in its manifesto that there was no need to render any special assistance to 'the great religion of the Buddha'. The party further took pride in the fact that it had treated all religions alike. The Kotelawala government for its part helped finance the renovations to the Temple of the Sacred Tooth of the Buddha, subsidised the Vidyalankara Pirivena in its programme for revising the Buddhist scriptures and compiling an encyclopaedia on Buddhism in the English language, and in 1956 took an active interest in the Buddha Jayanti celebrations. But the fears of the Buddhists were aggravated when the government, in its election manifesto of 1956, insisted that while it had taken note of the fact that Buddhism was being practised by the vast majority of people, it would, 'consistent with the true principles of democracy continue to recognise the policy of non-discrimination on religious grounds which is embodied in our constitution'.

The unofficial Buddhist Committee had in its Report demanded a ban on Christian activities and more specifically that Ceylon should not be allowed to become 'an eastern outpost of the Vatican'.[11] Further, it asked that: (1) statutory provision be made for the head of state, the prime minister, the chiefs of the armed forces and heads of all important departments of state to be Sinhalese Buddhists; (2) admissions to the universities and the public services be in proportion to the island's racial and religious composition; and (3) that the state follow the traditions of the ancient Sinhalese kingdom, accord Buddhism adequate recognition on ceremonial occasions, and give it the status of an official religion.

The M.E.P. government went to some lengths to accommodate

these demands but was not prepared to go all the way. Between 1956 and 1959 it established a department of cultural affairs with the emphasis mainly on Sinhalese Buddhist culture, effected a reallocation of public holidays in favour of the Buddhists where formerly these had been weighted in favour of the Christians, raised the two main seats of Buddhist learning, Vidyodaya and Vidyalankara pirivenas, to university status, reorganised the system of *ayurveda* (indigenous medicine), appointed a Buddha Sasana Commission to make recommendations for the reform of the *sangha* (the Buddhist clergy) and for 'according Buddhism its rightful place in Sri Lanka', and took steps to curb the proselytising activities of Christian organisations by terminating the services of Roman Catholic nursing nuns in state hospitals and bringing the income and properties of religious bodies under taxation, but these failed to satisfy the Buddhist militants.

The nationalisation of schools by Mrs Bandaranaike's S.L.F.P. government (1960–5) as well as other steps taken during its term of office reassured Buddhist opinion. The government's proposal to control the construction of places of religious worship was aimed at Christians. It was not proceeded with, but it had the desired effect. When Mrs Bandaranaike coalesced with the L.S.S.P. in 1964, the new coalition government proposed to guarantee Buddhism its proper place while assuring freedom of worship to other religions. But before legislation could be enacted, the coalition was defeated on a parliamentary vote of no-confidence on the question of its failure to bring down the cost of living.

When the U.N.P. regained office in 1965 as the senior partner in a seven party 'national government' headed by Dudley Senanayake, it showed greater concern for the problems of the Buddhists than it had done in its 1948–56 phase. The new government proceeds to substitute the Buddhist *poya* weekend for the sabbath.[12] The change estranged the Catholics. Nor did it impress the Buddhist militants. The latter were sceptical of the government's *bona fides* in view of its alliance with the two principal Tamil political groupings, the F.P. and the C.W.C. Further, the government shied from its promise to the Roman Catholic Church of providing a measure of relief to privately run schools. The hierarchy was angered.

The Sinhalese Buddhists came closest to their objective with the promulgation of a new republican constitution in May 1972 by Mrs Bandaranaike's U.F. government. The second chapter of the constitution is entitled 'Buddhism' and it declares that the republic 'shall give to Buddhism the foremost place and accordingly it shall be the duty of the state to protect and foster Buddhism' while assuring other religions of their due rights. When this is translated into legislation, it could amount to Buddhism having almost the status of an official religion.

It was on the third aspect of the Sinhalese Buddhist problem – language – that bitter conflict arose between the Sinhalese and Ceylon Tamlis. The demand to make the Sinhalese language the sole official language arose from a mixture of motives. Primarily the motivation was cultural and economic. There was widespread anxiety that the process of deracination gaining ground among the middle and upper rungs of Sinhalese society would ultimately destroy the Sinhalese language, Sinhalese culture, and Sinhalese Buddhism. There was besides fear of Tamil 'domination' from south India. But above all there was antagonism to the presence of large numbers of Ceylon Tamils in the public services.

The U.N.P. governments of 1947–56 had, far from helping towards allaying these fears, actually aggravated them by their indifference and lack of sympathy for any moves to give the Sinhalese language a place of prominence. Even as late as in 1955, for instance, English was the primary language of debate in Parliament, while in the administrative sphere the English language continued to be used for almost all official purposes except in transactious or correspondence with the general public, when Sinhalese or Tamil was utilised, more as a matter of discretion than as a fact of accepted state policy.

By having Sinhalese made the *only* official language, the Sinhalese-educated hoped that they would dethrone the English-educated (both Sinhalese and Ceylon Tamils) from their priviledged positions and consequently have greater employment opportunities made available to them. They achieved a measure of success in the latter objective, but their hopes were not realised in regard to the former. They succeeded only to the extent that they had English removed from its position of primacy in the official sphere, and as the medium of instruction in the educational sector both in the secondary schools and at university levels.

Fear of cultural swamping from south India has also been a matter of concern to Sinhalese Buddhist nationalist opinion. Bandaranaike himself gave expression to these misgivings during the language debate in the House of Representatives in October 1955 when he said:[13]

> I believe there are a not inconsiderable number of Tamils in this country out of a population of eight million. Then there are forty or fifty million people just adjoining, and what about all this Tamil literature, Tamil teachers, even the films, papers, magazines, so that the Tamils in our country are not restricted to the northern and eastern provinces alone; there are a large number, I suppose over ten lakhs, in Sinhalese provinces. And what about the Indian labourers whose return to India is now just fading away into the dim and distant future? The fact that in the towns and villages, in business houses and in boutiques most of the work is in the hands of Tamil-speaking people will inevitably result in a fear, and I do not think an unjustified fear, of the inexorable shrinking of the Sinhalese language. . . .

Fifteen years later, a leading L.S.S.P. theoretician articulated similar views when, in explaining the minority complex of the Sinhalese vis-à-vis the Tamils of Ceylon and south India, he wrote:[14]

> . . . in the same way as it is necessary to provide special assurance to the smaller nationalities in other countries for building national unity, it is necessary to provide special assurance to the Sinhalese people for the sake of building national unity in this country.

The Sinhalese language movement was driven by a sense of urgency in the years from 1953 onwards because of (1) the misunderstandings created by the current interpretations given to the formula 'parity of status' for the Sinhalese and Tamil languages, which of course was skilfully exploited by those sections of the Sinhalese political leadership eager to ride the Sinhalese wave; and (2) the refusal of the U.N.P. (in the beginning) and left-wing parties at that time to toe the line.

Many sections of Sinhalese opinion believed that 'parity of status' implied a quantitative proposition which in its ultimate form would mean that all official records without exception would have to be maintained in both languages throughout the length and breadth of the island. There was further the almost universal view among Sinhalese that such a policy would lead to every Sinhalese child having to learn Tamil. Some sections of the Sinhalese elites felt that a step of this nature could lead Sinhalese children to become increasingly attracted to adopt the Tamil language since the latter, because of larger population and better financial resources, would have a more advanced literature to offer than the Sinhalese language.

The U.N.P. prime minister of the time, Sir John Kotelawala, added to the prevailing confusion and aggravated existing fears and anxieties by his ill-considered pronouncements, contradictory and sometimes equivocative, on the language question. At first the prime minister publicly pledged that he would legislate for parity of status for both languages. Later the U.N.P., in the face of mounting Sinhalese opposition, at its special conference in February 1956, reversed this position and declared for Sinhalese as the *only* official language. The move failed to convince the militants. The S.L.F.P. too changed its stance, earlier than the U.N.P., from Sinhalese and Tamil as official languages to Sinhalese as the *only* official language. But the party also added that it would allow provision for 'the reasonable use of the Tamil language'. The militants willingly accepted the *bona fides* of the S.L.F.P.

In office, the S.L.F.P.'s leader, Bandaranaike, would have preferred to bide his time in implementing his pledges on language. The prime minister's initial draft contained many provisions for the use of the Tamil language. These were rejected by his parliamentary group for a one-sentence legislative proposal that Sinhalese shall be the one official language throughout the island subject to the proviso that its full implementation could be postponed till 31 December 1960, depending on the conveniences of the administration. The prime minister utilised this saving clause to postpone an immediate switch-over to Sinhalese. He was well aware of the problems facing the administration. He also wished in the interim period to seek an accommodation with the Tamils.

In August 1958 Bandaranaike had Parliament enact the Tamil Language (Special Provisions) Act which provided for the use of the Tamil language in secondary and university education, in all public examinations, for correspondence with public officials and for certain 'prescribed administrative purposes' in the Tamil-speaking northern and eastern provinces. Regulations were necessary to give effect to these 'prescribed administrative purposes' and parliamentary sanction had to be obtained for their implementation, but these were not framed during the prime minister's lifetime.

During Mrs Bandaranaike's first term as prime minister (1960–5) the implementation of the official language was enforced with greater thoroughness. There was an obvious reluctance on the part of her S.L.F.P. government to make adequate concessions to the Tamils.

In December 1960 legislation was enacted to ensure the use of Sinhalese as the language of parliamentary business with provision for translations in Tamil and English. In the following year, despite strong protests from the Tamils, Parliament legislated for the use of Sinhalese as the language in which the courts of justice would have to give their decisions. In the same year regulations were proposed by two of Mrs Bandaranaike's ministers for a very restricted use of the Tamil language in the Tamil-speaking provinces – for registering births, issuing of licences and for official correspondence with the public. These were rejected by the Tamils.

During 1965–72 the Tamil language made further progress in the quest for official recognition due to (1) the support the 'national government' of Dudley Senanayake (1965–70) received from the F.P. and the C.W.C., and (2) the fact of the two traditional Marxist parties, the L.S.S.P. and C.P. (Moscow) with their conciliatory stances on Tamil joining hands with Mrs Bandaranaike in a United Front formed in 1968 and returned to office in 1970.

In January 1966 the 'national government' enacted the Tamil Regulations which provided for Tamil being a parallel official language in the Tamil-speaking provinces. There was strong opposition from the U.F. parties but the latter has not repudiated them from the statute book. But they have also not been implemented and remain, for all intents and purposes, a dead letter.

In 1972 the U.F. government incorporated provisions in their republican constitution for the use of the Tamil language in the administrative and judicial spheres.[15] These were a considerable advance on the earlier inflexible attitude of the S.L.F.P. Tamil political parties have, however, rejected them on the ground that they do not go far enough to provide the Tamil language an assured status. In particular, the Tamils feel indignant that it is specifically stated in the constitution that the provisions relating to the Tamil language can be amended by ordinary legislation whereas the provisions relating to Sinhalese are constiutionally entrenched.[16]

It is significant that in all the disputed spheres, in administration, in education and in religion, the extremist solutions demanded by the Sinhalese militants were rejected for 'the middle path' advocated by a pragmatic type of Sinhalese political leadership that emerged in the post-1956 phase. In part this could be attributed to the Buddhistic ethos which seeks moderation and compromise. As important was the realisation that intransigence could produce national disintegration and a hindering of the country's economic progress.

The Indian Question

Basically the problem is a Sinhalese–Tamil one with the political and economic aspects intermixed, though the political tended to dominate more often than not. But it was also one which involved Sri Lanka's relations with a powerful neighbour.

At the time of independence and for many years thereafter a number of important personalities in Sinhalese nationalist and political quarters felt a sense of urgency in regard to the need to find a solution to the Indian problem. The currently held view then was that as long as Nehru was in charge of affairs, an equitable solution could be obtained. There was apprehension that after him, the state of Madras might exercise pressure on a weak central government, or that Indian nationalism would take an aggressive turn.

The problem also had its local implications. The presence of more than a million Indian Tamil estate workers in the heart of the Sinhalese country, as it were, and that too in the island's economically most rewarding sectors (the tea and rubber plantations) posed both a political and an economic threat to the Sinhalese people, especially to the Kandyan Sinhalese.

Its origins could be traced back to the reluctance of the

Sinhalese to take to the regimented life of the estates. In a situation where nature is bountiful and where the average peasant owns even a fragment of land, where feudal and rigid social considerations keep him tied to the rural framework, there was, until the pressures of population and lack of employment opportunities began to be felt, an understandable reluctance to take to the barrack style labour required by the plantation sector.

The Indians posed a threat to the Sinhalese only when the question of representation in the legislature became an issue in the 1920s and thereafter. To have given large numbers of Indians the vote, as the Donoughmore Commission recommended in 1928, would from the Sinhalese point of view have meant (1) a dilution of the electoral strength of the Kandyan Sinhalese in most of the constituencies in the Kandyan areas; (2) the possibility of Indian Tamils being returned as representatives of Kandyan Sinhalese constituencies in the event of the splitting of the Kandyan Sinhalese vote between rival candidates; and (3) the likelihood, especially at the time of the Donoughmore reforms, of British planters, and/or Indian estate *kanganies* (overseers) herding the Indian vote in favour of the candidate of their choice. The Donoughmore recommendation was therefore, because of strong Sinhalese opposition, modified by the imperial government.

Even in the 1930s, except for protests from the Labour Party and Trotskyist leaders, there was no wholesale disapproval of the Indian presence. Sinhalese opposition was to the granting of voting and citizenship rights.

There was growing Sinhalese concern in the 1940s. In 1939 the Indian workers had formed their own political organisation, the C.I.C., at the instance of Nehru when he visited Ceylon. And the Ceylon Tamils and Indian Tamils tended increasingly to come together on common political issues against the Sinhalese. Further, the C.I.C. was accused by the Sinhalese, by using alien Gandhi and Nehru slogans, of having deliberately manipulated the Indian vote at the general election of 1947 for the benefit of their own as well as of anti-U.N.P. candidates whom they supported. The C.I.C. bosses were also faulted for going to Madras and New Delhi to discuss the Indian problem instead of dealing with accredited Sinhalese leaders.

The Soulbury Commission in 1944–5 was well aware of Sinhalese anxieties, and despite strong representations from Ceylon

Tamil and Indian Tamil organisations, decided that the Indian question was an internal matter to be disposed of by the future legislature. In 1940, 1941 and 1947, the Sinhalese ministers under the Donoughmore constitution made attempts to resolve the issue with the government of India but failed because of the difficult terms they postulated.

In 1948 an independent Sri Lanka framed its own laws in regard to citizenship and the franchise. In effect, however, the legislation in question, the Ceylon Citizenship Act of 1948 and the Indian and Pakistani Residents (Citizenship) Act No. 3 of 1949, put into legal form the rigorous conditions that conservative Sinhalese political leaders had envisaged from the 1930s and even before. In fact there were some among the latter who felt that the conditions were not exacting enough.

The first Act relating to Sri Lanka citizenship (No. 18 of 1948) created two categories of citizenship, (1) by *descent*, and (2) by *registration,* and postulated the conditions under which citizenship could be obtained in terms of each of these categories. Further, the Act gave the minister a discretionary power of granting citizenship to not more than twenty-five persons a year who had rendered distinguished service in various spheres of public life and/or have been naturalised as British subjects in Sri Lanka.

The provisions of the Citizenship Act of 1948 were by no means intended to cover all resident Indians. They were excessively rigid and could not have benefited more than a few. Provision was therefore specifically made in 1949 for those Indians and Pakistanis who wished to become citizens. Under the Indians and Pakistani Residents (Citizenship) Act No. 3 of 1949, Indians and Pakistanis who possessed an 'assured income of a reasonable amount', had no disabilities which made it difficult for them to conform to the laws of Sri Lanka (such as those relating to marriage), had their wives and dependent children residing with them during the required qualifying period of residence, and had renounced any other citizenship if they possessed it, could apply for citizenship if they had been resident in Sri Lanka before 1 January 1946 for a minimum period of (1) ten years if unmarried or divorced or widowed or a widower, (2) seven years if married.

These two Acts were followed by a third one, the Ceylon

(Parliamentary Elections) Amendment Act, No. 48 of 1949, which laid down among other things that no person who was not a citizen could have his name entered or retained in any of the registers of electors.

The sum effect of all three Acts was (1) to disfranchise the overwhelming majority of Indians who had up to date possessed the right to vote, and (2) to make it extremely difficult for those Indians and Pakistanis who wished to become citizens to qualify.

It was in the administration of the provisions of the second Act (No. 3 of 1949) that charges of discrimination and deliberate delays on the part of officials investigating claims were made. The Act fixed an appointed day (5 August 1949) and a two-year limit (5 August 1951) within which applications had to be filed with a commissioner appointed for the purpose.

The C.I.C. at first chose to register its opposition to these Acts by calling on Indians to desist from filing applications. It demanded the removal of the distinction between citizenship by *registration* and citizenship by *descent* and wanted citizenship granted on the basis of 'a simple and easily ascertainable factual test of residence' and a declaration of intention to settle permanently in Ceylon.[17]

Opinion in India, particularly in Madras from which state most of the Indians came, was condemnatory of the Acts in question. The Madras Legislative Assembly wanted citizenship conferred on the basis of a five-year test of residence, the abolition of the distinctions based on *descent* and *registration* and provision for 'continuance of essential human ties between Indians settled in Ceylon and their relations and dependents in India'.[18]

Locally, the Marxist parties (the L.S.S.P., B.S.P. and the pro-Moscow C.P.) and a number of anti-U.N.P. members of Parliament opposed the Acts on the score that it discriminated against an important section of the working class. Marxist candidates had obtained the support of the C.I.C. at the general election of 1947 in constituencies where the C.I.C. did not contest. The Marxists also had their trade unions in the plantation areas and hoped to organise the Indian workers in their fight against 'the capitalist class'.

A majority of the Ceylon Tamil M.P.s in the T.C. who had by this time joined the D. S. Senanayake government supported the legislation – in a way an achievement for the prime minister, because it divided the two Tamil groupings, Ceylon and Indian, where previously they had acted together for common political objectives. But in the process the T.C. splintered, and a rival Ceylon Tamil grouping, the F.P., emerged to champion the rights of the Indians.

For most of the two-year limit within which applications had to be filed, the C.I.C. persisted in its boycott. Then a few weeks before the expiry of the deadline, the boycott was lifted and a spate of inadequately completed applications flowed in. One hundred and sixty thousand of the 237,034 applications were submitted in the last ten weeks. The processing and final disposal of these applications involved long drawn out investigations and tedious delays and it was only in 1962, some thirteen years after the enactment of this legislation, that the task was completed. Of the 825,000 Indians claiming citizenship (in the 237,034 applications filed) only 134,188 were admitted to citizenship, approximately 16.2 per cent of the total.[19]

The Indian problem was not allowed to rest with the legislation of 1948 and 1949. It became both a matter of internal politics and the subject of a continuing dispute with the government of India. Neither the latter nor local political parties were willing to permit it to become a settled fact of political life.

The government of India made it clear that it would not accept responsibility for those Indians whose applications for citizenship were rejected by the Sri Lanka commissioner for the registration of Indian and Pakistani residents. Articles 5 and 8 of the Indian constitution made it difficult for Indians resident outside India to qualify for Indian citizenship and this was made even more difficult by the enactment of a separate citizenship law by the government of India in 1955. Nor did the high commissioner for India in Sri Lanka show any ready willingness to accommodate Indians in Sri Lanka who applied for Indian passports.

Meanwhile, between 1949 and 1953 various amendments were made to the Acts in question by Parliament with a view to closing loopholes where necessary, and relaxing procedures which were considered cumbersome or too heavy a burden on applicants. But none of these went to the heart of the problem.

In June 1953 the prime minister at the time, Dudley Senanayake, took the opportunity when he was in London to attend the queen's coronation to discuss the problem with Nehru. A solution seemed in sight but for the fact that the government of India was not willing to accept the three hundred thousand Indians who would not have qualified for Sri Lanka citizenship as Indian nationals.[20] The Indian government held that only one-half of this three hundred thousand would qualify. Besides, Nehru took up the position that he could not agree to the principle of repatriating all these three hundred thousand Indians, as similar requests would be made by countries like Malaya, Burma and South Africa where there were large populations of Indian origin. Dudley Senanayake had agreed to an estimated four hundred thousand resident Indians being admitted to citizenship, but it later transpired that this figure was only an *estimate* and that it did not in any way commit his government. As for the balance of 250,000 Indians (the total local Indian population at this time was estimated at 950,000), they were to be granted permanent resident permits and their future status reviewed after ten years. It was agreed that if within this period any of them desired to return to India and opt for Indian citizenship, the government of India would not raise difficulties. These discussions did not end in anything tangible.

With a view to making another attempt at settling the issue, Nehru extended an invitation to Dudley Senanayake's successor, Sir John Kotelawala, to have outstanding problems more fully discussed. This was accepted and the outcome was the Indo-Ceylon Agreement of January 1954. As far as Sri Lanka was concerned, the agreement established certain gains.[21]

For the first time the government of India acknowledged the existence of an illicit immigrant problem for Sri Lanka and acquiesced in the amendment to the immigration law which cast the burden of proof on any person accused of being an illicit immigrant. Illicit immigration had at this time become a political issue with the leading opposition party, the S.L.F.P., and other Sinhalese political groupings alleging that the government was not taking meaningful steps to stop the 'influx'.

A greater political gain for the Kotelawala government was the Indian prime minister's willingness to have Indians who became registered citizens to be placed on a separate electoral register for a ten-year period. These citizens would elect a certain number of members to Parliament, the actual number to be decided in consultation with the government of India.

On the citizenship question, the arrangement was that Indians not registered as citizens (and it was estimated by the Sri Lanka prime minister that their number would in all total five hundred thousand) would be provided with (1) facilities by the local Indian High Commission, and (2) inducement by the government of Sri Lanka if they wished to have themselves registered as Indian citizens under Article 8 of the Indian constitution. It was further proposed (and agreed) that Indians admitted to local citizenship would be obliged to acquire a knowledge of 'the language of the area' as proof of the fact that they had an abiding interest in Sri Lanka and not in India.

The last-mentioned aspect created a domestic political issue and was exploited by rival parties for their own ends. 'Language of the area' meant Sinhalese and no more, but S. W. R. D. Bandaranaike on the other hand insisted that the prime minister had implied 'language of the area' to mean Sinhalese *or* Tamil, not Sinhalese *only*.

Sinhalese nationalist opinion had at this time come round to the view that the Indian Tamils would have to be accommodated in some kind of way, especially in view of the obvious hesitation on the part of India to take most of them back. In the circumstances, they sought to compel the Indian Tamils in the plantation areas to adopt Sinhalese as their mother tongue. In this way the Indians could, they hoped, be absorbed.

Like all the Indo-Ceylon Agreements that followed the Agreement of January 1954, conflicting interpretations arose as to the intentions of the parties concerned.

The government of Sri Lanka assumed that there would be only two categories of Indians under the agreement – Sri Lanka and Indian nationals – and that those not admitted to local citizenship would *per se* be automatically registered as Indian nationals under Articles 5 or 8 of the Indian constitution. The government of India on the other hand assumed a third category of Indians – the 'stateless' – who might well fail to qualify for either Sri Lanka or Indian citizenship. This was stoutly rejected by Sri Lanka. Further, some of the inducements the latter offered were negative rather than positive, the very opposite of what the negotiators on the Indian side had envisaged.

In view of these divergent interpretations, a further conference was held in New Delhi at the request of the government of Sri

Lanka in October 1954 to resolve the differences. Some progress was made, but though it was hailed as a step in the right direction, in actual fact very little was achieved.[22]

When the M.E.P. government took office in 1956, it was expected that the new prime minister would work hard to arrive at a settlement with the government of India as the attitude of Bandaranaike and the Sinhalese nationalists in his S.L.F.P. on this vexed question was only too well known. It was hoped that Nehru would be more disposed to solve the issue in a manner satisfactory to Sri Lanka because of the new government's acceptance of nonalignment and neutralism as the guiding principles of its foreign policy. However, Bandaranaike had little time to address himself to the problem owing to his preoccupation with domestic issues. Also, Bandaranaike took up the position that the process of registration of Indians as Indian or Sri Lanka nationals had first to be completed before negotiations could be commenced on what should be done with the rest.[23] This process was not completed during his lifetime, but only in July 1964, by which time a total of more than eight lakhs (800,000) of applications had been investigated. Of these 134,187 were granted citizenship.

It was left to Mrs Bandaranaike to negotiate a settlement on the remaining Indians. The Indo-Ceylon Agreement of October 1964, often referred to as the Sirima-Shastri Agreement, was the outcome. From Sri Lanka's point of view, it was a definite gain.

The Agreement took into consideration the fact that there were 975,000 Indians in Sri Lanka without citizenship rights. It was agreed between the two governments that:

(1) Five hundred and twenty-five thousand of this number and their natural increase would be repatriated to India on a phased programme over a period of fifteen years.
(2) Three hundred thousand and their natural increase would be admitted to Sri Lanka citizenship over the same period, on the basis of an agreed ratio as between those repatriated to India after being granted Indian citizenship and those admitted to Sri Lanka citizenship. It was later agreed that the ratio would be seven to four.
(3) Indians to be repatriated to their country would be allowed

to continue in employment till they reached their fifty-fifth year or until the completion of their registration according to the phased programme, whichever was earlier. They could take back with them (per family) assets up to a maximum of Rs 4,000.

Difficulties in the interpretation of the Agreement arose over (1) the question of compulsion in repatriation, the Indian officials arguing that India had never agreed to the principle; (2) the method of registering those Indians given citizenship as voters, Mrs Bandaranaike's government insisting that this was a matter of domestic concern and wanting to place them on a separate electoral roll and the government of India protesting against such discrimination; and (3) the proposed Control of Employment Bill which would have prevented Indians registering as Indian citizens to continue in their occupation subject to the conditions stated.

The Ceylon Tamil political groupings, the F.P. and the T.C., and the main organisations of the Indian workers, the C.W.C., were opposed to the element of compulsion and the placing of Indians in separate electoral rolls. Mrs Bandaranaike's government assumed that compulsion may have to be used to ensure the implementation of the phased fifteen-year programme of repatriation, while both the S.L.F.P. and U.N.P. favoured the idea of a separate electoral roll.

Before these difficulties could be resolved Mrs Bandaranaike's government suffered defeat in Parliament in December 1964 and later at the ensuing general election of March 1965.

The Indo-Ceylon Agreement Implementation Act of 1968 enacted by the succeeding Dudley Senanayake 'national government' proved acceptable to all the Tamil parties. Senanayake was under an obligation to the latter. The element of compulsion was removed and the earlier intention of assigning Indians registered as citizens to a separate electoral roll was abandoned. The Kandyan Sinhalese interests were angered. The prime minister spoke in terms of setting up multi-member constituencies in electoral districts where the Indian interests clashed with the Kandyan Sinhalese. This did not satisfy the latter. Moreover the prime minister abandoned the principle of relating the grant of Sri Lanka citizenship to the physical repatriation of Indians opting for Indian nationality on the score that the crisis in the foreign exchange situation did not make it possible for his government to permit Indians wishing to leave to repatriate their assets up to the agreed maximum of Rs 4,000 per family. Those Indians granted Indian citizenship were therefore allowed to remain till they reached retiring age. Consequently the seven to four ratio was not adhered to. Hence at the end of the five-year term of the Senanayake government only 12,798 Indians had gone back while 7,316 obtained citizenship.[24]

The U.F. condemned the legislation of 1968 as doing violence to the spirit of the Sirima–Shastri Pact – especially the abandonment of the principle of linking conferment of citizenship to the physical repatriation of Indians from the island. With the U.F. in office in May 1970, steps were taken to reinsert this principle in amending legislation enacted in January 1971.

Meanwhile the Indian high commissioner in Colombo, Y. K. Puri, put forward a plan in 1971 for speeding up the process of implementing the 1964 Agreement.[25] It received favourable consideration from the U.F. government. Under it, Indians who wished to return to their country could do so regardless of whether in the first instance they received Indian citizenship or not. They could take away assets up to the Rs 4,000 maximum. Once on Indian soil, the government of India would investigate their claims for Indian citizenship and would endeavour to accommodate them without creating unnecessary delays or difficulties. It was estimated that under this plan, fifty thousand Indians, fifteen thousand more than the number stipulated under the 1964 Agreement, would leave the shores of Ceylon annually.

The estate workers are one of the most neglected of groups. The overwhelming majority of them are Indian Tamils, but there are at least 150,000 among them who are Sinhalese. These estate workers are among the most efficiently unionised groups. Their difficulties, however, arise partly from this very fact. They are in the effective grip of two excessively powerful trade union organisations, the C.W.C. and D.W.C.

The denial of citizenship rights deprives the Indian Tamil workers of the opportunity of participating in parliamentary elections, among other disabilities. And all estate workers, both Indians and Sinhalese, are not allowed to vote at local government elections, the argument being that their segregation in plantations automatically prevents them from taking a direct interest in the affairs of the towns and villages around them. Further, their isolation also deprives them of the benefits of the co-operative movement and access to rural development societies, and marketing, food production, agricultural and credit institutions.

Unemployment and under-employment is widespread. All estate children of fourteen years of age are registered for employment, but the management in the plantations cannot find work for all who are employable and the work load is therefore distributed. Wage rates are extremely low and remain at bare subsistence level.

The situation is made worse by other social miseries. The school-going population do not have the educational facilities available to the rest of the island community. Medical facilities are meagre and sanitation and housing are substandard. Meanwhile the only means of redress available are through the major unions which exercise a vice-like grip over these hapless people.

The Kandyan Sinhalese

Differences between the Low Country Sinhalese and Kandyan Sinhalese are not of any great cultural significance apart from those that arise from the fact of the latter's isolation from the lowland districts during Portuguese and Dutch rule. Even the British conquest of the Kandyan kingdom in 1815 and the administrative and political unification that followed the recommendations of the Colebrooke–Cameron Royal Commission of Inquiry some eighteen years later did not minimise distinctions appreciably. Nor did intermarriage or commercial contacts help to cast both groups into a single mould.

The Low Country Sinhalese, especially in the maritime areas, were exposed to Portuguese, Dutch and British influences. Consequently Roman Catholicism, Protestantism, the Roman Dutch law and a comparatively greater spread of English education made more of an impact on the lowland Sinhalese.

The Kandyan districts on the other hand were not as readily accessible to the westerners or to Christian missionary endeavours. Besides, the Kandyan Sinhalese themselves did not readily take to

British rule; in fact they staged two major rebellions against the colonial administration in 1817–18 and 1848.

The Kandyan Sinhalese were therefore able to preserve and maintain their own social organisation, and it is best exemplified in their laws in regard to marriages, guardianship, minority, adoption, legitimacy, parent and child, gifts, intestate succession and service tenures. During the time of the Sinhalese kings, Kandyan law was a territorial law and not a personal one. For a good part of the nineteenth century, Kandyan law was interpreted at different times by the courts as personal law and territorial law, till in 1891 it became a settled fact that Kandyan law applied only to Kandyan Sinhalese and their descendants and to no one else.

There used to be a certain measure of Kandyan antagonism, largely at the middle-class level, to the Low Country Sinhalese, but this is now fast disappearing. In 1927, a number of Kandyan Sinhalese political organisations insisted before the Donoughmore Commission that the Kandyan Sinhalese had 'never ceased to regard the Low Country Sinhalese as foreigners' and some of them went so far as to suggest a federated Ceylon in which the Kandyan Sinhalese provinces could, as one of three units, look after their own affairs and enjoy a measure of autonomy.[26] By the end of the period of the Donoughmore constitution, however (1931–47), both Sinhalese groups had forged close political links.

The problem of the Kandyan Sinhalese is at both the middle-class and peasant levels and their grievances encompass all sectors – economic, social and political.

More than 90 per cent of the Kandyan Sinhalese population live in the rural areas, a good many of them in plantation-locked villages. The possession of land carries with it a certain social status, inclusive of those in the non-*goigama* caste groups, not excluding even members of the under-privileged castes. Land fragmentation, joint ownership and landlessness have therefore reached crisis proportions in especially two of the Kandyan Sinhalese provinces – the central province and the province of Uva.

The situation was aggravated by the sale of unoccupied lands in the Kandyan areas at ridiculously low prices to investors (mostly British) in coffee and later tea and rubber during the middle and later decades of the nineteenth century, a process which was facilitated by (1) the Crown Lands (Encroachments) Ordinance, No.

12 of 1840; (2) the Registration of Temple Lands Ordinance No. 10 of 1856; and (3) the Waste Lands Ordinance of 1897. These laws in effect presumed all forest, waste, unoccupied or uncultivated land and unclaimed temple land to be the property of the crown unless the contrary could be proved. They affected the Kandyan Sinhalese peasant extremely adversely because it was his practice to clear and cultivate plots of forest land (called *chena* or *hena*) adjacent to his paddy fields on a rotational basis.

With increases in population, the absence of primogeniture and lack of land space, the individual sizes of paddy landholdings in the Kandyan Sinhalese districts have come to be the smallest for the island as a whole.[27] In two Kandyan provinces (central and Uva) the majority of paddy lands, except in one district (Nuwara Eliya) are below half an acre in extent.[28] In two other districts, in the Kandyan provinces of the north-west and Sabaragamuwa, the average holding is a little over one acre.[29] Further, a recent survey carried out by revenue officers in a number of Kandyan Sinhalese divisions indicated that there were many families who owned no land at all.[30]

Many Kandyan peasants also suffer hardship in the cultivation of paddy lands they lease out from exploitative landlords. The basis of payment is referred to as *ande* cultivation, under which the lessee gives a share of the crop, usually half, to the owner. Again, however, with pressure on land caused by a rising population, the owner's bargaining power has increased considerably. With more people bidding for the same land, the existing occupant is obliged to perform various other services to the owner as well as make a bigger preliminary payment (called *madaran*) for the land in order to ensure that he obtains a regrant of it. It might be noted that tenancy generally lasted for a year at a time. The Paddy Lands Act of 1958 and subsequent amendments to it have helped to protect these tenant cultivators from such exploitations and has assured them fixity of tenure.

The extent of the impoverishment of the Kandyan Sinhalese is seen in their income distribution revealed in the two Surveys of Ceylon's consumer finances. The Survey for 1963 recorded that in terms of average income by sectors, the Kandyan Sinhalese of all the communities in the island received the lowest average income in rural areas.[31] Between 1953 and 1963 the per capita income of Kandyan Sinhalese increased by only one rupee (from Rs 52 to

Rs 53) which in real terms meant a nearly 7 per cent fall in income.[32]

In education too their progress has been unsatisfactory. The Survey of 1963 recorded that the number of Kandyan Sinhalese who went for higher education remained the same (0.7 per cent of the population) between the years 1953 and 1963.[33] Consequently they are poorly represented in the public services, the professions and the private sector.

The opening up of plantations in the Kandyan Sinhalese country brought in its wake social and economic consequences which did not benefit the people of the area. With the plantations came trade, commerce and other entrepreneurial skills. The tradition-bound Kandyans, many of them already impoverished, did not seize the opportunities presented. Instead Low Country Sinhalese, Muslims, Ceylon and Indian Tamils made the most of the situation, the result being that in towns of the two Kandyan provinces of central and Uva, members of these groups far outnumber the Kandyan Sinhalese. To this day the Kandyan Sinhalese remain largely a rural population.

Sri Lanka's first post-independence government appointed a commission in January 1949 to investigate the conditions of the Kandyan peasantry in the two provinces referred to. The report published in August 1951 has since served as the guide to governmental policies and action.[34] In particular the commission urged the improvement of road communications, acquisition and distribution of lands to the landless, expansion of social, medical and educational services and provision of better housing. The cabinet accepted, in principle, these recommendations in January 1953, and in March 1956 the Ministry of Home Affairs, after considerable deliberation, produced a five-year implementation programme to cover the period 1955–6—1959–60. This has, from time to time, been extended for further periods.

The annual reports of the commissioner for Kandyan peasantry rehabilitation indicate extremely satisfactory progress for the period 1961–2—1968–9 – a total of 269 schools, 169 rural water supply schemes, 11 medical buildings and 326 miles of roads constructed were in the two provinces concerned.

The presence in their midst of an Indian Tamil population further constitutes a social problem and a political threat to the Kandyans.

Absorption of the Indian population is seriously suggested as a viable solution. A prominent Kandyan Sinhalese state councillor suggested in 1942 and again in 1945 that Sinhalese should be taught in all estate schools. In later years the view was advanced by many Sinhalese political leaders and Sinhalese educationists that Sinhalese should be made the compulsory medium of instruction in all estate schools. In 1962, seven of the twenty members of the National Education Commission including its chairman recommended that Sinhalese should be made the medium of instruction for the Indian Tamil population in the plantations as a means of 'integrating the estate population with the indigenous population surrounding them'.[35] They argued that the Sinhalese language should assume the same role as the English language in the United States in the acculturation process of the immigrant population. Two years after, Mrs Bandaranaike's government in a White Paper (1964) put forward the proposal that all estate schools should be taken over by the state and that the medium of instruction in them should be the official language (Sinhalese). The proposal was not given legislative sanction as the government suffered defeat in Parliament towards the end of the year.

It does not now seem likely that the Indian Tamil population will accept the Sinhalese language as their medium of instruction, as opinion has been and is still being created against the proposition by the various political organisations working in their midst. But there is no objection in most Indian Tamil quarters to Sinhalese being taught as a second language in estate schools.

The political aspects of the Indians in the Kandyan Sinhalese areas have been dealt with in a previous section. The Kandyan Sinhalese elites in particular as well as their Low Country counterparts resent the inclusion of Indian Tamil voters in constituencies in the Kandyan Sinhalese areas. Kandyan Sinhalese members in the House of Representatives have always supported legislation directed against the 'Indian presence' and have stoutly opposed any concessions that governments have at times tried to make to the Indians. In 1968, the Kandyan Sinhalese lobby organised the opposition to the Indo-Ceylon Implementation Bill of the Dudley Senanayake 'national government' in the Senate and they nearly secured its defeat in that chamber.

Consequently, from the point of view of parliamentary representation, the Kandyan Sinhalese areas have benefited greatly at the expense of the Indian Tamils. The citizenship laws of 1948 and 1949 resulted in mostly Kandyan Sinhalese annexing the seven seats held by the Indians in the House from 1952 onwards. When a fresh delimitation of constituencies took place in 1959, the Kandyan Sinhalese areas stood to gain once more. For, in apportioning seats in relation to population to the various provinces, the delimitation commission was directed to take into account the Indian population even though the vast majority of the latter had no voting rights. Kandyan Sinhalese parliamentary representation was thus considerably augmented and since 1960 the Kandyans have become a strong and reckonable political force. A Kandyan Sinhalese (Mrs Bandaranaike) has twice been prime minister (1960–5 and 1970–), a Kandyan Sinhalese (William Gopallawa) was governor-general from 1962 to 1972 and became the first president of the republic in 1972, a Kandyan Sinhalese functioned during 1960–5 as chairman of the Public Service Commission and other Kandyan Sinhalese have come to hold important positions in the public sector. Also, every cabinet has had in it at least three Kandyan Sinhalese ministers and they have in various ways used their positions to promote the interests of the Kandyan areas.

Sinhalese Caste Rivalries

Caste in Sinhalese society is the result of the impact of Brahminical Hinduism on a Buddhistic social structure wedded more to egalitarian concepts of birth and status.[36] However, the Hindu influence was able to make itself felt because the Buddhist view of karma and re-birth could readily be accommodated to the social divisions that Brahminical Hinduism ordained. Consequently caste divisions permeate Sinhalese society though its effects are not as unfortunate as those which plague Ceylon Tamil society in the Hinduistic northern and eastern parts of Ceylon.

Nevertheless even the Buddhist priesthood in contemporary Ceylon today finds itself divided on caste lines – the dominant majority Sinhalese *goigama* (cultivator) caste having its own sect, the *siam nikaya*, while the *amarapura nikaya*, started in the early nineteenth century as a protest against the *goigama* exclusiveness of the *siam nikaya*, has its monks from the lesser *karava* (fisher), *salagama* (cinnamon peeler) and *durava* (toddy tapper) castes, and the *ramanya nikaya*, a recent creation of some members of the *siam nikaya* is more active in promoting greater discipline among its members and effectively publicising Buddhist doctrine.

Buddhist doctrine, however, does not recognise caste differences and all Buddhists irrespective of caste are free to enter the Buddhist *vihare* and Buddhist preaching halls. But in practice members of particular castes, especially in the low-country Sinhalese areas, tend to worship in a temple which relates more to their relevant monkish sect or subsect. In the interior, these differences recede because most of the temples are the property of the *siam nikaya.* Monks of this *nikaya*, however, will seldom solicit alms from any persons of the lower caste groups.

In the Sinhalese social structure, there is no priestly caste such as the Brahmins of India. At the top of the social ladder are the *goigamas* or cultivators who form more than half the population. Not all *goigamas* are cultivators nor are all cultivators *goigamas.* Cultivation has however been their traditional occupation. There are various gradations among the *goigamas*, the *radalas* among the Kandyan Sinhalese and the *mudalis* among the low-country Sinhalese being socially the most prestigious. Among the influential castes below the *goigamas* are their immediate challengers, the *karavas* whose traditional occupation was fishing, the latter's rivals, the *salagamas*, many of them originally cinnamon peelers of south Indian origin whom the Dutch put to great use in the pursuit of their cinnamon monopoly, and *duravas* or toddy tappers.

The *karavas*, *salagamas* and *duravas* stand about midway in the Sinhalese caste ladder. The *navandannas* or *achariyas* who are artisans and smiths of all types come immedately after. Further down are members of the low caste groups.

Marriage by and large follows endogamous lines, though there are the exceptions more at the middle-class and urban levels.

Caste is of relevance in political life. The board of ministers in the explanatory memorandum to their draft constitutional scheme (1944) envisaged the advisability of providing representation in the legislature to certain caste groups. The Soulbury Commission was more specific when they recommended the creation of multi-member constituencies 'particularly where divisions of caste in the same community are prominent',[37] while Section 41(4) of the

Ceylon constitution of 1946–72 provided among other things for the representation of caste interests. The first delimitation commission in its report of September 1946 felt that caste divisions should not be unduly encouraged and was therefore very sparing in its recommendations on this subject. The commissioners recommended the demarcation of the two-member electoral district of Ambalangoda-Balapitiya in the low-country Sinhalese areas to enable the *karava* caste there to return one of its number to Parliament, as they were satisfied that the existence of more than one caste group in this area (the other being the *salagama* caste) gave rise to 'unusually intense communal tension at the time of election'.[38] They further recommended a two-member electoral district in Kadugannawa in a Kandyan Sinhalese area to help out the underprivileged caste group here.[39] In other areas the delimitation commissioners were unwilling to accede to demands put forward by organisations of underprivileged caste groups for separate representation. While they held that accurate figures on caste concentrations were not easily available, they noted that they were left 'with certain impressions that the so-called underprivileged classes dwell in some considerable degree of concentration in certain areas'.[40] They therefore placed them 'as far as possible undivided within an electoral district, to give these groups a greater voice in the election of representatives than they have hitherto possessed'.[41] On this principle they carved the Gampaha constituency in the low country and the constituencies of Kegalla, Gampola, Kurunegala and Bingiriya in the Kandyan areas.

Both S. W. R. D. Bandaranaike (1956–9) and Mrs Sirima Bandaranaike (1960–5 and 1970–) made use of the prime minister's power under the 1947 constitution of recommending to the governor-general the appointment of six members to the House of Representatives, to include among these recognised personalities from the underprivileged castes. In the selection of prime ministerial nominees to the Senate, too, caste was a material consideration.

Further, the caste factor has always been taken care of by prime ministers in the construction of their cabinets and appointments to parliamentary secretaryships. Members of the *goigama* caste are always in a majority in cabinets, not by deliberate choice but because it is in the order of things for the major group to have the larger number of representatives. A further consideration is that from this group is also available a wider spread of political talent and administrative ability. But invariably all cabinets have had in them representatives of the other two important caste groups, the *karavas* and the *salagamas*, and sometimes representatives from the underprivileged castes as well. The Bandaranaikes in particular have paid careful attention to a proper social construction of their cabinets. The adequate representation of caste groups in a government could provide it with electoral support from the appropriate quarters at election time.

A fact to note is that all prime ministers and leaders of the major political parties are from the *goigama* caste. The only exception was in the short phase, December 1959 to March 1960, when fortuitous circumstances led a non-*goigama* (S.L.F.P.) leader from the *salagama* caste, C. P. de Silva, to make a bid for the premiership on two separate occasions. His claims did not succeed for other reasons. But some leading personalities of the *salagama* caste complained that he was overlooked on caste grounds.

The stratifications imposed by caste are a prickly problem in some of the Sinhalese areas. It is not insignificant that the Marxist-oriented rebellion of rural youth organised by the P.L.F. in March–April 1971 had strong support from the underprivileged caste groups, especially the *wahumpuras* in the Kandyan Kegalle district and the *karavas* and *duravas* in the low-country southern districts. These groups were not only protesting against economic hardships and frustrations but were also struggling for upward social mobility.

Sinhalese-Ceylon Tamil Relations

There are historical, educational and sociological factors besides barriers of language and psychology that divide the two communities. Most important, economic contraction generates sharp antagonisms because of competition for the limited employment available in the public and private sectors.

Historically, there has been the tradition of wars between south Indian invaders and Sinhalese kings. The history books used in schools emphasise more these facts than the evidence of the long years of peaceful coexistence there has been between the two communities. A recent investigation on the subject of national harmony reveals that 'there is no school in Ceylon where there is a positive, well integrated, and graded programme for racial integration, working hand in hand with the community agencies, for the realisation of the aim of making our children better Ceylonese citizens'.[42] Separate schools provide education in one or other of the national languages and there is therefore little opportunity for Sinhalese and Tamil children to meet and interact. The same applies to even the few schools which have both language streams, for instruction is exclusively in one language or the other. A common medium of communication, English, operates only in the rare two-stream elitist schools.

A further inhibiting factor is the geographical isolation of the Ceylon Tamils in the northern and eastern parts of the island. The latter are, besides, generally conservative and community-conscious. Even when opportunities for employment and commerce took them to the Sinhalese areas, they developed there flourishing self-contained settlements of their own.

The psychological barriers are just as great. The Sinhalese, as already stated, tend on occasion to group the indigenous Tamils with the Tamils of south India and view them in their entirety as 'the Dravidian peril'.

The average middle-class Sinhalese is in sharp competition with his Ceylon Tamil counterpart for white collar jobs and the commonly held image of the latter is that he is hardworking, clever, industrious and intensely communal, the last mentioned view being reinforced by the fact that, until 1956, Ceylon Tamils in positions of authority tended to prefer their compatriots in the matter of public service appointments and promotions. On the other hand, sections of the Ceylon Tamil intelligentsia look on the average educated Sinhalese as being 'lazy and foolish'.[43] Such an extravagant and self-defeating communalism could not but produce, as it did after 1955, an equally intense communal reaction from sections of the Sinhalese intelligentsia. The deterioration of Sinhalese–Tamil relations in the years after 1956 can be largely attributed to this fact.

During most of the British period, the two groups seldom clashed. On the contrary their English-educated worked in close liaison on the question of constitutional reform. In 1912, an all-island constituency styled 'the educated Ceylonese seat' returned a Ceylon Tamil over a Sinhalese. In 1915, the Ceylon Tamil leadership supported the Sinhalese in the Sinhalese Buddhist–Muslim riots. During 1917–19 leaders of both groups co-operated in inaugurating the Ceylon National Congress and it was a prominent Ceylon Tamil, Sir Ponnambalam Arunachalam, whom the Congress elected as its first president. Thereafter, however, differences arose over the question of ratios in communal representation between the different groups, and more specifically over the refusal of the Sinhalese to agree to the creation of a separate communal electorate for the Ceylon Tamils of the western province. The Sinhalese leadership was becoming increasingly antagonistic to the communal principle. Up to this time (the mid-1920s) the Ceylon Tamils often regarded themselves and the Sinhalese as the two major communities in the country, while referring to the other groups as minorities.[44] This notion continues to die hard even to the present day and is part of the reason for the Ceylon Tamil minority not being able to adjust itself to the rapid political changes that have been taking place since 1931.

With prospects of further reforms in the constitutional structure materialising in the late 1920s, differences became sharper. Sinhalese political elites wanted representation in terms of population. Their objectives were realised when the Donoughmore Commission in 1928 condemned the evils that communal representation had given rise to and recommended in its place territorial representation and universal adult suffrage.[45]

Universal suffrage and territorial representation came to be narrowly interpreted as meaning the need to respond to the pressures of the Sinhalese majority. Though communal representation had been abolished, communal thinking gathered strength. The formation of the pan-Sinhalese board of ministers in 1936 and the emergence of communal organisations such as the S.M.S. (1937), C.I.C. (1939) and T.C. (1944) indicated the trend. The minority groups, especially the Ceylon Tamils, felt they were being discriminated against. The Sinhalese politicians on the other hand argued that they were trying to redress the balance caused by what they said was neglect of the Sinhalese areas during the colonial period. There was the added fact that there were disproportionate numbers of Ceylon Tamils in the public services, the Ceylon Tamil areas having benefited from the good schools that American missionary organisations had set up in the Jaffna peninsula where the majority of Ceylon Tamils reside.

Ceylon Tamil fears of 'Sinhalese domination' produced the demand for 'balanced representation', that is, that 50 per cent of the seats in the legislature be reserved for all the minority groups and that statutory provision be made for not more than half of the members of the cabinet to be chosen from any one community. The Sinhalese political elites rejected this demand outright but they were agreeable to a compromise under which a measure of weightage in representation would be provided for the Ceylon Tamils and Muslims in the sparsely populated areas of north and east Ceylon where both these communities were mostly concentrated. The Soulbury Commission too rejected the demand for 'balanced representation' on the ground that 'a system which purported to reimpose communal representation in the rigid form contemplated' would be 'static rather than dynamic', would not promote the growth of a healthy party system and that 'any attempt by artificial means to convert a majority into a minority is not only inequitable, but doomed to failure'.[46] The Commission, however, recommended various constitutional safeguards which they hoped might allay the fears of discrimination. These safeguards ceased to have much meaning when power was ultimately transferred to the Ceylonese in February 1948.

In the early post-independence phase, some attempts were made by the premier conservative politician among the Sinhalese, D. S. Senanayake, to forge a measure of unity among the middle and upper classes of the various groups in Sri Lanka's multi-communal society. This was reflected in the kind of Ministry, comprising representatives of the various groups, which he constructed on 26 September 1947, shortly after the general election held between 23 August and 20 September under the Soulbury constitution. Senanayake's U.N.P. also had similar objectives in view. But a rift developed between the two groups with the enactment of the citizenship laws of 1948 and 1949. It was the immediate pretext for the formation of the strongly Tamil nationalist F.P. in 1949.

The F.P. concentrated on three objectives: (1) an autonomous region for the indigenous Tamil-speaking peoples comprising the northern and eastern provinces linked to the rest of the island under a federal set-up; (2) parity of status for the Tamil language with the Sinhalese language; and (3) citizenship rights for all Indian Tamils who wish to make the island their permanent home. To pinpoint their grievances, the F.P. protested against what they alleged was the planned settling of Sinhalese in those government-sponsored colonisation schemes launched in 'the traditional homelands of the Tamil speaking peoples' in the northern and eastern parts of the island, and the dilution of Tamil parliamentary strength as a result of the disfranchisement of the Indian Tamils under the laws of 1948 and 1949.

The F.P. did not make headway till the Sinhalese language movement gathered momentum. It then became the principal spokesman of the Ceylon Tamils, replacing its rival the T.C. which had advocated 'responsive co-operation' with the U.N.P.

The party succeeded in gaining its point on colonisation in the agreements it forced on Bandaranaike in 1957 and Dudley Senanayake in 1965. Both prime ministers pledged that they would not utilise the instrument of colonisation to disturb the Tamil-speaking majority in the northern and eastern provinces. Both prime ministers also agreed to provide a measure of official recognition to the Tamil language which they put into legislative effect in 1958 and 1966. But the grievance remains that these pieces of legislation were never adequately implemented.

The same is true of the provisions for the use of the Tamil language in the 1972 constitution. Regulations have yet to be framed for the use of the Tamil language, as the U.F. government is of the opinion that the Tamil Regulations of 1966 are *ultra vires* the Official Language Act of 1956. Effect was, however, given by legislation enacted in 1973 to the proviso in section 11(1) of the 1972 constitution for the National State Assembly to legislate for the use of the Tamil language along with Sinhalese in all judicial proceedings in the original courts of the northern and eastern provinces. Further, there are other detailed provisions in the 1972 constitution which ensure that Tamil-speaking persons involved in proceedings before judicial institutions would have statutory rights to obtain translations of all such proceedings in their own language. These, together with other provisions in the 1972 constitution which obligate translations of all laws into Tamil, etc. imply an official status for the Tamil language. They do not, however, amount to parity of status with Sinhalese which all Tamil political groupings keep demanding. Besides, the provision in section 8(2) of the constitution that any regulation framed under the Tamil Language (Special Provisions) Act of 1958 shall 'not in any manner be interpreted as being a provision of the constitution but shall be deemed to be subordinate legislation' wounds Tamil sentiment. The view is that such regulations should have the same constitutionally entrenched status as Sinhalese.

The years 1956 to 1965 were the most disturbed phase in Sinhalese–Ceylon Tamil relations and reached a climax in the bloody riots of 1958. In February–April 1961, the northern and eastern provinces were once again, under F.P. leadership, engaged in a massive civil disobedience protest campaign against the pro-Sinhalese language policies of Mrs Bandaranaike's S.L.F.P. government, and the armed forces had to be used to bring the situation under control. In 1963, the F.P. spearheaded a campaign for the use of the Tamil language in all correspondence and transactions with government departments.

1965–70 was a period of reconciliation with the 'national government' of Dudley Senanayake in office with the U.N.P. and F.P. as its main components. For the first time since 1956, a Ceylon Tamil, the F.P.'s representative, was included in the cabinet. Ceylon Tamils in the public services who had suffered hardship in the earlier phase as a result of the enforcement of Sinhalese as the official language were afforded a measure of relief. The Tamil Regulations of January 1966, though not enforced fully, provided for Tamil being a parallel official language with Sinhalese in the northern and eastern provinces.

A controversial issue at this time was the demand of all Ceylon Tamil groupings for the Tamil language to be the compulsory medium of instruction for Tamil children. This was not satisfactorily resolved due to opposition from pro-Sinhalese elements in the 'national government'.

Senanayake was also not able to implement that part of his agreement with the F.P. for the institution of district councils enjoying administrative autonomy under the control and direction of the central government because of a threatened revolt of a sizable section of his parliamentary supporters. The F.P., for this and other reasons, felt disenchanted and quit the 'national government' in the latter half of 1968, but Senanayake, nevertheless, was by and large able to continue to retain the goodwill of the Ceylon Tamils.

With the return of the U.F. government in May 1970, there has been some deterioration in the relations between the two communities. But Mrs Bandaranaike has tried not to alienate the Tamils. She has included a Ceylon Tamil in her cabinet whilst her left-wing partners continue to retain their support bases in the Tamil-speaking areas.

The F.P., however, as the leading party of the Ceylon Tamils, walked out of the Constituent Assembly's proceedings in June 1971 and has emphatically rejected the constitution of May 1972.

The Sinhalese-Ceylon Tamil dispute thus remains still unresolved. But the severity of the conflict, as it existed in the 1956–1965 phase, has been mitigated somewhat. It would be reduced further if and when legislative effect is given to the sections of the 1972 constitution providing for the use of the Tamil language.

Ceylon Tamil Casteism

In the Ceylon Tamil areas of the northern Jaffna peninsula, saivaite Hinduism, with its ban on members of the depressed castes entering the inner courtyards of temples on the ground that they will defile the premises, has produced serious caste tensions which have on occasion resulted in violence.

Unlike Buddhism, Hinduism is intolerant, and though the brahminical structure is not strictly reproduced, caste divisions in these Tamil areas are rigid even to the extent of the classification of outcaste groups.[47]

Among the Ceylon Tamils, there are the 'clean' castes comprising the *brahmins*, the *vellalas* (cultivators) who form the majority in the same way as the *goigamas* among the Sinhalese, the *karaiyars* and *mukkuvas* (fisher folk), and the *koviyars* whose traditional occupation is being cooks and domestics to the *vellalas*, in that order. There are then the various craftsmen castes such as the *thattar* (goldsmiths), *nadduvar* (musicians), *vannar* (laundrymen), etc. There is finally a category of 'unclean' castes also referred to as depressed castes or minority Tamils.

The non-*vellala* castes, except for the *karaiyars*, are not concentrated in sufficient strength in any sizable area to warrant their separate representation in Parliament. Various associations and leaders from among them made representations to the Soulbury

Commission and to the three delimitation commissions appointed since 1946 urging the demarcation of special constituencies. The Soulbury Commission suggested the creation of multi-member constituencies in the Jaffna peninsula to enable their representation, but the delimitation commission of 1946 felt that these groups 'are scattered all over the peninsula and that the creation of a multi-member electoral district however large would not assist them'.[48]

The depressed castes have a voice in determining the result in a few constituencies in the Jaffna peninsula whenever the contest has been a close and sharp one. But generally their political organisations support left-wing candidates who, with a few exceptions, receive most of the depressed caste votes at elections. Consequently, left-wing parties are looked on with disfavour by the majority *vellala* Tamils, especially because these parties have been insistent and emphatic in their advocacy of the rights of the depressed-caste Tamils.

In the recent past the depressed castes have been active and militant in their campaigns for their social rights in the Jaffna peninsula. They are concentrating mainly on winning their rights to enter Hindu temples, public eating houses and hairdressing saloons. Numbers among the depressed castes have embraced Buddhism as a protest against Hindu intolerance.

The Christians

The Roman Catholics and Protestants both among Sinhalese and Tamils wield considerable influence in the political and economic life of the country, an influence quite out of proportion to their actual numbers – the Roman Catholics (being the larger group) to a greater extent than the Protestants. Evidence of this can be seen in the fact that five out of six prime ministers had their secondary education in Christian schools – four in Protestant institutions and one in the leading Roman Catholic convent in Colombo. And a majority of members of all cabinets up to date have also had their secondary education in Christian institutions. Further, most cabinets have had a Protestant or Roman Catholic or representatives of both these religious groups appointed to them.

Politically, the leadership in both religious groups up to the time of the general election of May 1970 tended to support the U.N.P. as against the S.L.F.P. and the Marxists. For instance, the head of the Roman Catholic Church in Ceylon, Archbishop Thomas Cooray, warned on the eve of the general election of 1952 that 'no Catholic with even an atom of Christian conscience can vote for a candidate who subscribes to a political creed banned by the Church – be it communism or any other'.[49] The statements of the heads of the Church of Ceylon and the Methodist Church in Ceylon at all general elections inclusive of that of May 1970 were indicative of support for the U.N.P. as against its opponents. Judging however from the results in constituencies with a majority of Christian voters (especially Roman Catholics) it is clear that the faithful have not taken these directives too seriously. The S.L.F.P. has always had its own share of support from the Christian groups, and many prominent Roman Catholics and Protestants have identified themselves with that party.

After the return of the U.N.P. and its allies to power at the general election of 1965, the Roman Catholic Church hoped to gain a measure of relief for its schools from the 'national government' of Dudley Senanayake but was disappointed. During this phase there also took place perceptible changes in the thinking of the Roman Catholic priesthood as well as of important sections of its laity. Two leading Roman Catholic priests – Fathers Tissa Balasuriya and C. A. Joachim Pillai – sought to involve the Church with the movement for social justice.

Father Balasuriya, as rector of the Aquinas University College in Colombo, was responsible for organising seminars and lectures which were clearly intended to acquaint the Roman Catholic priesthood and laity with the thought processes and political stances of parties that sought to eliminate privilege and restructure society on socialistic lines. Father Joachim Pillai, as the head of the National Seminary in Kandy, ensured that the priests his institution turned out were men who could identify themselves with the rural Catholics as well as the underprivileged Catholics. These priests were very different from their predecessors, who had been far removed from the ordinary mass of Roman Catholics.

Besides, up to this time, the Church had been closely identified with the right-wing order as represented by the U.N.P. There was a determination to remove this impression once and for all. It was no surprise therefore when, after the general election of May 1970, the Roman Catholic bishops of Ceylon in a public appeal on the occasion of the ceremonial opening of the seventh Parliament of Ceylon called on the faithful to 'give their loyal and enlightened co-operation to the new government for the realisation of those noble ideals to which it is pledged'.[50] The appeal had greater significance because it was a call to support a government which had in it leaders of the Trotskyist and communist (Moscow) parties.

We have already referred to the Sinhalese Buddhist position vis-à-vis the Christians in respect of the latter's schools and social welfare activities.

The Buddhist leadership during the years after 1956 was more conciliatory in its attitude to the Protestants, especially as the latter had shown a greater willingness to understand the Buddhist position and to accept Parliament's decision in regard to the schools. Being a much smaller group, the Protestants could not possibly have embarked on any other course of action.

The Roman Catholics on the other hand were severely criticised by leading Buddhist militants such as L. H. Mettananda, C. D. S. Siriwardena, Gunaseela Vitanage and T. U. de Silva, among others. These leaders directed their attacks against what they alleged were the workings of 'Catholic Action' in the public and private sectors.[51] 'Catholic Action' they insisted, with supporting evidence, was an exclusive mutual benefit organisation and an employment bureau for Roman Catholics. They also condemned the property interests and 'business activities' of the Roman Catholic Church. It is doubtful whether these strictures had the desired effect.

Nevertheless it is evident that since 1956, and especially after 1960, important changes have been taking place in the thought processes of members of both Christian groups. There is greater anxiety to understand the Buddhist viewpoint and to come to terms with it. There has been a shift from the earlier position of complacency.

The Muslims

The Ceylon Muslims comprise two groups – the Ceylon Moors mostly of Arab and Indian extraction who came as traders to the island during the seventh to the fifteenth centuries and intermarried with the natives, and the Malays of more recent origin, descendants of Javanese mercenaries brought by the Dutch.

A fair proportion of the Muslims on the east coast are herdsmen and cultivators, but generally there are Muslims engaged in minor commercial pursuits and these activities take them to the interior and remote parts of the island. Their ubiquitous disposition in regard to trade make them the only community in the island that has a percentage distribution of at least more than one in every district in the island. But they are also more than 35 per cent of the population in the Batticaloa district, and more than 25 per cent in the districts of Puttalam, Trincomalee and Mannar. They also form a sizable proportion of the population in the city of Colombo and in the towns of Galle, Kandy, Jaffna, Kalutara, Gampola, Matale and Negombo, while they are the majority in the towns of Puttalam and Beruwala. This wide dispersion as well as concentration in the important towns make the Muslims a force in parliamentary politics, for their votes do help to determine the results in those constituencies where they are a significant proportion of the population. Political organisations among the Muslims are not slow in exploiting this advantage.

A majority of Muslims are Tamil-speaking and they live adjacent to the Ceylon Tamil community residing in the northern and eastern parts of the island. The Muslims living in the Sinhalese districts are Tamil-speaking but they are proficient in the Sinhalese language as well.

The fact that the Muslims are a Tamil-speaking group gives rise to competition for their support between the Sinhalese and Ceylon Tamil political leadership. The Muslim political leadership, unlike the Ceylon Tamil, does not have strong feelings on the question of the Tamil language. Some of their leading political organisations are in favour of Muslims adopting the Sinhalese language as their mother tongue. But on this matter there is a divergence of opinion between the Muslims of the Sinhalese areas and the Muslims residing in the Tamil-speaking areas. In the latter case, there is a demand for Sinhalese being taught, but mainly as a second language.

Though a few Muslim personalities have from time to time supported the Ceylon Tamil political leadership, the general trend has been for the Muslims to identify themselves with the Sinhalese leadership in national politics. They see in such identification many advantages. For instance, until recent times the Muslims as a community, for various reasons, had not taken to higher education and the professions as the other communities had done. Since 1956 increasing attention has been paid by successive ministers of education, particularly W. Dahanayake (1956–9) and Badiuddin Mahmud (1960–4 and 1970–) to improving educational facilities available to the Muslim population.

There is a measure of economic and political rivalry between the Muslims and the Ceylon Tamil's which, however, is not a seriously complicating factor in ethnic relationships. Politically, many in the Muslim elite feel that when the Ceylon Tamils benefit, it is at their expense. This accusation has often been made by some of their leading politicians.

Important sections of the Muslim leadership strongly opposed the principle of district councils because they feared that it would result in their fellow men ending up as a minority within a minority in especially the Tamil-speaking areas. For example, the S.L.F.P. Muslim leader, Badiuddin Mahmud, stated in the Constituent Assembly in July 1970 that 'the geographical distribution and historical experience' of the Muslim community obliged them to fight all 'divisive tendencies'.[52] They would, he insisted, 'oppose strongly any attempt at the division, whether directly or indirectly, of the country'.[53] He urged that special provisions be included in the new constitution to avoid any such division.

The trend towards increasing control of trade and commerce by the state since the U.F. government took office in 1970 has created some concern among those Muslims who are engaged in these pursuits. In October 1970, Badiuddin Mahmud invited a representative gathering of his fellow religionists to a 'tea party' at his residence to explain to them the socialist policies of the U.F. government. Mahmud himself stated that it was his duty to inform them that 'vast changes are going to be made' and that it had therefore become 'necessary for the community to consider their future without trying to hit their heads against a stone wall'.[54] He asked the members of his community 'to think of small business enterprises' if they could not in future engage in big business enterprises.[55] They should also, he advised, take to other fields such as tourism and agriculture instead of being wholly dependent on trade.

The Burghers

Though a very small minority, the Burgher community, especially those of its members who were descendants of the Dutch settlers, during British rule wielded an influence in the public life of the island quite disproportionate to its numbers. They adopted English as their mother tongue.

With independence and the switch to nationalistic goals, their situation has become increasingly difficulty. It became almost untenable for those of them belonging to the middle classes, with the decision in 1956 to switch to Sinhalese as the official language and the steps taken thereafter to abandon English as a medium of instruction in the schools and the universities. Large numbers of Burghers as a result have migrated to Australia while others have settled in Britain and Canada.

CONCLUSION

It will thus be realised that in a plural society like that of contemporary Sri Lanka, with solidarity patterns based upon shared religion, language, ethnic identity, caste and region commanding a loyalty rivalling at least in some situations that which the nation state itself is able to generate, a national consensus on basic social and political goals is hard to establish.

However, an overwhelming number of middle-class Ceylon Tamils in the north and east look towards the Sinhalese south and the capital city, Colombo, for economic gain and political preferment. This inhibits the development of a separatism that looks to south India as an alternate focus of loyalty, though in times of stress there has been an attraction to extra-national movements such as the D.M.K. and a turning to Madras for succour.

On the other hand, as the Sinhalese Buddhists are politically and socially divided, and are unsure of their own strength and cohesion, they tend to regard the non-Buddhist minorities, especially the Ceylon and Indian Tamils and Roman Catholics, as a greater threat than they actually are.

In a sense, therefore, there are two nationalisms in Sri Lanka, a Sinhalese nationalism and a Tamil nationalism which vacillates, depending on the degree of intensity of Sinhalese Buddhist political consciousness, between a terminal loyalty to the Tamil nation and an overriding loyalty to a Ceylonese nation.

But there is a balancing factor. The Sinhalese power elites are keenly aware of the need to maintain national unity. They have therefore not pushed Sinhalese Buddhist nationalism too hard so as to bring about the break-up of the nation itself. The Buddhist ethos of moderation acts here as a deterrent to extremism.

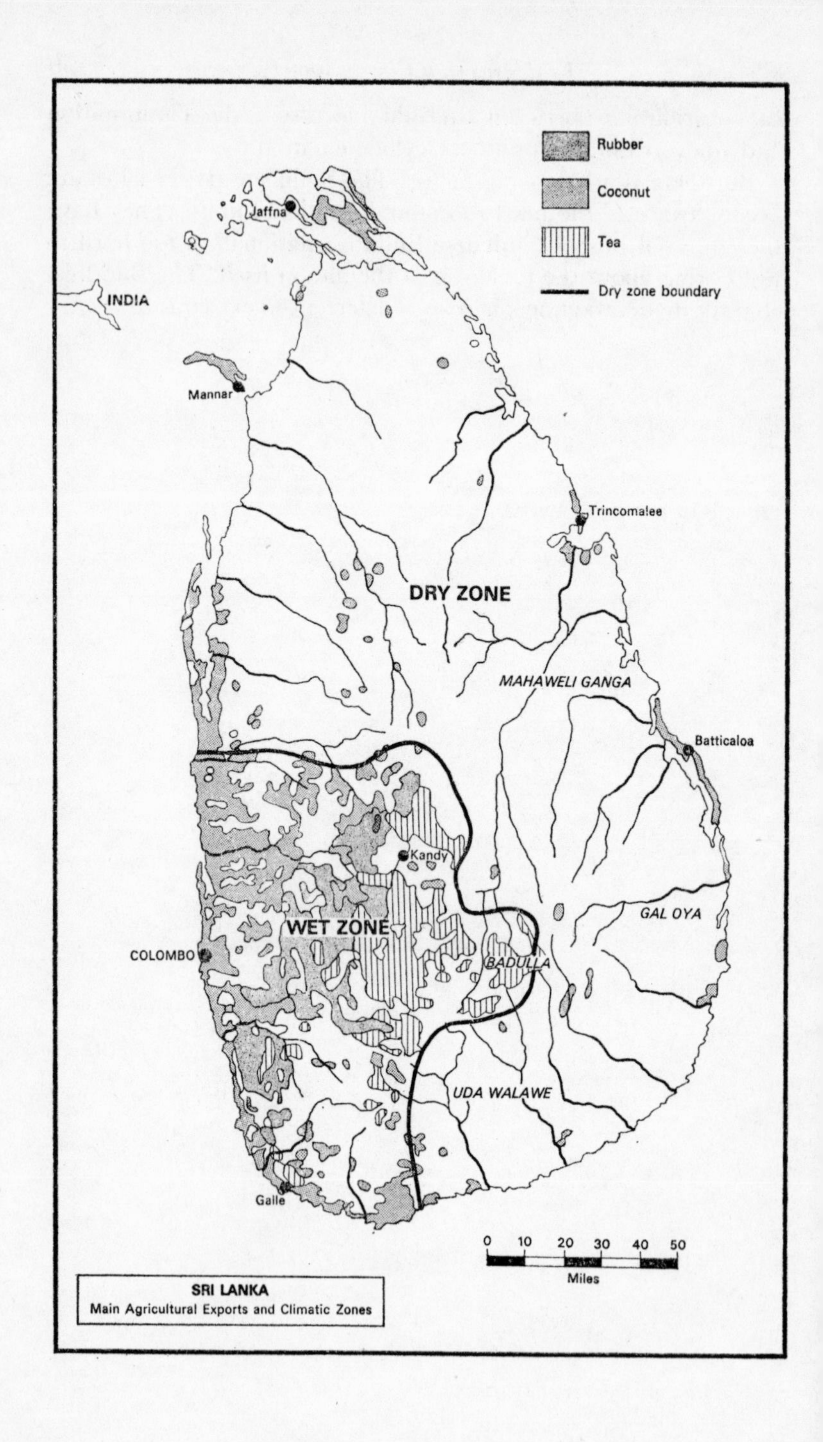

SRI LANKA
Main Agricultural Exports and Climatic Zones

3 Economic and Social Progress

POPULATION

Sri Lanka's economic dilemma lies in that she has to cope with the problem of a rising population. It is made more difficult by the fact that at the disposal of this population has been placed a whole range of welfare services, unequalled in Asia, which the country's resources can ill-afford to sustain. The political consequences of tampering with these services are so explosive that most governments have desisted from resorting to such measures.

The rate of increase in population, especially since 1946, is largely due to the widening gap between mortality and fertility rates brought about by the rapid expansion of medicare services and the virtual elimination of malaria by the efficient organisation of D.D.T. spraying campaigns. Table 3.1 gives the figures of population growth from the first census held in 1871 by the British colonial administration to the most recent one held in 1971.

It will be noticed that in the space of a hundred years the population has more than quintupled, while between the censuses of 1931 and 1963, the population had doubled itself. Though the annual rate of increase is now on the decline (from 2.8 per cent in 1953, it came down to 2.4 in 1968 and 2.3 in 1971), partly because of the use of contraceptive devices and postponement of marriage by women, it is nevertheless anticipated that if the present trend persists, population will double itself in twenty-nine years compared with the three score years and ten that developed nations take to double their population. The biggest problem facing governments since independence has therefore been to have economic development keep pace with increases in population. Efforts to popularise methods of birth control have so far met with only minimal success.

There are other aspects of this population problem which are incapable of speedy solution. There is, first, the fact of the relative youth of the island's population.[1] It is estimated that 52 per cent of the population is below nineteen years of age and 40 per cent is under fourteen. This implies greater dependence of the young on the old and an additional strain on the nation's welfare system. Further, the accelerated rate of population growth brings a corresponding increase in the work force. The estimated work force of 3.4 million in 1956 will rise to about 7 million in 1981, creating problems for the country in the field of manpower planning and employment.[2] And because of the undiversified and ill-planned structure of secondary and higher education in the country,

TABLE 3.1

POPULATION GROWTH 1871–1971

Census	Population (millions)	Average Annual Growth Rate (percentage)
1871	2.4	—
1881	2.8	1.42
1891	3.0	0.86
1901	3.6	1.72
1911	4.1	1.42
1921	4.5	0.91
1931	5.3	1.67
1946	6.7	1.52
1953	8.1	2.84
1963	10.6	2.75
1971*	12.7	2.3

* *Census of Population 1971, Preliminary Release No. 1*, Department of Census and Statistics, June 1972.
Source. *Research and Industry*, Industrial Development Board of Ceylon, March 1970.

labour is at a surplus in the traditional sectors of the economy while there is a marked shortage of technically and vocationally qualified personnel. In 1969 there were some 14,000 university graduates, and 112,000 young persons with the general certificate examination, ordinary level qualification without employment. A significant fact is that unemployment is more prevalent among the youth. Sixty-eight per cent of the total unemployed in 1968 belonged to the age group 15–29.[3] This age group numbered 1.69

million (of the workforce) in 1968 and it is estimated that it will be 2.3 million in 1978, or roughly 40 to 42 per cent of the total workforce.[4]

Unemployment is more widespread in the rural areas than in the urban. Over 75 per cent of unemployment is in the countryside.[5] There is as well under-employment in the form of seasonal or casual work, again more prevalent in the rural than in the urban areas. One consequence of this rural unemployment and under-employment is an aimless drift from the countryside to the towns, especially by youth in search of better opportunities.

Many attempts have been and are being made to tackle the unemployment problem. During 1965–70, youth settlement schemes, an agricultural development corps popularly referred to as the land army, and a national service programme organised by a national youth service council which was specially set up to look into the problems of the youth, sought to alleviate the problem.

With a new government in office in 1970, a portfolio of employment was specially created and taken over by the prime minister herself. A national apprenticeship scheme designed to absorb unemployed graduates who would be trained at administrative and managerial levels in the public sector, in industry and trade and in the co-operative movement was successfully got under way.[6] A sum of Rs 200 million was also set apart in the government's budget proposals for 1970–1 as capital expenditure to be utilized for sixteen projects in village and agricultural development to create job opportunities for about a hundred thousand people.

Widespread dissatisfaction still persists, despite the steps that have been taken towards improving the unemployment situation. The alarming proportions of the youth insurrection of March–April 1971 was evidence of the impatience of young people with the efforts that were being made by the U.F. government to come to grips with the problem.

THE SOCIAL SERVICES

The relative youth of the island's population places a greater burden on the welfare services. Most of the social expenditure is on the free public education and health services, housing, the provision of subsidised food and transfer payments. The objective is not so much to develop the social infrastructure as to enable rival political groupings to capture and retain political power. The system worked well during the good years – in the first half of the 1950s when rubber prices received a boost in 1950–1 due to the Korean War, and tea prices picked up rapidly in the 1955–1956 phase – but became a strain thereafter with export prices declining and increasing pressure of population.

The Rice Subsidy

This has proved to be the severest drain. Between 30 and 40 per cent of government expenditure and a considerable sum of foreign exchange are spent on providing this service. The subsidy is in fact a double one involving a guaranteed price for paddy to domestic producers and a weekly ration of rice which has varied in quantity and price from time to time but is generally made available to the consumer at prices well below those prevailing in the open market. For instance, during 1960–6, four pounds of rice a week was provided to each adult person at a price which was approximately half that prevailing in the world market.

This double subsidy on rice absorbed nearly one-fourth of all revenue, blocked public savings for public investment, increased the use of foreign exchange for imports of rice and discouraged domestic production of substitutes for rice because rice was available at cheaper rates than those substitutes.

Education

All education in the island from the kindergarten to the university has been free since 1 October 1945.

As a result of legislation enacted in late 1960 and early 1961 the majority of schools imparting primary and secondary education are now state-owned. Previously most of them were managed and run by Christian denominational bodies while there were still a few others which were controlled by Buddhist, Hindu and Muslim religious organisations. All of these were financed by a system of state grants. Parallel to these were 'central schools', run by the state, imparting secondary education.

Over 75 per cent of children between the ages of five and fourteen attend school. The enrolment ratio is high compared to other countries in the Asian region; and non-attendance in the 5–14 age group and dropouts at the 11–14 age level are very low. In 1966 the school-going population was estimated at 3 million and the figure will go up to about 5 million in 1981.

The rapid increase in the school-going population entails a considerable investment in expenditure on education, thereby imposing further burdens on the island's depleted exchequer. State expenditure on education per head of population is already the highest in Asia. The literacy rate is more than 82 per cent.

It is realised that the kind of education imparted hitherto is quite unsuited to the needs of a developing country, the emphasis having been more on the liberal arts and humanities than on technical, scientific and vocational skills. There is consequently a marked shortage of middle-level technicians, foremen, draftsmen, supervisors, etc.

The immediate need is to establish a multi-purpose, multilateral senior secondary school system which will be geared to the manpower needs of a developing economy. Some progress has been made in this direction with the establishment of provincial polytechnics, junior technical schools and various institutions for the training of craftsmen. But the most pressing need is for laboratory equipment in the schools in order to encourage students to take to scientific education. There is at present a scarcity of science teachers in the Sinhalese medium.

Table 3.2 compares the position with regard to education and unemployment for the years 1953 and 1963, establishing the fact that educational advancement outstrips availability of employment opportunities.

The imbalance in education was further worsened by the decision of the M.E.P. government of S. W. R. D. Bandaranaike in 1958 as part of its programme to give Buddhism its proper place to grant university status to two of the best known traditional centres of Buddhist learning in the island, the Vidyodaya and Vidyalankara *pirivenas* (training seminaries). These new universities began with an emphasis on cultural and liberal education and it was only later in the 1960s that they expanded in the direction of scientific education.

The disequilibrium became more emphasised when the Ministry of Education decided in 1965 that all 4,042 students who qualified for admission to the universities, the majority of these being in the liberal arts and humanities, should be admitted to the universities instead of the 1,550 for whom places were available on a competitive basis. In 1968, the Colombo campus of the University of Ceylon was converted into a separate university.

TABLE 3.2

UNEMPLOYMENT BY EDUCATIONAL STATUS, 1953, 1963 AND 1966

Category	Involuntarily Employed		
	1953	1963	1966
No schooling	16.6	6.0	10.5
Some primary	16.4	10.5	21.0
Some secondary	17.9	23.0	44.0
Passed G.C.E.	25.0	39.3	n.a.
Some higher education	2.9	13.9	21.5
Technically educated	—	3.8	n.a.

These figures have been extracted from
Sources. (1) International Bank for Reconstruction and Development and International Development Association, 'Ceylon: Preliminary Survey of Education', Colombo, Ministry of Planning and Economic Affairs, 1966 and
(2) *Research and Industry*, Industrial Development Board of Ceylon, 1970.

All these steps taken together aggravated further the problem of graduate unemployment. But admissions to the universities have gone on apace without proper reference to the kind of skills needed for development.

In 1966 a College of Technology was established in Katubedde, obviously with a view to correcting the imbalance, but as we have stated earlier the problem has to be dealt with at the school level where scientific education is still undeveloped.

Enrolments in all institutions of higher education at present (1971) exceeds fifteen thousand a year. This works out to less than 1 per cent of the population in the age group 18–24, though it is claimed that the proportion compares favourably with other countries in the Asian region.

As a consequence of this ill-planned expansion of higher education, and the many frustrations that the university-going population are faced with, the universities themselves became heavily politicised and a breeding ground for trouble, violence and extremist movements. In a vain effort to control and regulate the universities, the Dudley Senanayake 'national government' enacted a Higher Education Act in 1966 which only brought about further deterioration. The National Council of Higher Education which was set up under the Act, with powers greater than that of the usual university grants committee, functioned more as the instrument of the 'national government's tactless minister of education than as an autonomous body carrying out its declared objective of promoting and rationalising the conduct of university education.

In April 1971, shortly after the abortive insurrection of the ultra-Marxist youth organisation, the P.L.F., the U.F. minister of education appointed a committee to recommend changes in the higher education set-up. This committee advised a restructuring of courses, drastic reduction of the arts faculties and the amalgamation of the four universities and the College of Technology into a single university. The Higher Education Act of January 1972 embodied most of these recommendations.

In the schools, a 'new education policy' has been put into effect from the beginning of 1972.[7] The main objective is to alter the white collar oriented type of education that was sought after and imparted in schools. As the minister of education himself remarked, the proposed reforms would 'enable our educational machinery to be geared to socio-economic development at grass roots levels'.[8] Its design is to lay the foundations for job orientation at the grade six level (eleven plus). Pre-vocational guidance will be provided in subjects such as metalwork, pottery, woodwork, etc. and, depending on the geographical environment of the school, in fishing, gemmology, agriculture, etc. As the programme gets under way from grades six to nine, the vocational or occupational prospects available in the different districts will increasingly influence the teaching of subjects like science, geography, history, mathematics, etc. in the schools of a given district.

Further, the English language will be compulsorily taught in all schools from grade six onwards. As more teachers become available, it is planned to introduce its teaching from grade three upwards.

With a view to redressing the imbalance in the teaching of science, this subject is to be taught to all students from the sixth grade upwards.

The other objective of the 'new educational policy' is to reduce the differences between the privileged and the poor and between urban and rural children. The U.F. minister has stated that during the next ten years he proposes 'to develop a hundred schools in the less developed areas to the level of the good Colombo schools so that the present inequities in educational facilities from area to area are corrected'.[9] While this is the long-term remedy, the immediate solution proposed is to put all students from the sixth to the ninth grade through a common programme of studies which will include subjects in the social sciences, mathematics, science, English and pre-vocational studies among others. This would do away with the practice hitherto adopted of streaming students into science, arts, commerce, etc. in preparation for their first public examination which was the G.C.E., ordinary level. This change has been introduced, as has been officially stated, because otherwise 'the pupils from the remote areas where the facilities for science teaching are inadequate have the more favoured science stream less accessible to them'.[10] All students will therefore be equally placed when they sit their first public examination at the end of grade nine – the national certificate of education.

A more far-reaching change to ensure equalisation of educational opportunities is what is proposed after the national certificate of education examination. It is at this level (grades ten and eleven) that competition for admission to the universities begins. The numbers that will be allowed to proceed beyond the national certificate of education level will be determined on an area quota basis, consistent with the maintenance of proper standards.[11] Entrance to the university would therefore no longer be on the basis of merit, which it is argued is grounded on the fact of availability of opportunity, or on the student's good fortune in having middle-class parents, or education in one of the better urban schools. Under the area quota scheme students from the less developed parts of the country will no doubt have a greater chance of going in for higher education than they hitherto had.

It is recognised however that ultimately it is only a little less than 1 per cent of the school-going population that enters university each year. Government policy is to put an end to the rat race in the schools to enter the universities and for the schools to concentrate on the large majority who will not enter but who would nevertheless be needed by the country to man the various middle levels in the different sectors of the economy. With this end in view, the curriculum at the post-national certificate of education level will also be restructured to ensure that students are properly advised and directed to the employment avenues available.

Health

Health services are reasonably efficient and their improvement over the years is reflected in the rapid decline in mortality rates and the considerable increase in life expectancy.

Medical services until 1971 were available free of charge in government medical institutions to all sections of the population which could not afford to pay for treatment. A very nominal charge has been imposed since 1971. The ratio of doctors to population in the country is about 1:4,900, which compares very favourably with other countries in south-east Asia. Effective programmes for the eradication of malaria and the elimination of such diseases as tuberculosis, filaria, V.D., leprosy, etc. have been put into execution.

The emphasis was both on the curative and preventative services, but in the period 1965–70 there was a shift in emphasis to the latter. It was decided that the best use should be made of the limited resources available and that greater attention on the preventative side could reduce the burden on the already congested hospitals. The present bed strength is 3.2 per thousand of the population for the country as a whole, while the official target is to increase it to ten beds per thousand of the population.[12]

Since 1956 when the M.E.P. took office, the state has also given increasing recognition to the role of ayurvedic (indigenous) medicine in the curative health services of the country. There are over thirteen thousand ayurvedic medical practitioners of whom some six thousand are officially registered in the private sector and they obtain various kinds of assistance from government. There are a number of state ayurvedic hospitals. Further, a government institute for research in ayurvedic medicine was established in 1961.

The most neglected aspects of health are sewerage and water supply. Of all the urban areas in Ceylon, only Colombo has a water carriage system of sewerage disposal and even this is available to only about 60 per cent of houses. In the congested and slum areas of the city, sanitary facilities are altogether lacking.

Governments since 1956 have been interested in developing and extending the water supply system, and the target is to make supplies available to 80 per cent of the population. At present, of the one hundred and twenty urban areas in the island, sixty-six towns have public water supply services and thirty-eight have inadequate facilities. Rural areas obtain their supplies of drinking water from unprotected wells, rivers, streams, water holes, etc.

On the whole the prevailing system has produced very satisfactory results. The crude death rate per thousand of the population has dropped from 26.6 in 1920–2 to 7.9 in 1968 and life expectancy has during the same period increased from 32.7 years to over 66.

Housing

With rapid population growth, housing is an urgent national problem but for reasons of national economy tends to be a generally neglected sphere. For instance, the Ten-Year Plan in 1959 recommended that the public sector should be responsible for only one-third of the total outlay envisaged while the remaining two-thirds, it suggested, should be undertaken by the private sector. The Five-Year Plan in 1971 makes provision for various facilities and incentives for house construction but does not come to grips with the problem of finding accommodation for the increasing population.

The congestion in Colombo is most acute, it being estimated that there are in the city over 70,000 shanty dwellers and more than 240,000 living in substandard houses.[13] The latter category occupy some six hundred acres, which works out at four hundred people per acre (a very high density), with all the attendant evils of insanitation, vice and potential epidemic. A special committee on housing appointed in 1961 estimated housing needs by 1972 to be 945,000, 207,400 for urban areas and 738,400 for the rural. The committee estimated the cost of construction to be in the region of Rs 2,945 millions inclusive of the cost of land, or an average annual expenditure of Rs 295 millions for the ten-year period beginning in 1963. The total public sector investment for the period 1959–69 has in fact been about Rs 40 million a year.[14]

A special committee on housing appointed in 1970 (the Alif Committee) by the communist minister of housing estimated that housing requirements have gone up considerably. It recommended among other things a scheme to take over privately owned houses and to distribute them to their present tenants and others in need of accommodation. Another committee (the Maureen Seneviratne Committee), appointed a little earlier, reported on selected aspects of the rent laws. Government housing policy up to this time was to encourage private sector participation in the construction of residential quarters. But the results, according to the minister of housing, have been far from encouraging.[15]

The U.F. government therefore launched on a policy of regulation and control by the state. The reports of the two committees referred to formed the basis of a consolidated Rent Act passed by Parliament in February 1972.[16] This new Act is in effect a tenant's charter. It extends rent control to all rented residential premises in the private sector and provides the tenant with adequate security against capricious evictions and exploitative landlords. Further, it makes it easier for those who wish to build houses for themselves and their children to obtain the necessary facilities. To this end a Building Materials Corporation was set up to rationalise and facilitate the supply of materials to prospective house builders, as well as to stimulate research on producing building material from local raw materials. More important, legislation was enacted in 1973 to limit the ownership of houses and restrict their ownership to the number of persons in a family. Tenants of the surplus houses were given the first choice of purchasing them.

The Transport System.

The island had no commercial shipping of its own until 1971 when a state sponsored Shipping Corporation was established which at present owns five cargo ships with a tonnage of 40,000. The state operates a very modest airline, an omnibus passenger transport system and a railway, all monopolies. The last two are a part of the social service framework and are therefore a considerable burden on the exchequer.

Ports

Colombo on the west coast ranks first in importance, with Trincomalee on the east coast coming next, and then Galle in the south. Kankesanturai in the north is a minor port of only domestic value.

Colombo port had the advantage that it was situated at the junction of east-west sea routes and was the port of call for all ships on this lane when the Suez Canal was in use. From the domestic angle too it has a huge advantage over the other ports because on its hinterland are the most commercially productive areas of the country (tea, rubber and coconuts) with a network of roads and railways all converging on the city itself. Also, within an eighty-mile radius of the city reside 75 per cent of the population who also carry on their occupations within this broad arc.

Due to rival trade unionism, personal power struggles of union leaders and the active intervention of political parties, mostly Marxist-oriented, the port of Colombo is beset with constant labour disputes and strikes. The situation was considerably worse during the period before 1958 when the handling of cargo was the business of private stevedoring firms.

In 1958 the M.E.P. government nationalised the port of Colombo and placed it in the charge of a Port Cargo Corporation. Among other benefits that accrued from this action was the fact that negotiating with labour became much easier. But labour troubles did not disappear. On the contrary, politically inspired strikes by the Marxist unions were a dominant feature during the last years of the M.E.P. government in 1957–9, and were not uncommon in the succeeding phase when Mrs Bandaranaike was prime minister, 1960–5. In 1964 the government of Mrs Bandaranaike had the port of Galle brought under the control of the Port Cargo Corporation, and in 1967 the nationalisation of all the ports of Ceylon was completed when Dudley Senanayake's 'national government' had Trincomalee placed in the charge of the Corporation.

Trincomalee and Galle have acquired some importance because of the unsettled labour conditions in Colombo. But they suffer from the fact that neither commands sizable economic activities in their hinterlands. Colombo still handles the bulk of all cargo. Kankesanturai, the least of the ports, derives its importance from handling cement and the raw materials for cement – the town being one of the centres of the cement industry.

The importance of Colombo as a port of call for international shipping is expected to decline when the Sethusamudran Canal alongside India's southernmost coast is completed. It will become unnecessary for ships to circumnavigate Ceylon. Instead of calling at Colombo for the transhipment and re-shipment of cargo especially, they could have easier access to the Indian ports of Cochin and Tuticorin.

From the point of view of government expenditure the biggest burden is the drain on foreign exchange resulting from the heavy freight surcharges imposed by the Conference lines because of delays to shipping on account of labour troubles and operational difficulties.

Civil Aviation

The international airports are in Katunayake and Ratmalana, both within short distances of Colombo. Katunayake airport (renamed Bandaranaike airport) was completed with the help of aid from the government of Canada under the Colombo Plan. Ratmalana airport is not equipped to handle big jet aircraft. There are besides a number of landing strips in some of the important towns which are utilised for domestic flights.

Air Ceylon operates all domestic flights and flights to Bombay and Madras. For the longer international services it worked in association with KLM and later BOAC. In 1972 an arrangement was worked out with UTA French Airlines. Air Ceylon has so far functioned with a minimum deficit on its income account.

The Sri Lanka Government Railway

The Railway operates 922 route miles, of which 835 miles are broad gauge (5′ 6″) and 87 narrow gauge (2′ 6″). The latter is being run to obsoletion as it is unsuited for present-day purposes. The railway has a staff of some twenty-five thousand, all government servants. This staff is considered excessive.

Apart from excessive staff and frequent absenteeism, the prime cause for the railway's operational losses is its ridiculously low passenger fares which remained unchanged from 1953 to 1971. Government employees paid even lower fares. No attempts were made to increase fares, as governments were not happy about the possible political repercussions. On the other hand, the charges on goods traffic in the context of competition from road hauliers are comparatively high. Consequently the railways suffer an annual operating loss of Rs 25 million and if unpaid interest and capital charges are included, this works out to an annual burden of Rs 60 million to government. In 1971 changes were introduced in regard to fares, but these still remain very cheap.

The Sri Lanka Transport Board

Public dissatisfaction with the services provided by private bus operators was the prime cause for the nationalisation of all bus companies on 1 January 1958 by the M.E.P. government. Omnibus transport was thereafter placed under the control of a Transport Board.

As in the case of the railway, fares are extremely low and until 1971 governments were reluctant to increase these. Employment on the board's staff is based on political patronage and is excessive and wasteful. A visiting team of German experts reporting on the existing fares (prior to nationalisation) stated that in India, with which Ceylon transport conditions could be compared, 'fares are higher than in Ceylon, although the standard of living is lower in India'.[17] The pre-nationalisation fares were more or less maintained until 1971 when changes were made. But travel by omnibus is still very cheap.

In comparison with the railway system, the public omnibus transport system takes the first place. For instance in 1965–6 it moved just under 700 million passengers for nearly 4 million passenger miles whereas the railway moved a little over 70 million passengers for about 1.5 million passenger miles.[18]

In the first four years of its operation, the board incurred losses,[19] but from 1962 to 1966 it recorded fair profits. During 1965–70 the board was greatly inconvenienced because of unwarranted political interference especially in the matter of job creation and the granting of employment to constituents and political supporters.

Power Supply

In November 1969 power supply was transferred to the control of the Sri Lanka Electricity Board.

Despite the fact that the charges for electricity are considered to be low by international standards, it is nevertheless high in the local context, judging from the number of domestic consumers, which in 1964 was estimated at a mere 6 per cent of the total population. And since the average consumption in that year was around 1,600 kwh per household, at a cost ranging from 10 cents per unit (in Colombo and a few other towns) to 36 to 85 cents per unit (in other local authority areas), it could only be an article of consumption for the better-off sections of the community.[20]

Since installation costs are high, the expansion of supply has been far from rapid. A further retarding factor is that the island has to depend on her water resources for her electricity and one in every four years may be a dry year. In 1962 only 382 square miles of the island were supplied with electricity and two-thirds of this area covered only two of its nine provinces. There were large sections of provinces with no supply whatsoever.

A further consequence is that rural electrification, an agent of modernisation, which could also help the peasant farmer in his agricultural pursuits and provide employment opportunities to others, has suffered retardation. In August 1968 the minister of finance announced a four-year scheme for the electrification of five hundred villages at a cost of Rs 25 million. But this comprises only a fraction of the village community as there are some twenty thousand villages in the island as a whole.

Until the various hydro-electric projects inclusive of those which will be commissioned when major irrigation schemes get under way are completed, industrial development will suffer and benefits that will accrue to the domestic consumer will have to be postponed. At the present time there is considerable waste of resources in view of the fact that a large number of industrial enterprises, including the tea industry, have their own private generating plants. The Department of National Planning in its *The Development Programme 1964–65* opined that electricity will have to be made available at prices considerably lower than they are now available if manufacturing costs are to be anything like competitive.[21]

These investments in the social infrastructure raise many questions. The conventional argument that they are a waste and a drag on economic development need not detain us for long. The expenditure is in effect a method of re-distributing wealth in a society where there are wide disparities of income. It has been, besides, one of the most effective means of ensuring the continuance of the democratic system in Sri Lanka. Social discontent was not, until the P.L.F. insurrection of April 1971, permitted to go below the level which would leave the underprivileged with no option but to resort to extra-parliamentary action in order radically to alter the political process. An I.B.R.D. team headed by Manfred Blobel visiting the island in 1971 estimated that the state devoted 55 per cent of its total outlays on social services for the financial year 1968–9, which it said worked approximately to Rs 150 per head of population – a very high figure.[22]

More pertinent is whether the available finances are being put to the best possible uses in the area of social welfare. In other words, the argument is that the social services should not be politically motivated. Expenditure on the social infrastructure, it is now being argued in government circles, should ensure outputs which are relevant for national development – the familiar cost benefit analysis.

AGRICULTURE

Land Development

Active interest in reclaiming the abandoned desolate dry zone areas (which occupy about two-thirds of the island) for cultivation of paddy, began to be manifest in the 1930s when the minister of agriculture under the Donoughmore set-up, D. S. Senanayake, pioneered a number of important colonisation schemes in what had hitherto been malaria-ridden territory.

Land development has had a fourfold purpose.

First, it seeks to transfer population from the overpopulated and congested parts of the country to newly opened-up lands. A variety of schemes have been organised for this purpose.

Village expansion systems. These take the form of (1) allocation of crown land within the vicinity, which serves to extend the residential plot already available to the villager so that it will be of assistance to the dependants of his family; (2) alienation of economic units of paddy land under minor irrigation schemes to villagers in the vicinity; (3) highland schemes, also referred to as 'accelerated' or 'major village expansion schemes', under which villagers obtain economic units of crown land close to their dwelling places and financial assistance for the cultivation of specified commercial crops such as tea or coffee; and (4) acquisition of estate lands, also for distribution to villagers in the area. It has, however, been established that lands distributed under this category are not utilised for the cultivation of the specific crops for which they were allocated, and as a result valuable agricultural lands have been lost. Greater care is therefore taken now when such lands are acquired.

Major colonisation schemes. Originally these allotments were given out in lots of five acres of paddy land and three acres of high land. It was found that this was too large an allotment for the colonist to manage and was reduced to three acres of paddy land and two of highland. In 1963–4 the area of paddy was further reduced to two acres and of highland to one. This last-mentioned reduction was decided upon with a view to making land available to as many settlers as possible, but the viability of such units is questioned.

Colonists were assisted with liberal subsidies for constructing their dwelling places and for bringing their land under cultivation. In addition they received a whole range of inducements, such as fertilisers and agro-chemicals, at subsidised prices and, or on credit, loans of seed paddy, crop insurance against failure from drought or floods, agricultural training through extension services, and a guaranteed purchase scheme under which the state purchased the produce at prices well above world market levels, often at prices twice those prevailing in the open market. Colonists could also raise easy loans from co-operative societies. These benefits, it might also be noted, were made available to cultivators in general.

From the point of view of returns, the official assessment is that the paddy lots had not produced adequate yields, nor were the highland plots put to proper use.[23] However, with the increasing use of high-yielding varieties of paddy seed and Japanese methods of transplanting the young paddy stalks, there has been some significant improvement in production. During the period 1961–6 paddy cultivation per acre generally increased on an average from 36 to 39 bushels. Yields, however, varied from 40–60 bushels per acre for the different districts. In the period 1967–1970 there was a rapid improvement in yields per acre due to sustained government interest in promoting paddy production (see Table 3.4, p. 85, for details).

High colonisation schemes. These were started in 1957 as the land available under the major colonisation schemes was not adequate to meet the demands of the landless. Landless families were resettled in economic units of land, though within the same district as their original homestead. They had to be cultivated with permanent commercial crops such as tea, rubber and coconuts.

Middle-class schemes. Persons with incomes above a certain level and in a position to develop the lands allocated to them came within this category. The extent of land alienated under these schemes has not been great owing to the pressure of demand from the poorer sections of the community.

Marginal land sales. Prior to 1962 blocks of fifty acres per person in areas with water or rainfall were allocated to middle-class applicants for the cultivation of paddy or commercial crops. From 1962, larger blocks of land for which there was no demand from the peasantry were made available. It has since been established that the majority of such lands have been misused. Their valuable timber has been removed, they have been exposed to erosion, and little or no cultivation has taken place.

Youth settlement schemes. An organised scheme for senior school certificated youths and for those who had passed out from the farm schools was put into operation from 1965. Prior to this, youths with these qualifications were given preference in the allocation of a percentage of lands under the major colonisation schemes. A number of special schemes for the cultivation of tea, rubber, coconut or rice was also organised for this type of youth. However, these schemes were not successful because they lacked proper planning, supervision, and financial inducements. In the special schemes, it was found that the senior school certificate youths who were settled in them abandoned their allotments as soon as they obtained employment which did not require manual labour.

After 1965 more effort and planning were put into these youth schemes as part of government policy to alleviate unemployment. The target was to settle twenty thousand youths during the period 1965–70.

Special land leases. To encourage the cultivation of subsidiary food crops such as onions and chillies, and the rearing of cattle and goats, from 1965 the government offered large tracts of land not required by the peasantry on a twenty-five-year lease with tax incentives and other concessions to large-scale private enterprise, including limited liability companies, for development. It was hoped that this would help promote self-sufficiency and arrest the drain of foreign exchange. In a number of instances such special leases were abused and it cannot be said with certainty whether they met with any measurable success.

Government corporations and agencies. A River Valleys Development Board was established in 1965 with responsibility for two important schemes, the Uda Walauwe and the Gal Oya projects. The latter until this date was in the charge of the Gal Oya Development Board which was set up in 1949. The Gal Oya scheme was a multi-purpose agricultural project. During the period of the Gal Oya Board's existence from 1949 to 1965, irrigation was provided for the development of 53,550 acres of new land, 35,500 acres of old paddy land and 8,300 acres of sugar cane and tobacco. In all, some 120,000 acres come within the purview of this scheme and 10,648 families were settled under it during 1949–65.[24] The developed left bank was in 1961 placed under the administration of the government agent of the Amparai district within which the scheme is situated. The right bank is being developed by the present board.

The scheme has not been a complete success because the greater part of the inland paddy area had light sandy topsoil and required systematic and intensive manuring which has not always been done by the colonists.[25] Further, the sugar area has also been found to be low-yielding because of the poor draining of the soils.

The Uda Walauwe project is expected to bring 60,000 acres of irrigable land under a planned scheme of cultivation of paddy, cotton, sugar cane and citrus.

But by far the biggest scheme to be launched is the one that was inaugurated in 1970 to develop the potentialities of the basin of the island's biggest river, the Mahaveli. The scheme is in the charge of the Mahaveli Diversion Board set up in 1970. Its total cost is approximately Rs 6,000 million phased over a twenty-year period. Each stage of its implementation will be an economically viable proposition in itself. It envisages the construction of fifty-eight reservoirs and diversions of the river with a capacity to irrigate 650,000 acres of new land and 250,000 acres of land already cultivated. The first phase of the scheme is already under way. It is estimated that when the scheme is in full operation it will generate 900 megawatts of power. The I.B.R.D. and the International Development Association are providing loans to implement the scheme. It will confer huge benefits to the country's economy in agriculture and industry, and in absorbing the large numbers of unemployed persons.

Of the state-sponsored agencies (1) the Sugar Corporation, which was established in 1957, is now responsible for sugar cane cultivation projects and has a factory which has an intake capacity of 1,500 tons of cane per day. The factory at present works below capacity because the acreage covered by sugar cane is not adequate to feed the factory to capacity, and yields from 3,300 acres under cultivation is poor due to bad drainage. The corporation aims however at bringing 50,000 acres under cultivation. (2) The National Textile Corporation has a limited acreage under cotton cultivation. (3) The Sri Lanka State Plantations Corporation established in 1958 runs a number of estates and tea factories. It seeks to develop crown land with commercial crops and to provide employment for indigenous labour.

Table 3.3 provides a resumé of the lands alienated up to the year ended 1966 under the various schemes referred to above and the number of allottees who have benefited under each of them.

Secondly, it should be realised that these state policies in regard to land development and distribution constitute an attempt to alleviate unemployment and social distress. In this respect, all these schemes come within the framework of government welfare policies in view of the heavy subsidies that are provided to colonists and the moneys expended on developing such lands. Again

TABLE 3.3

ACREAGE OF LANDS ALIENATED AND NUMBER OF ALLOTTEES SETTLED UNDER STATE SCHEMES

Scheme	Acreage	Number of Allottees
Village expansion	663,869	504,154
Major colonisation		
Paddy	181,466	59,672
Highland	105,345	
Highland colonisation	31,498	8,853
Middle class	147,301	11,613
Marginal land	70,000	n.a.
Youth settlement	7,116	2,880
Special leases	57,415	174

Source. Ceylon Sessional Paper No. XI, 1968.

the relevant question is raised as to whether the outputs justify the inputs that go to make the system work – in effect whether the best possible use is being made of the resources available to the state. This has been a recurring theme of the criticisms of political opponents as well as of observers and experts both local and foreign.

The gestation period of irrigation colonisation schemes is reported to vary from eight to fifteen years for initial production to commence, twelve to twenty years for capacity output to be obained, and anything more than fifty years for them to pay back their full cost to the country.[26] The cost of providing irrigation facilities under the major schemes is approximately Rs 2,500 an acre and under minor schemes Rs 750 to Rs 1,000 per acre.[27] The former is regarded as prohibitive, the latter compares favourably with the heavy expenditure under the major schemes. It is estimated that a colonist's allotment costs the government anything between Rs 15,000 to Rs 18,000. The social service component of these schemes, such as the construction of houses, schools, hospitals, etc., absorbs the major part of government expenditure – 80 per cent of expenditure on village expansion schemes and 30 per cent on colonists' allotments in the colonisation schemes.[28] However, it is argued that this expenditure is justified to the extent that these services are a prerequisite for the settlement of families in the dry zone areas.

The recoveries levied from the allottees are ridiculously low – an annual payment of Rs 20 per acre in respect of the new schemes, and Rs 10 per acre for the old ones – and do not even cover the cost of maintaining and administering them. Nor are the payments even regular. In contrast, it is pointed out that the irrigation rates charged in India are double or treble that levied in Ceylon. The Short-Term Implementation Programme of 1962 estimated the cost benefit ratios as being uneconomic, between 0.56 and 0.67 (project costs being amortised over fifty years).[29] On the other hand the capital/output ratio was estimated to be over 17:1 when averaged over the four years 1961–2 and 1964–5.[30] It was also estimated that the allotments yielded the government an annual negative revenue (that is an annual net financial loss) of Rs 357 per acre.[31]

From the employment angle too the results were far from encouraging. During the five-year period 1962–7, less than 6 per cent of the annual increase in the workforce, which was estimated at between 90 to 100,000 per annum, was absorbed in these agricultural development schemes.[32]

These agricultural schemes, thirdly, became a prominent and essential aspect of the government's policy of promoting self-sufficiency in food production with a view to arresting the drain of foreign exchange on imports not only of rice but other essential foodstuffs like onions, chillies, potatoes, garlic, pulses, etc. Besides the various inducements provided to paddy cultivators referred to earlier, guaranteed prices were fixed for other essential foodstuffs as well.

In addition to owner cultivators of minuscule plots, each of which are very often separated from one another in small parcels, there are also a large number of tenant farmers cultivating under various schemes of share cropping.

Minuscule plots, scattered parcels and ownership of a single plot by several persons jointly, act as a disincentive to effort. This kind of situation is endemic in most parts of the island. The census of 1953 estimated that 591,852 acres of land in smallholdings, town and village gardens, and paddy representing 32.8 per cent of the total cultivated land in this class remained idle, fragmentation being one of the reasons for this waste.

The conditions of tenant farmers is far from satisfactory. Their greatest handicap is lack of security. In 1967 it was estimated that there were 400,000 acres of paddy, representing a little less than one-third of asweddumised land in the country under cultivation by some three hundred thousand tenant cultivators.[33] In 1971 an economist of the Central Bank of Ceylon concluded that more than 50 per cent of paddy lands in the island are held under share-cropping or leasehold arrangements.[34]

Despite the phenomenal increase in the area under paddy cultivation between the years 1962 (518,128 acres), 1946 (913,239 acres) and 1966 (1,313,239), rice still remains a smallholders' crop with 85 per cent of all holdings less than two acres and 60 per cent less than one acre.[35]

What is more significant is that despite all the interest shown by governments since 1931 in the promotion of paddy cultivation, very little was done to improve the conditions of the tenant cultivator till 1958. Previously, in 1952, legislation was enacted to secure this category of cultivators, but the Act lacked teeth and there was very little official or political enthusiasm to even invoke its weak clauses in their interests. In 1958, S. W. R. D. Bandaranaike's intrepid Marxist-inclined minister of agriculture, Philip Gunawardena, had the Paddy Lands Act accepted by Parliament, but only after some of its beneficial provisions had been excised by the latter's democratic socialist S.L.F.P. adversaries in the cabinet. The latter were apprehensive that the Act would give the minister the opportunities to broaden his political base.

The same minister was also responsible for the Co-operative Development Bank Bill of 1957 which again sought to ease credit facilities available to the cultivator, but it was adopted once more only in an emasculated form.

However, since its adoption the Paddy Lands Act has been amended at various times, in 1958 itself, 1961 and 1964 in the direction of providing additional safeguards for the cultivator.

In addition to seeking to provide the tenant cultivator with security of tenure, the other main features of the Paddy Lands

Acts of 1958 were the provisions for cultivation committees. These were expected to function as a catalyst in promoting paddy production. The committees were elected by cultivators for the management and adoption of advanced methods of cultivation and the improvement of minor irrigation works in the areas which came within their purview. There is also increasing liaison between the committees and the officials responsible for food production in the various government departments. An important instance of such co-operation was the decision in 1966–7 to conduct training classes in thirty-nine centres for cultivation committee personnel in regard to their function, duties and obligations especially in relation to the national food drive organised by the Dudley Senanayake government in 1967. The response was described as 'magnificent' and the classes were 'always extremely well attended'.[36]

A 'package programme' on the lines of that sponsored by the Ford Foundation in India whereby a pilot project in a designated area, in this case Elahera to begin with, was organised for 'farming on a planned basis' under which improved seeds, fertilisers, agro-chemicals, farm machinery and implements, better credit, improved extension services, and provision of adequate storage and marketing facilities were supplied. This initial project proved a success and was extended to other 'special project' areas from 1968–9.

The national food drive of the Senanayake government made a significant contribution towards self-sufficiency in rice. The immediate reason for the drive was the shortage of rice in the world market and the consequent rise in rice prices during the latter part of 1966. The Senanayake government reacted by halving the rice ration and adopting measures to increase the production of paddy. As a further incentive, the guaranteed price of paddy, which was introduced in 1948 and had been fixed at first in relation to world market prices (c.i.f. Colombo), but pegged at Rs 12 a bushel from 1952 onwards despite the fact that it was almost double the price prevailing in the world market in the years thereafter, was increased to Rs 14 a bushel. But government purchases under the guaranteed scheme tended to decline from 1967 due to the fact that rice fetched a higher price than Rs 14 in the open market.

For the reasons mentioned, as well as because of the use of

igh-yielding varieties of seed paddy, better cultivation practices, nd the use of improved varieties of fertilisers, the food drive esulted in a greater production of rice during 1967–70 than in 960–5 (see Table 3.4) when a different government in office nded to concentrate more on a policy of import substitution in range of industrial goods.

Table 3.4
Paddy Yields 1956–70

Year	Production in Thousand Bushels	Average Yield Per Acre
I. *During the Term of Office of the M.E.P. Government 1956–60*		
56–7	31,322	32.34
57–8	36,600	34.73
58–9	36,440	35.18
59–60	43,068	36.46
II. *During the Term of Office of the S.L.F.P. Government 1960–5*		
60–1	43,199	36.19
61–2	48,069	37.85
62–3	49,154	37.94
63–4	50,506	38.76
64–5	36,252	29.40
III. *During the Term of Office of the U.N.P.-oriented 'National Government' 1965–70*		
65–6	45,787	35.47
66–7	54,917	41.42
67–8	64,569	46.01
68–9	65,860	49.72
69–70	76,800 (estimates)	50.85 (estimated)

urce. Department of Census and Statistics.
ote. 1964–5 and 1965–6 were bad years due to adverse weather conditions.

The last aspect of land development is that it had the effect bringing the two communities, Sinhalese and Ceylon Tamils, in ntact with one another, in areas where they had never pre-ously come face to face. A number of these schemes were in eas adjacent to those inhabited by Ceylon Tamils or in the idst of Ceylon Tamil and Tamil-speaking Muslim settlements. t least two of Ceylon's best-known ministers responsible for rigation and land development (D. S. Senanayake 1931–46 and

C. P. de Silva, 1965–70), made little effort to disguise their inte
tion of getting the populations to intermingle with a view
promoting their fusion (D. S. Senanayake) or to undermine th
position of the Ceylon Tamils in 'strategic' areas (C. P. d
Silva).[38] Both ministers encountered strong opposition from th
main Ceylon Tamil political groupings. The latter feared th
the identity of the Ceylon Tamils as a separate cultural grou
was being threatened and that their parliamentary representatio
was being adversely affected by the influx of Sinhalese colonis
into constituencies where their position had been fairly secur
For instance, between 1946 and 1958 the proportion of Sinhale
to the rest of the population in the Tamil-speaking eastern pr
vince increased from 7.8 to 11.6 per cent while the number
Ceylon Tamils declined from 46.5 to 40.0 per cent.[38] The effe
was to exacerbate Sinhalese–Ceylon Tamil ethnic tensions.

Exports

Tea, rubber and coconuts, in that order, account for 93 per ce
of Sri Lanka's export earnings, of which tea alone contribut
some 63 per cent. They account for nearly one-third of th
country's national income besides sustaining a number of oth
economic activities. Other export crops, of little importance, a
arecanuts, cinnamon, cocoa and citronella.

The important fact in the island's economic situation is that
good part of tea, about 45 per cent, is owned by British con
panies, and 13 per cent by companies registered locally whe
ownership is divided between Ceylonese and non-Ceylones
while about 33 per cent of rubber is in the control of British cap
tal. Most tea and rubber is in large estates of a hundred acr
and above whereas coconut is a smallholders' crop and is almo
entirely owned by Ceylonese. The management and supervisio
of the large estates in (especially) tea and rubber and (occasio
ally) coconut are vested in agency houses which are almost whol
British-owned.

All three argricultural exports depend for their prices on th
vagaries of the foreign market. Tea was at its peak till about 19
(see Table 3.5). Thereafter there has been a steady declin
especially during the 1960s when prices were considerably d
pressed, though this was to some extent offset by an increase

the volume of exports. Between 1947 and 1970, export volume increased by 60 per cent, but the value of total tea exports improved by only 10 per cent. The drop in prices is partly due to the lower quality of teas exported as the tea industry is utilising its machinery to excess capacity. The machinery in the factories is considerably run down, besides being outdated. An urgent problem is the need for modernisation of factory equipment.

Sri Lanka is the world's second largest producer of tea and its produce has a high reputation for quality. Her principal customers are Britain, the United States, Australia, Canada, South Africa and New Zealand. She has also a fair market for her low- and medium-grown teas (low quality) in the countries of the middle east.

Rubber finds a market mainly in China, the United States, West Germany, the Soviet Union, Poland, Japan and Britain. It has maintained slightly better price levels than tea. Between 1947 and 1970 (see Table 3.5) the volume of exports rose by 95 per cent while export receipts increased by 85 per cent. In 1950–1951 there was a sharp rise in prices caused by the outbreak of the Korean War, while the rice–rubber barter agreement with the People's Republic of China signed in 1952 and renewed thereafter from time to time has helped the industry to keep going. In 1964 and 1970, China purchased 157.6 million lbs and 186.8 million lbs of rubber from Ceylon, which was 50.1 per cent and 52.7 per cent respectively of the total exports for these years. China fixes the price in keeping with those prevailing in the Singapore market. In return Ceylon obtains most of her total imports of rice and some of her other essential commodities from China. China offers favourable terms for this rice, sometimes at prices below the world market level. Rubber prices declined in 1956–7, 1962–4, and reached their lowest in 1967–8.

Coconut products, in contrast to tea and rubber, have fetched much better prices despite the fall in the volume of exports of coconuts, especially in 1958, 1969 and in 1970 (see Table 3.5).

When all three export commodities are taken into account, the increase in export earnings in the twenty-year period 1950 to 1970 is a mere 4 per cent, or 13 million U.S. dollars, which is minimal when compared to the rise in population over the same period. Nor is this minimal increase the only evidence of declining returns. The revenue from export duties on tea and rubber declined gradually during the years 1955–6 to 1965–6, from 25.5 per cent or approximately one-quarter of total government revenue in the former year, to 13.9 per cent or one-seventh of the total government revenue in the latter year.[39] And this despite the fact that there was a large increase in the volume of tea and rubber exports during the ten-year period in question – the volume of tea exported having increased by 31 per cent and rubber by 23 per cent.

TABLE 3.5

EXPORT VOLUMES AND EARNINGS OF TEA, RUBBER AND MAJOR COCONUT PRODUCTS 1947–70

Year	TEA		RUBBER		THREE MAJOR COCONUT PRODUCTS		Total Exports* Value $ m.
	Volume million lbs	Value U.S. $ million	Volume million lbs	Value $ m.	Volume million nuts	Value $ m.	
1947	287.3	170.8	182.2	39.2	572	28.0	267.8
1948	296.0	177.7	207.3	43.1	970	46.1	304.5
1949	297.6	195.8	197.0	37.7	940	50.6	320.2
1950	298.1	158.0	265.1	85.1	1030	52.1	328.4
1951	305.2	168.1	229.1	122.3	1263	67.2	400.0
1952	314.5	151.9	209.8	78.4	1454	48.7	315.5
1953	335.6	173.3	217.3	71.0	1262	51.3	329.4
1954	361.3	235.9	209.4	59.9	1171	44.5	380.0
1955	362.2	250.8	222.3	73.5	1531	47.3	407.6
1956	348.1	219.3	193.0	61.6	1418	44.7	364.5
1957	368.1	214.7	208.6	63.0	950	32.8	353.4
1958	411.2	237.8	207.2	54.2	890	34.5	359.5
1959	383.8	219.7	205.8	62.6	1140	51.3	368.5
1960	410.2	230.3	234.6	79.4	976	38.7	384.9
1961	426.0	234.2	197.3	54.6	1355	42.4	364.1
1962	452.0	241.4	224.5	60.9	1530	47.7	379.8
1963	455.9	239.5	209.5	54.0	1208	41.6	363.7
1964	455.7	239.9	253.2	60.9	1618	57.4	394.1
1965	494.6	254.2	266.8	63.9	1270	57.8	409.5
1966	441.3	215.8	298.4	70.8	1017	41.2	357.1
1967	477.7	222.9	290.9	59.2	940	35.1	355.0
1968	460.2	195.4	328.3	55.6	1096	55.6	342.0
1969	444.5	178.5	314.8	72.4	896	37.1	322.0
1970	459.7	188.2	354.2	73.9	874	39.8	341.7

* Includes re-exports.

Source. Central Bank of Ceylon, *Annual Report 1970*, and Ceylon Customs Returns.

Note. See also *Interim Report of the Tea Commission*, Sessional Paper No. VII, 1968 and *Report of the Tea Commission*, Sessional Paper No. XVIII, 1968.

At the same time the plantation companies (as well as other companies) have been subjected to a scale of taxation which is one of the highest in the world. All companies pay a non-refundable tax of 50 per cent of their income. In 1964–5 this company rate of taxation was the second highest in the world, next to Castro's Cuba. There were only 17 out of 150 countries which according to the Taxation Inquiry Commission imposed a corporate tax of 50 per cent or over.[40] In addition a study made by a committee which was asked to report on development and taxation in the plantation industry noted that (1) as much as 88.3 per

TABLE 3.6

TAXES, DIVIDENDS AND RESERVES AS A PERCENTAGE OF GROSS SURPLUS OF COMPANIES

Period	As a Percentage of Gross Surplus		
	Taxes	Dividends	Reserves
1951–9 (pre-Kaldor)	74.5	17.0	8.3
1957–9 (Kaldor + surcharge on income tax)	83.0	13.1	3.9
1960 (Kaldor + land tax and companies tax and *ad valorem* tax)	88.3	9.4	2.3

Source. *Report on Development and Taxation in the Plantation Industries* (unpublished).

cent of the gross surplus of companies was taken away as taxes in 1960; (2) that such taxes had increased from 74.5 per cent in the pre-Kaldor 1951–6 period to 88.3 per cent in 1960; (3) dividend income had progressively declined during this period; and (4) the percentage of reserves that companies held back for replanting capital development and other purposes had 'shrunk to dangerously low levels' by 1960.[41] Table 3.6 furnishes the data on this declining trend.

Table 3.7 below gives the value of the total assets of joint stock companies, and of partnership and proprietorships in the plantation sector as at 1964. When taken in relation to the total value of private sector assets and investments in 1964, the plantation sector contributed as much as 64.9 per cent of the total value.

TABLE 3.7
VALUE OF ASSETS, PLANTATION AND PRIVATE SECTOR, 1964

Type of Establishment	Value of Assets
Plantation companies rupee	413,292,225
Plantation companies sterling	515,004,913
Plantation proprietorships and partnerships	724,359,088
Total	1,652,656,226
Total value of all private sector assets	2,545,053,256*

* These include, besides the types of establishment mentioned, industrial companies, industrial proprietorships and partnerships, service companies, public and private and service proprietorships and partnerships.

Source. Central Bank of Ceylon, *Survey of Private Investment in Ceylon*, 1964, Parts 1 to 4. Bulletins of August 1965, November 1965, December 1965 and March 1966.

INDUSTRY

The Private and Public Sectors

One of the significant differences between the two main parties (U.N.P., S.L.F.P.) and their respective allies is their view of the extent to which private enterprise should be permitted to operate in the context of developing the country's economy. While the U.N.P. has stood for a greater degree of freedom for private enterprise, though even here with some measure of governmental control and direction, the S.L.F.P. and its allies wish the private sector to have a definite but assigned role within a national framework in which the public sector will have much the more dominant part to play.

For a variety of reasons, which we need not go into here, local enterprise was reluctant to enter the field of industrial production until the 1960s when the fortuitous circumstance of acute balance of payment crises led the governments of the time to impose a total ban on the import of various consumer items, thus providing the maximum encouragement to local entrepreneurs. In the 1930s and 1940s state enterprise in industry was more for the purpose of establishing a 'demonstration effect' for stimulating the private sector. These model projects did not, however, produce the desired effect.

After independence (1948) the vague outlines of a state industrial policy, albeit lacking coherence and definite purpose, began to take shape. This was during the U.N.P.'s first phase, from 1947 to 1956. Policy was (1) to develop basic and large-scale industries which could not be undertaken by private enterprise because the latter lacked sufficient capital and, in keeping with this, projects such as cement, paper mills and chemical factories were established; and (2) to invite and encourage private sector participation in state ventures wherever possible, and in fact to transfer ownership to it if this were feasible.

The emphasis on industry was nevertheless minimal. In the Six-Year Programme of Investment, 1954–5 to 1959–60, the investment on industry was to be a mere 4.4 per cent (approximately Rs 112 million) of the total outlay of Rs 2,529 million envisaged. The U.N.P. government in office at this time was fortified in its attitude by the encouragement it received from the I.B.R.D. mission's report of 1952. The mission favoured the development of small industries and advised second place for industry in the allocation of resources. Government therefore decided 'to create a favourable atmosphere in which the rapid establishment of large-scale industries by private enterprise becomes possible'.[42] To give effect to this policy, the Government Sponsored Corporations Act No. 19 of 1955 provided for the transfer and management of government factories to semi-autonomous public corporations and their transference *thereafter* to private enterprise by the disposal of government shares. The first step in this direction was the vesting of the state-owned plywood, leather, cement, paper and ceramic factories in public corporations. Before the government could transit to the second stage, a new government, that of S. W. R. D. Bandaranaike (M.E.P.) with a different orientation took office in 1956.

The M.E.P. government had decided views on the important role that industry should play in the economic development of the country. Some of the leading economists the new government invited to advise it also had pronouncedly favourable views on the need for industrialising the country. Nicholas Kaldor noted that industrialisation had hardly begun and urged that 'the full and effective utilisation' of Ceylon's manpower resources was 'only conceivable through industrialisation and the growth of tertiary [service] industries which are based on it'.[43] Oscar Lange said the same thing though in different words when he held that 'industrialisation is the factor which alone has the dynamic force of carrying forward the island's economy'.[44] John Kenneth Galbraith came out in favour of the public sector undertaking the responsibility. His view was that 'if private enterprise had been fully competent for the task in the presently underdeveloped countries, it would already have asserted itself'.[45] And he added, 'where, as in Ceylon or India, there is a strong political attachment to socialism, the role of the publicly owned enterprise will be that much greater'.[46]

The new M.E.P. government reversed the U.N.P.'s policy of turning over to private enterprise state projects in industry, as well as that party's negative approach to the whole subject of industrialisation. The minister of industries in 1957 in a statement of policy laid down the spheres in which the state would (a) involve itself, (b) join hands with private enterprise, and (c) leave industrial development and exploitation wholly to the private sector.

In the same year the State Industrial Corporations Act was enacted by Parliament. This did not, as the previous Act had, provide for the transfer of ownership of state industrial projects to the private sector. On the contrary, the Act was utilised by the new government and its successor to expand considerably the area of public enterprise in industry.

Most important were the provisions made for public sector participation in industrial development in the Ten-Year Plan formulated in 1959 by the M.E.P. government. Of the Rs 13,600 millions to be invested, Rs 2,714 million or approximately 20 per cent was set apart for industry. Most of the projects envisaged were to be in 'the planned sector' which was to be the responsibility of the state. The schemes actually drawn up to give effect to the Plan by the succeeding S.L.F.P. government of 1960–5, the Short-Term Implementation Programme covering three fiscal years, 1961–2, to 1963–4, and the Development Programme, 1964–5, also assigned the major proportion of investment to the public sector. However both the Ten-Year Plan and the implementation programmes also assigned a definite place to the private sector. The latter in fact was to gain increasing importance in the years ahead.

The emphasis on the public sector was seen in the growth and multiplication of state industrial corporations between the years 1956 and 1965 – the period of M.E.P. and S.L.F.P. governments. By 1965 there were some 119 state industrial corporations in which it was estimated that a total sum of about Rs 487.0 million had been invested. This was a major advance from the position at the end of the U.N.P.'s first phase of power in 1956 when there were six government factories in which a sum of Rs 91.8 million had been invested.

The pattern set by the M.E.P. and S.L.F.P. governments of the 1956–65 phase was not altered in any basic way when the U.N.P. regained power in 1965 and continued in office till 1970. In fact there was a further expansion of the public sector. By March 1969 there were twenty-two new industrial corporations in which the state had invested an estimated sum of approximately Rs 1,081.1 million.

Public industrial corporations have not performed as well as private enterprise, for a variety of reasons embedded in the public's concept of all governmental activity being in fact an extension of the paternal welfare state. Prices are fixed to subsidise certain groups of consumers and the corporations are expected to serve as employment agencies.[47] Further, employees in state corporations keep demanding terms and services similar to those in government service, on the mistaken assumption that both are identical. There has also been industrial unrest in this sector from time to time and disputes have been settled more on political considerations than on the ability of these enterprises to make adjustments and concessions within the framework of a commercial management. Productivity in the state sector is consequently low.[48] In addition to all this, state corporations are invariably manipulated by politicians who have political favourites appointed to their directorates and who in turn become their willing instruments especially in the matter of providing jobs to loyal supporters and constituents. Many state corporations have as a result more employees than are really necessary.

With a view to setting things right, in October 1970 the U.F. minister of finance, the Trotskyist leader Dr N. M. Perera, observed that state corporations and statutory boards hereafter 'must be efficiently managed with a view to ensuring adequate returns to the state on the investments which are being made at such great sacrifice by the people of this country',[49] and added that he would levy a sum of not less than Rs 60 million for 1970–1971 from these institutions.[50]

One other factor for the failure of public undertakings to provide adequate returns, a factor which is however outside the welfare concept, is the under-utilisation of existing capacities in some of them, especially in the textile, sugar, steel and tyre factories. The Five-Year Plan attributed this to raw material shortages, market limitations and to failures of management and workers at all levels.

Until the election of the U.F. government in 1970, a kind of anarchy existed in that part of the private sector in which Ceylonese interested themselves. At different times their enterprises took different forms depending on the prevailing political and economic climate. During the U.N.P.'s first phase (1947–56) investment was usually in the plantation sector (coconuts, rubber and tea, in that order) by the more dynamic Ceylonese entrepreneurs. Others invested in the wholesale and retail trade, in building construction or in moneylending operations. By the early 1950s investment in the plantation sector had reached a certain saturation point, and there was a shift more to commerce, then to finance and finally to industry. The last stage was reached when balance of payment difficulties resulted in increasing restrictions on the import trade, when the state in turn entered this field to ensure uninterrupted and cheap supplies of essential commodities to the public to the exclusion of private traders, and when in the 1960s the state imposed a total ban on the import of a whole range of consumer goods, thus opening the way for local entrepreneurs to make quick profits on import substitute industries.

The Ten-Year Plan took cognisance of the need for the state to interest the private sector in industrial development. It suggested targets which should be set for smaller-scale industries (the larger ones, for want of large-scale capital, to be the responsibility of the state) in which private enterprise should be encouraged to invest through incentives such as tax rebates and tariff protection.

A state organised banking system also came to the aid of the private sector. A Finance Corporation set up in 1956 with assistance from government was expected to help private enterprise, which it did in the next few years to the tune of Rs 25.1 million. The establishment of the state-sponsored People's Bank in 1961 further benefited small industrialists in particular, who had found it difficult to raise loans from the commercial banks.

Private investment in industrial projects was no doubt encouraged by the import restrictions introduced in 1960 and 1961 by the S.L.F.P.'s minister of finance, due to the crisis proportions that the balance of payments situation had reached. The same minister, in his budget speech of 1960–1, assured private foreign capital that all the benefits that accrued to local capital would also be made available to them in addition to the right (1) freely to repatriate their dividends and eventually their assets; (2) to bring in necessary technical and managerial skills and for the latter to remit abroad part of their earnings; and (3) not to be taxed twice over – that is, the avoidance of double taxation. It is believed that as a result of these incentives foreign capital to the value of Rs 12 million was invested in the private industrial sector during 1962–4.[51] In addition the Short-Term Implementation Programme had envisaged a total investment of Rs 125 million in private sector industry during 1962–4. But in view of the very favourable climate created, investment by the private sector during this three-year period exceeding all expectations, totalling Rs 370 million.[52] By 1964 the number of people employed in private industry numbered 17,900.

Industrial expansion during this period (1960–4), however, tended to be lopsided. There was a heavy emphasis on some consumer goods industries, mainly confectionary, plastics, textiles and garments, chemical products, metal products and tobacco, to the neglect of intermediate and investment goods. Part of the reason for the concentration on these industries was that initially these required smaller sums of capital. The incomes of entrepreneurs in this sector shot up considerably because of the five-year tax holiday the government allowed them and the absence of any form of price or quality control on the goods they produced.

Industries in the private sector had to receive prior approval from the Development Division of the Ministry of Industries. Between 1959 and 1963 over a thousand industries were approved by the Ministry and there were besides eight hundred other industries already in existence.[53] But 63.7 per cent of total industrial production represented consumer goods, 19.3 per cent intermediate goods and 7.0 per cent investment goods.[54] By 1964 it was realised that many of these new ventures were producing to excess because of their unplanned and lopsided growth, and the Ministry of Industries ruled that no further applications for new industries should be permitted. A further consequence of this wanton expansion was that these industries depended in varying degrees on imported raw materials and this meant a drain on the country's limited foreign exchange reserves. Besides, a majority of them (some 80 per cent) were heavily concentrated in and around Colombo and its environs to the neglect of the rural areas where unemployment and under-employment were considerable.

The unprecedented growth of industry without any proper co-ordination or relationship to national needs was soon realised in the highest governmental quarters and the minister of finance, as a consequence, announced a new industrial policy in his 1964–5 budget speech. Provision was now to be made for a scheme of national priorities. Due regard was to be paid to factors like the utilisation of local materials, cost of production, etc. However, before his policy could get under way, a new government with a different political orientation was returned to office in the spring of 1965 (the U.N.P.-orientated 'national government').

Steps to control wasteful growth in industry were adopted by the new government. In mid-1965 the Ministry of Industry set up a whole range of machinery for control, regulation supervision and encouragement of the private sector in industry. The practice of allocating foreign exchange to private industry according to national priorities established by the previous government during 1964–5 was continued. This was an effective means of cutting down waste and excessive production of non-essential goods. But it was put out of gear when the 'foreign exchange entitlement scheme'[55] was introduced in May 1968 under which industrialists were permitted to import raw materials within limits prescribed under open general licence.

During the period of the 'national government' (1965–70) every encouragement was given to private and foreign entrepreneurs to develop the industrial sector. In May 1966 an Industrial Development Board was instituted to provide promotional and research assistance to the private sector among other things. Earlier, in March 1966, the government had enunciated its policy on private foreign investment which provided the latter with the necessary guarantees on remittances, freedom from discriminatory treatment, expropriation, etc.[56] A fair number of private foreign capitalists came in with sizable investments, but they were reported to have made stupendous profits and remitted back the major part of their earnings. In July 1966 the Ministry of Industries defined the criteria it would employ for granting approvals to investment, thereby removing the climate of uncertainty that had prevailed earlier, especially on matters such as allocations for foreign exchange, further expansion of existing industrial projects, etc.

In the period 1966–70 the balance in industrial production shifted slightly in favour of intermediate and investment goods. The share of consumer goods decreased from 56.5 per cent in 1966 to 47.6 per cent in 1970 while that of intermediate and investment goods increased from 34.9 per cent and 8.6 per cent in 1966 to 36.0 per cent and 16.4 per cent respectively in 1970.[57] On the debit side, however, the Central Bank's Annual Report for 1970 noted that about three-quarters of the raw materials utilised by local industry originated from foreign sources.[58]

1960 to 1970 could rightly be called Ceylon's industrial decade. Over 2,500 new industries were established and the value of industrial production rose from Rs 350 million to Rs 1,500 million.[59] But growth was haphazard and ill-planned, bringing in its wake other problems which needed urgent attention.

With the election of the U.F.-oriented government in 1970, a Trotskyist minister in charge of finance, and a former Trotskyist (now turned S.L.F.P.) holding the portfolio of industries, it was only to be expected that industrial development would be restructured in the context of a socialist framework. Both ministers sought to correct the harmful trends that had been set in motion in the previous decade. Radical measures were therefore taken towards this end. Sectoral development corporations now coordinate all work within and among all sections of industry and are responsible for planning development, co-ordinating production programmes, allocating resources to various units in each sector and organising and encouraging research. They are further responsible for the management of public resources in each sector and for the regulation of private sector units. How these arrangements will affect the working of the private sector is still to be seen.

The public sector, it was decided, should be responsible for (1) heavy and capital goods industries; (2) industries processing selected mineral and natural resources; (3) industries which for reasons of scale, technology and policy, state ownership of them is vital to the national interest.[60]

Tourism

With the serious crisis in balance of payments in the 1960s, the possibilities of obtaining foreign exchange from tourism began to be explored. A beginning in this direction was made by the M.E.P. government in 1956. The government's Ten-Year Plan estimated that tourist earnings could be increased from Rs 10.3 million in 1957 to Rs 40 million in 1968.[61] This target was not realised because the organisational set up for tourism did not get under way until after the mid 1960s. Another factor was that a major share of foreign currency brought in by tourists found its way into the black market.

In 1961 the importance of tourism was emphasised when it was assigned to the Ministry of Defence and External Affairs, a portfolio in the charge of the prime minister. The prime minister herself (Mrs Bandaranaike) displayed a keen awareness of the potentialities tourism afforded and took an active interest in its promotion.

Foreign exchange earnings during the period 1957 to 1965, however, were not appreciable, the maximum earned being Rs 10.3 million in 1957. Thereafter till 1967 earnings continued to be stagnant.[62]

The private enterprise oriented 'national government' of 1965–1970 took concrete steps to set up the necessary organisational framework for an active tourist industry. The subject was assigned to a newly formed Ministry of State which was in the charge of the deputy head of the government. In May 1966 the Ceylon Tourist Board was established to promote tourism in Ceylon. In the same year the Ceylon Hotels Corporation was formed with a significant proportion of its capital subscribed by government and the government-owned Bank of Ceylon. It is actively involved in promoting hotel construction and development. In 1968 was enacted the Tourist Development Act which provided for the establishment of national holiday resorts, protection of highways and places of scenic beauty and the promotion of hotel development projects. The steps thus taken helped in the build-up of a fair tourist traffic and in 1970 there was a peak influx of 35,561 tourists (Indians excluded) which was double the number of such arrivals in 1961 (17,724). Foreign exchange earnings amounted to Rs 21.5 million in 1970, but they comprised only 1 per cent of Ceylon's total export earnings. A good proportion of the foreign exchange from this source still continued to find its way into the black market.

THE CO-OPERATIVE MOVEMENT

The co-operative movement dates back to some sixty years when in 1912 the first Co-operative Societies Ordinance was enacted at the instance of the British colonial administration mainly to regulate credit societies.[63] A second ordinance in 1921 provided for non-credit societies. But up to the inauguration of the Donoughmore constitution in 1931 the movement made little headway, the credit society being the kind that prevailed most. By 1932–3, the end of its first phase, the movement had a membership of 26,719 in 779 societies.

In its second phase, 1933–42, the subject of co-operation was assigned to an energetic minister of agriculture and lands, D. S. Senanayake, who provided the movement with a 'new look' with his Co-operative Ordinance of 1936. Besides seeking to remedy the defects of the ordinances of 1912 and 1921, the minister aimed at utilising this legislation to promote his pioneering agricultural schemes in the dry zone areas. The prospective cultivator was provided incentives through easily available loans from co-operative societies. However, even by the end of this phase, progress had not been impressive. The movement had touched only 7 per cent of the population, with a membership of 91,988 in 2,036 societies.

The third phase beginning in 1942 was marked by the critical turn the war had taken in the east with the Japanese occupation of Burma, a country which had been the island's principal source of rice, the cutting-off of another source, Thailand, the grave shortage of shipping space aggravated by the perils shipping was exposed to from submarine warfare, and the crisis caused to trade in the country after the Japanese bombings of Colombo and Trincomalee in 1942 when Indian shopkeepers who had controlled a large share of the trade in foodstuffs fled the country and their Ceylonese counterparts resorted to profiteering and blackmarketing.

All these factors combined to induce the government to utilise the co-operative movement as the instrument for providing the population with their food requirements at fair prices from consumers' co-operative stores, and to promote the campaign towards making the country less dependent on outside sources for its rice and other essential food commodities through the agricultural production and sale societies that were organised on a fairly extensive scale. By 1946–7 there were 3,961 co-operative stores serving nearly two-thirds of the island's population and in 1952 there were 339 agricultural production and marketing societies with a total membership of 82,000.

The consumers' co-operative societies virtually eliminated the Indian shopkeeper. They made considerable progress in the years after independence. A Co-operative Wholesale Establishment established in 1943 soon developed into the island's largest distributor of essential foodstuffs and textiles and functions as a corporation with its own board of directors. In January 1971 it was made the sole importer of essential cuttystuffs and other commodities. At the same time (January 1971) a Sri Lanka State Trading Corporation was set up with monopoly import rights in respect of certain essential and semi-essential commodities. Both these institutions utilise co-operative societies as well as the services of authorised distributors in the private retail trade to make available their goods to the general public. By the end of 1970 there were as many as 14,427 co-operative societies with a membership of about two million providing employment to some 23,000 people.

The agricultural production and sales societies helped rehabilitate the Ceylonese smallholders of coconut lands but, more important, relieved the peasant cultivator from excessive dependence on rapacious moneylenders and enabled him to secure his immediate needs for cultivating the land. Quite a few of these societies, in later years, enlarged the scope of their activities and developed into multi-purpose co-operative unions. Both types of institution became the main instrument for promoting the government's agricultural policies in the post-independence phase. Between 1947 and 1967 the state channelled Rs 314.8 million to cultivators through these institutions. In 1968–9 alone the latter ent as much as Rs 617 million to cultivators. They were also tilised by the state for its purchases of paddy and subsidiary rops under the various guaranteed price schemes.

In March 1972 a Co-operative Commission Act was passed by arliament. It brought the workforce of the co-operative institu-ons in the country under the supervision and control of a com-iission of not less than three members which among other things 'as empowered to categorise co-operative employees, fix their ilaries, and deal with disputes between employees and their istitutions.

The co-operative movement in Ceylon has been useful in pro-ioting state policies in the important spheres of trade and agri-ulture, in helping in the elimination of Indian petty traders who ended to send back most of their profits to the mainland, and in iaking the country increasingly self-sufficient in its food require-ients. It was not a movement which started from grass roots vel, rather from the opposite direction, with tremendous state ssistance. It has suffered from many defects and abuses, but has evertheless proved effective in the areas demarcated for it, and is today an important component of Ceylon's social and conomic set-up.

REDIT INSTITUTIONS

here is a whole range of credit institutions involved in pro-ding various types of financial accommodation to Ceylonese ntrepreneurs as well as to middle and lower income earners in e urban and rural areas.

At the apex of the system is the Central Bank of Ceylon. Next importance are the government-controlled credit agencies. hese are first the Bank of Ceylon which was established in 1939 a Ceylonese limited liability venture and is today a dynamic gency for the promotion of Ceylonese commerce and industry. here is next the People's Bank which was established in 1961. his bank was designed to meet the needs of low income earners ot catered for by the commericial banks, mainly peasants and nall agriculturists, wage earners, artisans and petty traders and isinessmen. It was also specifically intended to assist the co-erative movement. Both banks have a wide network of branches roughout the country.

In 1961 the S.L.F.P. government in office, with a view to cor trolling credit and assisting the credit operations of these tw bodies, banned the opening of new accounts by Ceylonese in an of the commercial banks. As a result, Ceylonese banks increase their share of deposits where formerly the foreign banks had th majority of deposits. Though the ban on the opening of Ceylones accounts was removed in 1968 (except in the case of the Habi Bank) by the U.N.P.-oriented 'national government' of 1965, a that the foreign banks were able to achieve was to arrest th declining trend in their share of total deposits with commerci banks.

The next set of government or government-sponsored instit tions is the Development Finance Corporation established in 195 to provide long-term financial assistance and technical an managerial advice to private industrial credit for agricultural pu poses only; the National Development Bank (1972) owned an run by the Central Bank to provide medium- and long-term cred for industrial, agricultural and commercial development in th public sector; the National Savings Bank (1972) whose objecti is to utilise all possible savings potential for development purpose and the Export-Import Bank (1972) designed specifically to he promote the export industry and cater to the import sector b providing the necessary market intelligence and purchase capita There is further the Insurance Corporation of Ceylon establish in 1961 with a monopoly over life insurance and gener insurance business in the country. Though it is not strictly credit-disbursing agency, one of its principal objectives is harness the savings of people, particularly in the rural areas, f insurance purposes. These people had up to this time be neglected by the private insurance companies.

Government also operates credit schemes for the rural sect through an 'extended credit scheme' operated by co-operati societies which obtain overdraft facilities for the purpose fro the People's Bank and rural banks, and through the 'new ag cultural credit scheme' which provides loans for paddy farme and cultivators of subsidiary food crops. The rural sector al obtains facilities from the commercial banks, the specialis credit agencies, and government departments dealing with ag cultural matters.

The last set of credit institutions is the commercial ban

British, Indian and Ceylonese owned. These banks do business only on their rupee deposits and have not brought much foreign capital into the country. They have besides not been very liberal in their assistance to Ceylonese entrepreneurs. Various attempts by the socialist-orientated governments in office since 1956 to squeeze these banks out of business have so far not met with much success. In 1963 the S.L.F.P. minister of finance complained that foreign-owned banks send out annual profits to the tune of Rs 5–6 million.[64]

BUDGETARY PROBLEMS

Prior to independence and for many years after, until about the late 1950s, Sri Lanka provided a classic example of a dualistic export economy. There was a well-organised export sector – tea, rubber and coconuts – very productive but isolated from the rest of the economy which was mainly based on agriculture at low subsistence levels. The major part of this export sector was in the hands of foreigners, mostly Britishers, but quite a few Indians as well. Profits and earnings from this sector were remitted abroad while the inputs which were required were also imported, mostly from Britain. Even the vast majority of workers in this export plantation sector were Indian Tamils, most of whom had ties of some sort with kinsfolk on the south Indian mainland to whom they sent a proportion of their earnings. These Indian Tamils also confined their day-to-day transactions to Indian traders, Indian moneylenders, Indian laundrymen, Indian-owned cinemas, etc. In addition to all this, trade and commerce in the island's most important sectors – imports of essential foodstuffs, of consumer goods, luxury items and requirements of machinery and other capital items – were controlled by British and Indian trading establishments.

In effect, the most productive sectors of the economy were controlled by non-Ceylonese and brought few benefits either in the form of improved incomes or employment to the nationals of the country. After independence in 1948, various steps were taken to correct the imbalance by the strengthening of the government-controlled co-operative movement, the provision of incentives and facilities to Ceylonese traders, government participation in productive ventures, and the cancellation of temporary residence permits to non-Ceylonese personnel employed in the plantations and the commercial establishments. But the impact of these measures on the economy was not very significant. It was only after the advent to office of the nationalist-oriented M.E.P., S.L.F.P. and U.F. governments in the post-1956 phase that a real shift took place. Their nationalisation programmes and their active involvement in the productive sectors of the economy helped to reduce the influence and power that the non-Ceylonese sector was able to wield over the rest of the economy.

A consequence of this twofold division of the island's economy without proper links with one another was that the pre-independent governments under the Donoughmore constitution (1931–1947) as well as post-independence governments tended to tax the export sector to provide social benefits to the underprivileged. This was done principally to ensure popular support and stave off discontent which was being exploited by left-wing parties bent on strengthening their own supports. But it was also claimed that such income transfers for welfare purposes were necessary to build up the social infrastructure in order to gear it for development efforts. The build-up, however, was undertaken with no planned purpose or direction. Domestic savings were not mobilised for a growth effort, not enough was done to improve productivity in the non-export sector, foreign exchange earnings were frittered away on imports of consumer goods and luxury items, and by the late 1950s the country was faced with serious balance of payments problems.

The budgets of Ceylonese governments classify expenditure broadly into three groups:

(1) Traditional government services, eg. national defence, conduct of external relations, the administrative and public sectors, etc.
(2) Social services and income transfers, most of which goes on education, health, housing, water supplies, low tariffs on passenger transport (rail and bus), subsidised food.
(3) Development expenditure.

The problem is to strike a balance between the second and third of these groups. But if there must be development, reduction on expenditure on the social services is an absolute. But any effort to economise in this direction spells electoral ruin. Further, expenditure on the social services and on development also necessitates the utilisation of the country's exchange earnings. But again, if expenditure of foreign exchange on the social services (as for example the import of rice) is channelled to development, the electoral consequences can be just as disastrous. Consequently development has been sacrificed in the interests of maintaining the welfare state.

During 1956–65, the balance of payments situation reached crisis proportions. After 1959, real per capita income fell by about 0.5 per cent a year, partly due to the adverse movement in the terms of trade. Consequently real incomes increased by only 2.3 per cent while real output increased by 3.2 per cent. In effect, between 1959 and 1965, 75 per cent of the increase in net export output was absorbed by declining prices. Table 3.8 provides figures of the deteriorating situation during this phase.

During the years 1957 to 1960, the M.E.P. government utilised the country's external assets to finance the resource gap resulting from the adverse terms of trade. About one-fifth of the resource gap was financed from project aid which up to 1960 did not exceed Rs 23 million, grants which comprised the major part of foreign aid and inflow of foreign capital which was hardly of any significance.

From 1961 the S.L.F.P. government in office could no longer fall back on the country's external assets to meet its foreign liabilities. More severe methods, such as a progressive imposition of exchange restrictions on imports, travel and remittances abroad inclusive of dividend payments, had to be resorted to. These restrictions stimulated the growth of a whole range of import substitute industries which, however, as stated earlier, were ill-planned and depended for their raw materials on foreign sources. In addition, recourse had to be made to I.M.F. drawings in 1961, 1962 and 1965 as well as to project aid, grants, private capital and short-term credits, though the amounts involved were not so large as to create any serious repayments problem.

The reasons for the deepening crisis could be attributed to the tendency of governments during this phase to (1) allow purchasing power to run ahead of real income despite adverse terms of trade marked especially by the fall in export prices and low economic growth; (2) employ expansionary financing with ever-increasing budgetary deficits to cope with rising government expenditure

TABLE 3.8
SRI LANKA'S EXPORTS AND IMPORTS 1956–69
(in Rs millions)

Year	Exports (f.o.b.)	Imports (c.i.f.)	Balance of Trade
I. *During the Term of Office of the M.E.P. Government 1956–9*			
1956	1772	1576	+196
1957	1669	1764	– 95
1958	1624	1713	– 89
1959	1773	1958	–185
II. *During the Term of Office of the S.L.F.P. Government 1960–4*			
1960	1796	2006	–210
1961	1707	1794	– 87
1962	1763	1906	–143
1963	1708	1869	–161
1964	1767	1960	–193
III. *During the Term of Office of the U.N.P.-oriented 'National Government' 1965–9*			
1965	1909	1922	– 13
1966	1700	2028	–328
1967	1690	1738	– 48
1968	2035	2173	–138
1969	1916	2543	–627

Source. Central Bank of Ceylon, *Annual Reports*.
Note. The government elected in 1956 went out of office in March 1960, that of 1960 in March 1965 and the government of 1965 in May 1970.

despite the slow rate of growth both of the economy and of per capita incomes (see Tables 3.10, 3.11 and 3.12). A disproportionate share of expenditure was on consumption, resulting in investment in development suffering. The emphasis during this phase was on effecting income redistribution, as Table 3.9 indicates.

The years between 1959 and 1963 were some of the worst in Ceylon's attempts towards economic progress. During this phase the net output of the export sector in agriculture (at 1959 factor cost prices) increased by 13 per cent. But due to the adverse terms of trade, which dropped from 142 in 1959 to 115 in 1963, the contribution of this sector to the increase in real national income was negligible.

In the non-export agricultural sector there was a slight increase in paddy output from 43,068,000 bushels in 1959–60 to 49,154,000 in 1962–3. But the value in this increase was offset by the expenditure on major irrigation works and land development schemes which raised the capital output ratio. In 1961–2 the capital output ratio was estimated to have been as high as 12:1.

TABLE 3.9

GOVERNMENT EXPENDITURE ON SOCIAL SERVICES AND ECONOMIC DEVELOPMENT, 1948, 1955, 1961

	1948–9	1955–6	1961–2
In Rs millions			
Social services	207.5	353.6	665.6
Economic development	246.1	389.1	707.5
In rupees			
Expenditure on services as per head of population	27.00	40.00	65.00
Expenditure on economic development as per head of population	33.00	44.00	68.00

Source. T. B. Illangaratna, *Economic and Social Progress, 1956–62* (Supplement to the Budget Speech, 1963), Ministry of Finance, Colombo, 1963.

Note. Social services here refer only to food subsidies, education and health.

Though in the industrial sector import substitution had gone on apace, the increase made little difference to the national product during this phase. It was the same in the public industrial sector. State industrial corporations took at least three years to commence production while investment in projects such as power and transport was capital intensive and took a long period to come into full operation.

The result of this slow growth, if not stagnancy, was that real income per head of population actually fell between 1960 and 1963, partly due to the increase in population from 9.8 million to 10.6 and also because of the loss to national income due to adverse changes in the terms of trade.

The private enterprise oriented 'national government' which took office in March 1965 sought to right the economy by a number of drastic measures. These produced some results but there were certain adverse financial consequences that flowed from them. They also affected the political fortunes of the government.

The first of these measures was the halving of the rice ration from 4 lbs per person per week at the highly subsidied price of 50 cents a pound to 2 lbs per person per week free of charge. The immediate pretext for this action was the rise in the world market price of rice. It was expected that substantial savings could be effected and utilised for development. These were hardly adequate.

TABLE 3.10

GOVERNMENT OF SRI LANKA, FINANCIAL POSITION 1956–70
(in Rs millions)

Year	Revenue	Expenditure	Deficit	Domestic Debt*	Foreign Debt*
I. *M.E.P. Government 1956–9*					
1956–7	1,260.5	1,456.9	196.4	1,132.2	231.7
1957–8	1,280.0	1,502.3	222.3	1,237.6	257.8
1958–9	1,330.4	1,743.8	413.4	1,559.5	277.5
1959–60	1,403.8	1,821.3	417.5	1,936.7	293.7
II. *S.L.F.P. Government 1960–5*					
1960–1	1,513.9	1,976.4	462.5	2,344.7	307.0
1961–2	1,630.6	2,076.6	456.1	2,695.7	345.2
1962–3	1,593.4	1,985.3	391.7	3,030.2	407.1
1963–4	1,759.0	2,220.7	461.7	3,375.3	412.1
1964–5	1,816.4	2,246.8	430.4	3,695.5	489.3
III. *U.N.P.-Oriented 'National Government' 1965–70*					
1965–6	1,833.3	2,399.3	566.0	4,194.5	548.8
1966–7	1,954.8	2,560.6	606.8	4,582.2	739.3
1967–8	2,156.4	2,872.1	715.7	5,196.5	1,074.3
1968–9	2,497.3	3,284.9	787.6	5,513.0	1,375.5
1969–70	2,736.4	3,672.0	935.6	6,294.8	1,578.4

* The debt is calculated as at the end of every September. For 1956–7 we have taken the debt position as at the end of September 1957.
Source. Central Bank of Ceylon, *Annual Reports*.

The action, however, impressed aid-giving countries and the international credit agencies as evidence of the government's determination to put the country's finances in order. They displayed a greater willingness to come to Sri Lanka's assistance. Such assistance became more than urgent because of the continuing downward trend in export prices. The import structure was in fact altered during this phase (1965–70) to ensure utilization of the limited foreign exchange available, for obtaining intermediate and capital goods. Extensive borrowing from foreign sources and generous aid from donor countries helped the government over its difficulties.

TABLE 3.11

G.N.P. (1960–65) AT 1959 FACTOR COST PRICES
(in Rs millions)

	1960	1961	1962	1963	1964	1965
G.N.P.	6,289	6,425	6,710	6,900	7,363	7,551
Rate of growth (percentage)	6.7	2.2	4.4	2.8	6.7	2.5

Source. Central Bank of Ceylon, *Annual Reports*.

During most of the period of the previous S.L.F.P. government (1960–5) capital flows from abroad for financing imports were insignificant. One reason was that the government's nonaligned foreign policy sometimes resulted in marked anti-west stances. The 'national government' on the other hand avoided alienating the west and the latter as a consequence became more sympathetic

TABLE 3.12

PER CAPITA INCOME (1960–65) AT 1959 FACTOR COST PRICES
(in Rs millions)

	1960	1961	1962	1963	1964	1965
Per capita income	635	632	643	648	675	676
Rate of growth (percentage)	3.78	-0.56	1.67	0.09	4.6	0.1

Source. Central Bank of Ceylon, *Annual Reports*.

to Sri Lanka's grave balance of payments problem. From 1965 to 1970 Ceylon obtained a total credit of Rs 723.4 million from the I.M.F. of which Rs 301.7 million was paid back, leaving a balance of Rs 421.7 million as of 20 May 1970.[65] During the same period the World Bank organised five meetings of donor countries at which a total of Rs 1,568.42 million of commodity and project aid was pledged. Up to 30 June 1969 commodity aid amounting to Rs 724.17 million had arrived.[66] Further, in 1969 and 1970 the government borrowed from commercial banks and credit institutions in Europe and America to meet its day-to-day obligations arising from the maturing of bills. At the end of its term of office in May 1970, these borrowings stood at Rs 350 million.[67] The end result was that the net foreign debt more than doubled itself between 1964 and 1968. On 31 December 1969 the country's external debt stood at Rs 1,718 million. Debt servicing began to become an intolerable burden, 14 per cent of the total export earnings for 1969 being utilized for this purpose.[68]

The strategy in regard to development during 1965–70 was to mobilise the private sector. The Development Finance Corporation received facilities from private banks and establishments in the west to finance private sector projects and these were guaranteed by the government itself. In other fields the private sector was associated in government ventures – a pattern which increasingly came into vogue during this phase and was most manifest in the many hotel complexes that were brought into existence to meet the anticipated boom in tourism. It was also noticed in the agricultural sector where large tracts of land were leased out by the state to big companies and individuals for exploitation and development.

These policies of the 'national government' instilled considerable confidence in the private sector and there was unprecedented investment in various projects by entrepreneurs, local and foreign. For instance, the Central Bank of Ceylon in its Annual Report for 1969 noted that the increase in investment expenditure for the year was the highest on record (government and private sector) and the rise in private sector investment was almost double that in the government sector.[69] Industrial output in the private and public sectors also increased considerably, from just 6 per cent of the gross national product in 1958 to 13 per cent of the gross national product in 1968. There was also a significant shift in emphasis from consumer goods to capital goods industries. The manufacture of fabricated metal products, machinery and equipment, and electrical machinery was a marked feature of industrial activity during the years 1965 to 1970.

Two other measures were taken by the 'national government'

to ease the foreign exchange situation. These were the devaluation of the overvalued Ceylon rupee by 20 per cent in November 1967 and the introduction of a foreign exchange entitlement scheme in May 1968. The latter was in effect a further depreciation of the exchange rate of the Ceylon rupee, but only in respect of certain specified transactions. In addition, a number of commodities many of which were needed for the developing industrial complex were placed under open general licence. The procedure for the remittance of profits and dividends was also liberalised.

The devaluation helped to improve the balance of payments situation somewhat, but not as much as was expected, and the liberalisation of exchange control procedures went some way towards inspiring international confidence in Ceylon.

It was on the agricultural front that the government focused most of its attention. The prime minister himself took charge of the campaign for the promotion of food production, the 'food drive' as it came to be called. Incentives of various kinds were provided to cultivators of paddy and other essential food items. The objective was to cut down on imports and conserve exchange. After the halving of the ration, the government also increased the guaranteed price of paddy from Rs 12/- to Rs 14/- a bushel, but the price of rice appreciated more in the open market, making it very profitable for the cultivator to sell his produce there than to the government's purchasing depots. This 'grow more food campaign' brought the desired results. Rice imports fell from 642,000 tons in 1965 to 344,000 tons in 1968. In 1968 locally produced rice constituted 74 per cent of total rice consumption as against 44 per cent in 1965. Government, however, was not able to benefit greatly from this improvement because of the rise in the price of rice in the world market.

The overall performance of the economy in the period 1965–70 was highly satisfactory, as Tables 3.13 and 3.14 indicate. There was a steady rise in the gross national product which reached an all-time high of 8.3 per cent in 1968, as well as an increase in per capita income. From 1965 to 1968 per capita income rose steadily, and in 1968 it increased by 6.1 per cent which was in fact a record figure. Thereafter there was a slight decline. But on the debit side, it could not be definitely established that the rising prosperity was felt by the poorer sections of community. Those who benefited were only a section of farmers besides private entrepreneurs and companies. On the other hand the poorer sections experienced greater hardships and this was seen in the steep rise in the cost of living during 1960–70. In 1960 the Colombo consumers' price index which was the official record of the cost of living situation was 103.5. By 1968 it had risen to 121.5.

TABLE 3.13
G.N.P. (1965–70) AT 1959 FACTOR COST PRICES
(in Rs millions)

	1965	1966	1967	1968	1969	1970
G.N.P.	7,551	7,834	8,181	8,862	9,316	9,695
Rate of growth (percentage)	2.5	4.2	4.4	8.3	5.1	4.1

Source. Central Bank of Ceylon, *Annual Reports*.

TABLE 3.14
PER CAPITA INCOME (1965–70) AT 1959 FACTOR COST PRICES
(in rupees)

	1965	1966	1967	1968	1969	1970
Per capita income	676	685	699	739	760	775
Rate of growth (percentage)	0.1	1.3	2.0	6.1	3.5	2.0

Source. Central Bank of Ceylon, *Annual Reports*.

ECONOMIC PLANNING

Development Plans and the Machinery of Planning

The U.N.P. governments of 1948–56 showed little or no interest in engaging themselves in any scientific planning of economic development for many reasons. Most of this phase was marked by some kind of prosperity. Agricultural exports generally fetched stable prices though there were occasional recesses, of no serious consequence. The island's sterling balances were in good shape and did not run down to dangerously low levels. They stood at

Rs 1,260 million in 1948. Unfortunately these were frittered away on imports of consumer goods. Had they been depleted according to an organised scheme of development the country could well have tided over the balance of payment crises of the 1960s.

Funds were available for each minister in the cabinet of 1948–1952 to draw up his own long-term schemes for the promotion of subjects assigned to his charge. These were presented in the budget speeches of the minister of finance for 1947–8 and 1948–9 after they had been looked over, tidied up, and pruned by the cabinet and the prime minister. They were collectively referred to as the First Six-Year Plan and covered the period 1947–8 to 1953–4. The Plan was merely a presentation of government proposals with no reference to the private sector at all. Expenditure on the social services was stressed, industry was all but ignored, while the main emphasis was on paddy cultivation in the dry zone areas, the objective being to achieve self sufficiency in this sphere. Paddy culture received priority because Ceylon's first prime minister, D. S. Senanayake, was firmly committed to the view that agrarian policies were the ultimate solution to the island's economic and social ills.

Another reason for the neglect of planning was that D. S. Senanayake showed little interest in the need for organised economic effort. Partly the successful economic climate inhibited interest. In part, the milieu of the civil service which advised him was drawn from a generation of men schooled in the classical and colonial traditions. They viewed the nation's finances as an exercise in housekeeping with a need for the inmates to be kept in reasonable contentment.

With the launching of the Colombo Plan in 1950, however, the D.S. Senanayake government was required to submit a six-year development plan commencing from mid-1951. The emphasis was again on agriculture and the social services. The plan as such was, as a commentator remarked, 'purely a *pro forma* exercise and probably had no influence on policy'.[70]

A further effort was made during Sir John Kotelawala's premiership. An I.B.R.D. mission which had visited the island in late 1951 produced a plan for economic development for the years 1953–9. The Kotelawala government accepted almost all its proposals and incorporated these in their Six-Year Programme of

Investment 1954/55 to 1959/60, released in 1954. Again the emphasis was on agriculture, but social services were slightly downgraded and some notice was taken of the need to diversify the economy by activating interest in industry by the private sector.

The Six-Year Programme was not a total national plan but it was nevertheless an attempt towards organisation for development. But the government was ousted at the general election of 1956 before the Programme could get under way.

The new M.E.P. government which took office in 1956 showed considerable awareness of the urgency for scientific planning and for co-ordinating the efforts of all sectors of the economy. It rejected the Six-Year Programme and bent its efforts towards a macroeconomic plan with long-term perspectives in view.

The rudiments of planning machinery had already come into existence when the M.E.P. took office. On the recommendation of the I.B.R.D. mission the Kotelawala government had set up a planning secretariat with a chief planning commissioner at the head to advise its cabinet planning committee. The M.E.P. government expanded this machinery beyond recognition. In September 1956 it established a National Planning Council comprising five ministers and seven men prominent in public life. Following the Indian pattern, the prime minister (S.W.R.D. Bandaranaike) chaired the council but he became so engrossed in the country's problems that he was not able to pay enough attention to its deliberations. However the council produced a carefully thought-out and co-ordinated Plan for long-term development. It had the prime minister's blessing and was accepted by his cabinet in June 1959. It was called the Ten-Year Plan, and covered the period 1959 to 1968. But the political crises that followed soon after the publication of the Plan, coupled with the assassination of Bandaranaike in September 1959, stalled its implementation.

The significance of the Ten-Year Plan lay in the fact that it took both the public and private sectors into consideration in the overall national effort. It envisaged a huge outlay of Rs 13,600 million for the ten-year period under consideration. For the first time industry was given an important place, almost on a par with agriculture. Whereas the latter was allocated 22.9 per cent (Rs 3,100 million) of the total outlay, industry obtained as much as approximately 20 per cent (Rs 2,714 million). At the same time there was as much importance attached to the social services. 'Social investments', as they were called, took 26.3 per cent of the total sum envisaged.

In 1960, with the S.L.F.P. under Mrs Bandaranaike in office, it was only to be expected that steps would be taken to implement at least the more important proposals contained in the Ten-Year Plan. But it was realised that a macroeconomic effort of such dimensions could not provide solutions to the immediate and urgent problems confronting the new government. The situation was aggravated further by the steep decline in the country's external assets. In the beginning of 1957 when S. W. R. D. Bandaranaike was in office they were quite high, amounting to Rs 1,179 million. By December 1960 they had droped to Rs 481.2 million, necessitating the imposition of strict exchange and import controls to arrest further decline.[71]

As a first step, the National Planning Council and Planning Secretariat were replaced by a Department of National Planning whose functions were to programme and co-ordinate the schemes of development drawn up by the planning committees which were set up in each Ministry. The National Planning Department also supervised proper co-ordination and implementation through (1) liaison officers appointed in each Ministry whose duties were to ensure elimination of delays in the programming and execution of stated targets; and (2) progress control, a system of periodical review within a year of the actual performances in relation to expected targets of the departments under the various Ministries, or of public corporations, these being in fact the agencies for implementing the development programmes in their respective sectors. The major decisions on all aspects of planning were the responsibility of a cabinet sub-committee under the chairmanship of the prime minister.

The outcome of these endeavours was the Short-Term Implementation Programme (1961–2 to 1963–4) which was, however, published only in its second year (1962)). The Programme itself recorded that its necessity arose from the fact that internal and external finance 'became serious bottlenecks' in the way of implementing the objectives of the Ten-Year Plan.[72] But it proposed nevertheless to achieve the latter's broad objectives. These were increased output, employment and a balanced international account, but they would be accomplished at a lower cost. For example, the three-year period covered by the Short-Term Implementation Programme envisaged a total investment of Rs 2,295.9 million whereas the expenditure for the same period under the Ten-Year Plan was to be Rs 3,844 million.

The Programme therefore aimed at a 4.8 per cent increase in national income and a 2 per cent increase in real income per capita per annum. It gave emphasis to short-term projects which required less capital and foreign exchange. It stressed the role that the public sector must play in development. More significant, government investment in industry gained added importance, amounting to Rs 436.6 million, or 19.0 per cent of the total outlay. If the investment expected of the private sector in industry is also included (Rs 125.0 million) the percentage envisaged for industry as a whole amounted to 24.4 per cent. With the usual emphasis on social goals by all Bandaranaike governments, the Programme provided for 16.7 per cent of the total outlay to be invested on the social services (health, education, housing).

The targets set out in the Short-Term Implementation Programme were not realised, due mainly to adverse circumstances such as changes in the terms of trade, the nation having lost Rs 363 million in the three-year period, and bottlenecks and snags in the way of achieving the goals that had been fixed. There was little change in the structure of production though there was an expansion of output in the domestic sector. Agriculture actually declined from 48.2 per cent of the total share to 45.7 per cent (due to a fall in prices of exports) while the increase in the share of industry and mining was minimal, from 4.4 to 6 per cent.[73] As one economist remarked, 'so far has the "welfare state psychology" displaced "development mindedness" in Ceylon that in recent years the consumption of domestic products plus imports has exceeded the production of commodities for domestic purposes plus export. In fact Ceylon has been consuming more than it produces. . . .'[74]

For the last year of the S.L.F.P.'s term of office, the Department of National Planning, at the request of the government, produced the Development Programme 1964–5. This provided for a total investment in the private and public sectors of Rs 1,225 million at 1960 prices of which the public sector share was Rs 769 million. It planned for a growth rate of 4.8 per cent (or 2 per cent per capita) for the year in question. The programme failed to get under way due to the political problems which beset the government in its last year of office.

It must be noted that other than the preparation of these development programmes to cover the period of office of the S.L.F.P. government, from 1960–5, little or nothing was done to organise the machinery of planning so as to make it an efficient agent for the supervision and implementation of planned economic goals. On the contrary, an I.B.R.D.–I.D.A. mission to Sri Lanka in its report to the meeting of the Aid Ceylon Group which met in Paris in March 1968 noted that even the existing planning organisation 'fell into disuse and disintegrated in the early 1960s'.[75]

Primarily, the cause for the failure of planning in the period 1959 to 1965 was political instability coupled with administrative inefficiencv. Added to this was the shortage of foreign exchange which could have to some extent been alleviated if government departments had made full use of the assistance offered to them by foreign governments. This indifference was further aggravated by government departments not spending all the money allocated to them for investment in the annual budgets. The additional money needed for such investment was raised partly from the sale of short-term treasury bills to the Central and commercial banks, such bills which were outstanding increasing from Rs 320 million in September 1959 to Rs 1,125 million in September 1963. The resulting inflation sent up the money costs of public sector projects. There was besides a woeful lack of detailed basic statistics which if available would have assisted in determining the capital requirements necessary for defined output targets. Absence of such statistical information was an important reason for the rise in the capital output ratio to about 5 for the period 1959 to 1963. For the 1950s it was 3.5. And above all these defects and shortcomings was the continuing scarcity in technological and managerial skills due to misallocation of resources in educational planning. It is not necessary to mention again here the absence of any planning or direction in the private sector. It was allowed to grow and expand as it pleased with only the minimum of controls by government.

When the U.N.P.-oriented 'national government' assumed office in March 1965, there was apparently a determination to update the machinery of planning and make it a meaningful instrument for co-ordinating and ensuring proper development. An added incentive for the interest was the prospect that detailed and adequate planning offered of attracting foreign aid.

A Ministry of Planning and Economic Affairs was created with the prime minister himself in charge and with such departments as those of National Planning, Foreign Aid, and Plan Implementation under its overall direction. A top-level planning committee of the cabinet was set up, comprising the prime minister, the deputy head of the government who was the minister of state, and the minister of finance. Further, four committees, comprising permanent secretaries, on Industry, Economic Overheads, Domestic Agriculture, Manpower and Education were constituted to deal with the stated aims of the new Ministry, viz. (1) a substantial breakthrough in agriculture; (2) stepping up the tempo of industrial development; (3) improving the economic infrastructure – roads, railways, ports, power systems, etc.; and (4) training and orientating human resources towards development. The new Ministry added that its immediate objective was 'to concentrate on the formulation of concrete programmes for the key sectors of the economy, and on the identification and preparation of specific projects suitable for early implementation and where relevant, for external financing'.[76]

The Ministry of Planning and Economic Affairs assumed increasing importance in the course of the next few years, becoming virtually the supervisor general of all other ministries in relation to their respective development programmes. The Ministry assumed responsibility for formulating the foreign exchange budget and the capital budget, besides evaluating the proposals put forward by the respective Ministries. It also had the system of national accounts, which up to this time was based on the needs of an open export economy, completely revised so as to provide insights and information on the structure of production for domestic use. Shortly thereafter an input-output table for the economy was completed. These steps no doubt helped to improve the realisation of targets set. Most important was the Ministry's setting up of a Central Progress Control Room. The latter's function was to monitor the progress of the development programmes of the respective Ministries and to recommend corrective action where necessary.

The Ministry was responsible for the formulation of two development programmes. In its publication entitled *The Development Programme 1966–1967* which it issued in 1966, it provided a plan setting out the overall growth possibilities for the five-year period 1966 to 1971. Broadly it aimed at an average growth rate of gross domestic product of more than 5 per cent for the period under consideration. The Ministry also produced a macroeconomic framework for the period 1967 to 1977 in which it envisaged an increase of real income per head of 2 per cent during this period. If a rise in population of 2.4 per cent per annum is taken into consideration, the overall growth rate would be roughly 4.5 per cent a year.

It was *The Development Programme 1966–1967* which gained immediate attention. Concentration on its implementation was more on a sectoral basis, as for example agriculture, industry (including fisheries), economic overheads, social overheads, etc. than on a departmental or Ministry basis. The 'national government' could not take corrective action on the results of this Programme as it was turned out of office in the general election of May 1970.

Economic planning under the successor U.F. government is an integral part of its programme of taking the country in the direction of a socialist democracy. The wide leeway permitted to the private sector under the previous government has been drastically curtailed. This sector is now obliged to function under strict governmental supervision and to operate only within the confines permitted it under the Five-Year Plan (1972–6) formulated by the Ministry of Planning and Employment.[77] The Ministry is in the charge of the prime minister.

The Five-Year Plan provides for (1) a considerable widening of the public sector coupled with a drastic curtailment of the economic privileges of in all some fifty thousand people who may be categorised as belonging to the better-off layers of Ceylonese society; and (2) a climate of investment for private enterprise. The latter is expected under the Plan to contribute approximately 52 per cent of the total investment of Rs 14,820 million envisaged. How the private sector can co-operate in the context of severe legislation enacted by the U.F. government to restrict it, such as the Business Undertakings (Acquisition) Act, a once and for all capital levy, ceilings on income and property, and the implementation of what has come to be called the 'package deal' (for details see below), is another question. The minister of finance warned in his closing speech on the 1971 budget debate that the government had legislation ready to compel the private sector to do its duty. But he added that this sector has expressed its willingness to co-operate in the implementation of the Plan.

The same question arises in regard to foreign investment. The Plan sets out in detail the fields in which foreign participation will be welcome – tourism, specified manufactures, and technical skills not locally available. But on the other hand, one or other of the Marxist parties in the U.F. government keeps demanding from time to time the nationalisation of foreign-owned plantations, commercial banks and mercantile or industrial concerns. Besides, left-inclined ministers in the government have derided the poor returns obtained by U.N.P. governments in the past from their efforts to create a favourable environment for foreign investors.

The Plan's principal objective is to achieve a growth rate of 6 per cent, raise domestic savings from the present level of 12.5 per cent of national income to 17 per cent, and to improve the living standards of some 40 per cent of the population who at present earn incomes which barely average Rs 200 a month. It is hoped that per capita income by the end of the Plan period (1976) would have risen from Rs 910 per annum to Rs 1,150 at 1970 prices.

The planners were keenly alive to the twin problems of population and unemployment. They therefore recommended extensive family planning, and framed a programme of development which would by 1976 absorb 810,000 of the 1,100,000 who would by then be in need of employment. The remaining 290,000, they hoped, would find jobs in the special works programmes envisaged in the rural, urban and plantation sectors.

Coupled with the Five-Year Plan was a 'package deal' which proposed a general redistribution of income and property.[78] It provided for (1) a ceiling on landholding, fixed at fifty acres per adult member in a family under the Land Ceiling Act of 1972 (foreign and local public limited liability companies owning land were exempted), the excess land acquired (with payment of compensation) to be made available to the landless and unemployed; (2) the government to purchase shares in plantation companies and to appoint directors to their boards with a view to ensuring their proper management and maintenance; (3) government directors to be appointed to public and private companies; (4) nationalisation of any trade or industry where necessary, or, in the alternative, acquisition by the state of at least a 51 per cent interest in them; (5) a ceiling on the ownership of house property and a land trust for acquiring all buildable land and providing incentives for house construction; (6) overhauling the wage and salary structure so as to reduce the disparities in income between manual and service or clerical occupations; and (7) a charter of workers' rights. In addition to all this, a ceiling on disposable incomes fixed at Rs 2,000 a month was imposed by the 1971 budget.

Other measures have also been taken to ensure a greater degree of state control over the economy. A Gem Corporation (1971) which brings the entire gem trade under governmental supervision was set up to put an end to the smuggling of gems and their under-invoicing which had hitherto entailed the loss of several million rupees' worth of foreign exchange to the country. On 30 December 1971, the Sri Lanka Petroleum Corporation completed the nationalisation of the petroleum trade when it took over the handling of aviation fuel from Esso, the last of the foreign oil companies operating in the island. On 21 January 1972 the State Film Corporation went into business, becoming the sole authority responsible for the purchase and distribution of films, local and foreign, throughout the country. On 25 January 1972 the Paddy Marketing Board Act came into operation, taking under its control the entire paddy trade in the island. In March 1972 a state trading tea corporation was established to control the 40 million pound domestic tea market, while the State Trading Corporation (Consolexpo) established in January 1972 handles the entire tea trade with countries that have bilateral trade agreements with Sri Lanka. Legislation was also enacted in 1972 obliging persons or companies proposing to alienate estates of over a hundred acres to offer these for sale in the first instance to the Ministry of Plantation Industries.

The objective of all these measures inclusive of the Plan is to change the hitherto prevailing concept of the public sector as a mere welfare agency which also ensured law and order to one that will play a major productive role, and by this means to raise the 'poverty line' in the country.

For purposes of implementing the Plan detailed annual programmes are being worked out by the Ministry of Planning which provide for targets in public and private sector expenditure and for a foreign exchange budget. Sectoral committees have also been set up in the Ministry to review Plan performances and to take necessary and remedial action where indicated. A Planning and Progress Control Division in the Ministry is responsible for the overall supervision of the implementation of the Plan.

Whether the Plan would make any measurable progress is a moot question. The 1971 budget recorded a huge deficit of Rs 400 million, and finances for its implementation from governmental sources are therefore considerably curtailed. And the economy in 1971 performed very poorly. A mission from the Asian Development Bank which visited Sri Lanka in August 1971 reported that slackness was due, besides the P.L.F. insurrection of April 1971 to the tight import restrictions, to the uncertainty on the part of the private sector over the eventual shape of governmental policies, and to the downward trend in the export sector.[79] As a result the gross national product, the mission reported, rose by only 1 per cent in 1971. In per capita terms the gross national product was expected to register a negative growth rate of about 1 per cent. The mission added that the G.N.P. growth rate for 1972 could not be expected to differ very much from that of 1971 and it attributed this to the country's serious balance of payments problem. In addition to all this there was a considerable shortfall in foreign aid during 1970–1.[80] Project aid anticipated for the year was Rs 111.3 million but the actual aid received was only Rs 20.1 million. Non-project (commodity) aid for the same year was estimated at Rs 525 million but aid received amounted to only Rs 169 million. Though all these facts do not relate to the Plan period, but just precede it, they are a pointer to the difficulties that lie ahead especially by way of enthusing the private sector and of attracting assistance from foreign sources.

CONCLUSION

The solution to Sri Lanka's economic and social problems, it will be realised, are not available within the country itself. There are external constraints, of which the vagaries of the international market in respect of export crops and the difficulties of obtaining a market for even the products of the new industries that have emerged in the post-1960 years are the most important ones. Not only are markets not readily available, the recurring shortages in hard currency make it impossible for many industries which depend on imported raw material components to maintain themselves at normal capacities throughout the year. Add to this the fact of political instability goaded by the advent of socialist governments which are frowned on by Sri Lanka's principal aid-givers – the international credit agencies, western countries and Japan – and the problem reaches near insoluble proportions.

The situation is further complicated by the inter-group tensions that are now a perennial feature of the country. The resources are simply not enough to go round, and consequently in a contracting economy with an expanding population in the under-nineteen age group and educated with skills that have no market, an explosion is surely inevitable. The surprising fact is that it came later, the P.L.F. outbreak of April 1971, than earlier. Whether discontent can any longer be contained for a sufficient time to overcome some of the more immediate problems is a moot point.

The strivings of governments since independence have been to find ways and means of answering the urgent questions of the day – controlling population, striking a balance between expenditure on economic growth and the welfare services, providing employment and maintaining national unity.

Two definite strands of political thinking have identified themselves as being fit to provide viable solutions. The U.N.P. with its emphasis on the private sector, the recognition of the need to maintain the welfare system, concentration on agricultural productivity and pro-west stances in foreign policy did operate within the democratic framework with a fair measure of success in its two phases of power, 1947–56 and 1965–70. The S.L.F.P. with its socialist orientations, stress on the public sector and industry, neutralism, and a constitutional framework to achieve the objectives of a socialist democracy, has widened the area of interaction with the public and successfully enlisted the participation of the have-nots in society. The real test arises in its second phase of power, from 1970 onwards, and it is yet too early to hazard a prediction.

The various exercises in planning, especially in the post-1956 phase, have helped in some way to determine directions but not to achieve targets. Governments cannot be altogether blamed for the failures because they have inherited impossible situations and their success depends on factors over which they have no control.

A pruning of the welfare services has taken place in the last few years but these are not adequate to make up the funds needed for economic development. Nor have they impressed the aid-givers.

On the other hand the drive towards socialism has not enthused the underprivileged towards a concerted national effort though it has brought the private sector to a virtual halt through the numerous disincentives imposed.

A measure of authoritarianism may help tide over present difficulties but unless this is accomplished with a mammoth effort at development, the odds are that Sri Lanka could well slip into a state of inflationary chaos and constriction of the democratic process.

4 Political Behaviour and Political Forces

PATTERNS OF POLITICAL CONDUCT

The Social and Religious Ethos

As already stated, the history of Sinhalese–Tamil wars serves as a constant reminder to the Sinhalese of the dangers from the Dravidian foe.

There is also the fact of the Tamil kingdom in north Ceylon which ceased to exist in 1618. This provides inspiration to Tamil separatism.

To complicate matters further, Sinhalese Buddhists regard Sri Lanka as *their* land in which must be preserved *theravada* Buddhism in its most pristine form. Many Sinhalese Buddhists believe that the future of the Sinhalese race is tied up with the very existence and continuance of this kind of Buddhism in Sri Lanka. Hence their antipathy to powerful minority groups such as the Tamils (Ceylon and Indian) and the Roman Catholics.

But this antipathy is tempered by the tolerance of Buddhism.[1] The Buddhist tenets of *metta* (loving kindness), *karuna* (compassion), *mudita* (sympathetic joy) and *upekha* (equanimity) provide a foundation for the advocacy of peace and compromise and of middle-path solutions to vexed problems. There is also much to be said for the Sinhalese temperament, which is an accommodating one. A combination of these factors mollifies political tensions.

Legacies of British Rule

The British welded the island into a cohesive whole through the network of communications which they developed and through their unified administrative structure. Their educational system also contributed to the emergence of an English-educated westernised middle class comprising members of the administration, personnel in the commercial establishments from clerical hands upwards, professional men such as lawyers, doctors, teachers and journalists, and landed proprietors owning mostly coconut and some rubber lands. Quite a few of these people went to the metropolitan country for studies while others had their education in British-oriented schools in the island which among other things imparted knowledge of British constitutional history and parliamentary institutions.

With time, the 'England returneds' and the local intelligentsia desired similar institutions in their country. They also wanted the administration progressively Ceylonised – the obvious result of increasing education and specialisation. These bonds and attitudies produced a unity of outlook culminating in the formation of the Ceylon National Congress in 1919.

Progressive reforms and gradualism in constitutional development characterised the demands of the Ceylonese nationalists. In this sense Sri Lanka was the ideal colony which saw a peaceful transition from dependence to self-government. In neighbouring India, independence and unity was forged in the fires of a common struggle based on mass participation. Sri Lanka's independence was won by negotiation and diplomacy, and craft cannot altogether be excluded.[2] It was the top elite that was involved, not the lower layers.

The stages through which Sri Lanka progressed to independence shed light on the economic circumstances influencing her political evolution.

The constitution of 1924 provided for a limited franchise and placed the unofficial members of the Legislative Council in a position of 'power without responsibility' leaving the British-dominated executive in a hopeless minority situation.[3] The upshot was limited internal self-government under the Donoughmore constitution of 1931 with its executive committees, a board of ministers, without collective responsibility except for the annual budget and universal suffrage.[4]

Such a constitution encouraged individualism and lopsided growth, with the able minister forging ahead with his grandiose schemes. It therefore inhibited the emergence of a proper party system. Members of the State Council (the legislative body) placed undue emphasis on servicing their constituencies and on social welfare programmes. It was the same with the board of ministers. The larger issues of economic development tended to be overlooked.

This type of political conduct also had its roots in the past. There had been a kind of authoritarian but paternalistic form of administration from the days of the Sinhalese kings. The British up to the time of the Donoughmore constitution followed similar policies by providing a quantum of social welfare in order to keep the people of the country contented. The Ceylonese ministers who took office from 1931 onwards continued the system, but in benevolent forms since they operated in the context of universal suffrage and democratic institutions. The Buddhist concept of providing alms to gain merit and the acceptance of these *danas* or alms as a normal feature of Sinhalese social life has also contributed to the widespread notion that the state is and should be the supreme almsgiver. This, when translated into contemporaneous idiom, implies nothing more than the social service state.

Parallel to these developments, there had also emerged a left-wing movement in the early 1930s organised by young intellectuals returning from abroad. Their militancy was to some extent tempered by the British education they had received. In a way this could explain the accident of Trotskyism in Ceylon with its liberalism and determined opposition to Stalinism. The Trotskyists came to be more influential than the Moscow communists.

Both left-wing groups have been responsible for radicalising politics during the last four decades.[5] The spread of literacy as a result of the introduction of a free education scheme from the kindergarten through the university in October 1945 helped them in their campaigns. This process of radicalisation led to further expectations and demands for welfare services, redistributive justice and legislation in a socialistic direction.

The conservative governments in office from 1931 to 1956 pandered to these demands as a way to secure their positions. Major agricultural schemes transferring population from the impoverished, densely populated regions of the south to lands freshly irrigated in the dry zone areas in north-central Ceylon were launched, coupled with generous social welfare measures such as rice at prices heavily subsidised by the state, free education, free medicare, etc. These social services have been a heavy drain on the country's exchequer to the detriment of its economic development.

Political Ecology and the Basis for Political Competition

The island is an underdeveloped export-import economy with tea, rubber and coconut products (in that order) playing the dominant role of foreign exchange earner, but these have fared poorly in recent times.

On the other side of the picture is the island's rising population, made more serious by increasing unemployment owing to slow economic growth. More pertinent to this economic crisis is the fact of the relative youth of the island's population which results in greater dependence of the young on the old and further burdens on an already severely strained welfare system.

The bulk of the island's population is rural based, 73.7 per cent as against an urban population of 15.4. The rest is in the plantation sector. The majority of the population lives at subsistence level or a little above it. The distribution of income is glaringly disparate. Twenty per cent of the national income goes into the pockets of 1.5 per cent of the population.[6] Ninety per cent of the population earns less than Rs 175 a month, 60 per cent less than Rs 85 a month.[7]

Political leadership at the higher levels comes from a relatively small category of professional men mostly from the legal profession, retired public servants including school teachers, a few medical men, industrialists and business men. There is also a minuscule group of full-time professional politicians who generally form the top rung leadership in all parties. Although some 52.3 per cent of the population is engaged in agriculture, this sector hardly provides a recruiting base, though at the middle and lower levels of politics some farmers take an active interest in local government and constituency politics. But even at these levels, it is the big and small shopkeepers and traders, the local legal profession, the Buddhist monks, the native physicians, the *swabasha* (vernacular) school teachers and trade union workers that form the major component of local bodies and the constituency organisations of the political parties.

Electoral demarcation (see Chapter 5) provides a terrific weightage in representation to the rural sector as against the urban. The backward and sparsely populated areas enjoy a premium. The result is that the urban voter is placed at a disadvantage.

The electoral system has also worked to the detriment of radical and left-wing parties. The rural voter is generally suspicious of their economic programmes and their non-sectarian political beliefs. Conservative parties have a lead, and repeated frustration has in recent times driven left-wing parties to discard Marxism for a type of Sinhalese Buddhist-oriented socialism in their search for parliamentary goals.

The bias towards ruralism poses a problem to the higher echelons of the Sinhalese power elites, who are mostly English-educated and more secular and modern than tradition-bound in their political beliefs. Consequently their political styles and vocabulary have not seldom been in conflict with their actions and policies, especially when in office. They make extravagant use of the language of Sinhalese Buddhist chauvinism on public platforms, especially in the rural areas. But in Parliament, in the committee rooms, in the cabinet, at the bureaucratic levels and in the centres of social intercourse there is willingness to deal rationally with problems and to work out compromises.

The need to adopt such schizophrenic political styles is reinforced by the fact that 67.4 per cent of Sri Lanka's population is Sinhalese Buddhist and the latter suffer from numerous economic, social and cultural disabilities, the result of the neglect and oppression of colonial powers, and indifference to their problems on the part of the island's westernised intelligentsia.

Further, political, social and economic pressures from the Sinhalese are felt most, in view of the fact that 60 per cent of the island's population of over twelve million people live within the south-western quadrant of the island, with population densities of over one thousand per square mile along the coastal strip. To put it in another way, about 75 per cent of the island's total population (the majority of this 75 per cent being Sinhalese Buddhists) live and earn their livelihood within a radius of eighty miles of the capital city of Colombo. From the point of view of social and political tensions, this concentration makes it difficult, if not sometimes impossible, for governments in office or for the major political parties to make any major concessions to the Tamils without courting consequences in the form of hartals, violence and/or electoral defeat. It would be easy for agitators and extremist groups to exert the maximum pressure on a government that is within so easy reach of them in Colombo. It would be the same if any government attempted to make drastic cuts in expenditure on the island's welfare services.

The attenuating factors in an otherwise rigidly complex situation are (a) the dangers of political instability, and (b) the retardation of economic progress that would follow attempts on the part of governments to pursue purely chauvinistic policies.

Since 1960, the number of seats in the House of Representatives has been increased from 101 to 157. This has made it difficult, though not impossible, as the general election of 1970 proved, for Sinhalese political parties to obtain a clear majority in the House without the support of Tamil parties in the House and/or the marginal votes of especially the limited number of Indian Tamils who have recently obtained the franchise as well as of the Ceylon Tamils and the Muslims in Sinhalese constituencies.

POLITICAL PARTIES

The U.N.P.

The U.N.P. was organised in September 1946 by D. S. Senanayake and other conservative-minded political notables with the backing of a number of ethnocentric political groupings such as the S.M.S. and the Ceylon Muslim League and of sections of Ceylon and Indian Tamils.[8]

The new party had the support of almost the entire national press, the 'big families', the landed interests, the *mudalalis* (shop-owners) and the higher and middle rank government officials, as well as some in the lower ranks.

Basically the U.N.P is democratic socialist, committed to a mixed type of economy with greater emphasis on the private sector, agrarian based, well disposed towards foreign especially British investors, willing to permit, consonant with political circumstances, a measure of elbow room to the minority socio-ethnic groups, and in external affairs desirous of maintaining the Commonwealth connection and ties with the west, though for form's sake professing to adhere to neutralism. The party has been slow to adapt itself to the rapidly changing economic and political situation.

The party's prime ministerial figures also represented certain categories of thinking – D. S. Senanayake (1947–52) and his nephew Sir John Kotelawala (1953–6) in its first phase, and Dudley Senanayake and his deputy J. R. Jayawardene in the second (1956–70) and third (1970–) phases.

The first phase (1947–56). During this phase, the U.N.P.'s approach to the economic problem was to concentrate on the opening up of the dry zone areas with irrigation schemes, etc. to provide employment and to alleviate pressure of population in the densely populated south-western quadrant. D. S. Senanayake pioneered many of these schemes as minister of agriculture during the Donoughmore phase.[9] When prime minister, he entrusted the portfolio to his son, Dudley. He paid little attention to the question of overall national planning. Nor did he care very much for industrialisation.

Part of the reason for the lack of interest in industry was because of the very satisfactory balance of payments situation. The island had sizable sterling balances in Britain, export produce fetched good prices and rubber received an added boost after the outbreak of the Korean War. But foreign exchange was frittered away on luxury and other non-essential imports.

In its manifesto for the 1947 general election the party promised to strive for five freedoms – freedom from foreign domination, want, unemployment, ignorance and disease. It added that all these could not be attained in the five-year term of Parliament, but that 'the essential foundations would be laid in that period'. However, it was known that D. S. Senanayake had not favoured the system of free education from the kindergarten to the university inaugurated under the Donoughmore constitution in October 1945. The party capitalised on the fact that it won independence for Sri Lanka in February 1948.

The party claimed that it was the protector of the nation's civilisation from the Marxists who, it charged, were agents of foreign powers. It alleged that religion stood in danger from Marxism. At the 1947 general election, posters depicting temples, churches and mosques in flames with the caption 'save the country from the *sama samaja* [Trostkyist] fire' were freely distributed by party propagandists. Similar cries were raised by the party at every subsequent general election.

The party claimed that it was the instrument of national unity. In its anxiety to placate minority groups it alienated layers of Sinhalese Buddhist nationalist opinion. It was extremely reluctant to switch to the national languages in administration in case this alienated the Ceylon Tamils – for in the process primacy would have had to be given to the Sinhalese language. It refused to involve itself any more in the provision of state patronage and state protection for Buddhism. On the contrary, section 29 of the constitution (which D. S. Senanayake helped to frame) afforded safeguards to the Roman Catholics and other minority groups from discrimination.

Senanayake's irrigation policies, however, roused the opposition of a section of the Ceylon Tamils who formed a new party, the F.P., in 1949. Senanayake's refusal to accommodate the immigrant Indian Tamil population alienated the latter and gave a handle to the F.P. in its campaigns against the T.C., which became the ally of the U.N.P. from the latter half of 1948.

The party was decidedly anti-Marxist. Marxist constituencies were neglected by U.N.P. governments and the rights of the Marxist opposition during 1947–56 hardly respected.[10] The Public Security Act of 1947 and the Trade Union (Amendment) Act of 1948 were designed to curb Marxist attempts to disturb the social order. U.N.P. governments were convinced that the Marxists were aiming to destroy Parliament and refused therefore to do business with them.[11]

There could not have been a stauncher advocate of the Commonwealth connection. It was Senanayake who negotiated the defence and external affairs agreements of November 1947 with Britain. It was to him that the British government felt it could confidently transfer power in February 1948. The prime minister reciprocated by his refusal to consider any proposals for the nationalisation of British interests, particularly British-owned tea estates. He flatly declared that 'it would be foolish to kill the goose that laid the golden egg'.

Senanayake backed the Colombo Plan of 1951 in which his minister of finance, J. R. Jayawardene, had an important role to play along with the Australian minister of external affairs, Percy

Spender. His government organised the Colombo Plan Exhibition of March 1952.[12]

In foreign policy, the Ceylonese leader claimed to follow 'the middle path', but there was no doubt that most of the actions of his government were directed at giving support to the west.[13]

D. S. Senanayake's successors, Dudley Senanayake (March 1952–October 1953) and Sir John Kotelawala (1953–6) pursued similar policies. But on the domestic front the social services had to be contracted because of the deteriorating balance of payments situation. The cut in the price of subsidised rice in July 1953 brought about Dudley Senanayake's resignation in October of that year. Cuts imposed by his successor in other fields contributed to the defeat of the U.N.P. in 1966.[14]

The U.N.P.'s reluctance to countenance the demands of Sinhalese Buddhist pressure groups contributed most to its rout in 1956. It refused at first to be drawn into the language imbroglio and Kotelawala persisted for a while with his party's position on parity of status for the Sinhalese and Tamil languages. Then, in the face of mounting Sinhalese opposition, the party at a special conference in February 1956 changed to 'Sinhalese only'. The *volte face* failed to convince the Buddhist militants and disgusted the U.N.P.'s Tamil supporters.

The party, however, was unwilling to be drawn into the controversy over special rights for Buddhism.[15]

In Commonwealth affairs, Kotelawala proved as redoubtable as D. S. Senanayake. He organised the visit of the queen to Sri Lanka in April 1954.

In foreign policy, Kotelawala was even more pro-west.[16] His stance at Bandung in 1955 gave the opposition ample ammunition. The latter alleged that Sri Lanka was fast becoming an American satellite with the attendant dangers of nuclear bases being set up in the country. This was an issue in the general election of 1956.

The second phase (1956–70). In the years 1956–9 the party excelled in its strategy to undermine and destroy S. W. R. D. Bandaranaike's M.E.P. government, embarrassing him particularly on his extravagant pledges to the electors on language, religion and economic relief. The party successfully led the opposition to Bandaranaike's pact of July 1957 with the F.P.

The U.N.P. further exploited the antagonism that developed

between the Marxist and democratic socialist wings in the Bandaranaike cabinet. The fact was that the latter's (the democratic socialist wing's) ideological framework was not much different from that of the U.N.P.

The party's anti-Tamil chauvinism reached its climax at the general election of July 1960. At the preceding general election of March 1960, Dudley Senanayake, having failed to secure an overall majority, tried to enlist the co-operation of the Tamil federalists who, however, laid down terms which were in the circumstances impossible to concede. The U.N.P. thereupon let loose a barrage of anti-Tamil propaganda, accusing its rival the S.L.F.P. of having a secret pact with the Tamil federalists. It called on the electors to give a clear verdict so that the Tamil federalists would not be in a position to bargain. Ironically the electors responded to Senanayake's plea by returning the S.L.F.P. with an absolute majority.

In the next five years (1960–5) the party adopted a more temperate attitude. It gave the public the impression that it was regretful of the errors it had committed during its first phase, 1947 to 1956.

During these years the party's main platform was that the country's economy was being ruined, the cost of living was soaring, and that national unity was being systematically disrupted by the government's alienation of the Roman Catholics and the Tamils.

The party also constantly harped on the theme that the freedoms of a democratic society were being abused by Mrs Bandaranaike's government and were in danger of being destroyed. It capitalised on the many attempts Mrs Bandaranaike's government made to nationalise the Lake House Press which at the time published some 60 per cent of the newspapers in the island, and stepped up its campaign of 'democracy in danger' when Mrs Bandaranaike coalesced with the L.S.S.P. in June 1964. It eventually succeeded in securing Mrs Bandaranaike's parliamentary defeat in December 1964.

Despite its claim of having transformed itself into a new democratic party, the U.N.P. showed little evidence of fundamental change. Its two most important policy formulations – *Progress through Stability* adopted in March 1958 and *What we Believe* adopted in September 1963 – bore evidence of this fact.

On national questions, the leadership still spoke the old language. In a message to his party before the general election of March 1960, Dudley Senanayake spoke of national unity having received 'severe reverses', adding that during the recent past 'the forces of disruption represented by the extremists' have exploited 'race, religion, poverty and the most susceptible and inflammable passions of the people to confuse and destroy the national structure'.[17] Its stance on the language question was liberal compared to that of its rival, the S.L.F.P. But the party's decision to retain English for some further time in the administration, though intended to help public servants not proficient in the official language, was taken as evidence of its unwillingness to accommodate the Sinhalese-educated intelligentsia.

On both education and religion the party failed to sense the winds of change. On the schools question the party said that 'a religious environment is an essential part of a child's environment', but for this purpose it would organise a system of 'state-denominational schools' while providing at the same time assistance to the existing state-aided denominational schools.[18] The party declared that in pursuance of this policy denominational schools would not be taken over by the state.

The U.N.P. was further unwilling to concede the demand for special rights for the Sinhalese Buddhists. In its policy statement of March 1958 (*Progress through Stability*) there was no reference to how it proposed to deal with the problems of the Sinhalese Buddhists. There were vague pronouncements such as that there was the need for 'religious education and upbringing' and for 'the spread of spiritual values'. These were slightly revised when the party issued its manifesto for the general election of March 1960. There were references to the pressing problems of the Sinhalese Buddhists, but that was about all.

These attitudes were no doubt laudable from the abstract angle of nation-building, but in actual fact the U.N.P. had failed to come to grips with the realities of the problem.

It was the same with the economic question. No amount of camouflaging could hide the fact that it was still the party of private enterprise and that it had the support of powerful vested interests.

In its manifesto for the 1960 general election it stated that it would not resort to 'the forcible acquisition of foreign-owned tea and rubber plantations which now bring in most of Ceylon's foreign income'.

Its penchant for private enterprise was expressed in more precise terms in its policy statement entitled *What We Believe* adopted at the party's annual sessions in September 1963. It took pains to declare that its policy was 'not socialism alone, but democratic socialism'. Such a socialism, it said, had as its cornerstone 'a greater dispersal and decentralisation of political and economic power', and in the latter sphere, it would imply 'co-operative ownership and management where feasible, public ownership and management were necessary in the public interest, and private monopoly and management sensitive to its responsibilities for the welfare of the community'.

The party emphasised that what it was seeking to do was to steer clear of total state ownership on the one hand and ownership and management by a few capitalists on the other. This was greatly amplified in the party's manifesto for the general election of 1965. There was a separate section in it on 'free enterprise' where it was clearly stated that the party believed in 'the co-existence of the public and private sectors'. It went on to say that 'human initiative enthusiasm and energy are greater than machines', adding: 'What free enterprise can achieve in some sectors of the economy, a government department or corporation cannot achieve, except at greater cost and slower speed. . . . We shall boldly plan', it went on, 'together with the private sector, to make best use of human energy, skill and managerial ability, to create new wealth, employment and prosperity for all.'

The manifesto deplored the fact that a large number of national traders and industrialists had had their businesses 'strangled' by the S.L.F.P. government. These would, it pledged, be assisted by a U.N.P. government.

On organisational matters, however, the U.N.P. did make considerable progress during 1956–65, mainly due to the endeavours of J. R. Jayawardene. It interested itself in fields in which it had not been so keen up to 1956. It organised youth leagues and regular conferences and study classes for the members of these leagues. It also made a determined entry into an area which up to that time was regarded as the preserve of the Marxists – trade unionism. In both these sectors the party met with fair success.

The U.N.P. fought the general election of March 1965 not

on a go it alone policy, but for the first time as a senior partner in a broad front of 'democratic forces' forged to fight 'the totalitarianism of the left' which it said had become evident with the L.S.S.P. and C.P. entering into a coalition with the S.L.F.P. Its allies were a disparate group comprising the pro-Sinhalese S.L.F.S.P., M.E.P. and J.V.P., and the Tamil organisations, the C.W.C. and T.C., with the F.P. lending it indirect support. This broad front emerged victorious and formed a 'national government' under Dudley Senanayake's leadership.

The 'national government' during its five-year term achieved a limited success in its attempts at affecting national reconciliation through its handling of the language and Indian questions. Senanayake could not, however, implement his promise of district councils under central control and direction to the F.P. and this eventually led to their quitting his 'national government'.

The switch to the *poya* weekend and the government's refusal to provide relief to the private schools of the Roman Catholic Church did not reassure the Buddhists. On the other hand Catholic support for the U.N.P. declined.

On the economic front, the U.N.P. reverted to the principle of a mixed economy with the balance tilted in favour of the private sector. There was considerable private investment in 1965–9, almost double that in the government sector.[19] The government did not, however, restore to private enterprise the undertakings nationalised by the Bandaranaike governments of 1956–65. It was the prime minister's view that it was not possible to 'unscramble scrambled eggs'.

The party's organisational network tended to be neglected during 1965–70. Much store was placed in the charismatic potentialities of Dudley Senanayake's personality at the expense of a proper and streamlined organisation in the constituencies. This neglect was a major contributing factor to the U.N.P.'s defeat in the general election of 1970.

The U.N.P. leadership, especially its cabinet, also kept aloof from the rank and file, from party supporters and constituents. Its backbenchers quickly sensed this growing alienation and the more critical among them organised a gingergroup to keep an eye on the activities of ministers and their officials. One of its leaders, Festus Perera, was persuaded by the prime minister to disband the group on the assurance that he (the prime minister) would ensure ministerial and administrative efficiency.[20] But the evidence indicates that the prime minister failed to remedy the situation.

The third phase (*1970–*). After its 1970 rout, the party went through the motions of a major crisis from which it managed to emerge, though somewhat shattered.

Immediately after the results, Senanayake threw in the sponge and the leadership of the opposition devolved on J. R. Jayawardene. The ex-prime minister however returned to the fray after a while. He had a special committee of twenty members of the party's working committee appointed to re-vamp the party's policies with a view to giving it a new image. But the differences between him and Jayawardene, which up to the time of the general election had been contained, came into the open.

Jayawardene took up the position that the U.N.P. had no future. He set out his reasons for this conclusion in a confidential memorandum entitled '*The UNP in Opposition, 1970*'.[21] The substance of his thesis was that the party was considered by the majority of voters 'to represent the "haves", the affluent and the employer' whereas its opponents are accepted as the representatives of 'the have-nots, the needy and the employed'.

It was Jayawardene's view that a country such as Sri Lanka, going through the crises of balance of payments deficits, economic stagnancy, etc. could not afford the luxury of an opposition. He therefore advocated support for any unpopular measures the U.F. government may take to solve these difficulties. He further advised co-operation in all socialist measures the U.F. government would take within the context of a democratic framework. But he also insisted on opposition to any measures that 'violate the democratic freedoms'.

With much reason Jayawardene criticised the attitude his party had taken during 1956–65. He asked:

> Are we to criticise all government proposals and also government members, raising issues even of a personal nature, seeking to poison public opinion against the government individually and collectively, as we did from 1956 to 1965, with the results that we have seen?

Jayawardene developed this theme further after the ultra-left P.L.F. insurrection of March–April 1971. He urged that in a national crisis of such proportions the democratic forces in the country should close their ranks and join in the formation of a national government.[22]

The majority in the U.N.P.'s working committee opposed Jayawardene's proposed line of action, adopting, at its meeting on 18 December 1971, Senanayake's resolution to oppose the U.F. government 'uniquivocally'.[23]

In early 1972 the Senanayake section in the U.N.P. made a bid to oust Jayawardene by having a disciplinary committee investigate his conduct and public pronouncements. Jayawardene foiled it by obtaining an injunction from the Supreme Court. Shortly thereafter, in April–May 1972, other sections in the U.N.P. not immediately involved helped in effecting a reconciliation between the two leaders.[24]

In the autumn of 1972 the party had its constitution revised and democratised. It is now concentrating on an all-out opposition to the policies of the U.F. government. With Dudley Senanayake's death in April 1973, the leadership of the party devolved on Jayawardene.

The S.L.F.P.

The S.L.F.P. was launched by S. W. R. D. Bandaranaike in September 1951 shortly after he resigned his portfolio of health and local government in the administration of D. S. Senanayake. For a few years before he severed his connections with the U.N.P., Bandaranaike had given broad expression to his views on the social and economic problems of the country, but these went unheeded, for they were radical opinions, and the right wing of the U.N.P. was firmly entrenched at the time.

In a press release on 15 July 1951, Bandaranaike stated that his organisation would be 'a middle party between the U.N.P. of the extreme right and the Marxists on the extreme left'.[25]

There are three identifiable phases in the evolution and development of the S.L.F.P. The first was when Bandaranaike himself was its sole law-giver, as it were, from 1951 to his untimely death in September 1959. The second was when his wife took over the leadership of the party and ran it with the assistance of her late husband's nephew, Felix Dias Bandaranaike. The third phase commences from June 1964 when Mrs Bandaranaike teamed up with the two major left-wing groups in the country, the L.S.S.P. and the C.P.

The first phase (*1951–9*). With Bandaranaike's exit from the D. S. Senanayake government, anti-U.N.P. opinion in the country developed confidence in the possibilities of an alternative government being formed under his leadership. Such a government was formed in 1956 when Bandaranaike succeeded in overthrowing the U.N.P. as head of a Sinhalese Buddhist-oriented united front, the M.E.P., comprising his S.L.F.P., Philip Gunawardena's Marxist V.L.S.S.P., the pro-Sinhalese Bhasa Peramuna (language front) of W. Dahanayke, and a group of independent M.P.s led by I.M.R.A. Iriyagolle.

Shortly after its inaugural meeting the S.L.F.P. put forward a radical socialist programme which stood in contrast to the U.N.P.'s conservative, go-slow, benevolent paternalism.

In the sphere of foreign policy as well, important changes were advocated. Bandaranaike's concept of 'dynamic neutralism' was evident in the proposal that Ceylon should establish friendly relations with all countries and steer clear of any of the major power blocs. For this reason the granting of military bases to any foreign power was opposed. This meant the cancellation of the defence agreement with Britain and the removal of British military bases in Katunayake (air) and Trincomalee (naval). When Bandaranaike took office in 1956 he successfully negotiated the transfer of these bases to Sri Lanka.

As prime minister (1956–9) Bandaranaike was more anxious to make an impact on the international scene. His government established diplomatic missions with a number of communist states which U.N.P. governments had shunned. Trade and aid agreements too were concluded with these countries.

The S.L.F.P. had earlier advocated Sri Lanka's exit from the Commonwealth and assumption of republican status. But when Bandaranaike took office in 1956, he decided that Sri Lanka should, while declaring herself a republic, remain within the Commonwealth.

The S.L.F.P. proclaimed its commitment to constitutional methods and its acceptance of the parliamentary system of government. This, among other things, implied giving the opposition a fair deal. It was Bandaranaike's view, contrary to U.N.P. beliefs and practices, that Marxist parties should not be ignored. During his term as prime minister the Marxist opposition groups were given ample accommodation.

The S.L.F.P. was not satisfied with the existing constitutional arrangements. At the general elections of 1952 and 1956 it called for a constituent assembly to look into the unsatisfactory features of the constitution. As prime minister in 1956, Bandaranaike had a parliamentary joint select committee convened for the purpose of restructuring the constitution, but its work could not be completed because of the other urgent problems engaging the attention of his government.

It was the S.L.F.P.'s view that the laws relating to elections and electoral arrangements needed complete overhauling because of their undemocratic features and the advantages they gave to parties and individuals with superior material resources. A select committee of Parliament was therefore appointed by Bandaranaike to go into these matters and on its recommendations the electoral laws of the country were democratised.

It was in its economic and social policies that the S.L.F.P. differed materially from the U.N.P.

The S.L.F.P. drew attention to the fact that successive U.N.P. governments had not paid enough attention to the need for developing the country industrially. In its initial statement of policy (in 1951) it said that cheap power should be made available to the villages so that cottage industries might be promoted. Industrialisation, it added, should be encouraged as a means of eliminating unemployment.

The party declared its opposition to unrestricted freedom for all forms of enterprise. It stated that it would nationalise in a gradual way all essential industries, and this would include the large plantations, and the transport, banking, and insurance concerns in the country. These were further elaborated in the M.E.P.'s election manifesto of 1956 when it pledged that all key industries would be run by the state, small industries would be left in private hands, and an overall national plan would be formulated.

With a view to effecting a proper redistribution of incomes, the new party promised (in 1951) to impose a supertax on all incomes in excess of Rs 50,000. It proposed the introduction of such measures as death duties and a progressive scale of income taxation.

When faced with the challenge of implementing these economic policies, Bandaranaike told the House of Representatives in August 1956, shortly after he became prime minister, that his government was faced with the difficult problem of trying to transform 'a stagnant, narrow, plantation, colonial economy' into a modern one.[26]

But despite the obstacles, the port of Colombo and the omnibus services were nationalised in 1958. Peasant cultivators obtained a measure of security with the passing of the Paddy Lands Bill in 1958. A national provident fund was instituted to help the lower income groups. The system of taxation was overhauled with a view to encouraging savings and investment and providing relief to the lower income groups. A national planning council was set up and by 1958 a serious, scientific Ten-Year Plan was put out.

The S.L.F.P.'s social policies were just as far-reaching. During 1951–3, the party stood for Sinhalese *and* Tamil as the official languages and at the general election of 1952, Bandaranaike claimed that if returned to office he would effect the switchover from English in twenty-four hours.[27] In 1955–6, in the face of mounting pressure from Sinhalese Buddhist militants, the party changed to 'Sinhalese only' with provision for 'the reasonable use of the Tamil language'. The objectives were to make the administration accessible to the ordinary *swabasha* majority in the country and to give importance to the *swabasha*-educated intelligentsia.

As prime minister, Bandaranaike encountered opposition from the Sinhalese militants and the Ceylon Tamils in seeking to give effect to his pledges on language. In June 1956 he had Parliament enact the Official Language Act in the wake of Sinhalese-Tamil clashes following an F.P.-organised *satyagraha* against the proposed legislation.

Relations between the two ethnic groups rapidly deteriorated thereafter. In July 1957, in the context of a crisis that was threatening to envelop the whole country, Bandaranaike concluded a pact with the F.P. which was a compromise on its principal demands.[28] The pact provided for legislation to make Tamil a language of administration with Sinhalese in the northern and eastern provinces, and for the devolution of powers to district councils.

There was strong opposition from Sinhalese extremists and from the U.N.P. to this *rapprochement.* Both groups accused Bandaranaike of betraying the Sinhalese and seeking to divide the country. In the face of this growing opposition, the prime minister became discouraged and took no action to implement his pact.

The F.P., wearying of this reluctance and delay, sought an opportunity to register its protest, which came when the minister of transport sent nationalised omnibuses with the Sinhalese letter *sri* on their number plates to the Tamil-speaking areas. The F.P. responded with two anti-*sri* campaigns which provoked retaliatory action from extremist Sinhalese groups in the Sinhalese areas. The mounting crisis resulted in the prime minister succumbing to the pressure of the extremists and abandoning his pact in April 1958. There then followed the violent race riots of May and June.[29] In August 1958 Bandaranaike, in a vain attempt to conciliate the Tamils, had Parliament pass the Tamil Language (Special Provisions) Act, but it failed to make any impact on them.

The S.L.F.P.'s policy on religion was decidedly pro-Buddhist. At the general election of 1956 Bandaranaike declared, with reservations, that his M.E.P. 'generally approved' of the recommendations of the unofficial Buddhist Committee of Inquiry.[30] In office he was reluctant to nationalise the schools though in many other spheres his government took steps to encourage Sinhalese culture and Buddhism and to control the activities of the Christians.

Bandaranaike's M.E.P. of 1956 was, however, a complex coalition of contradictory forces riven most of the time by sharp rivalries between strong and ambitious personalities of rightist and leftist persuasions vying for primacy within its confines.

In early 1959 relations between the right and left wings in the M.E.P. government reached crisis point. The rightist 'democratic socialist' ministers, a majority, led by W. Dahanayake, demanded the dismissal of the V.L.S.S.P. Marxist minister, Philip Gunawardene, whose growing influence they viewed with apprehension. Gunawardene had authored two controversial but popular Bills, one on paddy lands which was passed in an emasculated form, and the other on co-operative banks which was rejected by the Government Parliamentary Group. Both Bills provided relief to the peasantry and the rural population. The crisis ended with the prime minister being forced to restrict Philip Gunawardene's portfolio (agriculture) and the latter resigning from the cabinet along with his V.L.S.S.P. colleague, P. H. William de Silva, minister of industries and industrial research, in May 1959.[31]

Bandaranaike reconstituted his government on 9 June 1959. It was now a wholly S.L.F.P. government, with its right wing on the ascendant. It subsisted on a threadbare majority for the next few months until the prime minister's assassination in September 1959.

The second phase (*1960–64*). With the prime minister's assassination the S.L.F.P. entered a traumatic phase with its leadership invested in W. Dahanayake. Dissensions in the government over the way in which the investigations into the assassination were being handled finally ended in Dahanayake getting rid of his S.L.F.P. colleagues in the cabinet and forming a new party, the L.P.P., to fight the general election which he had called for March 1960.[32] The S.L.F.P. leadership then passed on to C. P. de Silva for a brief while until Mrs Sirima Bandaranaike decided to involve herself actively in its affairs. On 7 May 1960 the S.L.F.P. elected her its president, and in July 1960 she led the party to a convincing victory at the general election held in that month. Her plea to the electors was that she should be given a mandate to continue her husband's policies.

In office (July 1960–March 1965), Mrs Bandaranaike effected significant changes in the cultural and economic spheres.

In late 1960–early 1961 most of the schools were nationalised despite Roman Catholic opposition. During the same period her government proceeded to give effect to its policies on the switchover to Sinhalese and encountered in the process a massive civil disobedience protest movement launched by the F.P. which it eventually crushed in April 1961.[33]

Important nationalisation measures were put through during this period. In 1961 the minister of finance at the time, Felix Dias Bandaranaike, nationalised the Ceylonese-owned Bank of Ceylon, the biggest commercial bank in the island. It was proposed to get this bank to assist local enterprise in a more liberal way than it had done in the past. Likewise, with a view to helping with easy credit facilities the rural sector, small industrialists and petty traders, the minister of commerce, trade, food and shipping, T. B. Ilangaratne, the principal left-wing socialist in the cabinet, had people's banks established in many towns in the island. The same minister effected the takeover of almost the entire petroleum and insurance businesses in the island. Ilangaratne was further instrumental in expanding the commercial activities of the Co-operative

Wholesale Establishment which now became responsible for the import and distribution of essential commodities, virtually elbowing out the private trade.

The government's nationalisation programme, labour unrest in the country, trade union action by left-wing parties and religious and communal troubles (from the Roman Catholics and the Tamils) made right-wing elements in the higher rungs of the armed services and the police feel that they must act 'to save the nation'.[34] In January 1962 plans for a *coup d'etat* by these sections were uncovered, but only after these had been abandoned. A number of high-ranking army, navy, and police officers and a few civil servants of the higher grades had planned to arrest left-wing leaders, the minister of finance, Felix Dias Bandaranaike, and some of the senior civil servants who were supporters of Mrs Bandaranaike's government. Thereafter they were to ask the governor-general to suspend the constitution and hand over authority to 'a government of national safety' comprising leading members of the U.N.P., some of the right-wing politicians of the S.L.F.P. and other prominent persons in public life.

When the government was made wise to these plans, it was Felix Dias Bandaranaike who was invested with the responsibility of investigating the conspiracy.

The S.L.F.P. government exploited this abortive *coup d'etat* to its political advantage for the suspects were all Christians.

Another major crisis for the government developed with the budget of 1962. It marked the beginning of the decline of Felix Dias Bandaranaike's position of importance in the cabinet. As minister of finance, he proposed a cut in the rice ration in view of the government's grave economic difficulties. This was opposed by S.L.F.P. backbenchers though it had the support of the prime minister. The minister was obliged to drop the proposal and subsequently resigned.

The third phase (1964–). There followed a succession of finance ministers none of whom could help to right the economy. This fact among others led Mrs Bandaranaike in June 1964 to re-form her government by coalescing with the L.S.S.P. The L.S.S.P. at this time was part of the U.L.F., comprising itself, the C.P. and the M.E.P. formed in August 1963. The U.L.F. had a list of twenty-one demands and was planning to take action on these. Mrs Bandaranaike realised the dangers. It was also evident to her that without electoral co-operation from the left the S.L.F.P. could not hope to win a general election.

The L.S.S.P. coalesced on a fourteen-point programme agreed to between the two parties. It marked a further leftward direction to S.L.F.P. policies and a more conciliatory approach to the Tamil problem.

The new coalition was viewed with apprehension by the conservative right-wing elements in the country. The government's decision to forge ahead with legislation to nationalise the Lake House group of newspapers and to institute a press council to discipline the press was the rallying point for all the diverse and sometimes conflicting forces that were at variance with it. The U.N.P. under Dudley Senanayake provided the necessary leadership. It ended in the parliamentary defeat of the government in December 1964 followed by an electoral defeat in March 1965.

Representatives of leading Buddhist organisations in their evidence before the press commission headed by a retired supreme court justice who was also a Buddhist activist, K. D. de Silva, appointed by the S.L.F.P. government, had condemned the press for its anti-national and anti-Buddhist activities. The Commission in its interim report of August 1964 endorsed these crticisms and recommended that an independent press council be established and newspapers be placed under a broadbased corporation.[35] But with the Trotskyists in the government, the fears of the Sinhalese Buddhists were aroused by the propaganda of the government's opponents. These Marxists would, the government's opponents insisted, take control of the press and then undermine democratic institutions. Since they were 'materialists' they would destroy religion. It would, they said, be the end of the Sinhalese Buddhist civilisation.[36]

The move to nationalise the press undermined the confidence of sections of the Buddhist public and clergy in the government. Some of the S.L.F.P. members of Parliament, who had had misgivings earlier about the wisdom of coalescing with the Marxists led by C. P. de Silva who was at the time deputy head of the government, were persuaded by the leaders of the opposition to defect and vote against the government's throne speech of 20 November, 1964, which contained the controversial proposal. On 3 December, C. P. de Silva and thirteen of his followers crossed the floor in what they claimed were the interests of democracy and voted against the throne speech. The government was defeated at the division by 74 votes to 73 and Parliament was thereafter dissolved on 17 December, and a general election was fixed for 22 March 1965.

The foreign policy of Mrs Bandaranaike's government was one which trod the nonaligned path, with Ceylon taking up a critical attitude to the west in most matters. During this period there was increased identification with the Afro-Asian powers. Mrs Bandaranaike also successfully negotiated a settlement of the Indian issue with the Indian prime minister, Shastri, in October 1964.

In opposition (1965–70) the S.L.F.P. and its Marxist allies at first concentrated their fire on the U.N.P.'s alliance with the two Tamil groups, the F.P. and the C.W.C. – sensitive isses in the Sinhalese areas. Thereafter, however, other issues arose, just as important, which they exploited.

In their campaign, the opposition met with much success because they had united under the leadership of Mrs Bandaranaike. Both in Parliament and outside they worked in close co-operation. Further, during this phase, the left-wing leadership of the S.L.F.P. organised a Socialist Study Circle, of a Fabian Society type, which arranged discussions, seminars, and study groups on various aspects of the programme that an S.L.F.P. left-wing coalition would implement if returned to power.

In March 1968 the S.L.F.P. and its two Marxist allies, the L.S.S.P. and C.P., set the seal to their unity when they agreed to form a Samagi Peramuna (U.F.) and to implement a twenty-five point programme of work if returned to power. They made it clear that they would form a people's government of all three parties under Mrs Bandaranaike and that they were not merely entering into an electoral arrangement as in the past to defeat the U.N.P.

The Common Programme made it clear that the S.L.F.P. had decided to move further to the left from the left-of-centre position it had earlier taken. There was agreement on the need to regiment the economy and therefore to increase governmental control of the economy. When spelt out, it meant among other things that foreign-owned and local commercial banks and the import trade in essential commodities would be nationalised, agency houses (mostly British-owned) controlled, the plantation industries guided and directed by state agencies established for the purpose and the state's entitlement to acquire shares in both foreign and local companies. Further, there would be a considerable extension of the public sector. Heavy capital goods and suitable basic industries would be state-owned and other industries would be assigned to co-operative societies and private enterprise. The role the latter would have to play would be minimised considerably.

In the agricultural sector, the Common Programme promised land reforms and other amenities to the peasant. It pledged that it would have the terms imposed by the World Bank for the Mahaveli Diversion project revised so as, among other things, to have the raised water tax lowered.

Employment would be provided for the 750,000 without jobs inclusive of fifteen thousand graduates.

The Common Programme promised to restore the cut in the rice subsidy imposed by the 'national government' and to extend greater social benefits to the people than were available to them at the time.

There was, further, a promise of reforms in the constitutional and administrative spheres. A constituent assembly would be convened to draw up a new constitution. People's committees, employees councils and advisory committees in government offices would ensure greater participation of the people in government and administration. The large majority of public servants would be given political rights, and workers were promised a comprehensive charter of rights. The university population would be provided with a reformed and democratised university structure. All repressive legislation restricting democratic rights would be repealed.

On the perennial question of majority-minority relationships, the Common Programme promised to give Buddhism its 'rightful place' while guaranteeing to other religions their 'due rights'. The Tamil Regulations framed by the Senanayake government in January 1966 would be replaced with another set of regulations acceptable to both the Sinhalese and Tamils.

In external affairs, the Common Programme specified the principles that would guide a U.F. government in its relations with other countries. It pledged that it would follow the non-aligned path, oppose imperialism, colonialism and racism while supporting national liberation struggles, extend diplomatic relations to the German Democratic Republic, the Democratic

Republic of Vietnam, North Korea and to the Provisional Revolutionary Government of the Republic of South Vietnam. There was also a pledge to suspend diplomatic relations with Israel until such time as the government of Israel arrived at a settlement with the U.A.R., Syria and Jordan acceptable to these Arab states, or conformed to the U.N. Security Council's resolutions of 22 November 1967 and subsequent dates.

At the general election of May 1970, the U.F. scored a resounding success, winning 118 of the 135 seats it contested.[37] The S.L.F.P. secured a majority of seats (90) in its own right but Mrs Bandaranaike, in keeping with her pledges to form a U.F. government with the two Marxist parties, the L.S.S.P. (19) and C.P. (6), assigned the key portfolios of (1) finance, (2) communications, (3) plantation industries and constitutional affairs, to senior Trotskyist parliamentarians, and (4) housing to one of the most senior of the C.P. M.P.s. In addition, two other important portfolios, that of internal and external trade, and industries and scientific research, were given to prominent left-wing socialists in the S.L.F.P. As evidence of the U.F. government's determination to solve the unemployment problem, the prime minister created a new subject of Employment and assigned it to herself.

In the first two years of office, the U.F. government proceeded to take steps to implement the more urgent aspects of its Programme. A constituent assembly convened in July 1970 completed its endeavours in May 1972. But in the meanwhile the second chamber, the Senate, with its U.N.P. majority was abolished by constitutional amendment in September 1971. Appeals to the Judicial Committee of the Privy Council were also done away with and a Court of Appeal was set up in its place in November 1971.

Further, workers' councils, advisory committees in government offices, and people's committees on a territorial basis were duly constituted. Divisional development councils were also organised, and a measure of administrative decentralisation was introduced.

On the economic front the new government was confronted with grave problems. The Trotskyist minister of finance stated that he could not proceed with the U.F.'s pledge to nationalise the foreign commercial banks as the previous Senanayake government had borrowed extensively from commercial banks in West

Germany and Britain. In its second year of office the government found the social services financially intolerable and proceeded to impose additional levies on some of them.

In January 1972 further pruning of the social services took place when the Higher Education Act providing for the amalgamation of the four universities in Ceylon and the College of Technology into a single university structure was enacted. This would reduce the intake of students in the liberal arts.

Additional burdens were also imposed on the better-off sections of the community – a ceiling on individual incomes (Rs 2,000 net a month), on company dividends (12 per cent for the year, but not many companies could declare up to this limit), a once-and-for-all capital levy on individual and family wealth (net) of Rs 200,000 and over on a graded scale, and a compulsory savings scheme for income earners above a certain limit and for companies, operative for one year but extendable on a yearly basis.

After the P.L.F. insurrection of March–April 1971, the U.F. government, realising the need for urgent economic and social reform, announced plans for economic development (the Five-Year Plan) and a 'package deal' which proposed a general redistribution of income and property.

The government's plans for the public sector were intended to reduce private initiative to an accessory role. The minister of finance in his first budget speech (1970) indicated that public sector expansion would provide an infrastructure for co-operative, private and small-scale industry.

In the agricultural sector too there has been increasing state control. In January 1972, the Paddy Marketing Act which nationalised the entire paddy trade in the island came into operation. A State Agricultural Corporation was also established in the middle of 1972 to purchase and market agricultural produce, the intention here being to protect the small producer from exploitative middlemen. Further, legislation was enacted in the same year obliging persons or companies wishing to dispose of estates of over one hundred acres to obtain the prior approval of the Ministry of Plantation Industries The latter would have the right of first refusal.

These measures go far in the direction of a socialist set-up and have resulted in the imposition of burdens on middle and high income earners and on the entrepreneurial class. There has consequently been a flight of talent. In 1972 the U.F. government enacted legislation obliging Ceylonese income earners abroad to remit up to a maximum of 10 per cent of their foreign earnings to their home country.

In its foreign policy, the U.F. government acted with speed in proceeding to fulfil its election pledges. It suspended diplomatic relations with Israel and extended diplomatic recognition to the communist states referred to in the Common Programme. In the process it alienated to some extent the support that Ceylon had obtained from the countries of the west.

The Traditional Left

The traditional left still maintains its influence and comprises (1) the L.S.S.P. (founded in December 1935) which pioneered Marxism and turned Trotskyist in the late 1930s in protest against the Moscow trials and the attempts of the Third International to make national communist parties instruments of Soviet foreign policy; (2) the C.P. (founded July 1943), a breakaway from the parent L.S.S.P. in 1939 which took at first the name United Socialist Party; and (3) the M.E.P., a splinter from the L.S.S.P. in 1950, led by Philip Gunawardene (died 1972) which at that time called itself the V.L.S.S.P.

The traditional left is continuously involved with the questions of left unity, electoral support, parliamentarianism versus revolution and trade unionism.

Left unity. Under pressure from their rank and file, the L.S.S.P. and C.P. made many efforts during 1947–63 to come to a united front and agree on a common programme. These failed because of ideological differences especially on the questions of Trotskyism and Stalinism.

Matters were made worse by the fact that between 1945 and 1954 there were further splinterings in the L.S.S.P. itself. In 1945 the B.L.P.I. (later the B.S.P.) comprising the orthodox theoreticians and intellectuals of the L.S.S.P., splintered and functioned as a separate organisation till June 1950 when after protracted negotiations they agreed to unite 'into one party which shall be called the L.S.S.P.'[38] Philip Gunawardene, one of the founding leaders of the L.S.S.P., disapproved of this reunion and in protest formed his V.L.S.S.P. in the same year. After the general election of 1952, another section led by P. H. William de Silva broke off, on among other grounds the failure of the L.S.S.P. to make tangible efforts towards establishing an anti-U.N.P. government headed by Bandaranaike at the 'lowest level' or an L.S.S.P. government at the 'highest level'.[39] This group merged with the V.L.S.S.P. prior to the 1956 general election.

The V.L.S.S.P. for its part followed a chequered course. In April 1951 it entered into a united front with the C.P. which broke up a year or so (in early 1955) before the general election of 1956 when the former entered the M.E.P. forged by Bandaranaike. In 1959 when the V.L.S.S.P. leaders, Philip Gunawardene and P. H. William de Silva, were elbowed out of the M.E.P. government, they formed a new political party which took the name M.E.P. P. H. William de Silva, however, did not remain for long in the M.E.P. At the general election of 1965 this M.E.P. joined with the U.N.P. and the latter's allies to oust the S.L.F.P.-L.S.S.P. coalition. Philip Gunawardene served in the 'national government' during 1965–70 and at the general election of 1970 partnered with the U.N.P. in the latter's campaign against the U.F. After the defeat of the 'national government' in 1970, Philip Gunawardene declared his support for the ultra-left P.L.F.[40]

The C.P. escaped unscathed till 1963 when Maoist elements led by its trade union stalwart, N. Sanmugathasan, broke off in opposition to the C.P. joining the U.L.F. These elements had also supported the Chinese in the Sino-Soviet conflict at the time. But the C.P. continued to remain the stronger group for the next few years.

From 1971 differences between two groups in the C.P., one led by S. A. Wickremasinghe and the other by Pieter Keuneman who had a portfolio in the U.F. cabinet, developed over the extent of co-operation that the C.P. should give the U.F. government. The Wickremasinghe group was critical of the U.F. government's economic policies, which it felt were not 'progressive' enough, and its lack of commitment to the Soviet bloc in foreign relations.[41] These differences have resulted in a permanent rift with the Keuneman group supporting the U.F.

At the electoral level, there was sharp conflict between the Trotskyists and the C.P. at the 1947 and 1952 general elections. In 1947, the two Trotskyist parties (L.S.S.P. and B.L.P.I.) had a no-contest polls agreement but the C.P. clashed with them in at least six constituencies while a number of C.P. sympathisers contested Trotskyist candidates as independents. In 1952 the L.S.S.P. sought a left united front with the C.P. but this did not materialise. On the contrary, the C.P.-V.L.S.S.P. United Front clashed with the L.S.S.P. in seven constituencies while in other constituencies the front supported S.L.F.P. candidates against the Trotskyists. After the election S. W. R. D. Bandaranaike was elected leader of the opposition on the votes of the four C.P.-V.L.S.S.P. M.P.'s returned. The latter could have decided the issue in favour of the L.S.S.P. leader, Dr N. M. Perera.[42]

An opportunity for the two parties to come together arose when the Dudley Senanayake government raised the price of subsidised rice in July 1953. They organised an island-wide hartal on 12 August which resulted in violence, damage to property and loss of nine lives due to police action. It was a complete success and on 14 August the left leaders issued a joint statement 'congratulating the masses of Ceylon on their splendid response'.[43]

Disunity over what line of action they should pursue thereafter developed between the L.S.S.P. and the C.P. The latter feared repression from the succeeding Kotelawala government and in its secret circular of 27 January 1954 entitled Report on the Political Situation called for an 'anti-imperialist democratic government to save Ceylon from fascism'.[44] The L.S.S.P. rejected the proposal alleging that it was a device on the part of Stalinism in Ceylon to engineer a government of whatever complexion which would keep Ceylon out of the Cold War and of the hot war between the Soviets and the west that the C.P. was anticipating.[45]

At the 1956 general election however the L.S.S.P and C.P. had a satisfactory mutual aid polls pact with Bandaranaike's M.E.P. They concentrated on defeating the U.N.P. government and there were therefore no serious clashes between the two.

But things reverted to form at the general election of March 1960, the L.S.S.P. having earlier at its conference of July 1959 rejected the C.P.'s call for a united front of the 'progressives'.[46] The three left parties, the L.S.S.P., Philip Gunawardene's M.E.P. and the C.P., clashed with one another in many constituencies and the split in their votes resulted in a number of defeats which could otherwise have been turned into victories.

In July 1960 the L.S.S.P. and C.P., apprehensive of a possible return to power of the U.N.P., entered into a no-contest polls agreement with the S.L.F.P. But Philip Gunawardene's M.E.P. clashed with all three parties in a large number of constituencies.

In 1963 the three parties of the left, presumably tiring of their self-destructive warring, after long drawn out discussions agreed to a united front on a limited programme. Thus emerged the U.L.F. of August 1963 with its twenty-one demands and the threat of trade union action to accomplish these. But hardly had the ink dried on the agreement when there began negotiations for a U.L.F.-S.L.F.P. coalition government. Philip Gunawardene on behalf of his M.E.P. laid down conditions which Mrs Bandaranaike found impossible to accept, such as the expulsion of the 'reactionaries' from her cabinet including her deputy C. P. de Silva. The L.S.S.P. proved more responsive and in June 1964 abandoned the U.L.F. for a coalition with Mrs Bandaranaike. The C.P. though disappointed at its exclusion from the coalition gave its support to it.[47] Thus ended the short-lived U.L.F. of August 1963.

Since June 1964 the two left parties, the L.S.S.P. and C.P., have worked in concert with the S.L.F.P. to achieve the objective of a socialist-oriented anti-U.N.P. government. They worked together at the general election of March 1965 but failed to emerge victorious. In 1968 they entered into a United Front with the S.L.F.P. on a Common Programme, and at the 1970 general election achieved the supreme objective of a U.F. government comprising themselves and the S.L.F.P.

Electoral support. The left has never been able to command sufficient electoral strength to make a serious bid for parliamentary power. Only on one occasion did they make the effort, the L.S.S.P. and Philip Gunawardene's M.E.P., at the general election of March 1960 and both parties fared very poorly, winning ten seats each. However, each of the three parties (L.S.S.P., M.E.P., C.P.) have their traditional sources of support and they have been successful in retaining these fairly consistently over the years – the L.S.S.P. and M.E.P. in the Kelani valley areas and along some sections of the south-western sea board including the Colombo district, the C.P. in the south and in Colombo and the greater Colombo area.

The system of electoral demarcation which gives tremendous weightage to the rural areas at the expense of the urban has contributed in no small measure to the left's failure to make electoral headway. Their secularism and their Marxist-oriented socio-economic programmes do not make an impact on the rural voter. Their liberal stances from 1947–64 on the question of official recognition for the Tamil language and citizenship and voting rights for the Indian Tamil population, and their refusal up to 1964 to get involved in the demands of the Buddhist militants, alienated the average Sinhalese Buddhist from them. But the left failed to win support even when one of them, Philip Gunawardene's M.E.P., switched to a militant Sinhalese Buddhist-oriented socialist programme at the general election of March 1960. Nor did the L.S.S.P. or C.P. gain when they accepted the S.L.F.P.'s position on these matters at the general election of March 1965. The only conclusion that can be drawn is that the rural voter is suspicious of Marxian policies.

However despite repeated failures, the left continues to place some reliance on the parliamentary processes. That attitude has nevertheless never been consistent, veering at times towards revolution and extra-parliamentary methods, at other times toeing the constitutional line, depending very much, as their theoreticians are wont to aver, on the objective circumstances.

Part of the reason for the attraction to parliamentarianism was the surprising success that the left met with at the general election of 1947. The L.S.S.P, B.L.P.I. and C.P. had organised an alternative village leadership and sections of the rural and urban intelligentsia against the privileged English-educated middle class represented by the U.N.P. The left had also the support of the urban working classes as well as those in the lower ranks among government officials who had suffered disciplinary punishment after the massive strikes of 1946 and 1947. Further, the two Trotskyist parties made a strong bid to defeat some of the U.N.P. stalwarts in 1947 and in this they fared reasonably well. But they did not seek to win parliamentary power, utilising the election campaign to explain their revolutionary programme and to condemn the 'anti-working class character' of the U.N.P., its alleged corruption and nepotism, the 'fake independence' it had won and its pro-British 'proclivities'.[48] Between them they only contested thirty-eight of the ninety-five elective seats and won fifteen while the C.P. contested thirteen, winning three.

At the L.S.S.P.'s annual conference in January 1952 the

principal resolution adopted was that all the resources of the party should be directed towards forming a L.S.S.P. government in the next Parliament which need not 'necessarily mean a government of the party alone' but one pledged to implement its fourteen point programme.[49] The latter had in it the usual Marxist ingredients, but the C.P.-V.L.S.S.P. combine refused to respond.

The L.S.S.P. however contested only thirty-nine of the ninety-five seats and won nine. The C.P.-V.L.S.S.P. contested nineteen and won four. Both groups suffered because they were exposed to the U.N.P.'s attack that they stood for citizenship rights for the Indian Tamils.[50] Besides, the S.L.F.P. now came to be looked on as a viable democratic alternative. The opposition as a whole however lost to the U.N.P. The latter gained from the emotional impact that the passing away of its leader, the 'Father of the Nation', D. S. Senanayake, had on the electorate.

Between 1952 and 1955, the L.S.S.P. and C.P. indulged in manoeuvres and counter-manoeuvres regarding the possibilities of an alternate government to the U.N.P.

The C.P. was more realistic and wished to utilise the S.L.F.P. to bring into being an 'anti-imperialist democratic government' comprising the progressive forces inclusive of even 'non-fascist sections of the U.N.P.'. Such a government it felt could be formed 'on the basis of the S.L.F.P.'s own programme and no more', but it emphasised that this government would serve to pave the way to 'a people's democratic government' on the Soviet model.[51]

The L.S.S.P. proved more doctrinaire, its leading theoretician, Dr Colvin R. de Silva, arguing that their guiding slogan should be that they must 'replace the capitalist U.N.P. government with an anti-capitalist government' with the ultimate objective of 'a workers' and peasants' government'. This could, he insisted, be accomplished only by a united front of the working-class parties who must give leadership to the anti-U.N.P. struggle and to an anti-U.N.P. front.[52] How this could have been achieved in the context of the left's serious divisions and lack of a popular base was a matter for conjecture at that time.

However, before even any preliminary steps could be taken to form the anti-U.N.P. front both parties aimed at, though from different angles, the country was engulfed by the Sinhalese

Buddhist movement which put the left, except for the V.L.S.S.P., temporarily out of the current mainstream.

Prior to the general election of 1956, the L.S.S.P. and C.P. tacked themselves on to Bandaranaike's M.E.P. with a no-contest polls pact while the V.L.S.S.P. entered the M.E.P. as a constituent partner. The L.S.S.P. called on the electors to give their support to Bandaranaike and the M.E.P. The C.P. advocated a similar line. The L.S.S.P. contested twenty-one seats and secured fourteen while the C.P. fielded nine and won three. The L.S.S.P. had expected that it could form a coalition with the M.E.P. This failed to materialise owing to the latter's outright victory.

In the next few years the L.S.S.P.'s strategy was to undermine the M.E.P. government in the hope that it would be the alternative. It believed that the U.N.P. was 'dead and buried' and it feared that if the M.E.P. government succeeded, it could be a substitute to itself. But its stance on language made it unpopular and it fared disastrously at the Colombo Municipal elections of December 1956 when its leader, Dr N. M. Perera, lost to an S.L.F.P. tyro in politics. The party's hopes rose again when Dr N. M. Perera played the leading role in bringing to book the conspirators in the Bandaranaike assassination and in toppling the government of W. Dahanayake in December 1959.

The L.S.S.P. made its strongest bid therefore at the general election of March 1960 and fielded 101 candidates.[53] The exercise ended in a fiasco with fifty-two losing their deposits and only ten winning. Philip Gunawardene's M.E.P. fared just as poorly, winning ten seats after contesting eighty-nine.

Since then, the L.S.S.P. along with the C.P. came round to the ultimate view that their immediate future lay in co-operating with the radical and left-wing elements in the S.L.F.P. It was this realisation that led the L.S.S.P. to coalesce with Mrs Bandaranaike in June 1964 and for it and the C.P. to forge a United Front and a Common Programme in 1968.

Parliamentarianism versus revolution. As stated earlier, there is much ambivalence in the left's attitude to Parliament. The ultimate goal is its overthrow. For tactical reasons, however, they will utilise Parliament for an interim period.

After the general election of 1947 both the L.S.S.P. and B.L.P.I. refused to support moves by the other opposition parties to form an alternate government. The L.S.S.P. leader, Dr N. M.

Perera, claimed that his party was a revolutionary one and would not serve in a 'capitalist government' but would support a progressive alternate government.[54] At the same time, however, the L.S.S.P. wished that its leader, Dr N. M. Perera, should be recognised as leader of the opposition (in Parliament), a recognition which came only in June 1950 after the B.L.P.I. merged with the L.S.S.P. The L.S.S.P. would have liked to obtain the office for its leader in the 1952 Parliament but it went to the S.L.F.P. leader. In the 1956 Parliament the L.S.S.P. made a bid for the office and secured it.

The revolutionary aspect persisted for a few years after 1947. At its annual conference in 1951 the L.S.S.P. affirmed that their ultimate objective lay along that of 'a direct mass struggle alone and not through parliamentary devices and manoeuvres'.[55] But in the annual conference of the following year, the decision was that all the resources of the party should be directed towards forming a L.S.S.P. government in the next Parliament which need not 'necessarily mean a government of the party alone' but one pledged to implement the party's fourteen point programme.[56] In 1954 the party was back again to revolutionary class struggle as the method of achieving its basic objective of 'a peasant supported workers' state'.[57] But in 1956 and 1960 it vainly hoped that the Bandaranaikes would assign them portfolios in their cabinets, a hope which materialised only in June 1964 and again after the general election of May 1970.

The M.E.P. of Philip Gunawardene too began and ended in the same way. In 1950 Philip Gunawardene's V.L.S.S.P. was emphasising revolution and the class struggle. In 1956, the V.L.S.S.P. joined the M.E.P. of Bandaranaike and took office in the latter's government. In March 1965 Philip Gunawardene, now as leader of his own M.E.P., campaigned with the U.N.P. and joined the latter in the formation of the 'national government'. After 1970 Philip Gunawardene gave expression to revolutionary views and in a pamphlet he presented to his party in January 1971 entitled *The Present Political Situation* condemned 'the system of electing governments by the ballot'.[58] He scorned his erstwhile friends in the L.S.S.P. as 'the saviours of both the local and foreign capitalist classes' while he condemned the U.N.P. as being in the grip of 'capitalists and monopolists'.[59] He declared support for the P.L.F. With his death in March 1972 it is doubtful whether the M.E.P. will continue as a political party of any worth.

It was different with the C.P. From 1947 the latter kept consistently in view a government of progressives, in the popular front style, with a foreign policy which was well disposed towards the Soviet bloc.[60] This objective was realised with the M.E.P. victory of 1956 when the C.P. decided to sit in opposition and render responsive co-operation to the government formed thereafter. It withdrew its support after the exit of Philip Gunawardene from the M.E.P. government in 1959. In July 1960 it supported the S.L.F.P. government established under Mrs Bandaranaike. It eventually entered the U.F. in 1968 and its general secretary took cabinet office in the U.F. government in May 1970.

This does not imply that the traditional left has abandoned Marxism and the goal of a workers' state. Both the L.S.S.P. and C.P., even after participating in the formation of the U.F. government in May 1970, have reiterated their Marxist objectives.

The L.S.S.P. stands for a gradual transition, on the grounds that 'instant socialism' is not possible. Dr N. M. Perera has stated that 'the whole question had to be gauged in accordance with the feelings of the people' who, he said, 'wanted changes within the framework of the law'[61] while the L.S.S.P.'s deputy leader, Dr Colvin R. de Silva, in cautioning on the difficulties of effecting change speedily remarked that 'the pressure of circumambiant imperialism in Ceylon is powerful and even heightened'.[62]

The C.P. on the other hand has been critical of the U.F. government's slow progress towards socialism. After its first post-election plenary sessions, the C.P. insisted in September 1970 that in overcoming the financial crisis which the government faced, 'emphasis should be laid, not so much on sacrifices by the working people or the pursuit of loans from the west, as getting into state hands the financial resources of foreign banks, industries and plantations'.[63] This has been a recurring theme in the C.P.'s policy statements. The party also calls for closer collaboration with the Soviet bloc. The C.P. is able to take up this critical position because, unlike the L.S.S.P., it does not have as great a stake in the U.F. government.

The left, however, generally faces the prospect of being edged out of the U.F. government in the event of the right wing in the S.L.F.P. gaining ascendancy. Leslie Goonewardene, the L.S.S.P.'s general secretary, was well aware of such a possibility when he wrote,[64] 'while it is necessary in Ceylon to utilise one hundred per cent Parliament and a government set up within Parliament for the journey towards socialism, in the final analysis the L.S.S.P. reposes its trust only in the masses', adding that 'on the question how far the journey towards socialism can be made through Parliament and the parliamentary system, the L.S.S.P. has not made any final judgment... The answer to this question does not lie in our hands but in the hands of our enemies.'

Trade Unionism. A war to the death has characterised the trade union activities of all three left parties.[65] When one party's union strikes, the others abstain or give lukewarm support and consequently charges and counter-charges of sabotage and treachery are often levelled. Each party tries to gain kudos for itself in winning wage demands and in the process crimps members from rival unions.

Another feature of trade unionism is that the rival parties use the unions for political ends. But it cannot be gainsaid that there are occasions when the unions must strike at their party's call when legislation is likely to affect them adversely. There have also been times when they were also used for political objectives, pure and simple.

In 1946, L.S.S.P. and C.P.-controlled trade unions on strike demanded among other things the abrogation of the Soulbury constitution. In 1953 the trade unions of all three left parties joined in the one-day hartal called to protest against the increase in the price of subsidised rice imposed by the Dudley Senanayake government. In 1956, the L.S.S.P.'s trade unions went into action against Bandaranaike's M.E.P. government, showing a measure of political rivalry. In 1957, joint trade union action, mainly L.S.S.P.-organised, forced Bandaranaike to take the army off the streets which he had called in to curb labour unrest. In 1959 the trade unions launched a one-day general strike against Bandaranaike's amendment to the Public Security Act which the unions protested had dangerous implications for them. During 1960–3 the L.S.S.P. unions were restive and the abortive *coup d'état* organised by officers in the armed forces and the police was partly aimed at suppressing labour unrest. When the U.L.F. was formed in August 1963, Mrs Bandaranaike realised the repercussions it could have on her government, especially as the three left parties planned trade union action to achieve their twenty-one demands. In 1966, the L.S.S.P., C.P. and S.L.F.P. trade unions struck in protest against the Tamil Regulations of the 'national government'. Presently the L.S.S.P. and C.P. trade unions are refraining from strike action and actively co-operating with the U.F. government.

The Revolutionary Left

The Maoist C.P. and the Trotskyist L.S.S.P. (R.) command some trade union support while the Guevarist P.L.F. has influence among educated youth and young people in the rural areas.

The C.P. (Maoist). N. Sanmugathasan who controlled the powerful C.P. Ceylon Trade Union Federation opposed the formation of the U.L.F. in August 1963 and was expelled. He maintained his trade union base and launched his own Maoist organisation. At the March 1965 general election he ran four candidates all of whom forfeited their deposits. His C.P. boycotted the 1970 election.

In April 1971, Sanmugathasan was detained as a 'security risk' after the outbreak of the P.L.F. insurrection. He had nevertheless in May 1970 denied any 'truck with the so-called Guevara line' which he condemned as 'nothing but petit-bourgeois romanticism'[66] and in August 1970 his party had issued a pamphlet condemning the P.L.F. leader, Rohana Wijeweera, as one who had 'been trained by Soviet revisionists in Moscow's Lumumba University and sent here to sabotage the Marxist-Leninist movement from within'.[67]

As is to be expected, the Maoist C.P. is strongly critical of the Soviets and the United States. Its central committee in a statement in August 1970 denounced the American peace plan for the middle east as a 'sell-out' by the Soviets, adding that the peoples of the world must 'learn to identify Soviet social-imperialism as the greatest betrayers of the working class and of the national liberation movements all over the world'.[68]

Sanmugathasan and his party have been consistent in their denunciations of the parliamentary system as a 'fraud' and the democratic change of government through the ballot as 'a game of musical chairs' which they insist can never solve the fundamental problems of the people.

L.S.S.P. (R). In June 1964 when the L.S.S.P. coalesced with the S.L.F.P. government, the extreme doctrinaire Bolshevik elements splintered from the party to form their own organisation. Two L.S.S.P. M.P.'s Edmund Samarakoddy and Meryl Fernando, voted for the motion which brought down the L.S.S.P.–S.L.F.P. government in December 1964. Both were defeated in the general election that followed in March 1965.

The moving spirit behind the L.S.S.P. (R.) is the trade unionist Bala Tampoe, who controls the powerful white collar Ceylon Mercantile Union, which however is not committed to his Marxist policies.

The party did not contest the general election of May 1970, but it issued a manifesto reiterating the old Trotskyist ideals and condemning the L.S.S.P. leaders. In August 1970 Tampoe, in a public speech, stressed that there was 'no such thing as a slow march towards socialism' and called upon the country's youth 'to join forces with the working class to establish power under the leadership of that class'.[69]

The P.L.F. The P.L.F.'s origins date back to late 1964, the result of disillusionment on the part of a group of Marxist youths with the 'failure' of the S.L.F.P.–L.S.S.P. government of June 1964 to produce the expected results.[70] The movement developed a network of cells and branch organisations in great secrecy during the term of office of the 'national government'. With the return of the U.F. to office in May 1970 it came out in the open, but its leadership and organisational network maintained tight security.

Addressing its appeal only to Sinhalese Buddhists, the P.L.F. concentrated on the 16–25 age group.[71] Its hard core of support is not from workers or peasants but from jobless middle and lower middle-class youth, mainly from the rural areas, urged on by a fair number of teachers. The P.L.F. despised the older generation.

The P.L.F. programme is epitomised in 'The Five Lectures' which deal with Indian expansionism, the island's parlous economic situation, an economic analysis which seeks to prove that 80 to 90 per cent of the people have gained nothing from Sri Lanka's post-independence development, the failure of the island's traditional left leadership, and how to capture power in twenty-four hours. Their examples are China, Cuba and Albania. The revolution would take over the press and broadcasting system, do away with democracy and ban all political parties. All companies and plantations would be nationalised. But the P.L.F. leader, Wijeweera, declared that his front would not depend on the plantation economy. According to the U.F.'s Trotskyist minister of plantation industries (Dr Colvin R. de Silva), the P.L.F. had planned on seizure of power 'to uproot every tea, rubber and coconut plant in the country and replace them with edible yams'.[72]

The P.L.F. believes in violence organised in *blitzkreig*-like fashion to achieve its objectives.[73] Its first insurrection in April 1971 was put down ruthlessly by government forces. The front had an estimated force of ten thousand actives and seventy thousand others, and fighting was fiercest in the north-central, south-central and southern districts. In the latter two districts, large numbers of youths belonging to the underprivileged castes were involved. Eighty-five per cent of the 16,355 taken prisoner or who surrendered under the two amnesties offered them by Mrs Bandaranaike in May and June 1971 were youths with five credit passes in the general certificate examination, ordinary level.

The P.L.F. is at present proscribed and its leaders are facing trial before the criminal justice commission which the U.F. government set up in 1972 to bring them to book.

It is not possible to gauge the extent of popular support the front has. The fact that it failed so dismally will not stand it in good stead. But the possibility of it re-forming its ranks and making further attempts to disrupt law and order or even of engaging in guerilla warfare cannot be ruled out.

Ethnocentric Groupings

The T.C. Formed in 1944 under the charismatic leadership of G. G. Ponnambalam, the T.C. in the phase up to 1948 agitated for 'balanced representation' in the legislature. After 1948 it allied itself with the U.N.P. on the basis of 'responsive co-operation' with the Sinhalese. Ponnambalam received a portfolio which he retained until 1953 when Sir John Kotelawala dismissed him from the cabinet. Though Ponnambalam went out, the Congress kept its ties with the U.N.P.

The Congress swept all before it at the 1947 general election. It split on the issue of joining D. S. Senanayake's U.N.P. administration in 1948, the splitters forming the future powerful F.P. Differences arose over the Indian citizenship legislation issue, the T.C. supporting the U.N.P. government, the future F.P. leaders dissenting strongly. The T.C. disintegrated thereafter, faring poorly at the 1952 general election. It ceased to be a parliamentary force from then. But it represents the views of substantial sections of middle-class Jaffna Tamils who disapprove of the separatist politics of the F.P., and its leader continues as a prominent figure in Ceylon Tamil politics.

In the 1965–70 phase of the 'national government', the T.C. functioned as a pressure group of some importance within the U.N.P. Ponnambalam vigorously opposed Prime Minister Senanayake's attempts to placate the F.P. criticising it for concentrating on the issue of Tamil as a language of administration for *only* the northern and eastern provinces. His Congress, he insisted, was for parity of status for both languages throughout the island. The T.C. further opposed the F.P.'s demand during 1966–70 for a Tamil-medium university in Trincomalee, insisting that it should be sited in Jaffna or its environs.

The Congress fared disastrously at the 1970 general election, all three of its sitting members including Ponnambalam being defeated. It secured three other seats, but two of its M.P.s are now members of the U.F. parliamentary group, contrary to party instructions.[74]

The F.P. The immediate pretext for the F.P.'s emergence in December 1949 was the objection of two T.C. M.P.'s and a T.C. senator to the legislation of 1948 and 1949 against the Indian Tamils.[75] These leaders had also become wary of the state-aided colonisation schemes in the Tamil-speaking areas, which they alleged were being deliberately populatised with Sinhalese people. The sum effect of these policies, they said, would be to reduce Tamil representation in Parliament and make the Ceylon Tamils a minority in their 'traditional homelands' comprising the Tamil-speaking areas of the northern and eastern provinces.

Unlike the Jaffna-centred T.C., the F.P. seeks to unite under its leadership the Tamil-speaking peoples of the north and east, the Tamil-speaking Muslims, and the Indian Tamil plantation workers. They have from time to time had links with the Indian Tamil C.W.C. and D.W.C. and they have established a trade union of their own for Indian Tamil plantation workers. They had some Muslim support to start with but for some time now that support has been negligible.

F.P. activists represent Tamil subnationalism. In the beginning they advocated federation with a future Dravidian sovereign state of south India. Later opinion stabilised in favour of a 'Tamil homeland' federated to a Sinhalese Ceylon.

The leadership like the parent T.C. is ultra-constructive and is more at home with the U.N.P. than with the radicalism of the S.L.F.P. The party opposes nationalisation in principle on the ground that this would reduce employment opportunities for Tamils.

The party fared poorly at the 1952 general election but has been the leading Ceylon Tamil political grouping since then, from the 1956 general election and thereafter.

The F.P. has been essentially a party of crisis leadership. In June 1956 it led the opposition to the Sinhala Only Act and the action of its M.P.s and other leaders in staging a sit-down protest on the Galle Face Green, which is a couple of hundred yards from the precincts of Parliament, caused a chain reaction of violence between Sinhalese and Tamils in sensitive areas throughout the island.

The party's singular achievement was the pact it entered into with Prime Minister Bandaranaike in July 1957. Prior to this, the party had met in convention at Trincomalee in August 1956 where it presented a one-year ultimatum to Bandaranaike demanding (1) replacement of the 'present prenicious constitution by a rational and democratic constitution based on the federal principle'; (2) parity of status for the Tamil language with the Sinhalese language; (3) repeal of the existing citizenship laws which discriminated against the Indian estate Tamil population; and (4) immediate cessation of colonising the traditional Tamil-speaking areas with Sinhalese people.[76] The party threatened to launch 'direct action by non-violent means' to achieve these demands.

Tension built up in the months that followed but before the situation got beyond control, the party was invited for negotiations by the prime minister and the agreement reached was a compromise settlement. The federal demand was accommodated with a scheme for the establishment of regional councils for the various administrative districts or provinces in the island, including a single regional council for the northern province and two or more for the eastern. These councils would have powers delegated to them by Parliament in respect of a number of subjects.

The language demand was met by the offer that Tamil would be recognised as the language of a national minority and that it would, without infringement of the official language, be made a language of administration in the northern and eastern provinces.

On the question of colonisation, Bandaranaike conceded that his government would not utilise the instrument of colonisation to convert the majority Tamil-speaking population in the two provinces into a minority.

The citizenship issue, it was agreed, would be resolved with the C.W.C. and D.W.C.

The agreement however was from the F.P.'s point of view not a final solution but an 'adjustment'.

Opposition from militant Sinhalese Buddhist groups and the U.N.P. resulted in the abandonment of the pact in April 1958. The immediate pretext was the F.P.'s anti-*sri* campaigns of March and April which were launched because of the prime minister's reluctance to take steps to implement the pact. The F.P. replied by resolving to launch a non-violent direct action campaign, but before this got under way there followed the communal holocaust of May 1958. A state of emergency was declared, the F.P. proscribed and its M.P.s placed in preventive detention for several months. The emergency was lifted in May 1959.

The general election of March 1960 gave the F.P. further opportunity to bargain on its demands in view of the inconclusive results. The minority prime minister, Dudley Senanayake, refused to concede their demands and the votes of the F.P. M.P.s helped to bring down the government.

The opposition S.L.F.P. promised to revive the abandoned pact. But when it received an overall majority at the general election which followed in July 1960, it chose to ignore the F.P. Instead the S.L.F.P. government proceeded to enact legislation on the courts and in respect of parliamentary business (already referred to) besides enforcing vigorously Sinhalese in the administration, much to the chagrin of the F.P. The latter then launched a civil disobedience campaign during February–April 1961 which brought the administration in the north and east to a halt.[77] Before the government declared a state of emergency, on 17 April, the minister of justice, Sam P. C. Fernando, had talks with the F.P. leader, S. J. V. Chelvanayakam, but these ended in deadlock.[78]

In early 1964, the F.P. organised a 'Tamil only' campaign in which it appealed to the Tamil-speaking public to transact all their business with the state in the Tamil language. The campaign caused some problems for the administration. In mid-1964 the party announced plans for a direct action campaign, but before this could be organised, Mrs Bandaranaike's S.L.F.P.–L.S.S.P. coalition suffered parliamentary defeat and it was therefore abandoned.

The party's opportunity arrived again with the inconclusive general election of March 1965. The U.N.P. leader, Dudley Senanayake, was obliged to fall back on the F.P. to form his 'national government' and the F.P. secured from the U.N.P. leader terms similar to those it had obtained from Prime Minister Bandaranaike in July 1957, with some variations. Under the F.P.'s agreement of March 1965 with Dudley Senanayake, the latter agreed to (1) provide for Tamil as a language of administration along with Sinhalese in the northern and eastern provinces and to amend the Language of the Courts Act so as to provide for the use of the Tamil language in judicial proceedings in these provinces; (2) a scheme of district councils under the direct supervision of the central government; (3) preference for the people of the area in the allocation of lands under colonisation schemes in the Tamil-speaking provinces and, where sufficient numbers of such people were not forthcoming, consideration to be paid to Indian Tamil applicants from the plantation areas; and (4) relief to Tamil public servants who had failed to gain proficiency in the official language.

The provisions of this agreement were implemented, except for that dealing with district councils The prime minister had a Bill prepared for this purpose but had to drop it in July 1968 when faced with a revolt of his backbenchers. Shortly thereafter, the F.P.'s minister of local government in the 'national government', M. Tiruchelvam, resigned his portfolio over the reluctance of the prime minister to have the Konesar Temple area in Trincomalee, revered by the Hindus, declared a sacred area.

At the general election of May 1970, the F.P. suffered some reverses but maintained its position as the leading party of the Ceylon Tamils. The party was however rendered dysfunctional in Parliament owing to the overwhelming majority the U.F. obtained. It participated with some reluctance in the proceedings of the Constituent Assembly but withdrew from it in June 1971 when its demands on federalism, language and citizenship were rejected. It asked for (1) the division of Sri Lanka into five states in a federal set-up; (2) Tamil to be the language of administration and of the courts in the northern and eastern provinces; and (3) the mother tongue to be the compulsory medium of instruction for all Tamil children, Chelvanayakam arguing that otherwise the Tamil community 'will disappear'.[79]

Since then, the F.P. and T.C. have joined hands in a Tamil United Front (T.U.F.). They have rejected the republican constitution of May 1972. In March 1972 Chelvanayakam visited Madras and at a press conference there warned that 'the Tamil-speaking people might shortly have to agitate for a separate state for themselves'.[80]

The C.W.C. and D.W.C. Both these organisations were originally one – the Ceylon Indian Congress formed in 1939. Personality problems and internal politics led to a split in the leadership.

S. Thondaman is virtual boss of the more powerful C.W.C. and is politically conservative. He controls a very tightly knit organisation which is in a position to deliver the Indian Tamil vote in about fifteen to twenty-five constituencies in the plantation areas to any of the major parties.

In the general election of July 1960, Thondaman supported the S.L.F.P. for which Mrs Bandaranaike made him and another C.W.C. nominee appointed members of the House of Representatives (1960–5).

At the general election of March 1965, Thondaman switched to the U.N.P. partly as a protest against the terms of the Indo-Ceylon Agreement of October 1964. Thondaman and his C.W.C. negotiated an 'understanding' with Dudley Senanayake to have some of the clauses in this Agreement, especially those relating to the compulsory repatriation of Indians from Ceylon, rendered ineffective.[81] Thondaman boasted (to the writer) that he had achieved the near-impossible feat of varying the terms of an Agreement already entered into between two sovereign states. He was made an appointed member (1965–70) and a prominent member of his C.W.C. appointed to the Senate by Prime Minister Senanayake.

At the general election of May 1970, Thondaman again supported the U.N.P., but on this occasion the rival D.W.C. which backed the victorious U.F. obtained 'recognition' and its leader, Abdul Aziz, was appointed to the House and continues as an appointed member in the National State Assembly.

The D.W.C. is strong in at most two or three of the plantation districts. Aziz is a fellow-traveller of the communists and is sympathetic to the S.L.F.P. and the left parties and has always supported their candidates.

Both the C.W.C. and D.W.C. do not profess any political faith. They are essentially trade unions involved in politics insofar as the voting and citizenship rights of their membership are involved. In a close contest between the two major Sinhalese parties, the Indian vote could count.

The J.V.P., D.P. and S.M.P. All three are militant Sinhalese organisations which have faded from the political scene.

The J.V.P. achieved prominence during 1957–9 when S. W. R. D. Bandaranaike was beset with the communal problem and the language question.

An extremist Sinhalese Buddhist ginger group, it was mainly a husband and wife combination of the Rajaratnes advised by an able and skilful academic, F. R. Jayasuriya, the Ceylon University economist.

Though the J.V.P. had only the Rajaratnes in Parliament, it commanded much more influence than its parliamentary strength indicated.

The organisation claimed to stand for the rights of the Sinhalese Buddhists. Rajaratne vigorously opposed Bandaranaike's pact of July 1957 with the F.P., and in 1966 Mrs Kusuma Rajaratne opposed and voted against the Tamil Regulations of the 'national government'.

At the general election of March 1965 the J.V.P. joined hands with the U.N.P. in the front which defeated the S.L.F.P. and its left-wing partners. During 1965–70, despite differences on the Tamil question, the Rajaratnes made common cause with the

U.N.P. and continue to do so at the present time. At the general election of 1970 the J.V.P. failed to secure the election of any of their candidates to Parliament.

The D.S.P. came into existence prior to the general election of March 1960 under the leadership of L. H. Mettananda. It was

TABLE 4.1

PARTY POSITIONS AT GENERAL ELECTIONS, 1947–70

1947

Parties	Candidates	Seats Won	% Seats	Votes Polled	% Votes	Votes Per Candidate
U.N.P.	98	42	44.2	751,432	39.81	7,668
L.S.S.P.	28	10	10.5	204,020	10.80	7,286
B.L.P.I.	10	5	5.2	113,193	5.99	11,319
C.P.	13	3	3.1	70,331	3.72	5,410
L.P.	9	1	1.0	38,932	2.06	4,326
T.C.	9	7	7.3	82,499	4.37	9,167
C.I.C.	7	6	6.3	72,230	3.82	10,319
U.L.C.	2	0	0.0	3,953	0.21	1,977
S.P.	3	0	0.0	1,393	0.07	464
Independents	181	21	22.1	549,381	29.10	3,035
TOTAL	360	95		1,887,364		
Total no. of votes				3,052,814		
Percentage polled				61.3		

1952

Parties	Candidates	Seats Won	% Seats	Votes Polled	% Votes	Votes Per Candidate
U.N.P.	81	54	56.80	1,026,005	44.08	12,667
S.L.F.P.	48	9	9.5	361,250	15.52	7,526
L.S.S.P.	39	9	9.5	305,133	13.11	7,824
C.P.-V.L.S.S.P.	19	4	4.2	134,528	5.78	7,080
L.P.	5	1	1.1	27,096	1.16	5,419
T.C.	7	4	4.2	64,512	2.77	9,216
F.P.	7	2	2.1	45,331	1.95	6,476
R.P.	9	0	0.0	33,001	1.42	3,667
B.R.P.	3	0	0.0	3,987	0.17	1,329
Independents	85	12	12.6	326,783	14.04	3,845
TOTAL	303	95		2,327,626		
Total no. of votes				2,990,881		
Percentage polled				74		

1956

Parties	Can-didates	Seats Won	% Seats	Votes Polled	% Votes	Votes Per Can-didate
U.N.P.	76	8	8.4	718,164	27.44	9,450
M.E.P. (Bandaranaike)	60	51	53.7	1,045,725	39.96	17,429
L.S.S.P.	21	14	14.7	274,204	10.48	13,057
C.P.	9	3	3.2	119,715	4.57	13,302
L.P.	4	0	0.0	18,123	0.69	4,531
T.C.	1	1	1.1	8,914	0.34	8,914
F.P.	14	10	10.5	142,036	5.43	10,145
T.R.P.	2	0	0.0	387	0.01	194
Independents	64	8	8.4	289,491	11.06	4,523
TOTAL	251	95		2,616,759		
Total no. of votes				3,646,579		
Percentage polled				71		

March 1960

Parties	Can-didates	Seats Won	% Seats	Votes Polled	% Votes	Votes Per Can-didate
U.N.P.	127	50	33.1	908,996	29.62	7,157
S.L.F.P.	109	46	30.5	648,094	21.12	5,946
L.S.S.P.	101	10	6.6	322,352	10.50	3,192
C.P.	53	3	2.0	141,857	4.62	2,677
M.E.P. (Philip Gunawardene)	89	10	6.6	325,832	10.62	3,661
T.C.	8	1	0.7	38,275	1.25	4,784
F.P.	19	15	9.9	176,492	5.75	9,289
J.V.P.	2	2	1.3	11,201	0.36	5,601
L.P.P.	101	4	2.6	125,344	4.08	1,241
S.M.P.(I.M.R.A. Iriyagolle)	40	1	0.7	24,143	0.79	604
S.L.J.P.	1	1	0.7	11,115	0.36	11,115
B.B.P.	2	1	0.7	9,749	0.32	4,875
Independents	167	7	4.6	270,881	8.83	1,622
Others	80	0	0.0	54,775	1.78	685
TOTAL	899	151		3,069,106		
Total no. of votes				3,724,507		
Percentage polled				77.6		

July 1960

Parties	Candidates	Seats Won	% Seats	Votes Polled	% Votes	Votes Per Candidate
U.N.P.	128	30	19.9	1,143,290	37.57	8,932
S.L.F.P.	98	75	49.7	1,022,154	33.59	10,430
L.S.S.P.	21	12	7.9	223,993	7.36	10,666
C.P.	7	4	2.6	90,219	2.96	12,888
M.E.P. (Philip Gunawardene)	55	3	2.0	102,833	3.38	1,870
T.C.	10	1	0.7	46,803	1.54	4,680
F.P.	21	16	10.6	218,753	7.19	10,417
J.V.P.	2	2	1.3	14,030	0.46	7,015
L.P.P.	6	2	1.3	29,190	0.96	4,865
Independents	39	6	4.0	140,522	4.62	3,603
Others	6	0	0.0	11,167	0.37	1,861
TOTAL	393	151		3,042,954		
Total no. of votes				3,724,507		
Percentage polled				75.6		

1965

Parties	Candidates	Seats Won	% Seats	Votes Polled	% Votes	Votes Per Candidate
U.N.P.	116	66	43.7	1,579,181	38.93	13,614
S.L.F.P.	100	41	27.2	1,226,833	30.24	12,268
L.S.S.P.	24	10	6.6	302,095	7.45	12,587
C.P.	9	4	2.6	109,744	2.71	12,194
M.E.P. (Philip Gunawardene)	60	1	0.7	110,388	2.73	1,840
S.L.F.S.P.	32	5	3.3	129,986	3.20	4,062
T.C.	15	3	2.0	98,726	2.43	6,582
F.P.	20	14	9.3	217,986	5.37	10,899
J.V.P.	10	1	0.7	18,791	0.46	1,879
Independents	96	6	4.0	237,805	5.86	2,477
Others	10	0	0.0	24,932	0.61	2,493
TOTAL	492	151		4,056,467		
Total no. of votes				4,710,887		
Percentage polled				82		

1970

Parties	Candidates	Seats Won	% Seats	Votes Polled	% Votes	Votes Per Candidate
U.N.P.	127	17	11.3	1,876,956	37.92	14,779
S.L.F.P.	105	90	60.0	1,812,849	36.63	17,265
L.S.S.P.	23	19	12.7	433,224	8.75	18,836
C.P.	9	6	4.0	169,229	3.42	18,803
M.E.P. (Philip Gunawardene)	4	0	0.0	46,571	0.94	11,643
C.P. (Maoist)	1	0	0.0	3,485	0.07	3,485
T.C.	12	3	2.0	115,567	2.33	9,631
F.P.	19	13	8.7	245,747	4.96	12,934
S.M.P. (R. G. Senanayake)	50	0	0.0	20,429	0.41	409
Independents	87	2	1.3	225,559	4.56	2,593
TOTAL	437	150		4,949,616		
Total no. of votes				5,525,028		
Percentage polled				84.9		

Notes.

(1) These tables have been composed from the Reports of the Commissioner for Parliamentary Elections and from the *Ceylon Daily News Parliament of Ceylon* for 1947, 1956, 1960, 1965 and 1970.

(2) In 1947, 1952 and 1956, there were 89 constituencies inclusive of one three-member and four two-member constituencies returning 95 members. From March 1960 and thereafter there have been 145 constituencies, inclusive of one three-member and four two-member constituencies, returning 151 members.

(3) The B.L.P.I. (later B.S.P.) amalgamated with the L.S.S.P. in 1950. The C.P.–V.L.S.S.P. broke up into their constituent parts in 1955. The V.L.S.S.P. joined forces with Bandaranaike in 1955 and became part of his M.E.P. in 1956. In 1959 when the two V.L.S.S.P. ministers resigned from Bandaranaike's M.E.P. government, they formed a new political party which they called the M.E.P.

(4) In 1947 the U.N.P. ran 98 candidates in 75 constituencies, sponsoring more than one candidate in some constituencies owing to personal and caste differences between candidates seeking its label and as many as five candidates in one constituency. It did not repeat this in subsequent general elections.

(5) Some parties were ephemeral, not lasting more than one general election, the examples being the U.L.C., S.P. (1947), R.P., B.R.P. (1952), T.R.P. (1956), S.M.P., S.L.J.P., B.B.P. (March 1960), S.L.F.S.P. (1965) and S.M.P. (1970). The L.P.P. fought two general elections (March and July 1960) and went out of existence thereafter.

(6) The C.I.C. fought the 1947 general election but did not contest seats in any general election thereafter. It broke in two after 1947 – into the C.W.C. and D.W.C. Both organisations influenced voting at the general election of 1956 and every general election thereafter.
(7) The reference to 'Others' in March and July 1960 and 1965 is to unrecognised mushroom political parties.
(8) There were 150 seats contested at the 1970 election as one of the candidates died during the course of the election campaign and a by-election had to be held after the general election.

in alliance with Philip Gunawardene's M.E.P. and campaigned for Buddhist rights. It ceased to function after the general election of July 1960.

The S.M.P. was organised by R. G. Senanayake prior to the general election of May 1970 and put forward fifty-one candidates all of whom save the leader forfeited their deposits. It stood for Buddhist rights and for privileges for middle-class Sinhalese interests such as traders and public sector and private sector employees. It was ostentatious about Sinhalese Buddhist nationalism but failed to make any impact on the electors.

PRESSURE GROUPS AND INTEREST ASSOCIATIONS

Most matters of a social and economic character in Sri Lanka influence and are influenced by political attitudes. This is only to be expected from a state based on the paternalistic and welfare pattern. The high levels of literacy, growing political awareness stimulated by the exercise of the franchise since 1931, and the activities of Marxist and labour party-type politicians in unionising the working classes have all contributed towards the growth and multiplication of numerous group formations. Further, in the post-independence phase, the extension of state control to all important sectors of the economy has also compelled economic interests in the private sector to organise themselves for their own protection and advancement.

A noteworthy feature is that most of these organisations are concentrated in and around Colombo, the capital city. Some of them have branches in the cities and towns in other parts of the country. A few of the more powerful ones focus their activites in the plantation districts. But Colombo dominates everything and it is to Colombo that the organisers must come wherever they may be, if they must produce results.

Economic Groupings

These cover:

(1) Firms in the private sector, the most powerful of which is the Employers' Federation of Ceylon. Others which are influential are the Ceylon Chamber of Commerce, the Ceylon National Chamber of Commerce, the Mercantile Chamber of Ceylon, the Chamber of Commerce of Ceylonese by Descent and the All Ceylon Trade Chamber. Membership in these sometimes overlap. They are all linked together in a Federation of Chambers of Commerce and Industry. Some of the organisations mentioned in (2) are also members of this federation. At a lower level in commerce is the All Ceylon Federation of Authorised Dealers which comprises businessmen and shareholders at the middle and lower levels.

(2) Industries in the private sector. The bigger industrialists are members of the Ceylon National Chamber of Industries. The Manufacturers' Association has membership at the middle level, and at the higher levels as well, though not extensively. At a lower level is the small industrialists' association. There are also specialised associations such as the Approved Shirt Manufacturers' Association and the All Ceylon United Textile Weavers' Association.

(3) Commercial agriculture. The all powerful Ceylon Estate Employers' Federation covers most of the plantations. It is this body which must give its sanction to any agreement between estate labour and the plantation companies which belong to its membership. The Planters' Association comprises proprietorial and salaried planters. The Low Country Products Association is representative of Ceylonese agricultural interests in the low country districts.

(4) Foreign interests, the most important of which are the Commercial Banks Association and the Ceylon Association. The latter has its headquarters in Britain. Both are largely British in character and are strong pressure groups vis-à-vis the government.

All these groupings in some way or another touch the centres of power. They are involved with the government of the day in regard to (a) allocations of foreign exchange for the import of raw materials, (b) the role to be assigned to them in planning economic development, and (c) their relationships with organised labour. The government often intervenes in their disputes with organised labour.

The Press

The three biggest combines are the Associated Newspapers of Ceylon Limited (the Lake House Group), the Times Group and the Davasa Group. The last-mentioned came into prominence in the post-1956 period while the first two held sway till then, with the Lake House newspapers way ahead of the newspapers published by the Times Group. Together all three groups virtually monopolise the newspaper-reading public, publishing dailies in English and Sinhalese and, barring the Times Group, in Tamil as well. In 1973 legislation was enacted to broadbase the ownership of Lake House.

Though sales figures as such are not very impressive, the reading public could be reasonably estimated to reach the 1,500,000 mark if the newspaper-borrowing public and the reading aloud of a newspaper by a person possessing one to groups of listeners around him at boutiques and other such places during certain times of the day, are taken into consideration.

The press therefore wields a tremendous influence. The only qualification is that sections of the general public are sceptical of what is published by these three groups during the period of a general election.

The three newspaper combines mentioned enjoy a unique advantage in that they claim to publish national newspapers as distinct from the dailies and weeklies put out by party presses. They seek to create an impression of impartiality and fairness in the presentation of news and comments which, however, is not exactly their intention especially in matters which concern their proprietors directly – politically, socially and on questions of economics.

There is no strong tradition of journalism, editors tending to change, depending on the political sympathies of the proprietor or the political atmosphere of the time.

The Lake House Group was the monopoly of the Wijewardene family while the Davasa Group is controlled by the Gunasena family. The Times Group has a diversified ownership, but one or two individuals who own sizable shares in it influence directly or through their representatives the editorial policies of its newspapers.

The newspapers of the Lake House Group, until the advent of the U.F. government to office in May 1970, had consistently followed a policy which gave broad support to the U.N.P. and in particular to the Senanayakes – D. S. and Dudley. The Group was decisively opposed to the Marxists, and for this reason to the S.L.F.P. as well. At every general election from 1947 its newspapers came out openly in favour of the U.N.P. Owing to the proposal to nationalise it in 1964, the Group played an important part in the events leading to the parliamentary defeat of Mrs Bandaranaike's S.L.F.P.–L.S.S.P. coalition government in December 1964. It took an active interest in the general election campaign that followed (December 1964–March 1965) and during this phase was virtually an organ of the U.N.P. It played a similar role in the general election campaign of March–May 1970, though not in such an overt fashion as in 1965. After the election of May 1970, Lake House decided for various reasons to switch its support to the U.F. government. But despite this there were demands for its nationalisation by the L.S.S.P. and C.P. and by left-inclined members in the S.L.F.P.

The Times Group also followed a similar policy though for less obvious reasons. It is mainly an organ of conservative and anti-Marxist interests. Its English dailies also have a Roman Catholic or Ceylon Tamil bias and in addition they cater, generally, to middle- and lower middle-class interests. The Group's support for the U.N.P. has been more disguised and not seldom critical and qualified.

The Davasa Group articulates Sinhalese Buddhist opinion. Its support for the U.N.P. until the general election of March 1965 and for a while afterwards was conditional insofar as it felt that Sinhalese interests were not adversely affected. It became increasingly disillusioned with the 'national government' of Dudley Senanayake, especially because of the latter's ties with the Ceylon Tamil federalists and the Indian Tamil C.W.C. Its newspapers thereafter gave their full backing to the S.L.F.P. and the U.F. But the Group is wary of the Marxists.

There is besides a flourishing party press. The U.N.P., S.L.F.P., L.S.S.P., F.P. and C.P. have their respective organs.

The C.P.'s *Attha* (Truth) enjoys a wide circulation, and in the post-1965 years was a source of embarrassment to the 'national government'. It was critical of the U.F. government but in 1972, owing to adverse reactions from sections of the U.F. leadership, its editorial management was changed by the Keuneman Group in the C.P. and it changed to a soft line vis-à-vis U.F. policies. But this did not last for long.

Trade Unions

Most trade unions in Ceylon are politically orientated.[82] Compettition is sharpest among the Marxist parties for control of the unions. Until the early 1950s, it was they who had a virtually exclusive interest in unionising labour in all except the plantation sector. Since then, other political parties such as the U.N.P., S.L.F.P. and F.P. have organised their own unions. So have the Christian religious organisations among both the Roman Catholics and Protestants.

Strike action is fairly common in the labour sector but not as frequent in the white collar sector. Partly it arises from genuine grievance but rival Marxist parties are also jockeying for position. The tactic is for one union to take the initiative and launch a lightning strike in the hope of commencing negotiations thereafter and extracting as many concessions as possible. In this way kudos would come to the Marxist party controlling the union.

Strikes are therefore more the rule. Since independence (1948) each year has had its quota of strikes, in the 1950s and 1960s the largest number being recorded in 1957 and 1964 – 304 in each year. But 1970 was also a year of unprecedented strikes, totting up a record number of 319, involving 139,312 workers and a loss of 1,283,811 man days.[83]

The state has organised an elaborate system of wages boards, industrial dispute boards and industrial tribunals and other such conciliating agencies to arbitrate and mediate between workers and employers. Employees have stood to gain a good deal from these. The U.F. government has ruled that lawyers should not be allowed to appear before industrial tribunals as employers are always at an advantage, being in a position to hire superior legal talent.

Governments have also used pressure on employers to agree

to a settlement of matters in dispute between themselves and the workers. In 1957 the prime minister (S. W. R. D. Bandaranaike) intervened on a number of occasions to settle strikes. In that year his government threatened to invoke the relevant sections of the Public Security Act to compel the employers in the private sector to come to terms with striking workers. The threat itself had the desired effect. The 'national government' of Dudley Senanayake (1965–70) went further and used the Public Security Act to force the private sector to pay their employees an interim devaluation allowance at fixed rates. On 31 July 1971, the Employers' Federation of Ceylon, partly owing to pressure from the U.F. government, entered into a series of collective agreements covering the non-white collar categories of workers in the private sector.[84] These agreements were reached after eighteen months of hard bargaining. They initially benefited twenty-five thousand workers belonging to U.F.-oriented unions, but were extended later by the government to cover, in all, eight hundred thousand workers throughout the private sector. In return for the fairly substantial benefits obtained, the trade unions agreed to a comprehensive procedure for the settlement of disputes and gave a pledge of 'no trade union action' for the three-year duration of the agreement unless employers acted *mala fide*. Even in such instances it was agreed that at least seven days' notice would be given prior to strike action.

Non-U.N.P. governments have been anxious always to extend their patronage to the working classes. In 1956 the M.E.P. government declared 1 May a public holiday. The U.F. government has gone to great extents to please the white collar and non-white collar workers. Advisory committees in government offices, employees' councils in state run enterprises, and the appointment of workers to directorships in state corporations and boards have been some of the steps taken in this direction.

Further, in October 1970 legislation was enacted through the Ceylon (Constitutional) Amendment Act and the Local Authorities Elections (Amendment) Act to extend political rights to all public servants, except those belonging to the judiciary, the armed forces, the police, including persons exercising peace functions under the criminal procedure code and staff grades in the public services and corporations. The minister of public administration explained that since staff graders exercised discretionary functions, they would be tempted to utilise these with political motivations. All other public servants are allowed leave and other facilities to run for election to Parliament or to a local body. If they failed to get elected, they would have the right to revert to their positions in the service. But if elected they would have to choose whether to remain in service or take to political life. If it were the latter, they would have to resign, or retire with a pension if qualified for one.

The U.F. government has besides pledged that it would legislate for a comprehensive charter of worker's rights.

Trade unions cover: (1) Non-white collar workers in the industrial private sector, best organised in the tea export, rubber export, engineering, coconut fibre, fertiliser, motor transport and printing trades. Workers here are distributed among the S.L.F.P.-controlled Sri Lanka Independent Trade Union Federation, the L.S.S.P.-led Ceylon Federation of Labour, the C.P. Ceylon Federation of Trade Unions and the Maoist C.P. Ceylon Trade Union Federation. Workers in other trades and industries have also been unionised in some form or another either by political parties or by the workers themselves. (2) Non-white collar workers in the public sector. The larger sections of these are organised once again primarily in the L.S.S.P.'s Government Workers' Trade Union Federation, the C.P.'s Public Service Trade Union Federation and the S.L.F.P.'s Sri Lanka Government Workers' Trade Union Federation. Mention might be made here of the dock workers in the state-controlled Port Corporation who belong to unions organised by Marxist parties and by the S.L.F.P. and U.N.P. (3) White collar workers in the private sector. The unions with the most numerous membership here are the Ceylon Mercantile Union which has no party affiliation but has as its principal organiser and adviser the L.S.S.P. (R.) leader, Bala Tampoe, the United Corporation and Mercantile Union which is the L.S.S.P.'s counter to the latter union, and the Ceylon Bank Employees' Union and the All Ceylon Estate Staffs Union both of which have no ties with any political party. (4) White collar workers in the public sector. The most powerful union is the L.S.S.P.-controlled Government Clerical Service Union with some 150 branches and a membership of sixteen thousand. There are then the Tamil Government Clerical Service Union with F.P. sympathies and the Government Technical Officers' Trade Union

Federation and the Sri Lanka Jathika Guru Sangamaya (teachers' union), both U.F.-orientated. The Government Allied Health Professional Trade Unions Federation covering fifteen professional groups directly involved in the country's health services, the Local Government Clerical Service Union, the National Union of Teachers, the Ceylon Teachers' Union, the Graduate Teachers' Union and the Union of Secondary Trained Teachers have no direct political affiliations. (5) Workers in the plantation sector. The C.W.C. has the largest membership with 115,000 paying their dues but with an overall membership of 500,000; the D.W.C. comes next with a paying membership of 45,000; and the National Union of Workers forms the third largest union. Other unions are the L.S.S.P. Lanka Estate Workers' Union, the C.P. Ceylon Plantation Workers' Union, the Maoist C.P. Plantation Workers' Union, the F.P. Hill Country Workers' Union and the U.N.P. Lanka Jathika Estate Workers' Union.

The U.F.-orientated unions in the public and private sectors are linked together in the most powerful trade union combine in the country – the Joint Council of Trade Union Organisations. After the U.F.'s advent to office this Organisation, as well as the more vocal unions in it, have been agitating for the implementation of the socialist aspects of the Common Programme, especially those relating to nationalisation of foreign-owned concerns and plantations as well as local industrial and commercial organisations

Professional Organisations

Lawyers, doctors, accountants, university teachers, administrative officers in the higher and middle grades of the public service are the most influential interests.

The proctors have their Law Society, the advocates the Bar Council and the General Council of Advocates, and there are also a few other organisations which have distinct party sympathies. The Sri Lanka Democratic Lawyers' Association, for example, is left-oriented.

Among doctors, the Government Medical Officers' Association is an island-wide organisation which has since 1956 been able to bring pressure to bear on governments in matters connected with their conditions of service. The Medical Specialists' Association is concerned with promoting the interests of its specialised membership. The General Medical Practitioners' Association and Independent Medical Practitioners' Association relate to medical men in general practice in the private sector. Ayurvedic (native medicine) practitioners and homeopaths have their respective associations.

The accountants have the Institute of Chartered Accountants of Ceylon, an incorporated body, while the cost and works accountants have their own association.

University teachers are organised into associations in the different campuses. During the general election of May 1970, many university teachers campaigned for the major political groupings, and the more prominent among them were selected for important positions in government departments and corporations by the U.F. government.

The middle and higher rung public servants of the Ceylon administrative service are organised into three unions of which the more articulate are the Ceylon Administrative Service Association and the Association of the Officers of the Ceylon Administrative Service. None of these unions has political ties. They are more concerned with their conditions of service and were successful in obtaining a re-structuring of the service in 1971, in keeping with their demands.

Specialised Interests

The Income Tax Payers' Association is concerned with the state's taxation policies insofar as they involve individuals. Its membership comprises those in the middle and higher income brackets.

There are two influential groups which have been agitating for relief for tenants – the Rent Payers' Association and the Rent Control Association. The Rent Act of 1972 brought to a successful conclusion the campaign they had been conducting for a number of years for greater protection for tenants.

Religious, Cultural and Communal Interests

Various associations, some longstanding, others ephemeral, have become activated from time to time, depending on the controversies and burning questions of the day. The language question, the problem of Indians in Ceylon, the place for Buddhism in the country's constitutional set-up, the education system, the role of the national press, the rights of the various ethnic and religious groups, the proposed new republican constitution, are but some of the issues which rouse older associations from their somnolence and produce a crop of others to exercise pressure on the centres of power. Caste groups are more devious in their methods and less visible on the surface, since caste is a word seldom mentioned in the best circles. But though a factor not often openly articulated, it is nevertheless taken into account by the powers that be, and its pressures are made to be felt at the appropriate time.

The Buddhist clergy, unlike the Christian, is not organised in any sophisticated or articulate manner. The clergy comes together on occasions when their interests are affected, or when its politically motivated members feel that they must organise themselves for purposes of lending their support to one political party or another. Many Buddhist monks organised themselves into rival fronts to help the U.F. and U.N.P. at the general election of May 1970, while the E.B.P. is the outstanding example of a political organisation of Buddhist monks which contributed a major share in the victory of the M.E.P. in 1956.

The Buddhist laity is better organised, of which the best examples are the Buddhist Theosophical Society and All Ceylon Buddhist Congress. The latter is the more politically activated body insofar as political questions have a bearing on Buddhism or the Buddhists. The Congress has always interested itself in the state's excise policy, education, language, etc. In November 1964 the Congress, along with eight other Buddhist associations, among which were the Young Men's Buddhist Association, the Buddhist Theosophical Society, the Bauddha Jatika Balavegaya (the National Front for the Protection of Buddhism), the Mahabodhi Society and Buddhist Students' Federation, formed a joint action committee to fight the S.L.F.P.–L.S.S.P. government's proposal to nationalise the Lake House Press. In the same year the Congress along with other Buddhist organisations opposed what came to be known as the 'toddy proposals' of the Trotskyist minister of finance (Dr N. M. Perera) contained in his budget of that year. In 1972, also, the Congress expressed concern over the proposal of the minister of finance to establish liquor shops in every electorate. In 1968 the Congress went in deputation to the prime minister (Dudley Senanayake) to register its strong protest over the proposal to establish district councils.

The Bauddha Jatika Balavegaya has an extensive membership in the public sector, as well as outside. Its first president was L. H. Mettananda. In 1964 it opposed the move on the part of Mrs Bandaranaike's S.L.F.P. government to establish district councils. The organisation continues to be active in the public services in particular.

Less active but of some importance are the Sinhala Sanwardena Sanvidanaya formed in December 1971 'to promote education, employment and culture' among the Sinhalese, the Sinhala Tharuna Sanvidanaya (Sinhalese Youth Organisation), and the Sinhala Prajathanthrawadi Sangamaya (the Sinhalese Democratic Union) which has taken an active interest in regard to the position of the Kandyan Sinhalese and the place to be accorded to Buddhism under the new constitution. The Vihara and Devale Trustees Association headed by the Diyawadana Nilame (the lay custodian of the Sacred Tooth Relic of the Buddha) has also been active in the matter of the place to be given to Buddhism in the new constitution. Its influence can be gauged from the fact that a census taken for the very first time in 1971 by the Department of Culture Affairs of Buddhist institutions and clergy in Ceylon indicated that there were 18,670 monks and 152 Buddhist hermitages with 548 monks.[85]

The way in which the Sinhalese language should be used is a matter for dispute between rival Sinhalese literary groups, and has political repercussions. The use of 'standard Sinhalese' became a ground of conflict between the minister of education in the 'national government' of Dudley Senanayake and Sinhalese scholars interested in its promotion. Another organisation called the Hela Havula is also to some extent politically involved in that it is in the forefront of the agitation for the use of the Sinhalese language as set in vogue by the famous Sinhalese writer, the late Munidasa Kumaranatunga.

Interest groups among the Christians are not so open in their political activities. The Roman Catholic Church and the Protestant Churches involve themselves in political affairs insofar as their interests are concerned, but in a less obvious sort of way. The fact that they are readily identifiable minority groups make them function more cautiously than the Buddhists. Among the laity, the Catholic union of Ceylon, a middle-class organisation is the only one worthy of mention.

The Muslims have their main organisations in the Ceylon Muslim League, the Ceylon Moors' Association, the Islamic Socialist Front, and the International Islamic Institute of Ceylon to agitate in matters which concern them directly especially in regard to affairs concerning their religious, political and economic interests. The Malays have their own separate association.

The Ceylon Tamils operate mainly through their political parties, and the Indian Tamils through their principal trade unions. It is not unusual for the Ceylon Tamils in particular to organise unity conferences to which various groups are invited to discuss problems that are of common concern to all Tamils. A growing force among the Indian estate Tamil labour is the Ceylon D.M.K. which has both cultural and political overtones. Its organisation is not so widespread, but its cultural impact causes growing concern to the Sinhalese Buddhist nationalists.

Friendship associations that link Ceylon to foreign countries of the west and to the communist states have been flourishing, and have become part of Ceylonese political life since the 1960s. Some of the friendship associations of the communist states have the patronage of U.F. politicians. At the time of the P.L.F. insurrection there were some thirty-eight Ceylon–North Korean friendship associations in the country. The Ceylon–China Friendship Association has been more articulate than the others in making pronouncements on matters relating to China and Vietnam. The Ceylon Peace Council supports the socialist and communist states. The Muslim lobby, though not exactly organised as part of this friendship network, has played a part in helping to promote good relations between Sri Lanka and the Arab states (the Afro-Asian Society also sponsors the latter but its role cannot be exaggerated) and its influence cannot be discounted in the U.F. government's decision not to support Bangladesh in its war of independence against Pakistan.

Civil Liberties

The International Commission of Jurists and Amnesty International have branch organisations in Ceylon, the former under the chairmanship of a distinguished judge, T. S. Fernando, who is now the president of the Court of Appeal. Amnesty International interests itself in the cause of persons detained for long periods without trial, such as those who were suspected of involvement in the P.L.F. insurrection of March–April 1971. The parent organisation sent a representative, Lord Avebury, to investigate the situation in Ceylon vis-à-vis civil liberties, arising from the declaration of a prolonged state of emergency during and after the P.L.F. outbreak. Lord Avebury evidently proved an embarrassment to the U.F. government and was expelled shortly after his scheduled departure from the island. His report on the situation in Sri Lanka was given wide publicity in the British press.

But by far the greatest source of discomfort to the U.F. government is the Civil Rights Movement of Ceylon inaugurated in November 1971. Its founding members comprised eminent Ceylonese from the professions, trade unions, Buddhist and Christian clergy, and other walks of life. Its objective is the protection and promotion of the civil rights and liberties of the people at all times, more so, because, as its secretary emphasised, the organisation felt that these rights and liberties are 'a necessary accompaniment to radical social and economic change and the movement towards the egalitarian society'.[86]

The movement expressed its concern over the detention, without trial, of persons suspected of P.L.F.-inspired insurrectionary activities. It came in for harsh rebuke from the minister of justice during the debate in the House of Representatives on the Criminal Justice Commission Bill in April 1972 for its exposure of the rigours of this Bill and the serious threats it posed to the democratic rights of the people. The Movement was also critical of the Interpretation (Amendment) Bill of April 1972 which sought to define the powers of the Supreme Court and exclude the district courts of the country from making declarations in regard to executive action. It opined that this would result in 'the creation in the country of a large number of despots ranging from petty officials to ministers whose acts cannot be effectively challenged even where arbitrary and illegal'.[87]

CONCLUSION

Sri Lanka is not well equipped economically for successful parliamentary government but has worked the Westminster model satisfactorily since 1948. English-educated political elites and the Sinhalese Buddhist ethos of tolerance are the prime factors. But the electors have also had their fill of experience since 1931. There have been nine general elections so far and in five of these governments were turned out of office in a peaceful and constitutional manner.

Pressure groups and interest associations for their part do not jostle in a void but are involved in the political processes.

Democracy flourishes because debate, discussion and negotiations precede decision-taking on the part of the wielders of power. This is true both in regard to solutions to the vexed problems of ethnicity as well as of economics. More often than not compromise is the outcome rather than the implementation of one point of view to the exclusion of the other.

Politics follows a middle course and on this, save for extremist revolutionary groups of not very great reckoning, the major political forces are at one. There is, in terms of parliamentary politics, no extreme right or extreme left. The major parties veer towards the centre, though one is right of centre (U.N.P.) and the other left (S.L.F.P.), making for an ideal two party situation with the rivals agreeing on most fundamentals. The division arises from the fact that in Sri Lanka there is a strong conservative tradition with its respect for hierarchy, authority and the established order. On the other, radicalism and the desire for social change to facilitate social mobility motivate movement. The debate is on the rate at which change must take place. But the participants, left, right and centre, if such a categorisation can be made of all centrists, are the English-educated elite with a vested interest in orderly change.

A high degree of responsibility characterises those who possess and wield power. This is true especially of the top leadership. D. S. and Dudley Senanayake (U.N.P.), S. W. R. D. Bandaranaike and Mrs Sirima Bandaranaike (S.L.F.P.), Dr N. M. Perera and Dr Colvin R. de Silva (L.S.S.P.) and Dr S. A. Wickremasinghe and Pieter Keuneman (C.P.) have contributed towards moderation in political solutions. It stands to the credit of the Bandaranaikes that they socialised the Marxists and in the process railroaded them into parliamentarianism.

Both major parties (U.N.P. and S.L.F.P.) have also, at different times, accommodated the ethnocentric claims of feuding Sinhalese and Tamil groupings and in this way arrested the trend towards primordialism and national disintegration.

It is difficult, though, to conjecture as to how much longer the system can continue. For one thing an impatient younger generation which forms the majority of the population is tiring of parliamentary 'musical chairs' and demands an immediate solution to the problem of unemployment. For another, the English-educated elite is being replaced with a Sinhalese- and Tamil-speaking elite, and when the process is complete they will have neither a common medium of communication nor a common experience and heritage which at present enables them to meet on common ground. The process may take some time, and even when it happens it is possible that the English speakers will have transmitted their values to this new elite. But it would not be possible to say how this new elite will respond to the pressures of the rival groups in Sri Lanka's plural society. Will they wish to transform public opinion in an orderly fashion and effect change with moderation, or will they seek solutions that might bring the nation to the brink of disaster? It is difficult to hazard a guess.

5 Constitution and Government

THE CONSTITUTION FROM 1948 TO 1972

The Background

The constitution which came into effect on 4 February 1948 when Sri Lanka became an independent sovereign state was no more than the Soulbury constitution of 1946 with certain consequential changes. The latter in turn was, with a number of not unimportant modifications, based on the Draft Scheme of 1944 framed by the Ceylonese board of ministers functioning under the Donoughmore constitution (Sessional Paper XIV of 1944).

The constitution provided for an adapted version of the Westminster model which was, with a few exceptions, favoured by the local political elites.

Amending Procedure

Section 29 subsection 4 required that not less than two-thirds of the total membership of the House of Representatives, including those not present, had to cast their votes in favour of any Bill to amend or repeal any of the provisions of the constitution. Such a Bill, before it was presented for the royal assent had to carry a certificate from the Speaker that it had obtained the requisite majority. This procedure was availed of on a number of occasions to vary some of the provisions of the constitution. But at no time was it invoked to effect a total revision.

Part of the reason for the paucity of change was that only in two parliaments, that of 1952–6 and the one elected in May 1970 did governments have a two-thirds majority. In the Parliament of 1952–6, the U.N.P. government showed no interest in effecting a major overhaul. In the post-1956 phase, S. W. R. D. Bandaranaike, though his M.E.P. government lacked the required majority, had a joint select committee of both Houses of Parliament set up to look into specific aspects of the constitution and recommend change, but except for the amendments relating to the law on delimitation of constituencies enacted in 1959 no other significant revision was effected. The practice of setting up joint select committees was carried on by the succeeding governments, those of Mrs Sirima Bandaranaike (1960–5) and Dudley Senanayake (1965–70). These committees heard evidence and did a great deal of spadework but their efforts did not come to fruition because they did not have the necessary co-operation from other sections in Parliament to enable them to cross the two-thirds barrier.

The U.F. government of Mrs Sirima Bandaranaike returned at the general election of May 1970 had more than the required majority to effect change according to the procedure laid down, but it preferred the more dramatic method of implementing the sovereign mandate it had obtained by convening a constituent assembly for the purpose. This move had the support of all political groupings in the House of Representatives, though at first the U.N.P. and F.P. were hesitant. Thereafter the machinery for enacting a new constitution was set in motion by Mrs Bandaranaike's cabinet with the House of Representatives sitting as a constituent assembly during 1970–2. However, in the interim period the U.F. government seemed to contradict the position it had already taken when it made use of the normal procedures to effect two major changes in 1971 – the laws to abolish the Senate and appeals to the Judicial Committee of the Privy Council.

An alternative method of amending the constitution was available, but this was never utilised as it could have given rise to many embarrassing questions both in respect of the government of the day as well as in regard to Sri Lanka's position as a sovereign independent state.

Section 1 (1) of the Ceylon Independence Act, 1947, enacted by the British Parliament stated that an Act of the latter body could extend to Sri Lanka if it was 'expressly declared' in that Act that Sri Lanka had requested and consented to its enactment. Jennings stated that under this provision, legally, it would have been possible for an amendment to the Ceylon constitution to have been made by an Act of the British Parliament if a request to this effect was made by a Ceylonese government.[1] Other than routine change requiring uniformity in Commonwealth matters like sucession to the throne, British nationality, etc. no Ceylonese government which had a two-thirds majority in the Ceylon Parliament would have made a request to the British Parliament to enact the desired amendment. If it did not have the majority, and still made the request, it would have given rise to such serious political controversy that even the British Parliament may have hesitated to accede.

The Nominal Executive

While the neighbouring states of India and Pakistan opted to become republics within the Commonwealth, Sri Lanka's leading statesman at the time of independence, D. S. Senanayake, and his immediate successors (Dudley Senanayake and Sir John Kotelawala) decided that the links with the British monarchy should be retained. It was left to S. W. R. D. Bandaranaike to take the preliminary steps to effect the transition to republican status within the Commonwealth. Permission for this was secured by him at the Conference of Commonwealth Prime Ministers in 1956, but the declaration of a republic had to be put off until May 1972, as no government during the intervening period had sufficient time or the required majority to overhaul the constitution.

Until 1972 the British queen was therefore queen of Sri Lanka as well, a title which she assumed under the Royal Titles Act, No. 22 of 1953 which declared her to be 'Queen of Ceylon and her other realms and territories, Head of the Commonwealth'. Her representative in Sri Lanka was the governor-general whom she appointed on the advice of her Ceylonese prime minister. The governor-general held office during pleasure which in effect meant that he functioned as long as he was acceptable to a Ceylonese prime minister in command of a majority in the House of Representatives. Viscount Soulbury, the second governor-general of Sri Lanka described the unsure situation in the following terms:[2]

> Under a constitutional monarchy the prime minister of a Commonwealth nation is more powerful than he would be in a republic under a president. If for any reason he wishes the governor-general to be removed he has only to request the

British sovereign to recall him, and his request must be granted. A president however is usually elected for a term of years, and though he may be uncongenial or unco-operative cannot be removed speedily or without a possible political upheaval.

In view of the foregoing it was clear to me that constitutional proprieties required that I should keep out of politics and refrain from any activities which might give rise to the suspicion of political influence.

It was, however, customary for a new appointee to the post to be privately offered a five-year term by the prime minister recommending his appointment – which was the procedure followed in the cases of Lord Soulbury (1949–54), Sir Oliver Goonetilleke (1954–62) and William Gopallawa (1962–72). The latter two in addition received several extensions.

The post carries some political significance. For instance, an important group such as the Kandyan Sinhalese was pleased when William Gopallawa was appointed. Or the holder may make himself so very acceptable, as did Gopallawa, or extremely useful to the prime minister of the day, as did Sir Oliver Goonetilleke (who 'served' five successive prime ministers), that there is often some reluctance to effect a change.[3] Sir Oliver made himself indispensable to both Mr and Mrs Bandaranaike by the assistance he rendered them in quelling serious communal disturbances and in bringing under control the massive strikes organised by left-wing trade unions during the phase 1956–64.[4]

Reliability is the main consideration in a prime minister's decision to permit a governor-general to continue in office. When that goes there is no reason for his continuance. Thus Sir Oliver Goonetilleke became suspect in the eyes of Mrs Bandaranaike's government when it became known that the army and police organisers of the abortive *coup d'état* of January 1962 had planned to coerce him into suspending the constitution had they succeeded, though he, as far as investigations indicated, had had no hand in the conspiracy.[5] It was after this development that Mrs Bandaranaike decided that the governor-general should be replaced.

Most, though not all of the powers, authorities and functions vested in the queen under the constitution were exercised on her behalf by the governor-general. The powers not delegated to the governor-general related to the making of treaties, appointment of ambassadors and other diplomatic and consular agents, issuing of exequators to consuls and the declaration of war. In respect of powers delegated, there were occasions when the sovereign came to the island or sent a special representative to exercise some of these. In February 1948, King George VI sent his brother, the Duke of Gloucester, formerly to declare open the sessions of Sri Lanka's first post-independence Parliament and to read the speech from the throne. In 1954, Queen Elizabeth visited the island and during her stay participated in functions of state that were normally undertaken by her governor-general.

The powers, authorities and functions specifically assigned to the governor-general related mostly to the executive, legislative, judicial and administrative spheres. Under section 4 (2) of the constitution they were exercised usually on prime-ministerial advice. Jennings argued that on occasion it may have been necessary for the governor-general to be persuaded.[6] No serious differences of opinion however have been reported between a prime minister and a governor-general during the period of the constitution's functioning.

In two matters, however, the governor-general had a certain discretion.

There was first the question of the appointment of a prime minister, carrying with it the right of dismissal. The problem of choosing arose in March 1952 when the first prime minister, D. S. Senanayake, died unexpectedly. An importunate claimant, Sir John Kotelawala, who was at the time leader of the House and had acted as head of the government during times when the prime minister was away was passed over by Lord Soulbury for a comparative junior, Dudley Senanayake, the son of the late prime minister. Soulbury said that it was the late prime minister's wish that his son should succeed him.[7] Relations between Sir John Kotelawala and the governor-general thereafter were never satisfactory. When Dudley Senanayake resigned in October 1953, it was reported that J. R. Jayawardene who was a senior minister in the government at this time had also claims for the office, but Soulbury on this occasion had no choice but to appoint Sir John.[8]

In September 1959 a choice had once more to be made because of the assassination of the prime minister, S. W. R. D. Bandaranaike. The governor-general, Sir Oliver Goonetilleke, preferred to place the onus on the members of the outgoing cabinet. He had them summoned to his official residence in Colombo, directed them to one of the rooms, while he himself stayed outside and requested them to choose a successor.[9] The ministers selected W. Dahanayake who was then commissioned by the governor-general to form a government.

In April 1960 Sir Oliver could have appointed C. P. de Silva, the leader of the opposition, as prime minister on the defeat in Parliament of Dudley Senanayake's minority administration.[10] The governor-general preferred to accept Senanayake's advice and had Parliament dissolved.[11]

In July 1960 Sir Oliver Goonetilleke was faced with the difficulty of selecting a prime minister, as Mrs Sirima Bandaranaike who had led the S.L.F.P. to victory at the general election did not have a seat in either chamber. It was resolved by her being appointed to the Senate by the governor-general, presumably on her own advice, an action quite without parallel.[12]

The problem of dismissing a prime minister did not arise, but on two occassions pressure was brought to bear on the governor-general to exercise the power to which he did not however submit,[13] while on another occasion, in late 1961, Sir Oliver Goonetilleke was reported as having consulted the secretary to the cabinet at the time about his constitutional powers to dismiss Mrs Bandaranaike and her entire cabinet.[14]

On the second of the governor-general's discretionary powers, that of granting a dissolution, the rule was well established, namely to accede to the wishes of the prime minister. Only on one occasion was there doubt expressed when in April 1960 Sir Oliver Goonetilleke allowed the request of a minority prime minister, Dudley Senanayake, who *ab initio* had no majority in the House of Representatives to dissolve Parliament.[15] The governor-general was criticised by the leaders of the opposition parties for his action, but as the result achieved a stable government the criticism of partisanship was not persisted in.

The Cabinet

The constitution provided that the cabinet should be collectively responsible to Parliament, in effect the House of Representatives [section 46 (1)]. The prime minister headed the largest group in the House. He was usually a member of the House. Mrs Bandaranaike however functioned as prime minister during 1960–1965 while sitting in the upper chamber, the Senate. It was nevertheless realised, though all too late, that had she sat in the House and been more in contact with her supporters in the House, the revolt within her ranks in late 1964 which resulted in the defeat of her government at the division on the throne speech would not have reached the proportions it did.

Under the constitution, the prime minister was the authority for assigning subjects and functions to the various ministers. He could, as he sometimes did, also reallocate functions as between ministers. But this on one occasion produced a crisis. In 1959, S. W. R. D. Bandaranaike withdrew some of the subjects in the charge of his controversial minister of agriculture, Philip Gunawardene. The latter objected and resigned from the cabinet along with his colleague, William de Silva, who held the portfolio of industry and fisheries. On the other hand, in 1967 Prime Minister Dudley Senanayake took over the subjects of information and broadcasting from his deputy, J. R. Jayawardene, the minister of state, without even informing him beforehand.[16] The minister learned about it only next morning from the reports in the newspapers. But he did not think it important enough to make an issue of it.

Under the constitution the prime minister did not have a completely free hand in the allocation of portfolios. He himself was obliged to take on the portfolio of defence and external affairs. It is said that the British government at the time of independence wished to negotiate agreements relating to both these matters with the prime minister of the country and therefore made provision in the constitution for these subjects to be in his charge. Furthermore the constitution also provided that not less than two ministers, one of whom had to be responsible for the portfolio of justice, had to be appointed from the Senate (section 48).

There was no limitation on the size of cabinets. But the tendency was to have more ministers than was really necessary, due to the fragile nature of party ties and the need to satisfy the numerous social, ethnic and religious groups.[17] Every cabinet had in it representatives of the two Sinhalese groups (low country and Kandyan), the Muslims, Christians (sometimes Roman Catholics, on other occasions Protestants and on still others both Catholics and Protestants), and of the more important caste groups, especially of the *goigama*, *karava* and *salagama*, as well as on occasion the *duravas*, and on others the so-called depressed castes. Except for the phase 1956–65, Ceylon Tamils were always included in the cabinet.

The constitution further provided for the appointment of junior ministers, otherwise called parliamentary secretaries, to assist ministers in the exercise of their parliamentary and departmental duties. Their number could not at any time exceed the number of ministers (section 47). Also, the constitution specified that not more than two parliamentary secretaries should be appointed from the Senate. In the selection of these junior ministers, too, attention was paid to party as well as to community, religion and caste.

This method of constructing the administration proved politically useful. It enabled the government to draw its political sustenance from the widest sources possible. At the same time, any important grouping could not be left out, for when this happened, as for instance in 1965–7, when there was no Roman Catholic in Dudley Senanayake's 'national government', or during 1956–9 and 1960–5 when no Ceylon Tamil was appointed to the Bandaranaike cabinets, the leading opposition parties exploited the situation to play on the feelings of the aggrieved group.

The prime minister himself in the prevailing context of sectarian and communal politics was always from the majority Sinhalese Buddhist *goigama* group. Certain fortuitous circumstances in late 1959 and April 1960 led the S.L.F.P. to sponsor their leader, C. P. de Silva, a Sinhalese Buddhist from the *salagama* caste, for the office of prime minister, but this was because that party had had little time to resolve its leadership issue so soon after the confusion created in its ranks by the unfortunate assassination of its leader S. W. R. D. Bandaranaike. In December 1959 the S.L.F.P. decided to disown the leader whom it had chosen immediately after Bandaranaike's assassination, W. Dahanayake, and addressed a 'prayer' to the governor-general requesting that he be dismissed and C. P. de Silva be appointed prime minister in his place.[18] It bore no results. In April 1960, all opposition parties indicated their willingness to join hands with the leader of the S.L.F.P., C. P. de Silva, to form an alternate government after the defeat of the minority administration of Dudley Senanayake at the division on the throne speech. The governor-general preferred to grant Senanayake's request for a dissolution. By the time of the general election which followed in July 1960, the S.L.F.P. had changed its leader, Mrs Bandaranaike taking C. P. de Silva's place. Even while C. P. de Silva led his party, it often used to be said that he and his colleague A. P. Jayasuriya (from the Sinhalese Buddhist *goigama* group) were co-leaders of the S.L.F.P. Generally, however, all major Sinhalese political parties ensured that the requirements of race and religion were satisfied when choosing their leaders.

In the configuration of politics during the 1948–72 phase, membership of one of two leading Sinhalese Buddhist *goigama* families enjoying great political prestige and influence, the Senanayakes or Bandaranaikes, was a *sine qua non* for the premiership. All except one prime minister belonged to one or other of these families.

Further, all prime ministers save two (Kotelawala and Dahanayake) had a measure of charisma which gave a boost to their party's image. D. S. Senanayake won independence and was 'the father of the nation'. Dudley Senanayake's 'image' was that of the honest liberal democrat. S. W. R. D. Bandaranaike was the aristocrat who came down from Mount Zion to usher in the age of the common man. Mrs Sirima Bandaranaike inherited her husband's charisma, but soon developed one of her own.

For all these reasons, the prime minister was the key figure in the island's troubled political set-up. Though at times he and his government were involved in implementing sectarian or partisan policies, he was nevertheless looked on as a national figure. The island's various ethnic, religious and social groupings turned to him for mediation or arbitration in many of the serious differences that arose between and among them. In 1953, Dudley Senanayake was called upon to deal with the grave situation resulting from his government's decision to increase the price of rice. He chose resignation as the way out. In 1955, Sir John Kotelawala had to resolve the crisis caused by his party's (the U.N.P.) stand on having Sinhalese and Tamil as the official languages of the country. In the years 1956 to 1959, it fell to S. W. R. D. Bandaranaike to placate the Ceylon Tamils and handle the forces of Sinhalese extremism. Mrs Sirima

Bandaranaike came to an understanding with the Roman Catholic hierarchy in Sri Lanka in early 1961 over the crisis that arose from her government's decision to nationalise the schools, most of which were the property of the Church. Dudley Senanayake had to pacify many Sinhalese organisations which felt alarmed over the Regulations his government framed on the Tamil language in January 1966, and the concessions it made to Indians resident in Ceylon in enacting legislation in 1967 to implement the Indo-Ceylon Agreement (the Sirima-Shastri Pact) of October 1964. Very often the prime minister was called upon to settle trade union disputes. Nearly all prime ministers after 1956 were burdened with this problem.

The importance of teamwork in regard to the programmes and policies of governments in office was not sufficiently realised in political circles. Often a leading political figure in the cabinet, usually its deputy, with positive views on important matters of policy, was out of step with his chief. This was true of S. W. R. D. Bandaranaike in D. S. Senanayake's cabinet (1947–1952), Sir John Kotelawala in Dudley Senanayake's (May 1952–October 1953), C. P. de Silva in Mrs Sirima Bandaranaike's government of 1960–5, and J. R. Jayawardene in Dudley Senanayake's 'national government' of 1965–70.

Sometimes the prime minister had to take stern note of actions or pronouncements by his ministers which were critical or in conflict with the stated or implied objectives of his government.[19]

D. S. Senanayake requested the resignation of his minister of commerce when the latter advisedly walked out of the chamber at the division on the Indian and Pakistani Citizenship Act as a protest against a piece of legislation which he had strenuously opposed in the cabinet.[20] The same prime minister caused a memorandum dated 14 April 1948 to be circulated among his ministers on the full implications of collective responsibility.[21] It was mainly intended as a warning to his senior colleague S. W. R. D. Bandaranaike who at this time was making public statements which were tangentially and at times directly critical of government policy. But it failed to have any effect on the deviant minister. There were conflicts in Dudley Senanayake's cabinet of May 1952–October1953, especially between the prime minister and Sir John Kotelawala, whose frustrations and contempt for the Senanayakes was recorded in a document of dubious authorship called 'The Premier Stakes' which caused a furore in political circles, and between the minister of agriculture and food, J. R. Jayawardene, and the minister of trade and commerce, R. G. Senanayake, over the Rubber-Rice Agreement of 1952 that the latter was negotiating with the People's Republic of China.[22] The position was no worse under Sir John Kotelawala's premiership (October 1953–April 1956). His cousin, the minister of trade and commerce (R. G. Senanayake) was openly critical of the government's policy in regard to the Indian question and the decision to appoint Sir Oliver Goonetilleke as governor-general in succession to Viscount Soulbury.[23] The minister of industries and housing, Sir Kanthiah Vaithianathan, gave public expression to views on the Tamil language which were on one occasion embarrassing to his chief and on another directly in conflict with the rest of the cabinet.[24] In fact the differences between ministers were receiving such publicity that the prime minister said it would not matter if his cabinet met at the Galle Face Green (an open public park close to the House of Representatives).

The conflict between ministers reached dangerous levels in the coalition cabinets that became a feature in the post-1956 phase of Sri Lanka politics. S. W. R. D. Bandaranaike's first government (April 1956–May 1959) was a coalition of his democratic socialist centrist S.L.F.P. and the Marxist V.L.S.S.P. of Philip Gunawardene, among others. The S.L.F.P. ministers were generally suspicious of Philip Gunawardene's political ambitions and were therefore critical of most of his legislative proposals, in particular his Paddy Lands Bill and Co-operative Development Bank Bill, which they feared would invest him with power, patronage and an accession of political strength. The minister's agricultural policy was impeded by the actions of the S.L.F.P. minister of lands and land development, C. P. de Silva, who was also at this time the second-in-command of the government. Philip Gunawardene for his part was openly derisive of the rural development movement which came under the purview of the S.L.F.P. minister of home affairs, A. P. Jayasuriya. Bandaranaike had a code of conduct framed for his ministers in which, among other things, he advised them to refrain from referring to their colleagues by name when defending their policies in public. The only immediate effect this had was that ministers ceased to identify each other in their public pronouncements, but the references were none the less only too obvious. These skirmishes between the two wings in the cabinet reached crisis proportions when the S.L.F.P. ministers banded themselves together under the leadership of W. Dahanayake and refused to attend cabinet meetings in early 1959 until such time as the prime minister dismissed Philip Gunawardene from his government.[25] This 'boycott' continued for some time until Bandaranaike very reluctantly effected a reallocation of functions among his ministers to which Philip Gunawardene was not agreeable. It ended in his and his colleague's (William de Silva, minister of industries) resignation from the cabinet.

These conflicts and machinations soured the prime minister and made him pessimistic about the advisability of continuing the cabinet system in the context of Ceylon's poorly developed party situation at the time. Bandaranaike advocated the adoption of the Swiss type of executive or a return to the Donoughmore model of government by executive committees where ministers would carry out the wishes of the legislature and would not have to resign if their views were at variance with majority opinion in Parliament.[26] But this did not find ready acceptance.

The shortlived Dahanayake cabinet which took office in September 1959 on the assassination of S. W. R. D. Bandaranaike was torn with dissensions between rival groups which quarrelled over the manner in which the police investigations into the assassination were being handled.[27] One group faulted some of the ministers who were close to the prime minister. The latter, under pressure, dismissed two ministers who were connected with some of those alleged to be involved in the assassination conspiracy. Subsequently the prime minister found the situation intolerable, had Parliament dissolved on 4 December 1959, and in the weeks that followed dismissed most of his S.L.F.P. ministers who in turn expelled him from their party.[28] Dahanayake then formed his own party, the L.P.P., and fought the general election under its banner, a truly Gilbertian situation.

The situation was better under Mrs Bandaranaike, but a powerful group of senior ministers disapproved of the ascendancy in the government of her nephew, Felix Dias Bandaranaike, and petitioned for his dismissal. Differences between ministers however did not emerge into the open. But when Mrs Bandaranaike decided to coalesce with the Trotskyist L.S.S.P. in June 1964, a section in her party led by her deputy, C. P. de Silva, strongly opposed the move. It ended with C. P. de Silva and thirteen others leaving her government, thereby causing its defeat in Parliament.

The 'national government' of Dudley Senanayake from 1965–1970 worked reasonably well except for the open differences the prime minister had with his F.P. colleague, the minister of local government. These were not of a serious nature however and did not endanger the stability of his government, or confuse the general public.

The present U.F. government headed by Mrs Bandaranaike is a coalition of right-wing, centrist and left-wing elements. There are differences between the right and left groups within the cabinet and the government parliamentary group but they have not created embarrassments so far.

Part of the reason for these deviations from the norm can be attributed to the highly individualistic tendencies that the Donoughmore system of government, with its executive committees and its politically heterogeneous boards of ministers with no sense of collective responsibility except in the case of the annual budget, promoted. This tradition dies hard, so much so that the electors do not seriously expect complete unity and agreement at cabinet level. On the contrary, the public is more than ready to identify particular policies with particular ministers and to regard it as not abnormal for other ministers to be opposed to such policies.

This tendency towards associating ministers with specific policies gains further emphasis because of the recent trend of Parliament to enact what may be called framework legislation. Details are left to be worked out by ministers and their officials who as a result have acquired considerable administrative, quasi-legislative and sometimes quasi-judicial powers. In addition, the number of government-sponsored corporations that have come into existence after 1956 has increased ministerial powers of patronage and administrative direction.

But despite the conflicts and sometimes revolts in Ceylonese cabinets, it is the prime minister who dominates the political scene. His eminence is an established fact in Ceylonese political life and the tremendous influence that he is able to wield in shaping political direction is due to the immense powers which were vested in him under the constitution. These powers he wisely utilised to increase the prestige of his administration, especially in choosing ministers, parliamentary secretaries, appointed members of the House of Representatives, senators, and in recent times since the U.F. government assumed office, even key members of the administration such as permanent secretaries and heads of departments.

Further, it is the prime minister who is responsible for advising the governor-general to summon, prorogue and dissolve Parliament.

The device of prorogation was utilised by both S. W. R. D. Bandaranaike and Mrs Sirima Bandaranaike during 1956–65 to utilise the interval to recoup their falling majorities. The objection was to the unusually long period of prorogation.

The weapon of dissolution has also proved useful, though not always. In 1947 when D. S. Senanayake had only the support of the forty-two U.N.P. members and the six appointed members in a House of 101, it was said in political circles that he planned to have Parliament dissolved if he were defeated in the House.[29] The mere threat served to persuade the fairly large number of independent members elected to that Parliament to decide to support the Senanayake administration and to give it the majority it needed. However, the threat of dissolution by W. Dahanayake in December 1959 failed to coerce rebels in his party into supporting his government, nor did it make any impression on members of the opposition parties when Dudley Senanayake as minority prime minister in April 1960 stated that he would, if defeated, have Parliament dissolved. Earlier the prime minister's supporters and political brokers of various hues had tried without success to persuade opposition parties to join hands with the Senanayake administration.

The Government Parliamentary Group

The Group is important because of the complexities of the party system and the occasional tendency for members to think differently from ministers on controversial questions.

Besides granting approval to proposed legislation and on occasion amending it, and determining policy questions, the Group also helped to resolve disputes and iron out differences among its members.

The Group not only included members of the largest single party in Parliament (in both Houses) which may or may not have an overall majority, but also the six appointed members who in theory were supposed to act independently but did in fact, except on one or two occasions, always support the governments in office, and those independent members and smaller parties which threw in their lot with the government.

Generally at the beginning of each week during which the House assembled, the Group met to discuss parliamentary business for the week. Cabinet ministers were called upon to explain important policy matters and proposed legislation. Resolutions were usually moved by the more active members, and if adopted had to be acted upon by individual ministers or the cabinet, as circumstances demanded. There were occasions when ministers were criticised for their failure to give effect to the Group's decisions, or for the inefficient handling of affairs which came within the purview of their Ministry.

The Group's influence depended very much on the balance of forces within it, as well as on the personality of the prime minister.

In the pre-1956 phase, with the U.N.P. firmly on the saddle, the Group did not, except on one or two occasions, have as much opportunity to assert itself. The crisis caused by the decision of the Dudley Senanayake government to raise the price of rice in 1953 and the grave controversy resulting in the ill-timed and contradictory pronouncements of Sir John Kotelawala on the language question in 1955 were some of the rare instances in which the Group intervened to express its views.

In the post-1956 phase, however, with the emergence of coalition government, the Group was definitely on the ascendant. In 1956 it rejected S. W. R. D. Bandaranaike's first draft Bill providing for Sinhalese as the only official language, as it felt that too much leeway was permitted in its clauses for the use of the Tamil language, for a more forthright and brief sentence declaring Sinhalese as the *one* official language throughout the island. The Group had sharp, conflicting, and often confused views to express on the controversial legislative proposals of the Marxist minister of agriculture. During Mrs Bandaranaike's premiership of 1960–5, the Group very clearly expressed its opposition to the budget proposal of her minister of finance, Felix Dias Bandaranaike, in 1962, to reduce the rice subsidy, despite the fact that it had her full support. The Group also rejected several drafts of Bills presented by the minister of justice, Sam P. C. Fernando, for the state to exercise a measure of control over the press, on the ground that these did not go far enough.

Dudley Senanayake had greater difficulties with the Group because his government of 1965–70 comprised a coalition of politically disparate and irreconcilable groups. Rare and fortuitous circumstances had brought them together. In mid-1968, the prime minister had to abandon his proposed District Councils Bill because he was faced with a revolt of a section of his own parliamentary supporters.

In 1972 the Government Parliamentary Group of the U.F. government under Mrs Bandaranaike compelled the minister of finance to withdraw a number of cuts he had imposed on the welfare services in the annual budget. Members felt that the cuts were too severe and they feared the reactions of their constituents.

Parliament

The responsibility for making laws 'for the peace, order and good government of the island' was, subject to the provisions of the constitution, vested in Parliament. Parliament comprised Her Majesty the Queen and, until September 1971, two chambers, the Senate and the House of Representatives. The Senate was abolished with effect from September 1971 by constitutional amendment.

The Senate. The Senate consisted of thirty members, fifteen elected by the House on the basis of the single transferable vote and fifteen appointed by the governor-general on prime-ministerial advice. The constitution provided that in appointing senators the governor-general should endeavour to select persons who had distinguished themselves in public service, or in professional, commercial, industrial or agricultural life including education, law, medicine, science, engineering and banking [section 10(3)]. Senators had to be at least thirty-five years of age. Otherwise their qualifications were the same as those for members of the House of Representatives.

Senators held office for a term of six years, but the Senate functioned as a continuous body with one-third of its membership (five elected and five appointed) going out of office every two years. The term of office of a senator was therefore not affected by reason of a dissolution of Parliament.

The Soulbury commissioners had hoped that given the basis of its composition the Senate would make a valuable contribution to the political education of the country. Appointed senators were, however, not always drawn from the specialised fields of interest specified. Some distinguished persons in business and industry and with professional and educational skills were appointed or elected to the Senate and there is little doubt that they made extremely valuable contributions in political debate. Certain minority interests, ethnic, religious and caste, secured entry, but they were chosen more on political grounds than as a method of enabling the articulation of these interests. There were occasions when defeated candidates at parliamentary elections also found their way into the Senate, a practice which was quite contrary to the intentions of the framers of the constitution who had pleaded that such a chamber would be useful for those who wished to avoid the hurly-burly of electoral politics. Often members of this body were elected or appointed more as a reward for their services to the party which preferred them. More often than not they tended to repeat the arguments put forward in the House. The latter in fact was the focus of interest.

In regard to elected senators, the Government Parliamentary Group made its own selections with or without ministerial or prime-ministerial influence, and at the two-yearly elections secured three and occasionally four of the five seats. Opposition parties combined to pool their votes to secure one if not two of the elective seats, the seats in question going on a rotational basis as between the various groups.

In the matter of appointed senators, the prime ministers had a free hand in their selection.

The constitution provided that not less than two ministers, one of whom should be minister of justice, and not more than two parliamentary secretaries, had to be appointed from the Senate. The purpose in assigning the portfolio of justice to a senator was to ensure that the holder of the office would be a person not directly involved in the heat and dust of down-to-earth politics. Almost every minister of justice throughout the period filled the office with honour and dignity.

The Senate had at best only a power to delay non-money Bills for two sessions of Parliament, which meant a maximum delay of one year. It could not initiate money Bills and could delay these for only a period of one month. In actual practice a money Bill was interpreted as meaning the annual budget and no more. Supplementary financial estimates sanctioned by the House were not therefore presented to the Senate for its approval.

In its first twenty-three years (1947–70), the Senate rarely interfered with important legislation. Occasionally amendments of an inconsequential nature were suggested or made. When it did obstruct legislation, as in mid-1970, it incurred the wrath of the U.F. government which seized the occasion to have it legislated out of existence. The measure it opposed was not of great significance. But the U.F. government chose to act because it realised that the U.N.P. opposition with a majority in the Senate was bent on extracting concessions from it.

The House of Representatives. The House as constituted under the general elections of 1947, 1952 and 1956 comprised 101 members, ninety-five elected, and six appointed after a general election under section 11(2) of the constitution. The latter were appointed by the governor-general on the advice of the prime minister to represent unrepresented or inadequately represented interests. Of the ninety-five elected, eighty-four were from single-member and eight from four two-member constituencies while three were from one three-member constituency.

In 1959 a fresh demarcation took place under which the number of constituencies was increased to 151, 140 single-member, four two-member and one three-member. In addition there were the six appointed members.

The six appointed members were usually from the European and Burgher communities which have never been in a position to secure representation through the electoral process, and at various times from the Indian Tamil and Muslim (Ceylon Moors or Malays) groups. Occasionally caste groups from among the Sinhalese and Ceylon Tamils also obtained representation in this way.

Parliament could not vary the provisions of the constitution except in accordance with the provisions laid down in section 29 (4), already referred to.

Further, section 29(2) stated that Parliament could not enact legislation which (1) prohibits or restricts the free exercise of any religion; (2) makes persons of any community or religion liable to disabilities or restrictions to which persons of other communities or religions are not made liable; (3) gives to persons of any community or religion any privilege or advantage which is not given to persons of other communities or religions; (4) alters the constitution of any religious body except with the consent of the governing authority of that body. This provision was, in an *obiter dicta*, held by the Judicial Committee of the Privy Council in Bribery Commissioner v. Ranasinghe (66 N.L.R. 73) to be unalterable.

The Privy Council's opinion, though not binding on the government (since it was only an *obiter dicta*), caused a stir in political circles, especially among opposition parties at the time, which declared that the pronouncement was an additional reason as to why the 'British-imposed' Ceylon constitution should be abrogated.

On an earlier occasion, in 1952, the Citizenship Act, No. 18, of 1948 and the Ceylon (Parliamentary Elections) Amendment Act, No. 48, of 1949 were challenged on the ground that they discriminated against the Indian community and therefore contravened section 29(2). The argument was that the Acts in question in fact disfranchised Indians resident in Ceylon, who had earlier exercised the vote. These Acts confined the vote to citizens of Ceylon. The position of the Indian community was somewhat complicated in view of the Indian and Pakistani Residents (Citizenship) Act, No. 34, of 1949 which permitted only those Indians and Pakistanis resident in Ceylon who satisfied certain stipulated conditions to obtain Ceylonese citizenship. The revising officer, the district judge of Kegalle, N. Sivagnanasunderam, before whom the Acts No. 18 of 1948 and No. 48 of 1949 were challenged held that these were invalid on the ground that they sought to deprive members of the Indian community of the franchise. The Supreme Court however in Mudanayake *v.* Sivagnanasunderam (53 N.L.R. 25, 1952) quashed the decision on the ground that the Acts in question were clear and unambiguous, that the disqualification of a large number of Indians in Ceylon was not the necessary legal effect of the disputed Acts, and that the disqualifications in question would disqualify members of any other community in like manner as it would disqualify Indians. An appeal was taken to the Judicial Committee of the Privy Council which however held with the Supreme Court.

The organisation of business in the House was very similar to that of the British House of Commons. Government and opposition faced each other with a gangway separating the two sections, the earlier semi-circle arrangement of seats in concentric fashion in the State Council under the Donoughmore constitution, being abandoned. The House divided itself into committees just as the British House did, and legislative procedure followed the same lines.

The Speaker of the House until the last Parliament followed the traditions of his British counterpart, renouncing all party ties on his election. In fact in January 1949 a delegation from the British House of Commons made a presentation of a mace and a chair for the use of the Speaker.

Rules of debate and parliamentary practice were similar to those in Westminster, and recourse was more often had to Erskine May and Gilbert Campion, and on constitutional questions to Dicey, Berriedale Keith, Jennings, Laski and in recent times S. A. de Smith, than to authorities in other Commonwealth countries, even neighbouring India. The debates in the House until 1955 were almost entirely conducted in the English language. It was only in late 1960 that legislative provision was made for parliamentary business to be transacted in Sinhalese and Tamil, though it must be said that between 1956 and 1960 there was a progressive switch to the national languages.

What is more, the constitution itself prescribed that the privileges, immunities and powers of the Senate and the House, and of parliamentarians, should not exceed those 'for the time being held or enjoyed by the Common House of Parliament of the United Kingdom or of its members'.[30]

The House is elected for a term of five years unless earlier dissolved. Section 15(5) of the constitution, however, provided for a dissolved Parliament to be re-convened in the event of an emergency situation arising between the dissolution of the old Parliament and the date fixed for the meeting of the new.

The social composition of the House has changed significantly since 1956. The membership of the first two parliaments, that of 1947 and 1952, was drawn largely from the middle and upper layers of Ceylonese society. The overwhelming majority of members inclusive of those from the left-wing parties had had an English education in the better-known secondary schools, belonged to the professions, or were landed proprietors, businessmen and industrialists while a few were retired public servants of the higher and middle grades. At the higher levels of party leadership there were men of means who could freewheel on their own resources.

The social composition of the House after each general election from 1956 (March 1960, July 1960, 1965 and 1970) tended to become progressively democratised with members emerging from the lower layers of society. This was most noticeable in the House elected in May 1970.

Recruitment to the House nevertheless maintained a certain social optimum. All members had had a reasonably good secondary education and had a certain social reputation in their local areas. Membership did not descend to the poverty line nor did actual peasants and workers enter the House even in 1970, with one or two rare exceptions.

It was the S.L.F.P. which in fact opened its doors to the emerging rural middle classes and intelligentsia striving for social and political recognition. This could not be said of the U.N.P., the left-wing parties, or the Tamil groupings. Their parliamentary membership continued to be confined to the pre-1956 strata. The U.N.P. in competition with its S.L.F.P. rival gave nomination to a few farmers and workers, but it was more a window-dressing exercise than evidence of changed social attitudes.

The expenses involved in contesting an election have always been a heavy burden on the candidate, in the absence of proper party organisation and adequate party funds. Wealthy candidates as well as political parties which could fall back on powerful business and financial interests to provide them with the resources for transport, for the publication and disrtibution of literature, for the organisation of propaganda meetings, etc. were at an advantage.

Before 1956 it was the U.N.P. of all political groupings which stood to benefit in regard to these matters. After 1956, S. W. R. D. Bandaranaike took steps to lessen the burden which elections imposed on candidates and parties.

Legislation enacted in 1959 provided for (1) the deposits of candidates of recognised political parties to be halved; (2) a limited use of postal services free of charge for all candidates duly nominated; and (3) a ban on the display of propaganda material to promote the candidature of any person. In 1964, Mrs

Bandaranaike's S.L.F.P. government enacted legislation which further reduced the financial burdens on candidates. The more important aspects of this legislation were that candidates of recognised political parties had their deposits reduced by a further 50 per cent and voters hereafter were obliged to use, with certain exceptions, only public transport to get to the polling booths. This meant that political parties with the means to hire vehicles to transport their supporters to the polls no longer had an advantage.

Despite these useful changes, candidates are still burdened with sizable expenditure. A candidate has to possess some means of his own. For the rest he has to fall back on relatives and friends, as well as influential and wealthy supporters. On average, a candidate would require between Rs 15,000 to Rs 25,000 to fight an election seriously. The subscriptions that he receives from supporters in his constituency place him under obligation to them. It is therefore not an infrequent occurrence for the more prominent of these important supporters to manipulate a candidate who succeeds in winning his seat.

Members of Parliament have seldom the time or the opportunity to engage in occupations other than attending to the needs of their constituents. The situation is made worse for the member because he has increasingly tended to be a local man who resides in his constituency and not in some far away city from which he could visit his constituents at times convenient to himself. Most members are at the beck and call of their constituents at all hours of the day and night. In return for his vote, the constituent expects the member to perform all kinds of services for him. He must use his position and influence with officials and ministers to secure appointments, promotions and transfers in the public service or state corporations. At the local level, he is expected to assist in getting the children of constituents admitted to schools, patients into hospital, permits and licences for the entrepreneur, and sometimes even a birth certificate. The member either issues a letter to the constituent concerned, which in local parlance is referred to as a 'chit', or if the person or persons concerned are of some influence, he would use his official telephone or interview the authorities concerned to get the job done.

The member not only helps individual constituents. He must also look after the general interests of his constituency. Construction of or repairs to hospitals, schools, roads, bridges and culverts obliges him to be on good terms with ministers and their parliamentary secretaries. Backbenchers who snipe at ministers and their deputies will not receive a ready ear either from the minister or his officials. Even members belonging to the opposition are careful in criticisms they make.

In serving his constituency, it will thus be seen that the average M.P. has a fair amount of patronage at his disposal. But he has to act discreetly to make the best use of it. Generally opposition M.P.s receive a better deal from non-U.N.P. governments than from U.N.P. ones.

On important issues of vital political significance, however, backbenchers both on the government and opposition sides tend more often than not to reflect and articulate the views and reactions of their constituents.

This trend has been more marked in the post-1956 phase of Ceylonese politics with the entry of the low layers of society as well as the rural elites into the mainstream. The member of Parliament has had to submit to greater pressure from these demanding sections which had hitherto been kept outside the pale. Where his predecessor in the pre-1956 Parliaments was accustomed to be passive, or at best an arbiter between the well-shielded administration and his electors, the post-1956 member of Parliament has to cast himself in a more dynamic role as the 'people's representative'.

The Opposition

From a situation of one-party dominance during the first two Parliaments (1947–56) when the U.N.P. was strongly positioned, political alignments gradually moved towards a bi-polar confrontation of the two major parties, the U.N.P. and S.L.F.P., with the smaller groupings attaching themselves to one or the other.

The trends were apparent at the 1956 general election when Bandaranaike's political formation, the M.E.P., having forged no-contest electoral alliances with the L.S.S.P. and C.P., inflicted defeat on the governing U.N.P. Thereafter, save for the general election of March 1960 when each of the main anti-U.N.P. parties proceed on a go it alone policy and met with disaster, the forces opposing the U.N.P. have cohered around the S.L.F.P. – at the general elections of July 1960 (when they succeeded), 1965 (when they failed) and 1970 (victorious). In July 1960 and in 1965 they were united on the basis of no-contest mutual aid polls pacts. In 1968 they formed the U.F. on an agreed programme and rode to victory in 1970.

The U.N.P. for its part had been a lone operator up to July 1960. It succeeded in obtaining a clear verdict only once, in 1952. In 1947 it was in a minority situation but consolidated the government which it formed. It was in a similar situation in March 1960 but failed to make the grade as in 1947. In July 1960 it suffered defeat as it had in 1956. Thereafter it realised that only by joining forces with elements opposed to the S.L.F.P. and its allies could it succeed. In 1965 therefore the U.N.P. led a seven-party coalition (inclusive of itself) against the S.L.F.P. and the latter's Marxist allies and triumphed. In 1970 it operated on a similar basis but failed.

The end result is that there has been in existence since 1956 (March 1960 excluded) a virtual two-party situation comprising two opposing political coalitions willing to work within the parliamentary framework and through constitutional mechanisms.

A confusing factor is the role of the traditional Marxist parties in Parliament. Conservative democratic forces have been and are sceptical of their intentions, a view reinforced by the L.S.S.P.'s ambivalent attitude to the formation of an alternate government up to 1956.

But despite their lack of certainty as to which path (revolutionary or democratic) they should follow to achieve their ultimate goals, the L.S.S.P. proved anxious whenever opportunity presented itself to secure for themselves the leadership of the opposition. In Sri Lanka's parliamentary context this meant nothing more than Her Majesty's loyal opposition if not Her Majesty's alternative government.

In 1947 the L.S.S.P. laid claim to the office but failed to secure it until June 1950 owing to the differences they had with their splinter group, the B.L.P.I. (later B.S.P.) which until then refused to recognise the office,[31] while the C.P. persisted in condemning it as a 'reactionary British convention'.[32] Again in 1952 the L.S.S.P. wished to take the office but it went to the S.L.F.P. leader.[33] In 1956 the L.S.S.P. succeeded in getting its leader elected to the post.[34] This was an anomalous situation as the L.S.S.P. had co-operated with the M.E.P. in the election campaign which led to the latter's victory. Really the L.S.S.P. should therefore have been accommodated on the government benches.

In 1947 the L.S.S.P. declined to participate in talks summoned at Yamuna, the residence of a leading opposition member, Mr H. Sri Nissanka, K.C. on the grounds that it was 'a revolutionary party' and would not therefore serve in 'a capitalist government'.[35] They were willing to assist those who might take office in an alternative 'progressive government'[36] but their concept of 'progress' was obviously not acceptable to the other groups who gathered at Yamuna and the talks ended in a fiasco. A mushroom political formation of independents, the Lanka Swadhina Party, which had been formed to assist in the talks broke up as soon as it became clear that these would not produce results; consequently some of the founding members crossed over to the U.N.P. government.

Between 1951, when Bandaranaike crossed over to the opposition and inaugurated his democratic alternative, the S.L.F.P., and 1956, the L.S.S.P. veered between offers of support for a Bandaranaike government and advocacy of a revolutionary line leading to a government of workers and peasants.[37] The traditional democratic forces feared in the L.S.S.P.'s offers the possibility of the latter casting Bandaranaike's in the role of a Ceylonese Kerensky.

After 1956 the L.S.S.P. sought office in the various Bandaranaike governments but it was only in June 1964 that they realised their objective when they coalesced with Mrs Bandaranaike's S.L.F.P. government. The coalition was shortlived, suffering parliamentary defeat in December of the same year. In May 1970, with the return of the U.F. to power, the L.S.S.P. obtained key portfolios in what is a more stable set-up.

In the post-1956 years the L.S.S.P. declared its commitment to Parliament but its protestations made little impression on the traditional democratic forces in the country. The latter alleged that the L.S.S.P. was merely seeking to utilise Parliament to achieve its revolutionary goals.

The C.P. was more pragmatic from the point of view of its own interests in that it sought all the time to bring into being a popular front government not antagonistic to the Soviet Union. In 1947 it even conceived of the U.N.P. in this role.[38] Thereafter it concentrated on Bandaranaike and the S.L.F.P. The democratic forces referred to did not regard the C.P. as a serious threat.

The effect of these ambivalent intentions on the part of the L.S.S.P., coupled with the politically motivated trade union struggles which the L.S.S.P. and C.P. launched during the years immediately preceding and after independence, culminating in their successful hartal of August 1953, was that the U.N.P. governments of this phase proved most unwilling to extend to them any kind of accommodation. This intolerance of the Marxists in U.N.P. circles continues even to the present day. Further, the U.N.P. alleges that the Marxists are infiltrating the S.L.F.P.

Consequently the U.N.P. is chary of the Marxists in Parliament. Between 1947 and 1952 the U.N.P. seldom consulted the Marxist opposition in the arrangement of parliamentary business.[39] The Marxist opposition retaliated by staging protest walkouts on the ground that verbal protest was of no avail.[40] It was the same with motions and resolutions brought up by Marxist M.P.s. They were voted down as a matter of policy.[41] In June 1950 Sir John Kotelawala, explaining the U.N.P.'s intransigence, said that they had 'to fight the opposition not as an opposition but as enemies of the state', emphasising that 'once they got in they would not get out' and there would be 'no guarantee you would ever have a chance to go to the ballot again'.[42]

Generally, however, U.N.P. governments are neglectful of opposition constituencies, Marxist or otherwise. In 1954 the opposition censured the U.N.P. prime minister (Kotelawala) for his 'three boons scheme' which sought to inaugurate construction works proposed by government M.P.s for their constituencies.[43] The opposition also censured him for heeding the requests of defeated U.N.P. candidates and ignoring the representations of the sitting members. The U.N.P. did no better during their 1965–70 phase and there was substance in Dr N. M. Perera's charge that 'all defeated U.N.P. candidates were the unofficial members of Parliament in all constituencies'.[44] But there were many U.N.P. backbenchers who themselves complained with justification that U.N.P. ministers in 1965–70 had become arrogant and aloof and unwilling to entertain their requests.

The emergence of Bandaranaike as the democratic opposition leader after the general election of 1952 improved relations between the two sectors. In February 1953, Bandaranaike remarked that the U.N.P. prime minister (Dudley Senanayake) was 'trying at least in some way to follow closely democratic traditions than was the case in the past' but he cautioned that there was still a great deal to be done.[45] In November 1953 Kotelawala, more for reasons of political self-interest, asked for opposition co-operation on 'matters of grave national importance'.[46] Bandaranaike was included by the prime minister (Kotelawala) as a member of the official delegation which went to New Delhi in early 1954 to negotiate the controversial problem of Indians in Sri Lanka.[47] But in June 1955, Bandaranaike alleged that the Kotelawala government 'was fast drifting towards a form of fascism under the camouflage and guise of democratic practice'[48] and complained that the government had indiscriminately turned down motions brought forward by opposition members and was rushing Bills through the House without giving the opposition adequate time for their consideration.[49]

The Bandaranaike governments on the other hand have been characterised by their tolerance of the opposition. In fact in the debate on the first throne speech of Bandaranaike's M.E.P. government, the L.S.S.P. opposition leader offered his party's co-operation and referred to 'the very unusual feature which will normally never appear in any amendment to the Address of welcoming certain proposals of the government'.[50] Thereafter, however, relations between the government and the L.S.S.P. deteriorated, though the opposition as a whole was well treated.

It was the same with the S.L.F.P. government led by Mrs Bandaranaike (1960–5). Whenever possible, ministers and officials accommodated the requests of opposition M.P.s. F.P. M.P.s who were bitterly opposed to the language and educational policies of the government reported that many of their requests at the administrative level were granted and they attributed this to the fact that there were ministers in the government who suffered from 'conscience'.[51] On national questions such as the Indian question, Mrs Bandaranaike was in touch with the leader of the opposition (Dudley Senanayake) at the time she was negotiating the Indo-Ceylon Agreement of October 1964.

The role of the F.P. in the post-1956 phase has from time to time tended to put the parliamentary process off course, thereby creating serious problems for the government of the day. The adoption of extra-parliamentary methods with persistence to achieve redress of grievances is evidence of a refusal to accept Parliament as the ultimate arbiter. In 1957 the F.P.'s threatened *satyagraha* forced the Prime Minister (Bandaranaike) to enter into a pact with it which was a compromise solution to its principal demands. When this was abandoned in April of the following year, partly because of the crisis caused by the F.P.'s extra-constitutional protest campaigns, a communal holocaust of crisis proportions seized the island, resulting in a year-long state of emergency being imposed. In February–April 1961 a major confrontation between the F.P. and Mrs Bandaranaike's S.L.F.P. government resulted in the latter using the armed forces to quell the disturbances in the Tamil-speaking northern and eastern provinces and a state of emergency which was prolonged for a considerable period of time. During both 1958 and 1961 F.P. M.P.s were placed under detention. The use of such methods of protest with even a small measure of success can undermine confidence in Parliament.[52]

Electoral Demarcation

The framers of the constitution sought to give some surplus representation to minority groups. To accomplish this the territorial principle was modified by providing weightage to the sparsely populated and backward rural areas. This ensured a measure of additional representation for the Ceylon Tamils and Muslims who are resident in the thinly populated areas in the northern and eastern provinces. Provision was further made for multi-member electoral districts, the object being to improve the possibilities of ethnic (Indian Tamils in the plantation districts and Ceylon Tamils in the city of Colombo), religious (Roman Catholics and Muslims) and social (non-*goigama* castes) groups living in the Sinhalese areas securing representation. These arrangements did away with the need to introduce the communal element in the electoral structure.

Thus article 13 (2) and (3) of the Draft Scheme of the Ceylonese ministers ran as follows:

> The total number of persons who according to the census of 1931 was resident in the Province shall be ascertained to the

nearest 75,000. In respect of each 75,000 of this number the Delimitation Commission shall allot one electoral district to the Province and shall add a further number of electoral districts (based on the number of square miles in the Province at the rate of one additional electoral district for each 1,000 square miles of area calculated to the nearest 1,000) as follows:

Western Province	1	North Western Province	3
Central Province	2	North Central Province	4
Southern Province	2	Province of Uva	3
Northern Province	4	Province of Sabaragamuwa	2
Eastern Province	4		

In dividing a province into electoral districts the Delimitation Commission shall provide that each electoral district in the province shall have as nearly as may be an equal number of persons, but shall also take into account the transport facilities of the province, its physical features and the community or diversity of interest of its inhabitants.

The Soulbury commissioners for their part gave the Delimitation Commission a measure of discretion by allowing it to create electorates in those areas.[53]

> ... wherever it shall appear to the Commission that there is a substantial concentration ... of persons united by a community of interests, whether racial, religious or otherwise, but differing in one or more of these respects from the majority of the inhabitants of that area, it shall be at liberty to modify the factor of numerical equality of persons in that area and make such division of the province into electoral districts as may be necessary to render possible the representation of that interest.

The Soulbury commissioners further recommended the creation of multi-member electoral districts in appropriate areas.[54] This would enable minority groups if they were sufficiently united to concentrate all their votes on any one candidate to ensure his election.

These proposals of the Ceylonese ministers and the Soulbury Commission were incorporated in sections 40, 41 and 76 of the constitution.

The constitution provided for the appointment of a Delimitation Commission within one year after the completion of every general census of the island.[55] The Commission, the constitution stipulated, was to comprise three persons 'not actively engaged in politics'.[56] The membership of all delimitation commissions appointed (1946, 1953 and 1959) satisfied this condition. Commissions however have tended to fall in line with the wishes of the government that appointed them.

The first Delimitation Commission was required by section 76(2) of the constitution to demarcate electoral districts, on the basis of area and population, returning ninety-five members in all as shown in Table 5.1, vis-à-vis the island's nine provinces.

TABLE 5.1

DISTRIBUTION OF SEATS (HOUSE OF REPRESENTATIVES) BY PROVINCES, 1947–56

Western	20	Eastern	9
Central	15	North-Western	10
Southern	12	North-Central	5
Northern	7	Uva	7
		Sabaragamuwa	10

Source. *Report of the First Delimitation Commission*, 1946

The Commission demarcated eighty-four single-member electoral districts, four double-member and one three-member.[57] It used the census figures of 1931 to allocate seats on the basis of population as between the nine provinces, but those of the 1946 census to allocate seats within each province. The Commission's forecast of the communal distribution of seats, and the actual outcome at the general election conducted in 1947, were almost similar except where the Muslims were concerned. The relative figures are given in Table 5.2

TABLE 5.2

DISTRIBUTION OF SEATS (HOUSE OF REPRESENTATIVES) BY COMMUNITIES, 1947

Communities	Commission's Forecast	1947 General Election Results
Sinhalese	68	68
Ceylon Tamils	13 or 14	13
Indian Tamils	7 or 8	7
Muslims	4	6
Burghers	–	1

Source. *Report of the First Delimitation Commission*, 1946 and *Ceylon Daily News, Parliament of Ceylon 1947*, Colombo, 1947

The representation as between the various groups in Sri Lanka's plural society was thus based on a kind of balance, thereby enabling each group to obtain its fair share, in some cases even more than their proper due. The Kandyan Sinhalese and Ceylon Tamils, especially, stood to gain most because of the principle of granting weightage to backward districts and to area. The former, strictly on population, were entitled to twenty-five seats in 1947. They obtained between thirty and thirty-six. The Ceylon Tamils would have suffered if all electorates throughout the island were made equal in voting strength. But the districts where they were mainly resident obtained a bonus in seats on the area principle (additional seats for every 1,000 square miles). As a result they obtained thirteen seats, which was one more than their total island population entitled them to. The Indian Tamils on the other hand did not get their proportionate due. This was because their distribution was such as to make it difficult for the Delimitation Commission to carve out seats where they were certain to win, resident as they were in the landlocked plantations situated in the Kandyan Sinhalese areas. In the end they were fortunate to secure seven seats. But they counted in fourteen Sinhalese constituencies as well, and in these their votes went to the candidates of left-wing parties.

The Delimitation Commission of 1946 took into consideration the factor of caste in demarcating constituencies. At least two constituencies in the Sinhalese areas were made dual-member ones to enable defined caste groups to secure the return of one of their number. In other cases, the commissioners said that in drawing the boundary lines of electorates they had endeavoured whereever possible to include areas in which the underprivileged caste groups were resident within the electoral district concerned, so that the members of these caste groups could have a voice in the election of a representative.

The citizenship legislation and amendments to the elections ordinance of 1948 and 1949, already referred to, upset the arrangement of this structure of representation. Their effect was to exclude the vast majority of Indian Tamils from the franchise. As a result the voting strength in at least seven electorates was reduced to ridiculously low levels compared to what it had been in 1947, as the figures in Table 5.3 indicate.

A further consequence was that at the general election of 1952, the Sinhalese gained a greater number of seats than their population entitled them to, seventy-five as against sixty-eight, while the Indian Tamils lost all their seats. This situation was repeated at every general election thereafter. However those Indian Tamils who qualified under the Acts of 1948 and 1949 and were included in the electoral registers exerted some influence in constituencies where the contest was close.

TABLE 5.3
VOTING STRENGTH IN SELECTED CONSTITUENCIES, 1947 AND 1952

Constituencies	General Elections 1947	1952
Nuwara Eliya	24,295	9,279
Talawakele	19,299	2,912
Kotagala	17,092	7,749
Nawalapitiya	22,580	10,082
Maskeliya	24,427	8,703
Haputale	11,063	7,051
Badulla	43,396	28,151

Source. *Ceylon Daily News, Parliament of Ceylon 1947* and *Parliament of Ceylon 1956*

A census was held in 1953 and a Delimitation Commission appointed shortly thereafter. It was wound up by a constitutional amendment enacted in 1954.

In 1959 Parliament, by constitutional amendment, authorised the appointment of a Delimitation Commission, though no new census had been conducted.[58] The Commission was empowered to effect a fresh demarcation of electorates but was excluded from creating constituencies to help caste interests on the ground that caste promoted divisive tendencies. The Commission was further required to award representation to a province on the basis of one seat for every 75,000 units of population, citizens as well as non-citizens, while also retaining the earlier principle of one seat for every 1,000 square miles of area. However, the counting of citizens and non-citizens for the purpose of assigning seats to a province resulted in the Kandyan Sinhalese areas continuing to enjoy the over-weightage in representation they had secured from the disfranchisement of the Indian Tamils.

The demarcation effected in 1959 which became effective from the general election of March 1960 onwards provided for 145 electoral districts returning 151 members. Of these 145 electorates, 140 were single-member, four were two-member and one was three-member. The provincial distribution of seats on the basis of area and population is set out in Table 5.4.

TABLE 5.4

DISTRIBUTION OF SEATS (HOUSE OF REPRESENTATIVES) BY PROVINCES, 1960–70

Western	35	Eastern	11
Central	23	North-Western	16
Southern	19	North Central	8
Northern	13	Uva	10
		Sabragamuwa	16

Source. *Report of the Delimitation Commission*, 1959

The Commission's forecast of the communal distribution of seats and the actual results at the general election which followed immediately thereafter (March 1960) are set out in Table 5.5.

TABLE 5.5

DISTRIBUTION OF SEATS (HOUSE OF REPRESENTATIVES) BY COMMUNITIES, MARCH 1960

Communities	Commission's Forecast	March 1960 General Election
Sinhalese	124 or 125	123
Ceylon Tamils	18	18
Muslims	8 or 9	9
Indian Tamils	—	—
Burghers	—	1 [59]

Source. *Report of the Delimitation Commission*, 1959 and *Ceylon Daily News, Parliament of Ceylon 1960*

Though the Commission was specifically instructed not to take caste into consideration, it nevertheless carved out constituencies wherever the caste and economic factor coincided, as for example where the occupation of a caste was directly concerned with an economic pursuit such as fishing.

This system of representation from 1947 onwards was designed, as its author (Jennings) claimed, to provide weightage to the rural as against the urban population. Jennings argued that the urban population 'are necessarily much more highly organised' and that in the past they had provided most of the members of the State

Council even in the rural areas.[60] It was also his view that his system provided 'weightage to the backward areas as against the more populous and wealthier areas'.[61] In other words, its effect was to deprive those low-country Sinhalese areas which are more advanced and politically conscious of the representation that was their due. On the other hand, the Kandyan Sinhalese provinces with an overwhelmingly rural population which is generally respectful of tradition and status gained. The Delimitation Commission of 1946 estimated that the low-country Sinhalese population was, in proportion to their population, entitled to forty-one seats whereas under their delimitation they would probably obtain thirty-two. The Kandyan Sinhalese on a proportionate basis should have got twenty-five seats but were assigned roughly thirty-six by the Commission.

In its actual working, this scheme of representation placed left-wing parties at a disadvantage. Most of their propaganda had been concentrated in the low-country Sinhalese areas of the south-western coastal belt and the developed plantation districts to the south of the Kelani river. It is from these areas that they drew most of their electoral support. But it was these areas, among others, that lost the representation that was their proportionate due.

It was also clear from this that the principle of one man, one vote was not followed. This was because the provision for weightage for the backward and sparsely populated areas resulted in wide disparities in the voting strength of constituencies as between provinces. These disparities increased further with the disfranchisement of the Indian Tamil population. In the general election of 1947, out of ninety-five constituencies, there were twenty-three which returned members of Parliament with a voting strength of between 40,000 to 60,000, while there were twenty-six with a voting strength of between 5,000 and 25,000. The remainder had voting strengths distributed between these two sets of figures. At the general election of 1952, the disparities were more marked with the disfranchisement of the Indian Tamils. There were twenty-five constituencies with 40,000 to 60,000 voters and thirty-one with 5,000 to 25,000 voters. In the 1956 general election, there were nine constituencies with over 60,000 voters, eight with between 20,000–25,000, eleven with 15,000 to 20,000, two with 10,000 to 15,000 and three with 5,000 to 10,000. One constituency had a voting strength of below 5,000. With the fresh delimitation of 1959 the electoral districts within a province were made nearly equal in the numbers of voters, but the average voting figures in electoral districts as between provinces continued to remain as disparate as they had been in the past.

The Public Services

The public services are even today considered the main avenue of secure employment by the majority of high school and university-educated persons in the island. Good salary scales, automatic increments, except where efficiency bars have to be crossed, security of tenure, certain fringe benefits like restricted facilities for free rail travel and concessions in regard to charges levied in state hospitals, and pensions at retirement are the main attractions.

Further, the values that prevailed in colonial times, of staff appointments in the government sector being associated with status, power and the right to disburse some patronage still persist. The public servants of the executive and administrative grades continue to wield influence and authority and are regarded as socially well placed. They can, if they wish, improve their social and economic position through a matrimonial alliance which could bring a dowry and entry into the upper rungs of Ceylonese society. This used to be common practice, with the usual exceptions, in the immediate post-independence decade, but it is becoming less and less so as of recent times.

Other avenues for employment began to make themselves available as the years progressed. Ceylonisation of managerial and technical staffs by foreign concerns and increased Ceylonese participation in trade and industry provided alternate opportunities. But by and large the biggest employer of educated personnel next to the government departments are the quasi-government undertakings such as public corporations and state commercial ventures which multiplied in the post-1956 phase.

It was realised that in a socially heterogeneous society like that of Sri Lanka, with slow rates of economic development, the competition for jobs in the public sector was certain to create unhealthy inter-group competition and invite political interference from members of Parliament, parliamentary secretaries and from ministers under pressure from constituents and supporters alike. A constitutionally entrenched Public Service Commission could serve as a buffer against such possibilities as well as create confidence among minority groups of all types by impartial methods for the selection and promotion of personnel. It is precisely these purposes that the Ceylonese Public Service Commission was intended to serve when it was created.[62]

Section 60(1) of the constitution stated:

> The appointment, transfer, dismissal and disciplinary control of public officers is vested in the Public Service Commission subject to the proviso that appointments and transfers to the office of attorney-general shall be made by the governor-general.

Subsection 2 of the above section defined 'transfer' as meaning 'a transfer involving an increase of salary'. Section 61 stated:

> The Public Service Commission may, by Order published in the Government Gazette, delegate to any public officer subject to such conditions as may be specified in the Order, any of the powers vested in the Commission by subsection (1) of section 60. Any person dissatisfied with any decision made by any public officer under any power delegated as aforesaid may appeal therefrom to the Commission and the decision of the Commission on such appeal shall be final.

The Commission comprised three members appointed by the governor-general on the advice of the prime minister. The constitution stipulated that one at least of the members should be a person who had not held public or judicial office at any time during the five years immediately preceding appointment. Membership was for five years, with the possibility of reappointment. The Commission was constitutionally protected from undue political interference and influences.

During the twenty-five years of the Commission's existence, there were only four instances of members being asked to serve a second time. In one of these instances the prime minister was reported to have expressed the view that if the member was not reappointed he could be a source of political embarrassment to his government, as he would have been free to campaign against him and his party.

One of the members of the Commission was nominated by the governor-general (on prime-ministerial advice) to be chairman.

The choice of appointees indicated that the relevant considerations were (1) dependability, with some similarity in political outlook; and (2) the ability to represent the major ethnic, religious or linguistic groups in Sri Lanka's plural society. The first ensured a co-operative Commission which would not interpret its constitutional rights too rigidly. The second created a measure of confidence vis-à-vis the various important groupings. This type of construction did not however mean that political or communal factors always influenced the Commission when it made its decisions.

Had the Commission interpreted its powers and functions in the strictest constitutional terms, it would have isolated itself from the political executive and as a result imperilled the whole principle of ministerial responsibility. Ministers in the government could have laid the blame on an allegedly over-independent Commission for their failure to secure reliable officials such as they required in order to have their policies and programmes implemented honestly and efficiently. Fortunately this did not happen.

Since members of the Commission and its chairman were appointed for a fixed term of five years, their terms did overlap with changes in government and in the premiership. Yet at no time did there develop friction or deadlock between itself and the prime ministers of the day. Only on one occasion, in 1970, did all the members of the commission resign when the government which had appointed it was swept out of office at the general election held in May of that year. But its members resigned voluntarily, and did not have to be removed from office according to the procedure laid down in the constitution. Section 58(5) of the constitution stated that the governor-general (on the advice of the prime minister) could 'for cause assigned' remove any member of the Commission from office.

Under the constitution certain specified appointments were outside the purview of the Commission. Subject to these, the appointment, transfer, dismissal and disciplinary control of public officers was vested in the Commission.

On all important appointments the Commission acted in close consultation with the prime minister.[63] When senior positions had to be filled, the minister concerned indicated to the prime minister his preference. The prime minister, provided he was satisfied that no serious injustice was being done, informed the chairman of the Commission of the decision. The channel of communication was however through the prime minister. The Commission was persistent in its refusal to deal directly with any minister.

Other appointments to the public service were on the basis of open competitive examinations or selection by interviews conducted by specially constituted boards.

The Commission thus enjoyed a certain pre-eminence in the administrative and constitutional life of the country. It was insulated from the political branch of government but, as already said, it could not have afforded to be too independent for this would have brought it into conflict with the prime minister and the cabinet. But since it was not entitled to answer Parliament for its actions, there was the inevitable tendency for the government of the day to use it as a screen to make appointments on political and other grounds. The Commission consequently became a continuing object of criticism, and demands were made that its powers and functions be redefined.

The overall business of co-ordinating the work of departments within a Ministry and of assisting each minister in administering them was in terms of section 51(2) of the constitution vested in a permanent secretary. He functioned under the general direction and control of his minister. Under the constitution, he was appointed by the governor-general on prime-ministerial advice. The wishes of the minister concerned were of course ascertained. Ministers dissatisfied with a particular permanent secretary could have him transferred.

The Organisation of the Administration

With independence certain necessary changes were introduced. Permanent secretaries took on the task of co-ordinating the work of departments within their respective ministries. The Treasury was invested with greater powers. But the basic colonial pattern of administration was retained, and markedly so at the provincial level. The monopoly of most of the important and coveted positions in the administrative set-up by the exclusive civil service was also maintained till as late as the mid-1960s.

Until 1970 the Treasury stood at the apex of the governmental system. Its prime responsibility was to scrutinise and supervise the expenditure of the departments, look into matters of cadre, and manage the combined services which included the civil service (later the administrative service) and the more important sections of the clerical services. It also controlled those public servants who did not come under the authority of either the Public Service Commission or permanent secretaries or heads of departments. Its numerous duties and increasing volume of work made it a veritable bottleneck and the inevitable delays made it the repeated target of criticism by members of Parliament, the general public, public servants and even ministers of successive governments.

Some of the functions of the Treasury in relation to expenditure and approval of new appointments, expansion of departments, etc. which involved finance were taken over in 1965 by the new Ministry of Planning established by Dudley Senanayake's 'national government' in that year. The Ministry of Planning continues to perform these functions even today. A further erosion of the Treasury's powers took place in 1970 with regard to its management of the public services when the U.F. government of Mrs Bandaranaike created a new Ministry of Public Administration.

There are some two hundred government departments today, each in the charge of a head. The increase in the number of departments is phenomenal, the result of the multiplication of responsibilities within each department, making further specialisation necessary, and also because of subdepartments being elevated to departmental level. Departmental heads have tended to function in much the same way as during the days of the pre-independence Donoughmore constitution, making the task of co-ordination within a Ministry more difficult. Departments then were self-contained units with their heads being in overall charge.

The co-ordination of the work of departments within a Ministry is the responsibility of the permanent secretary. However, this official is more preoccupied with administrative duties which should really devolve on heads of departments.

At the provincial level the form of administration until 1970 was mainly an extension of, or modification of the colonial structure. Up to 1955, for administrative purposes the island was divided into nine provinces, each in the charge of a government agent. Each province was divided into a convenient number of districts, depending on its size and accessibility, each in charge of an assistant government agent who was under the overall supervision and control of the government agent of the province.

In 1955, this administrative structure was altered by Act of Parliament, but the change was only one of form. The district now became the principal administrative unit in the charge of a government agent. There were twenty-one such districts in 1955, increased to twenty-three subsequently.

The office of the government agent is called the *kachcheri*. During colonial times the *kachcheri* used to be the centre of provincial activity when, as the Commission on the Organisation, Staffing and Operative Methods of Government Departments stated in its report of March 1948, 'communications were more difficult than they are now, and it was considered expedient to place a senior officer in charge of a province with merely general instructions, leaving him free to direct every form of government activity in it'. The situation changed with the multiplication of government departments in Colombo and their being invested with island-wide functions. The government agent nevertheless still continues to be responsible for a number of not altogether unimportant functions. He has besides a responsibility not clearly defined for the general welfare of the inhabitants of the area in his charge.

The criticism against this system of provincial administration was that it was outmoded and a colonial relic unsuited to the requirements of modern government. It was said that its machinery was slow and cumbersome and that there was not enough local participation in an over-centralised Colombo-linked structure.

An important change was therefore introduced in 1971 when the government agent was entrusted with functions in regard to economic and social development. This was in keeping with the U.F. government's socialist policies in the area of planned economic development and democratisation of the machinery of administration. The *kachcheri* still continues to be the important centre of administration, but the government agent now functions in consultation with Divisional Development Councils which have been set up with the specific task of organising economic activity and promoting the development of the area over which they have jurisdiction (for a detailed description of their functions, etc. see below, p. 233).

An indigenous system of administration through officials specially selected, who until 1959 were assisted by native chiefs of various types, operates to assist the government agent in his manifold duties.[64] A district is divided into a number of divisions each in the charge of a divisional revenue officer who acts under the orders and instructions of the government agent. These divisions are now (since1972) being converted into new administrative units with the divisional officer's designation being changed to that of assistant government agent.

The divisional revenue officers are selected separately by competition examination, as vacancies occur, on an area-cum-linguistic basis, for the Kandyan Sinhalese, the low-country Sinhalese, Ceylon Tamil, and Muslim areas. They replaced the chief headmen – the *muhandiramas*, *mudaliyars*, *ratemahatmayas*, *maniagars* and *vanniyars* – of an earlier period who were selected by the government agents on family and caste considerations. This system was abolished in 1946 shortly before independence because it gave rise to many evils.

The divisional revenue officer's administrative area, the division, comprises a number of headmen's areas in charge of indigenous officials known as superior headmen. The latter were selected by the government agents, again for the influence they wielded in their area and for their family connections. Their duties varied from district to district. Generally they were expected to supervise the work of village headmen, inquire into petitions, investigate crimes in unpoliced areas, carry out certain duties in connection with crown lands, and provide general assistance to the divisional revenue officers.

A headman's area consisted of a group of villages which was in charge of a village headman. The latter stood at the very base of this indigenous administrative structure and was the link in the general provincial administrative system between the government and the people in the rural areas. Local influence, family, caste the ownership of some property were the grounds for the selection of these officials. Before improvements were made in the administrative system, the village headman was entrusted with a host of duties relating to policing, irrigation, rural development, land, excise and forests. His main responsibilities later were in connection with the preparation of voters' lists, distribution of social welfare and assisting his superiors in the general task of rural administration.

This native system of administration was made liberal use of by the Dutch and British, but was frowned on by the Ceylonese from about the 1920s because of its many defects – its feudalistic and oppressive methods, corruption, and the fact of it being ill-suited to the needs of modern administration. Various Commissions of Inquiry looked into the system, but though modifications were introduced the system itself was kept going. Even after independence, the conservative U.N.P. governments in office up to 1956 found the system useful, especially because it helped them politically. With a socialistically-inclined government returned to power in 1956, the process was set in motion for its abolition by decisions made in October 1956 and 15 June 1959. A category of officials styled *grama seva niladharis* specially recruited by examination took the place of these headmen and with this change the time-honoured system of government through native chiefs with local influence passed out of existence.

Participatory Democracy

It was the U.F.'s policy to bring the administration closer to the people and for the latter to exercise a measure of vigilance over public servants so as to ensure that power was not abused. The U.F., in its Common Programme for the general election of May 1970, had condemned the administrative set-up as a colonial inheritance and as being 'bureaucratic and inefficient' and 'thoroughly unsuited to ensuring the speedy fulfilment of today's needs'.

The democratic devices through which the U.F. said it would set right these defects were (1) people's committees; (2) divisional development councils; (3) elected employees' councils; and (4) advisory committees in government offices. All of these institutions have started functioning, though on a limited scale. The P.L.F. insurrection of April 1971 delayed their inauguration for a number of months as the U.F. government was not sure whether P.L.F. members or sympathisers would find their way into these bodies and utilise them for their purposes.

People's committees. Legislation was enacted in 1971 to regulate the membership and spell out the powers of these bodies. 1,786 of the proposed 9,000 committees were established in December 1971 with a membership of around 22,000. They were started on an experimental basis in one local authority in each electorate for a trial period of one year, the local authority concerned being designated by the relevant member of Parliament. The committees are indirectly constituted and nominations for membership are invited from M.P.s, local organisations, societies, trade unions and the general public. Nominations are sent to the officer in charge of these committees, called the Janata commissioner, whose office processes them and prepares a summary in respect of each electorate. The summarised list is put up to the minister in whose charge these committees are placed – the minister of local government, public administration and home affairs. The minister makes the selections. He also appoints the chairmen of these committees. In making the selections, the minister gives due consideration to the recommendations of the local M.P. The minister in fact circularised M.P.s requesting them to forward to him fifteen names of persons suitable for appointment, 'in the M.P.'s order of preference'.[65]

Each committee consists of eleven members, three of whom are between the ages of eighteen and twenty-five, and one is the elected member representing the ward (the electoral unit of a local authority) which constitutes the committee's area of authority. The minister appoints the others. Persons who are (1) guilty of specified criminal offences or against whom inquiries in respect of such offences were pending; (2) uncertified bankrupts; (3) of unsound mind; (4) less than eighteen years of age; (5) not ordinarily resident in the area of authority of the committee; and (6) M.P.s or government servants, are disqualified from membership. Further, a family cannot have more than one of its members serving on a committee.

Objections were raised as to the method of composition of the committees. Opposition members asked why these could not be constituted by direct election. The view of the minister in charge was that the organisation of elections for some 9,000 committees would be a physically impossible task for the department of elections with its existing staff and machinery. The minister also argued that if members were answerable to electors they would be subject to pressures and would not be able to carry out their functions efficiently and honestly. The committees, he said, would be representative in that the local M.P., whether of the government or the opposition, would play an important role in the selection of members, and they would go out of existence with the dissolving of each Parliament. The opposition argued that with the government having on its side 121 of the 151 elected members of Parliament, they could afford to justify such a procedure for the selection of members.

M.P.s were cautioned not to interfere with the work of committees, especially when these were proceeding against anti-social elements, even if the latter were their supporters. The committees for their part were advised by the minister in charge to work in close collaboration with their M.P.s whatever their party ties were.[66]

These committees are invested with fairly extensive powers in the areas over which they exercise authority. These include (1) exercising vigilance over the activities of government departments, local authorities and other institutions whether financed wholly or partly by government; (2) preventing the abuse of authority, wastefulness, neglect of duty, misuse of public funds and corruption; (3) watching the activities of dealers in essential commodities and initiating action to stop any irregularities; and (4) promoting liaison between the people and government institutions. The committees are also expected to agitate for and draw attention to local needs, and suggest remedial measures, and to assist local villagers to make representations on individual or group grievances. They also have the power to report public officers, write to government departments which are obliged to reply to them, institute legal action against persons in certain kinds of cases, and get copies of letters not considered confidential from state and state-assisted establishments. But the committees are prohibited from interfering with the judiciary or the armed forces and from entering the home of an individual or family.

Members were repeatedly advised by the prime minister, the minister in charge, and the Janata commissioner to refrain from exceeding their powers or using these to persecute or take revenge on their opponents.[67]

During the general election of May 1970 the U.N.P. alleged that these committees would become the instruments of a totalitarian dictatorship which would oppress the ordinary people. An opposition member also expressed misgivings about the possibility of these committees being converted into ready-made organisations for a general election for the ruling U.F.[68]

Worker's councils. These are elected by secret ballot by employees in state enterprises such as corporations, boards and factories and are representative as far as is possible of the various sections in the workplaces. Staff and supervisory grades are excluded from voting. The weightage to be given to the different sections in each workplace is determined by the Ministry concerned in consultation with the workforce in the enterprise involved. Term of office is a year.

These councils function only in an advisory capacity. They associate the workers in the process of management and they collaborate with the latter in all matters connected with production and the running of the concerns, changes in programmes, etc. The management in fact affords all facilities for the functioning of these councils. The latter are, however, not expected to assume the role of trade unions. But in the elections to a number of them there were the usual rivalries between trade unions affiliated to rival political parties.

Advisory committees. These were set up in most government departments and corporations. Generally they are intended 'to combat bureaucracy, inefficiency, corruption, sabotage and waste', and with these objectives in view they make representations to the authorities concerned. As yet there has not been any proper demarcation of their functions, different committees interpreting these in different ways. Some of them are reported to have involved themselves in trade union matters, which are beyond their prescribed areas of action. In other cases administrators had invited committees to send observers to meetings of selection boards (for appointments) so as to assure employees that there is impartiality in appointments, but some advisory committees are reported to have attempted to seize the opportunity to clamour for trade union rights. On the other hand, production committees, as these advisory committees have come to be called in this instance, set up at the work sites of the mammoth State Engineering Corporation are reported to have been highly successful.[69]

Divisional development councils. These institutions are agencies of the Ministry of Planning and Employment operating at grass roots level. They comprise (1) officials of the central government serving in the area concerned; and (2) the elected representatives of the people of the area inclusive of members of local government bodies. The government agents and district revenue officers help in running these institutions.

The councils are expected to work out small-scale development projects in agriculture and industry for their respective areas in collaboration with officials of the Department of Agriculture and the Ministry of Industries. They are then submitted to the

Regional Development Division of the Ministry of Planning for final approval. The central government provides the finances for these projects. These not only help to develop the local area in question but also provide employment to the unemployed and under-employed there. During the year 1971, these development councils and the Ministry of Planning and Employment were together able to create some 4,700 jobs involving 223 projects.[70]

THE REPUBLICAN CONSTITUTION OF 1972

The Making of the Constitution

At the general election of May 1970, the U.F. had asked the electors for a mandate to frame a new constitution in the following terms:[71]

> To permit the members of Parliament you elect to function simultaneously as a Constituent Assembly to draft, adopt and operate a new constitution. The constitution will declare Ceylon to be a free, sovereign and independent republic pledged to realise the objective of a socialist democracy; and it will also secure fundamental rights and freedoms to all citizens.

The U.F. received more than a two-thirds majority at the election, and in keeping with its pledges the prime minister (Mrs Bandaranaike) wrote individually to members of the House of Representatives inviting them to participate in the proceedings of a Constituent Assembly which she was specially convening on 19 July 1970. Two of the major opposition parties, the U.N.P. and Tamil F.P. at first hesitated but after considerable second thoughts agreed to the proposal.

The Constituent Assembly had its inaugural meeting *not* in the precincts of the House of Representatives but at the Navarangahala Hall.[72] This was evidence of a determination to effect a complete break with the past which to the U.F. government had all the connotations of an alien imposition. The prime minister herself, in moving formally the resolution convening the Constituent Assembly, underlined this fact in her opening remarks when she said:[73]

> The Constituent Assembly which we have met to establish, and

> the constitution which the Constituent Assembly will draft, enact and establish will derive their authority from the people of Sri Lanka and not from the power and authority assumed and exercised by the British crown and Parliament in establishing the present constitution of Ceylon nor from the constitution they gave us.

The prime minister indicated that there were three objectives which the new constitution would seek to achieve, *viz.* (1) strengthen the oneness of the nation; (2) establish a socialist society; and (3) safeguard the country's freedom, independence and national sovereignty.[74]

A minister of constitutional affairs was specially appointed for the purpose of organising the work of drafting the new constitution. In actual fact it was he who ultimately took on the responsibility of framing the thirty-eight basic resolutions which provided the groundwork for the new structure. These received the approval of the cabinet with minor emendations. The minister concerned was Dr Colvin R. de Silva, a Trotskyist who also holds the portfolio of plantation industries.

A ministerial subcommittee comprising the minister of constitutional affairs and six others was entrusted with the task of giving form and substance to the proposed constitution. Of its seven members, four were from the S.L.F.P., two from the L.S.S.P. and one from the C.P. A drafting committee of thirteen inclusive of the minister of constitutional affairs was appointed to put into legal shape the various matters that were to go into the new constitution. Most of its members (nine) were lawyers. Some of them did the spadework in looking up sources and reading up material from books and documents dealing with the constitutions of other countries.

The U.F. had given some thought to the question of launching a Constituent Assembly and formulating a new constitution about a year and a half before the general election of May 1970. A committee with Dr de Silva as its chairman had given expression to the 'ideas and principles' that should govern the constitution and these had been reported to the highest co-ordinating committee of the parties of the U.F. The co-ordinating committee had been presided over by Mrs Bandaranaike herself, and it had discussed and re-shaped the suggestions put forward by the Dr de Silva committee. The U.F. cabinet had therefore in the phraseology of Dr de Silva gone to the Constituent Assembly with 'broad ideas in reasonable shape'.

Dr de Silva was careful to emphasise on more occasions than one that the U.F. government did not carry a draft in their pockets which they would spring on the Constituent Assembly. The prime minister herself in her opening address when convening the Constituent Assembly said that regarding the content of the constitution she would not try to anticipate its deliberations. The 'broad ideas' were more in the nature of an expression of intentions and a criticism of some of the features of the existing constitution. But they did give a definite indication as to how the new constitution would be utilised to usher in the radical economic and social changes the U.F. was proposing.

Early evidence of how a U.F. government would make Parliament its instrument was provided at a seminar organised by the U.F.'s socialist study circle on 11 December 1969.[75] At this seminar Dr de Silva stressed that Parliament must, if the U.F. was to implement its socialist policies, be characterised 'by leadership and not consensus'. If it was to reflect the views of the people, it must, he said (1) do what it was elected for; and (2) realise that the people who elected it must be brought in direct support of the administration. In short, it was Dr de Silva's view that the parliamentary system should be made use of to introduce far-reaching reforms in the administration, including the army and the police, property ownership, and the political processes.

It is significant that most of the changes that Dr de Silva envisaged in regard to democratisation of the administration, control of business enterprises, and the imposition of a ceiling on incomes, etc. was effected under the old constitution and did not have to wait till a new basic law was established.

Further amplification of the U.F.'s views on the existing constitution was contained in a broadcast talk by the minister of constitutional affairs (Dr de Silva) in September 1970.[76] The minister attributed the defects of the existing structure to (1) its unalterable entrenched clauses which though intended to safeguard minority groups against legislative discrimination were looked upon as an infringement on the sovereignty of Parliament by the U.F.; (2) judicial review of legislation which could negate the intentions of Parliament; (3) the colonial-style administrative machinery; (4) the Second Chamber (the Senate) which 'frustrates the will of the people'; and (5) the inequality of the franchise which under the existing delimitation system 'results in one vote in some constituencies being equivalent to five votes in others'. Although Dr de Silva did not say so, this method of demarcating electorates, as stated by us earlier, placed voters in the left-influenced densely populated south-western seaboard and the Kelani valley area at a disadvantage while it worked to the benefit of rural-based parties such as the S.L.F.P. and U.N.P.

Again it might be mentioned here that the U.F. government made use of the existing machinery for constitutional amendment to do away with some of these defects – the abolition of the Senate and appeals to the Judicial Committee of the Privy Council in the last quarter of 1971.

The final product of the endeavours of the ministerial sub-committee, the various committees of the Constituent Assembly, and of the latter body itself was a constitution not very different from the one it replaced. Many of its features were retained, and where changes were effected these were adapted to existing procedures, such as for example the appointment and removal of the president of the republic, or they merely sanctioned practices and conventions that had become part of the country's accepted constitutional mores, like those relating to the procedure for making senior appointments in the public services. Further, wherever it was felt that there had been an abuse of power by authorities under the discarded constitution, care was taken to spell out their obligations in greater detail in the new constitution to ensure that similar situations would not arise again.

The new constitution was therefore rooted in the past. As one of its founding fathers, Dr N. M. Perera, the Trotskyist minister of finance remarked when he seconded the prime minister's resolution for the convening of the Constituent Assembly (on 19 July 1970):[77]

> We have had over forty years of experience of limited political freedom but with a full franchise. We have in some ways utilised the valued portions of that experience. We would have to discard some of the institutions associated with the recent period of our history. We would have to modify others and

> also construct new institutions. No people can build entirely a new constitution. All of us are circumscribed by our own past, by our social habits and inclinations.

But though tied to the past in various ways, the constitution thus framed was the result of the endeavours of the representatives of the Ceylonese people themselves and it was to this fact that the framers laid their greatest claim.

Procedures

Reference was made to the drafting committee of thirteen and the ministerial subcommittee of seven. The members of the latter could in fact be regarded as the founding fathers of the constitution. It was the body which approved every step regarding the drafting of the new constitution. Final sanction was of course given by the cabinet itself.

The Constituent Assembly, for its part, set up on 12 August 1970 its most important instrument for the preparation of a draft – the Steering and Subjects Committee with the prime minister herself as its chairman. The committee comprised seventeen members, nine from the S.L.F.P., two from the L.S.S.P., one from the C.P. and one from the T.C., making thirteen in all from the U.F. government and four from the opposition, comprising two members of the U.N.P. and two from the Tamil F.P.

Besides reflecting all shades of political opinion in the Constituent Assembly, this Steering and Subjects Committee was also representative of all the major groupings, save the Indian Tamils, in Ceylon's plural society – low-country Sinhalese (six), Kandyan Sinhalese (six), Ceylon Tamils (three), Muslims (one) and Burghers (one). The main organisation of the Indian Tamil plantation workers, the C.W.C., protested that the Indian Tamils had not been provided any representation in the Constituent Assembly.

The Steering and Subjects Committee entrusted the minister of constitutional affairs with the task of preparing a set of draft basic resolutions which could form the basis for its discussions and work. The minister was anxious to elicit as much public opinion as possible before preparing these resolutions and therefore with the approval of the committee and the Constituent

Assembly invited the public to send him their views so as to, as he himself said, 'influence the thinking of the men entrusted with this historic endeavour'.[78] The minister explained that a 'mountain of memoranda' as a result reached him from members of the public, as well as from numerous organisations including political parties.[79] Classified summaries were made of all the memoranda received and these were circulated among the members of the Constituent Assembly. The minister said that the drafting committee had 'read them all so that they were in our minds' when involved in the task of drafting the basic resolutions.[80] These were then discussed and approved by the cabinet before they were submitted to the Steering and Subjects Committee for its consideration. The minister claimed that he believed that the thirty-eight basic resolutions were 'completely in accord with U.F. and government policy'.[81]

The Steering and Subjects Committee released the thirty-eight basic resolutions to the public on 18 January 1971, who were invited for a second time to express their views on them in the form of amendments or additions or counter-resolutions. These representations were considered by the members of the committee when they met in February 1971. Members of the Constituent Assembly were also provided with the texts of these representations so that they could, on the basis of these, formulate their own proposals, if they wished to, when the resolutions came before the Assembly for its consideration.

Broadly the basic resolutions dealt with the place of Buddhism in the proposed new republic of Sri Lanka, principles of state policy, fundamental rights and freedoms, the National Assembly, the president of the republic, the prime minister and council of ministers, the constitutional court, the administration of justice, the public services, and the place of the Sinhalese and Tamil languages in legislation, administration and judicial proceedings.

In February 1971, the Steering and Subjects Committee, after considering the representations from the general public, etc. unanimously adopted the basic resolutions in the form in which these had been submitted by the minister of constitutional affairs. The committee did not think that any major changes needed to be made to the text. The resolutions were then officially published as those of the Steering and Subjects Committee and the general public were invited for a third time to submit any amendments, additions or counter-resolutions for the committee's consideration. These were considered by the committee which decided that no changes were necessary to the original text. The resolutions were then submitted to the Constituent Assembly where each of these was debated at length. They were adopted in their original form, without amendment, by a majority vote.

The Tamil F.P. opposed the resolutions relating to the Tamil language. It moved an amendment to the resolutions in question in which it asked that Sinhalese and Tamil be recognised as the official languages of Ceylon and the languages of the courts.[82] This was rejected by a majority in the Constituent Assembly. The party further opposed Resolution 23 which provided that the Sinhalese language should be 'the language of the courts and of tribunals empowered by law to administer justice' throughout the island. Resolutions 24 and 25, however, provided for all relevant documents and proceedings to be translated into the Tamil language, and for litigants in the Tamil-speaking northern and eastern provinces of Ceylon to transact judicial business and participate in judicial proceedings there in the Tamil language. Resolution 23 also stated that the future National Assembly *may* make provision for the use of a language other than the Sinhalese language in judicial administration in the original courts in the northern and eastern provinces.

The Tamil F.P. was not satisfied with these provisions. Its leadership argued that the word 'may' left the issue in doubt and provision for the use of a language other than Sinhalese could well mean the English language.[83] As a compromise, the spokesmen for the U.F. government agreed to make a public declaration in the Constituent Assembly that the National Assembly when created would 'give the topmost priority to the introduction of legislation to make Tamil a language of administration in the original courts in the northern and eastern provinces'.[84] The opposition U.N.P. agreed not to oppose such a move. The Tamil F.P. however took up the position that it could not place any reliance 'on the word of the leaders of the Sinhalese people'.[85] The relevant legislation was nevertheless enacted in 1973.

In a final attempt at compromise, an accredited spokesman of the Tamil F.P. stated on 25 June 1971 in the Constituent Assembly that his party would drop its demand for parity of status for Tamil if the provisions of Bandaranaike's agreement of

July 1957 with the F.P. were incorporated in the proposed new constitution, if Tamils wherever they lived in Ceylon were administered in their own language and if the Tamil language was declared the language of administration for the northern and eastern provinces.[86] He added that his party would not object to Sinhalese also being a language of administration in these provinces. These proposals failed to evoke the necessary responses from the government side and towards the end of 1 June the Tamil F.P. withdrew in protest from the proceedings of the Constituent Assembly. Later the minister of constitutional affairs asked the Tamil F.P. to return to the Assembly, participate in its deliberations and express its views 'right up to the last moment', but the party was unresponsive.[87]

The U.N.P.'s working committee, also seriously debated the advisability of its members of Parliament withdrawing from the proceedings of the Constituent Assembly but it did not take a final decision on this matter.

In particular, the U.N.P. was opposed to Basic Resolution 7 which provided that the existing Constituent Assembly should continue for a term of six years from the date on which the new constitution was promulgated, which in effect would have given the Parliament elected in May 1970 a run of about eight years at the maximum, unless Parliament was dissolved earlier. The party was also unhappy with Basic Resolution 4(1) (v) pertaining to 'Principles of State Policy'. This required the state, in enacting legislation, to provide for 'the development of collective forms of property in the means of production, distribution and exchange, such as state property and cooperative property'.

These 'Principles' are of course not legally binding, but they set a goal structure for Ceylonese society which makes it clear that it should be in the direction of a socialist democracy. U.F. spokesmen argued that these 'Principles' were based on the widest possible consensus of all sections of Ceylonese opinion. But the U.N.P.'s leader, Dudley Senanayake, argued that his party was pledged to realise 'democratic socialism', not the objectives of a socialist democracy, which he equated with increasing state control and governmental interference in the private sector. The U.N.P. leader deplored the absence of any provision for the safeguarding of the rights of private property.

The U.N.P. was finally strongly opposed to the provisions relating to the judiciary. It felt that these would detract from its independence. The minister of constitutional affairs argued that while he had provided for the independence of the judiciary, the U.F. government was not willing to permit the supremacy of the judiciary over the legislature.[88]

After the Constituent Assembly had adopted the last of the thirty-eight Basic Resolutions on 10 July 1971, the minister of constitutional affairs was requested by the Steering and Subjects Committee to prepare the first draft of the constitution, in conformity with these Resolutions, for its consideration. A draft was accordingly prepared and presented to the cabinet in December 1971. The cabinet approved it as being in accordance with the Basic Resolutions adopted by the Constituent Assembly. In the same month the Steering and Subjects Committee met and unanimously adopted the draft and on 29 December 1971 copies of the draft constitution were released to members of the Constituent Assembly.

The Constituent Assembly met on 3 January 1972 and gave its approval to the draft constitution as being in conformity to the thirty-eight Basic Resolutions it had earlier adopted. It then divided itself into eleven committees, each of which was entrusted with scrutinising a group of related subjects which the draft constitution dealt with. Ten of these committees were chaired by cabinet ministers (eight S.L.F.P. ministers inclusive of the prime minister, one L.S.S.P. minister and one C.P. minister) and one was chaired by the leader of the opposition (U.N.P.).

The public, for a fourth time, were given the opportunity to suggest amendments to the various sections of the draft. The amendments, it was specified, could only deal with details and not with the fundamental principles underlying the draft. In the light of the discussions they had, and the evidence submitted to them, these eleven committees prepared their reports and sent them up to the Steering and Subjects Committee in the third week of March (1972). Some of the committees suggested modifications, especially in regard to the public services and the place of Buddhism in the constitutional set-up, but these were not much at variance with the underlying principles already accepted.

The Steering and Subjects Committee, after considering these reports, prepared a revised draft which it presented to the Constituent Assembly on 8 May. The latter body considered this draft in all its detail, sitting in committee, and completed its deliberations on 12 May. The Constituent Assembly then adjourned until 18 May when it met for its last spell, after the twenty-two months it had spent on this endeavour, to debate and give its approval to the final draft. On the morning of 22 May the Assembly voted on the draft and adopted it by 119 votes to 16. The new republic was proclaimed the same afternoon. The U.N.P. and two independent M.P.s voted against while the F.P., persisting in its boycott, did not record its opposition. Three elected Tamil M.P.s, two from the T.C. and the third a self-styled independent, cast their votes in favour.

The U.N.P. leader, Dudley Senanayake, in a statement to the Constituent Assembly, explained at length the reasons for his party's decision to oppose the constitution.[89] While, he declared, the U.N.P. accepted the principle of 'a free, sovereign and independent republic', he held that the political climate in the country had not been conducive to the task of constitution-making, nor had the people been provided adequate opportunities to participate in the operation. He emphasised that it contained many defects and omissions, and above all could represent an erosion of the people's liberties.

At various stages in the process of formulating the constitution, members of the opposition proposed that the discussions be put off because of the crisis in the country caused by the insurrection of the P.L.F. in March–April 1971. It was argued that the prevailing state of emergency and the restrictions on public meetings and the censorship of the press which it imposed prevented the public from expressing their views and political parties and other organisations from conducting campaigns in the country for or against the proposed constitution. The U.F. government stoutly refused to give way to this request. The minister of constitutional affairs himself argued that to do otherwise would be to make the insurrectionists 'the key to constitution-making, not the Constituent Assembly or the government of this country'.[90]

General Character of the Constitution

The constitution is a fairly lengthy document running into fifty-four printed pages with two other pages containing two very short schedules. It is divided into sixteen chapters and 134 sections. The defunct constitution, in contrast, was a shorter document comprising nine parts containing ninety-one sections and two minor schedules and running into twenty-seven pages.

The solutions to the most controversial issues of the country's twenty-five years of post-independence history, as thought fit by the U.F. government, have been written into the constitution. The first five chapters deal with the problems of federalism, Buddhism, language, guide lines for state action and fundamental rights.

Chapter I of the constitution in particular sets out its principles in no uncertain terms and provides a key to the understanding of its entire framework.

Basically, it declares Ceylon's republican status, upholds the sovereignty of the people and leaves no doubt that hereafter there will be no separation of powers in the conventional sense of the term by the provision that all power – legislative, executive and judicial – resides only in the unicameral National State Assembly which is held now to be 'the supreme instrument of state power'. However, there is envisaged a separation of functions, with the Assembly exercising the legislative power, the president and cabinet of ministers carrying out the duties of the executive, and courts and other institutions performing judicial tasks. Further, it unequivocally rejects the federal demand by the assertion that the republic of Sri Lanka is a unitary state (section 2), a principle which is further reinforced by what is spelt out in section 45(1), namely that:

> The National State Assembly may not abdicate, delegate or in any manner alienate its legislative power, nor may it set up an authority with any legislative power other than the power to make subordinate laws.

It will be noticed that there is the saving provision for authorities exercising subordinate legislative power to be set up. This could mean the institution of regional or district councils under the control and supervision of the National State Assembly as was envisaged in the district council legislation proposed by the Bandaranaike and Senanayake governments of the recent past, as a concession to the federal demand. In fact this is made more clear in section 45(3)(a) which empowers the National State

Assembly to confer the power of making subordinate legislation for prescribed purposes on any person or body. These provisions also refer to the existing set-up of local government authorities.

All impediments save one to the exercise of the sovereign will of the people by the National State Assembly are removed under the constitution. The only brake, if there is one, is the constitutional court which is empowered to pronounce on the constitutionality of legislation. But even an adverse opinion by this body can be overridden by the special majority prescribed for amending the various clauses of the constitution.[91] Bills passed by the National State Assembly become law as soon as the Speaker or his deputy certifies that these have been duly passed [section 48(1)]. The nominal executive is not required to assent to Bills before they become law, as in the past. What is more, section 91 makes him responsible to the Assembly for all of his Acts under the constitution and under the law of the land, a provision which is not to be found in any other constitution which provides for a parliamentary system with a cabinet of ministers.

The extent to which the public services weighed on the minds of the framers is indicated by the elaborate provisions for the appointment, transfer, dismissal and disciplinary control of its members contained in sections 105 to 120 of the constitution which run into a little more than six of its fifty-three printed pages. Under these provisions, the public services become a more effective instrument of state policy, unlike under the old constitution where the middle and lower rungs were in large measure insulated from political control. There is however the danger of political jobbery and nepotism in appointments, much more than was prevalent previously.

The judiciary too assumed as much importance in the minds of the framers, the provisions relating to it covering five and a half pages and eleven sections (sections 121 to 131). There are detailed provisions regulating the appointment and discipline of the members of the judiciary other than members of the Supreme and Appeal courts. Adequate provision is made for ensuring the independence of judges.

The principles governing electoral demarcation are wholly taken from the discarded constitution. The attempt by left-wing parties, especially the L.S.S.P., to establish some equality in the franchise as between the rural and urban areas proved abortive.

Religion

A separate chapter (II), but comprising only four printed lines, is allocated to Buddhism. It nevertheless bears evidence of the fact of Buddhism being an important political issue in the years after independence.

Buddhism is also tied up with social and economic issues, and though leading Buddhist pressure groups and lobbies preferred more favoured treatment for their co-religionists, the framers were not prepared to go beyond what they provided for in section 6 (Chapter II), namely that Buddhism should be given 'the foremost place', and accordingly it would have to be the duty of the state 'to protect and foster' it.

The implications of this provision can mean no more than what the state has hitherto been doing for Buddhism – providing financial subsidies for Buddhist activities and observing a certain amount of Buddhist ceremonial on state occasions and governmental or quasi-governmental functions. But it could add up to very much more if a government decided in earnest to implement it.

The rights of other religionists to pursue their activities unhindered but subject to the usual requirements of law and order are ensured under section 18(1)(d). Section 18(1)(h) further protects them against discrimination in appointments in the public sector.

Language

Chapter III deals with the controversial question of language. Its detailed provisions on the official language, the language of legislation and the language of the courts and other institutions dispensing justice are evidence of the determination of the framers to find solutions to the most prickly aspect of Sinhalese-Tamil relations. But while these satisfied Sinhalese opinion, they did not go far enough towards meeting Tamil demands.

The Sinhalese language is guaranteed a pre-eminent position by virtue of sections 7, 9(1) and (3) and 11(1) of the constitution. Section 7 declares Sinhala to be the official language, section 9(1) makes it obligatory for all laws to be enacted in Sinhala and subsection 3 lays down that the law published in Sinhala is *the* law while section 11(1) states that the language of the courts and other related institutions shall be Sinhala throughout the island.

The provisions governing the use of the Tamil language make it clear that it is also an official language though only in a limited sense. They leave no room for doubt that the Tamil language will have a distinctly inferior position in the country's administrative and legal set-up. Section 8(1) provides for the use of the Tamil language in accordance with the Tamil Language (Special Provisions) Act of 1958. But Regulations framed under the Act shall, states the succeeding subsection, be treated as subordinate legislation, not as provisions of the constitution. As far as the U.F. government is concerned, Regulations have still to be framed. The minister of constitutional affairs categorically stated that the Tamil Regulations of January 1966, which to a large extent satisfied Tamil opinion, were *ultra vires*.

In respect of legislation, section 9(2) requires that a Tamil translation be made of every law enacted in Sinhala but, as pointed out earlier, the enactment that is valid for legal purposes is the Sinhalese version, not the Tamil translation.

Where legal and quasi-legal institutions are concerned, elaborate provisions are made for translations into Sinhala or Tamil of proceedings, records and legal documents that are relevant in all cases where the participants are not conversant with the language used.

More important, section 11(3) permits all parties involved in legal proceedings in the northern and eastern provinces and in Muslim divorce courts in any part of the island to submit their pleadings, applications, motions and petitions in Tamil and for them to participate in the proceedings in Tamil. Furthermore, the proviso to subsection 1 of section 11 authorises the National State Assembly to legislate for the use of a language other than Sinhalese (which in this instance means Tamil) in the original courts of the northern and eastern provinces and in all other legal and quasi-legal institutions in these provinces. This was done in 1973.

It will be seen that these provisions for the use of the Tamil language are an improvement on what had been permitted up to the time of the enactment of the constitution. But regulations have still to be framed for the use of the Tamil language under the Act of 1958. The fact that these will be regarded as subordinate legislation and not as part of the constitution, as in the case with Sinhala, wounds Tamil sentiment.

Principles of State Policy

These are spelt out in section 16 subsections 2 to 10 but are not legally binding. However, section 18(2) provides that the exercise and operation of fundamental rights and freedoms contained in section 18(1) shall, among other things, be subject to any measures the state may take to give effect to these Principles.

These Principles make it indubitably clear that the state should move in the direction of a socialist democracy by providing for full employment, equitable distribution of the social product, developing collective forms of property with a view to ending human exploitation, eliminating economic and social privilege, ensuring social security and welfare and enlisting the maximum participation of the people in the processes of government.

There is, further, the realisation that in the troubled conditions of Sri Lanka's plural society, it should be the endeavour of the state to promote communal amity and religious harmony. The directive Principles require in subsections 4, 7 and 9 of section 16 that this should be done.

Sri Lanka's ambitions in the direction of international affairs, especially under the aegis of the Bandaranaikes, are taken note of in subsection 10 of section 16 which declares that the state should promote peace and international co-operation.

Fundamental Rights and Freedoms

Chapter VI (section 18 of the constitution) deals with fundamental rights. In the context of Sri Lanka's ethnic, social, religious and economic rivalries and conflicts, these assumed considerable importance especially in a constitutional document that did away with the entrenched section 29 of the earlier constitution providing for minority safeguards. However the provisions seem inadequate, only one printed page being devoted to this complicated problem. They permit the usual freedoms available to citizens in a democratic state, guarantee freedom of worship, and prohibit discrimination on grounds of race, religion, caste or sex in regard to appointments in the public sector. Provision is also made for the rule of law to prevail in that there are safeguards against arbitrary arrest and imprisonment, while all persons are held to be equal before the law and entitled to equal protection of the law.

All rights are subject to restrictions that may be placed in the interests of 'national unity and integrity, national security, national economy, public safety, public order, the protection of public health or morals or the protection of the rights and freedoms of others or giving effect to the Principles of State Policy set out in section 16' [section 18(2)]. This is indeed almost a blanket provision empowering the National State Assembly to enact legislation that could infringe these rights or abridge them in the interests of the circumstances enumerated. However the constitutional court would have to determine whether any infringing legislation comes strictly within the confines of these circumstances.

The same blanket provision could be utilised by the president of the republic during a state of emergency, on prime-ministerial advice, to enact regulations under the Public Security Act that could infringe these rights.[92]

Further, section 18 subsection 3 of the constitution validates all *existing law* even if these are inconsistent with the rights listed in subsection 1. In other words, legislation such as that relating to Ceylonese citizenship which draws a distinction between citizens by descent and citizens by registration and discriminates against the latter in certain matters is validated.

The statement of rights makes no reference to the subject of private property. Given the principles enunciated in the directive Principles of State Policy, it is clear that there is no intention to safeguard the rights of property or to guarantee due and reasonable compensation in the event of property being taken over in the interests of state policy. Payment of compensation and its quantum will be determined at discretion and will not be available as a matter of right.

Amending Procedure

The constitution cannot be repealed unless it is replaced with another. Section 51(2) makes this explicit. In other words it will not be possible for any government or for Parliament to suspend the constitution or to leave a vacuum by abrogating its provisions altogether. The idea of explicitness is further reinforced in subsection 4 of section 51. This prohibits any attempt at repealing or amending the constitution 'by implication'. In effect, therefore, Bills for the repeal or amendment of the constitution must expressly state so. It is the duty of the Speaker, or in his absence his deputy, to ensure that this provision is conformed with. If it is not, the Speaker can refuse to let it be proceeded with unless the condition referred to is complied with [section 51 (3)].

Section 51(5) requires that such Bills to become effective must be passed by at least two-thirds of the whole number of the National State Assembly, including those not present.

It will be possible for the National State Assembly to enact legislation which may in some way be inconsistent with a provision of the constitution, without the need to amend or repeal the provision in question. In such an event the two-thirds majority procedure laid down must be adhered to.

A few of the provisions of the constitution do not have to conform to the two-thirds requirement and could be repealed or amended in the ordinary way. Such, for instance, is the important chapter (XVI) on public security. Section 134(1) of that chapter states that the National State Assembly can replace the Public Security Ordinance in the ordinary way.

The constitution requires the attorney-general to examine Bills for any contravention of the rules relating to the amending procedure. He must communicate his opinion to the Speaker. He may also recommend that the matter be referred to the constitutional court for its views, in which even the latter's decision will be binding on the Speaker.

The Constitutional Court

The framers were determined that the ordinary courts should have no jurisdiction over the Acts of the sovereign National Assembly. Being committed to a speedy and vigorous programme of implementing socialistic measures, they were anxious to avoid the delays that litigation could impose should the constitutionality of their measures be challenged in the ordinary courts.

It was necessary to have a body of persons who could with

expedition give binding opinion on Bills whose constitutional validity may be questioned. The result was the Constitutional Court. It bears a resemblance to the Constitutional Council of France's fifth republic but the similarity ends there. Whereas the latter was a product of Gaullism and was designed to be an instrument for ratifying the decisions of the general, the liberal and independent traditions that have influenced constitutionalism and the legal processes in Sri Lanka will make of the Constitutional Court a different mechanism. The latter could in fact, given the way in which it is constituted, become a source of irritation to a government which was not responsible for its composition or is not in command of a two-thirds majority in the Assembly. Moreover the terms of the Court (four years) and the National State Assembly (six years) overlap. This could result in friction between a newly elected National State Assembly and a court appointed during the term of the Assembly preceding it.

The court comprises five persons, appointed by the president on the advice of the prime minister, for a term of four years. Members of the court cannot be removed from office except on account of ill-health or physical or mental infirmity [section 56(c)]. Vacancies can occur only in cases of death, resignation, termination of office or as a result of removal from office on the grounds stated.[93] Nor can the membership of the court be altered during the period for which it was appointed [section 56(4)]. This would mean that a government confronted with a hostile court will not be able to overcome it by increasing its membership except by conforming to the requirements laid down for amending the constitution. The membership of the court as at present constituted indicates that it will be on the whole an independent body.

The court is activated in two situations – ordinary or urgent. In ordinary circumstances, the Speaker or his deputy will refer to the court for its decision any question as to whether any provision in a Bill is inconsistent with the constitution if (1) the attorney-general is, as provided under section 53, of that view; (2) the leader of a recognised political party in the Assembly, within a week of a Bill being placed on its agenda, gives written notice of any objection; (3) members of the Assembly equal to its quorum within the said period give written notice of an objection; (4) the Speaker or his deputy is of that view; or (5) any ordinary citizen within the time mentioned moves the court which will then have to advise the Speaker that there is such a question. The decision of the court must be given within two weeks of the reference together with the reasons. It is binding on the Speaker. Until the decision is given, the Bill in question cannot be proceeded with in the National State Assembly.

Bills which in the view of the cabinet of ministers are 'urgent in the national interest' must in terms of section 55(1) bear an endorsement to that effect and will have to be referred by the Speaker or his deputy to the court for its opinion, as to whether it is (1) constitutionally valid; (2) inconsistent with the constitution either as a whole or in part; or (3) it or any of its provisions give rise to doubt as to whether they are consistent with the constitution. The court's advice must, under section 55(2), be communicated to the Speaker 'as expeditiously as possible' and in any case within twenty-four hours of its assembling. Bills of this nature cannot be proceeded with until the court gives its advice. If the advice expresses doubt, or states that the Bill or any of its provisions are inconsistent with the constitution, it will then become necessary for the special majority required for amending the constitution to be adhered to if it must pass into law.

Decisions of the court are final and conclusive and under section 54(4) of the constitution cannot be questioned before any other institution administering justice.

Three members of the court chosen in accordance with its rules determine questions referred to it. The court does not have a permanent chairman. He is selected for the occasion as and when the court sits. Decisions are by majority vote and no member of the court present at a session can refrain from voting.

The court is adequately insulated from political interference. As already stated, its membership cannot be increased during its term of office, members cannot be removed except for the reasons already referred to, their salaries cannot be altered during their term of office and, as a final safeguard against possible political influence, no member of the National State Assembly can appear before the court in the capacity of an advocate or proctor.

The President

More than his counterpart under the earlier constitution, the governor-general, the president is a constitutional figurehead. The framers were alive to the fact that the discretionary powers the governor-general possessed left him room for manoeuvre which could, if he was so inclined, be abused. We have already referred to the role played by Sir Oliver Goonetilleke which at times was not strictly in accordance with the best principles of constitutional conduct, even after allowance has been made for the circumstances surrounding a newly emergent country such as Sri Lanka. The framers were aware of the dangers of such a situation repeating itself. The president's powers have therefore been considerably circumscribed to the extent that his relationship with the political executive has been carefully defined.

The president, like the governor-general, is dependent for his office on the prime minister. Appointment by the prime minister is an unusual feature not to be found in any other constitution in the world. He serves a term of four years but can be removed from office if a resolution to that effect is moved by the prime minister in the National State Assembly and is adopted by it, or if at least half the members of the Assembly sign a resolution calling for his removal and that resolution is passed by at least two-thirds of the entire membership of the Assembly including those not present. Other circumstances in which the office can become vacant is death, resignation or determination by the prime minister that the holder is incapable of performing his duties in view of mental or physical infirmity.

Provision is made for an acting appointment in the event of the president being unable to perform his duties due to illness, or for any other cause, or during his absence from the island. The prime minister is empowered to nominate an acting president for the period of absence. If no such nomination is made, the president of the Court of Appeal officiates for the president.

It is clear from section 27(1) that the president has very little opportunity to act in his discretion. He is obliged to act on prime-ministerial advice or on the advice of a minister to whom the prime minister may have delegated authority. However the president is protected from any legal proceedings in the event of his failing to comply with this provision.

In one instance the constitution invests the president with powers he need not share with anyone else. Section 98(3) provides that in the event of the death or resignation of a prime minister during the period between the dissolution of the National State Assembly and the conclusion of the general election, and if by chance there is no other minister available to fill the office, the president will have to exercise and perform the powers and functions of the cabinet of ministers until such time as the general election is concluded. He could however be asked by the new National State Assembly to answer for any of his actions as the paragraph below indicates.

More significant is the provision in section 91 of the constitution which seeks to emphasise the supremacy of the National State Assembly vis-à-vis the nominal head of the state. The president is required to be responsible to the National State Assembly 'for the due execution and performance of the powers and functions of his office . . .' He could, therefore, be called upon by the Assembly to explain his conduct or action in respect of matters for which he is answerable. In all normal circumstances the prime minister takes responsibility.

The emergency powers of the president are a category in themselves. In the exercise of powers vested in him under the Public Security Act, section 134(2) enjoins the president in all matters he is legally obliged to do, including the making of emergency regulations, to act on the advice of the prime minister.

The constitution invests the president with the usual powers available to the nominal executive. He declares war and peace, summons, prorogues and dissolves the National State Assembly, appoints the prime minister, other ministers and deputy ministers, judges of the Constitutional, Supreme and Appeal Courts, receives foreign ambassadors and accredits Ceylonese ambassadors, grants pardons and remissions of sentences in certain circumstances, and keeps the Public Seal of the republic. In all these instances save two the president acts on prime-ministerial advice. In the selection of a prime minister, and in considering a request for a dissolution of the National State Assembly made by a prime minister whose statement of government policy has been rejected by the Assembly at its first session, the president is constitutionally empowered to use his discretion.

The president is also head of the state and commander-in-chief of the armed forces.

The constitution has divested the president of the power of assenting to legislation which in all other constitutional systems is the responsibility of the nominal head. It is now the Speaker's duty to certify legislation. This was in keeping with the framers' objective of upholding the National State Assembly as 'the supreme instrument of state power'.

The Prime Minister

The prime minister is appointed by the president from among the members of the National State Assembly who in his opinion is most likely to command its confidence.

The prime minister's powers are in most respects no different from those exercised by the holder of that office under the previous constitution. In one important matter, however, namely the making of appointments to senior positions in the public service, the constitution divests the prime minister of the power he or she had under the old one of influencing the chairman of the Public Service Commission to accept his or her choice. Hereafter it is the cabinet of ministers which will make these appointments.

In another field the prime minister is under the constitution invested with undisturbed authority, unlike previously where in terms of the Public Security Act he or she may on occasion have had to persuade the governor-general to declare a state of emergency and enact regulations thereunder. Section 134(2) makes it clear that the president must act on the prime minister's advice, while section 45(4) provides for the National State Assembly to delegate to the president, which in this case means the prime minister, the power to make, for the duration of a state of emergency, emergency regulations which could even override, amend or suspend the operation of the provisions of any law except the provisions of the constitution.

It is the prime minister's responsibility to determine the number of ministers and Ministries and to assign subjects and functions to ministers. The president appoints such ministers and deputy ministers on the recommendations made by the prime minister. The prime minister can at any time advise the president to change the assignment of subjects and functions as well as the composition of the cabinet of ministers. In the latter event it will no longer be necessary, as was the earlier practice, for the cabinet to be re-formed or for the prime minister to resign his office and reconstitute the cabinet.[94] Further, ministers and deputy ministers can be removed by the president on prime-ministerial advice.

Important appointments in the public service, such as the secretary to the cabinet, the secretaries to the various Ministries, the heads of the army, navy, air force and police force, the attorney-general, the commissioner of elections and other state officers required by law to be appointed by the president are made by the latter on the advice of the prime minister.

The judges of the higher courts – Constitutional, Supreme and Appellate – are appointed by the president on the recommendation of the prime minister.

The constitution lays down in some detail the occasions on which a prime minister could be deemed to have resigned his office (section 99).[95] The framers were in particular influenced by the circumstances surrounding the appointment of, and subsequent dissolution of Parliament by, the head of a minority administration (Dudley Senanayake) in March–April 1960. Opinion among the constituent parties of the U.F. which were in the opposition at that time was that a prime minister who *ab initio* had no majority in the House and who met with defeat on his very first presentation to the House of his government's statement of policy (the throne speech) was not entitled to a dissolution, though he obtained one from a partisan governor-general.[96] The constitution accordingly lays down that a prime minister is deemed to have resigned his office (1) at the conclusion of a general election; (2) if the National State Assembly rejects the Appropriation Bill, or the statement of government policy at any session other than its first session, or passes a vote of no-confidence in the government and he fails to advise the president within forty-eight hours of his defeat to dissolve the National State Assembly and such forty-eight hours have elapsed; (3) if the National State Assembly rejects the statement of government policy at its first session and he advises dissolution within forty-eight hourse of such rejection and the president decides not to accept such advice, or if he fails to advise dissolution within forty-eight hours of the rejection and such forty-eight hours have elapsed.

The principles of collective responsibility are inscribed in section 92 for the constitution which provides for a cabinet of ministers answerable to the National State Assembly and charged with the direction and control of the government of the republic. The cabinet is deemed to have resigned on the death or resignation of the prime minister except during the interim period between the dissolution and convening of a new National State Assembly when it is required constitutionally to continue functioning until a new government is constituted.

Ministers are assisted by deputy ministers, to whom they can by *Gazette* notification delegate any of the powers or duties conferred or imposed on them.

The cabinet of ministers has been invested by the constitution with considerable powers in respect of the public services – responsibility for their appointment, transfer, dismissal and disciplinary control and matters relating thereto. The cabinet is also empowered to make appointments to posts of heads of departments and to such other positions as it may determine after receiving the recommendation of the minister concerned who before making such recommendation is obliged to consult the State Services Advisory Board (section 113).

The constitution makes the cabinet answerable for its actions to the National State Assembly whereas previously the Public Service Commission could not be made to answer for appointments it chose to make.

Electoral Demarcation

The principles of electoral demarcation laid down in the previous constitution are retained. Weightage is given to area. Persons and not citizens are counted for allocating electoral districts to a province on the basis of one electorate for every 75,000 of population. Hence resident Indian Tamil labour in the plantations situated mostly in the Kandyan Sinhalese provinces is counted, but the electorates in a province, it is provided, must have as nearly as may be an equal number of citizens. On this basis, the Kandyan Sinhalese provinces obtain, as previously, the greatest amount of weightage in representation.

The Delimitation Commission, as in the past, is required, in demarcating constituencies, to pay regard to the transport facilities, physical features, community or diversity of interests of inhabitants within a province. The Commission can also carve out electoral districts wherever in any area of a province there is 'a substantial concentration of citizens of Sri Lanka united by a community of interest whether racial, religious or otherwise, but differing in one or more of these respects from the majority of inhabitants of that area' [section 78(4)]. Under this provision it would be possible for the Commission to demarcate constituencies on caste lines as well. This, it will be recalled, was permited under the earlier system but withdrawn later.

The absorption of Indian Tamils as citizens under the terms of the Indo-Ceylon Agreement of 1964 gives rise to the possibilities of a clash of interests between the Kandyan Sinhalese and such Indians. The constitution seeks to meet this problem by empowering the Delimitation Commission to create multi-member districts within a province to enable any substantial concentration of citizens 'who are united by a community of racial interest different from that of the majority of the citizens of Sri Lanka in that province' [section 78(5)] to obtain representation.

The three-man Delimitation Commission is appointed by the president within one year after the completion of every general census commencing with the first general census completed after the inauguration of the constitution.

The National State Assembly

The supremacy of this unicameral body is the chief characteristic of the constitution. In it is vested the legislative, executive, and judicial powers of the people. However, provision is made for the executive and judicial power to be exercised respectively through the president and cabinet of ministers and through legal institutions (section 5). There is thus no formal separation of powers, only a distribution of functions. Further, the constitution authorises the Assembly to even enact legislation having retrospective effect [section 48(1)].

The framers have made it absolutely clear that it is the Assembly and no other authority in the land that is 'the supreme instrument of state power'. Section 45(1) of the constitution forbids the Assembly from abdicating, delegating or alienating its legislative power. The Assembly has however authority to confer subordinate law-making power for prescribed purposes on any person or body [section 45(3)(a)]. Further, under section 45(4) the Assembly may during a state of emergency delegate to the president the power to make law for its duration (on prime-ministerial advice).

The Assembly is subject to no external restraints other than those which it seeks to impose on itself. The Constitutional Court already referred to is one of these restricting influences but it can only pronounce on the constitutional validity of legislation prior to its passage in the Assembly, not after. The ordinary courts have no right to call in question their constitutionality [section 48(2)]. Bills passed by the Assembly become law as soon as they receive a certificate of endorsement from the Speaker (section 49).

The Assembly's duration is for six years, after the lapse of which it stands dissolved. The constitution provides for a dissolved Assembly to be re-convened in the event of a state of emergency being proclaimed after a dissolution, and for it to be kept in session until the meeting of the new Assembly. A new Assembly must meet no later than four months after the dissolution of its predecessor. The Assembly will consist wholly of elected members. The provision under the earlier constitution for appointed members is abolished.

Special arrangements were made in section 42 of the constitution for the first National State Assembly. It was provided that the members of the Constituent Assembly would form the first National State Assembly inclusive of the appointed members and that it should, unless sooner dissolved, sit for a term of five years from the date of its first meeting. This would give the present government a run of seven years if it lasts its full term.

All citizens of the age of eighteen years and over, unless disqualified, are entitled to vote at elections to the National State Assembly. Section 67 provides that laws relating to citizenship and rights of citizens prior to the constitution will continue in operation. This provision has particular bearing on the Indian Tamil population in the country.

Special provision is made in the constitution for an independent authority, the commissioner of elections, to be responsible for the conduct of elections to the Assembly (sections 82 and 83). He is appointed by the president and holds office during good behaviour.

The State Services

Ministerial responsibility is wholly ensured under the provisions relating to the appointment, transfer, dismissal and disciplinary control of state officers. It is the cabinet of ministers that is ultimately responsible for all these matters and ministers therefore are answerable to the Assembly for all their actions. It is open to the cabinet to delegate, with certain exceptions, its powers to individual ministers or to state officers, and for ministers to whom such power has been delegated to delegate such power, with the concurrence of the cabinet ministers, to state officers. In the latter instance the minister concerned can himself at any time exercise the powers so delegated. In every such instance the minister must make his decision after receiving the recommendation of the State Services Advisory Board. Where the minister seeks to appoint a person from a Ministry or department other than his own, he is required to do so after consultation with the minister in charge of that Ministry or department.

The exceptions are with regard to appointments to posts of heads of departments and to such other positions as the cabinet of ministers may decide on. Section 113 of the constitution requires that these appointments be made by the cabinet of ministers after receiving the recommendation of the minister concerned who in turn must submit his nomination after consulting the State Services Advisory Board. If the nomination is from another Ministry or department, the minister must make his recommendation after consulting the minister in charge of that Ministry or department.

The constitution protects the cabinet, individual ministers and the two boards responsible for the state services from any legal action in respect of the powers invested in them [section 106(5)].

The two boards concerned are the State Services Advisory Board and the State Services Disciplinary Board. Each board comprises three people, one of whom is chairman. They are appointed by the president on the advice of the prime minister for terms of four years. A member of one board cannot be appointed to the other. Members of the National State Assembly or state officers are not eligible for appointment. Some constitutional provision is made for the independence of members in that their salaries are charged to the consolidated fund and cannot be diminished during their term of office. But this is negated by the provision that members can be removed from office by the president on prime-ministerial advice. Under the earlier constitution a member of the Public Service Commission could only be removed for cause assigned.

It is the responsibility of the State Services Advisory Board to make recommendations to ministers on appointments to the state services and carry out other functions that are entrusted to it in accordance with the constitution.

Transfers are the responsibility of the cabinet of ministers which can delegate this power to individual ministers who in turn can, with the concurrence of the cabinet, delegate their powers to state officers. A minister can himself exercise the powers so delegated with the approval of the cabinet. Section 120(4) of the constitution defines a 'transfer' as meaning 'the moving of a state officer from one post to another post in the same service or in the same grade of the same Ministry or department with no change in salary'.

The State Services Disciplinary Board makes recommendations to ministers with regard to the dismissal and disciplinary control of state officers. The cabinet of ministers is the ultimate authority for exercising the power of dismissal and disciplinary control. It can delegate to individual ministers any of these powers. The minister in turn can, with the approval of the cabinet, delegate these powers to any state officer.

A state officer aggrieved by an order of dismissal by a minister is entitled to make a single appeal against such an order to the cabinet of ministers which can either confirm or vary the order. A state officer aggrieved by the decisions of a state officer to whom power in relation to disciplinary matters and dismissal has been delegated has the right to make a single appeal to the State Services Disciplinary Board except in regard to an order of dismissal. In the latter instance he can make one more appeal to the minister concerned who has power to vary the order. In all other matters the decision of the State Disciplinary Board is final.

The Judiciary

The constitution makes elaborate provisions for the independence of judges.

Judges of the higher courts (Appeal and Supreme) are appointable by the president on the advice of the prime minister, hold office during good behaviour and cannot be removed except by the president upon an address of the National State Assembly. Their salaries are chargeable to the consolidated fund and cannot be reduced during their term of office. Neither can their age of retirement be reduced during their term of office.

The appointment, transfer, dismissal and disciplinary control of all other judges, state officers constituting labour tribunals as well as those whose principal duty is the performance of functions of a judicial nature are vested in two boards, a Judicial Services Disciplinary Board, whose members are, except for their chairmen, appointed by the president (on prime-ministerial advice) for terms of four years. The chairman of both boards is the chief judge of the highest court with original jurisdiction (the chief justice). Members of the Judicial Services Advisory Board other than the chairman can be removed from office by the president. The board comprises five members in all. The Disciplinary Board consists of the chairman and two other judges of the highest court exercising original jurisdiction (the Supreme Court) appointed by the president (on prime-ministerial advice). There is no provision in the constitution for the removal of members of this board by the president as in the case of members of the Judicial Services Advisory Board.

The Judicial Services Advisory Board makes recommendations regarding appointment of judges other than those of the higher courts to the cabinet of ministers. The constitution requires the board to submit to the cabinet a list of recommended persons together with the list of applicants [section 126(2)]. The cabinet can make an appointment from among applicants not included in the recommended list. In such an event, the constitution requires that the cabinet of ministers shall table in the National State Assembly the name of the person they have appointed, the reason for their not accepting the recommendation of the board, together with the list of persons recommended by the latter [section 126(4)]. This requirement is evidently intended as a safeguard against the recommendations of the board being set aside without proper reason. A debate could always be raised in the Assembly on a decision such as this and the cabinet would be hard put to it to explain its action unless there were proper grounds.

The Judicial Services Advisory Board is also responsible for effecting the transfer of judges and other state officers performing judicial functions placed in its charge. Transfer here means a transfer not involving an increase of salary. Officers can, if they wish, appeal to the minister of justice against a transfer order of the board.

The Judicial Services Disciplinary Board is vested with disciplinary control and responsibility for recommending dismissal of all judicial officers over whom it has jurisdiction. Dismissals in fact are made by the president upon an address of the National State Assembly to which body the report recommending dismissal is submitted by the Disciplinary Board. The constitution stipulates that the findings of the board are final and cannot be debated on by the National State Assembly [section 129(4)]. It is presumably assumed that the Assembly will ratify the decision of the board. But this may not always be the case.

Section 131 of the constitution specifically safeguards the judiciary from outside interference. Judges are protected from 'any direction or other interference proceeding from any other person, except a superior court or institution entitled under law' to direct or supervise them in the execution of their judicial functions. The penalties for improper interference are stiff.

CONCLUSION

A careful examination of the constitution indicates that though a greater proportion of the totality of power is vested in the National State Assembly than in the past, that power is not lodged in the Assembly as a whole but dispersed in a number of institutions within and without it.

Moreover, a distinction has to be drawn between a government in possession of a two-thirds majority and one which does not have it. In the latter instance the opportunities for the exercise of power are not as great as in the former. Only twice in twenty-three years did governments secure two-thirds majorities

– 1952 and 1970 – and in neither instance can it be said that they utilised their majorities for anti-democratic ends.

The dispersal of power is provided for in the following ways:
(1) There is no longer a separation of powers in the conventional sense. But there is provision in section 5 of the constitution for a separation of functions – the Assembly exercises legislative power, its executive power is exercised through the president and the cabinet of ministers and its judicial power through courts and other institutions created by law.
(2) A Constitutional Court which is adequately insulated from political interference examines the constitutionality of legislation. Its term of office is fixed (four years) and it can overlap with a new National State Assembly which has a government of a different political complexion from that which constituted it. During its term of office there can as well be a different prime minister from the one who constituted it. A government not in possession of a two-thirds majority would find it difficult to challenge the authority of the court or override its decisions.
(3) Neither the president, prime minister or the Speaker are too powerful. The first two under the former constitution enjoyed considerable power. The president is now answerable to the National State Assembly whereas the governor-general was not. The prime minister is not, as previously, the sole authority for making important appointments in the public service. It is the cabinet of ministers which does this now. Further, a prime minister in a minority situation or defeated in the National State Assembly in certain circumstances has no option but to resign or dissolve. And a request for dissolution in the event of defeat in the first session of a National State Assembly can be refused by the president. A prime minister is deemed to have resigned at the conclusion of a general election. He cannot therefore hope to collect a majority using his position as prime minister before facing the National State Assembly.

The Speaker under the new constitution is vested with greater authority than before. But he is the creature of the majority in the Assembly and cannot afford to outrage its feelings. Nevertheless a healthy tradition of respect for the Speaker's rulings has been established and most Speakers for their part have not misused their power.

(4) The constitution makes adequate provision for the independence of the higher judiciary. Though the latter is divested of the former power it had to determine the constitutional validity of legislation, it is nevertheless the body which will interpret the meaning of legislation.

A constitution ultimately depends on the *mores* of political elites and the kind of ethos which informs them. The evidence of the years since independence indicates that taken in the round political elites have wielded power responsibly despite many temptations to abuse it. And the Sinhalese Buddhist qualities of tolerance, compromise and humanism moderate the sharpness of political conflicts and rivalries. There is almost a trend towards auto-limitation.

6 Foreign Policy and Defence Arrangements

GENERAL CONSIDERATIONS

A small country, and an island at that, dependent for its hard currency on the vagaries of a foreign market which buys its export produce, and on the goodwill of the developed countries and international credit agencies for assistance in its economic progress, totally incapable of defending itself against major aggression from without has in the end not much space for manoeuvre in the conduct of an independent line of action in regard to questions of external import.

But on two matters the island could play a role depending on the skills of its political leadership. Sri Lanka is strategically placed on the world map and could use this position to advantage in attracting attention to what goes on within, politically, and as regards her economic plight. The fact that the country is non-committed and not too powerful gives her statesmen the opportunity to undertake the function of mediator, conciliator, emollient or intermediary in the conflicts between the powers in and around the south and south-east Asian region. In both, Sri Lanka's statesmen have displayed considerable adroitness in exploiting developments to further their political prestige and in the process garner benefits for their country.

The attitude of statesmen in their formulation of policies on matters of external concern reflects, in a sense, their involvement in domestic politics. All three U.N.P. prime ministers – D. S. Senanayake, Sir John Kotelawa and Dudley Senanayake – were dedicated opponents of Marxism and were in direct conflict with local Marxist parties. S.L.F.P. prime ministers did not look on the Marxists as being a serious threat to the parliamentary system. On the contrary, they realised that only by alliance with Marxist political groupings could they ensure the defeat of their U.N.P.

rivals. They tended to believe that Marxist political leaders could be pressed into the service of the democratic state and in this way be socialised into the political order. These differing approaches were therefore obviously manifested in the foreign policies of U.N.P. and S.L.F.P. governments or in governments in which either of these parties were the major components.

U.N.P. governments proved traditional in their foreign outlook, preferring to maintain the colonial heritage of ties with Britain, and in general to look to the west for military and economic succour. The first U.N.P. prime minister, D. S. Senanayake (1947–1952), was not inclined to be loud in proclaiming the virtues of such a policy but was rather cautious and restrained. Sir John Kotelawala (1953–6) on the other hand was brash in the expression of his anti-communist views, which brought him further difficulties both at home and abroad. Dudley Senanayake (1965–70), who was anxious to mobilise as much foreign aid as possible to ensure the survival if not success of his government, did not therefore offend the west, but generally cooled off his relations with the communist states.

Both D. S. Senanayake and Sir John Kotelawala enjoyed a distinct advantage in that during their terms of office, neither the local elites nor the general public, except for the Marxist groupings, displayed any abiding interest in the foreign involvements of their governments. The traditional view prevailed that matters of external concern were best left to the care of governments in office, or better still to their prime ministers, a view reinforced by the fact of the portfolio of defence and external affairs being, under the constitution at the time, invested in the head of the government. Besides, the elitist view backed by most sections of the dominant westernised intelligentsia was that Britain was a safe bet, the Marxists needed watching, and India could be a possible aggressor.

The S.L.F.P. prime ministers, S. W. R. D. Bandaranaike (1956–9) and Sirima Bandaranaike (1960–5 and 1970–) on the other hand proved more enterprising and dynamic in their foreign approaches. They took Sri Lanka into the Afro-Asian mainstream and sought a clear identification and rediscovery of Sri Lanka's personality in the councils of the nonaligned nations of the world. Their policies paid dividends to the extent that Sri Lanka ceased to be any longer taken for granted by the west.

Her patterns of trade came to be diversified as a result of bilateral arrangements with the communist states, and what is more, foreign aid hereafter proved available from both power blocs.

Marxist groupings were sympathetic to the foreign policies of the Bandaranaikes, for even though these were not in full accord with theirs – and there are serious differences between the Trotskyists and communists – nonalignment for them was a preferable alernative to the pro-west stances of U.N.P. governments.

Besides, after 1956, when S. W. R. D. Bandaranaike established diplomatic and cultural contacts with the communist states for the first time since independence, many organisations of the friendship type emerged anxious to promote friendly relations between Sri Lanka and foreign countries. Local elites and their supporting intelligentsia began to show a growing awareness of the implications of Sri Lanka's involvements with rival powers, a healthy development no doubt. Foreign policy was no longer viewed as the preserve of the top echelons of government.

All the country's statesmen have utilised the concept of Sri Lanka's uniqueness as the preserver of Buddhism in its purest and pristine forms to bolster up the positions they have taken on international questions. D. S. Senanayake spoke of the middle path in foreign policy, Sir John's rantings on the international stage extended to the teachings of the Enlightened One (the Buddha), while the Bandaranaikes have consistently maintained that their dynamic neutralism is in conformity with Buddhist doctrine.

But in actual fact, the *realpolitik* in Sri Lanka's foreign policy is determined by her economic circumstances. The attitude of governments towards membership of the Commonwealth, to the United Nations and its related agencies, and to the states of the western, non-aligned and communist world, is one that in the last analysis looks to the national interest, especially in regard to foreign markets for export produce and foreign aid for economic survival and economic development.

STRATEGIC SITUATION

The ports of Colombo, Trincomalee and Galle served as a vital link in the sea routes between east and west when the Suez Canal was open, and though their utility has declined altogether with the closure of the canal, there is little doubt that they will resume their position as a useful junction as soon as the canal is reopened for traffic. Further, the principal airports of Katunayake (the Bandaranaike airport) and Ratmalana function as a stopover for many airlines operating routes between east and west. In times of international crisis, the airport gains added importance. For instance during 1949, when the Indonesians waged their war of independence against the Dutch, Ceylon denied transit facilities to Dutch aircraft transporting troops and war material to the Indonesian front. But in May 1954, the prime minister of the time, Sir John Kotelawala, permitted American *Globemasters* carrying French troops to Indo-China to make use of one of the airports in the country.[1] Again in February 1971 when India withdrew landing and overflying rights for Pakistani planes after the hijacking and subsequent blowing up of an Indian plane at Lahore, Sri Lanka granted Pakistan International Airlines these rights at the request of the government of Pakistan. Consequently aircraft of this airline made 103 technical landings (for refuelling only) at Bandaranaike international airport in the month of March and forty landings in April. Further in March 1971, sixteen east-bound and fifteen west-bound Pakistani air force planes touched down at Bandaranaike international airport. These landings acquired much significance because of the continuing crisis in relations between the eastern and western sectors of Pakistan at this time. But the minister of communications, Leslie Goonewardene, insisted that the flights took place only during the phase when the Awami League leader, Mujibur Rahman, was involved in negotiations with the government of Pakistan. He emphasised that during the months of May to September there 'were practically no flights other than scheduled flights' through the Bandaranaike airport and denied that there was any complicity on the part of the government of Sri Lanka in regard to transport of troops or arms from West Pakistan to East Pakistan.[2] However, Indian opinion seemed to take a contrary view and there was strong suspicion that the flights involved soldiers and war material despite the minister's contention that of the 143 technical landings in March and April, only two involved flights from Karachi to Dacca.[3]

With the establishment of a Royal Air Force base in the

Maldivian island of Gan after the decision of the M.E.P. government in 1956 to withdraw all military facilities permitted in the island to Britain under the Anglo-Ceylon defence agreement of 1947, and the setting up in 1971 of an Anglo-American communications centre in the Indian Ocean atoll of Diego Garcia, it may be said that the utility of Sri Lanka's airports is no longer of immediate relevance to NATO powers seeking to operate in the area.

But even for the NATO powers, as well as for their rivals, the island is of immense value, if only for its geographic location. For a distance of nine thousand miles south of Sri Lanka, there is no patch of land until one hits the Antarctic. The sea distances between land are also very great. From Cape Town to Singapore it is 5,631 nautical miles, from Cape Town to Calcutta 5,480 nautical miles and from Suez to Jakarta 5,510 nautical miles. Added to all this is the fact of a scarcity of natural harbours. There are fewer good harbours in this ocean area than there are in any comparable length of coastline in the world. And above all, huge harbours like those at Madagascar and Trincomalee are not readily available.

For all these reasons the island is of great significance to rival powers in search of air and naval facilities, and if viewed in the context of Russian and Chinese interests and designs in the Indian Ocean area, Sri Lanka acquires immense strategic importance. Since 1967 there has been a Russian naval presence, with fleet trains comprising supply ships for their fighting vessels capable of staying in the area for months at a time, operating as a potential challenge to the American and British navies in this area. China for her part would like to have access to those states in central and east Africa with whom she has established friendly relations as well as to the Persian Gulf. A pro-Soviet or Maoist government in Sri Lanka would therefore be a tremendous accession of strength to either of these powers. Despite, however, repeated governmental affirmations that bases in the island would not be leased to foreign powers, there have been reports from time to time that the Chinese, in March 1971 for instance, and the Soviets in May of the same year had made requests for base facilities in the great natural harbour of Trincomalee. The Ministry of Defence and External Affairs had thus to issue a categorical denial on 15 May 1971 that any such requests had been made, adding that one of the fundamental principles of Sri Lanka's policy of nonalignment was the denial of bases to foreign powers.[4]

The island would further count for a great deal in the event of war in the Indian Ocean area. It is especially of supreme relevance to India as regards the defence of her southernmost flanks. These would be completely exposed in the event of a hostile government being in office in Sri Lanka, since the only major cantonment of the Indian armed forces closest to Sri Lanka is as far north as Secunderabad. (Although south India is the recreation and training ground for the Indian armed forces.) The defence of south India would therefore entail a huge drain on India's resources. The situation is similar to that of Eire vis-à-vis Britain, or Cuba vis-à-vis the United States.

A new development which is of greater significance than all these is the fact of Sri Lanka being strategically placed on the nuclear map of the globe.[5] Military strategists are of the view that there is a conjunction of forces in the island in the context of nuclear warfare which is very rare on the surface of the globe. It is said that if two circles are drawn with the radius of the firing range of a nuclear missile from a submarine, one circumscribing the Soviet Union and the other China, these two arcs would cut each other at a point 180 miles south of Galle – an important city in south Sri Lanka, some seventy-two miles south of Colombo. In other words a polaris or poseidon nuclear missile located in this area could hit both the Soviet Union and China. So that from the point of view of powers opposed to either of these countries, the waters to the south of Sri Lanka afford vast possibilities.

More relevant are the physical features of the Indian Ocean. It has several deep trenches, one of which runs from the Ganges basin and reaches down to Trincomalee. Some naval experts argue that a nuclear submarine setting out from its base under the Antarctic ice cap could linger on in the bottom of this ocean canyon to come up for firing at any appropriate time. It would be more difficult to locate such a movable menace than, for example, a fixed nuclear landbased launching pad.

DEFENCE

Sri Lanka does not have any military tradition worth speaking of, in the sense of her armed forces being battle-hungry or anxious to meet external aggression or domestic insurrection. Nor is the officer class sufficiently politicised to have ambitions of seeking complete control of the administration of the country. Even those involved in the abortive coup attempt of January 1962 had no plans of following the patterns set by Ne Win in Burma, Ayub Khan in Pakistan or Neguib and Nasser in the United Arab Republic. They intended, if they succeeded, to hand over power to a 'government of national safety' comprising some of the most experienced conservative politicians in the country. And the suspected coup of Buddhist army officers of 1966–7 had no serious design, and it is in fact doubtful as to whether the officers implicated had actually had any hand in the plots they were accused of having hatched against the U.N.P.-dominated government of the day.

In effect the island's armed forces are mainly organised for purposes of domestic peace-keeping, such as controlling communal unrest or industrial turbulence in times of crisis, curbing attempts of illicit immigrants to gain entry into the country from the south Indian coast, and putting an end to the flourishing two–way smuggling that goes on between the northern shores of Sri Lanka and the southern tip of the south Indian mainland. In these operations they are assisted by the local police force.

Internal security has assumed importance since 1956 when communal violence, trade union troubles and political unrest became increasingly endemic, culminating in the P.L.F. outbreak of March–April 1971. The armed forces were in fact not prepared for the insurrection of March–April 1971 when its six thousand or so active combatants had to engage rebel forces variously estimated at anything up to twenty thousand actives. There are no definite figures available as to the actual strength of the army, navy and air force. The army commander, Major General Attygalle, in a briefing to foreign correspondents during these troubles said that his forces numbered fewer than seven thousand trained men.[6] A *New York Times* correspondent assessed the strength of the army at a total of twelve thousand in all inclusive of the volunteer force, and the navy and air force at approximately five thousand.[7] The police force numbered 11,323 men in 1969.[8] It had more than doubled in strength since 1947 when there were 5,380 men in service.[9] After the insurrection, the armed forces and police were considerably strengthened. A two thousand strong National Service Regiment with 210 officers was recruited on 19 April 1971 as part of the Ceylon Volunteer Force.[10] In addition under the 1971 budget, provision was made for a thousand new recruits for the army, 2,300 for the air force, 280 for the navy and four thousand for the police.[11] The total expenditure on defence and the police in the 1971 budget reached an all-time high, but despite the unprecedented increase these sectors rarely absorb more than 5 per cent of annual budgetary allocations.[12]

A National Security Council which is part of the organisation of the Defence Ministry is responsible for maintaining internal security. Its meetings are attended by the secretary of the Ministry, the three service commanders, the police chief and the police superintendent responsible for the criminal investigation network.

The control of illicit immigration is a recurring priority in the defence policies of governments. A scheme for the registration of every person over eighteen years of age and for the issuing of identity cards containing their photographs and other particulars was put into operation during March–August 1972. Its objectives are to safeguard the country against the entry of illicit immigrants and to provide every adult with 'an adequate and ready means of identifying himself for any purpose'.[13] In addition, an organisation called the Task Force Illicit Immigration (T.A.F.I.I.) comprising personnel and equipment from the three services, patrols 225 miles of Sri Lanka's coastline in the north-western and north-eastern parts from Kalpitiya to Trincomalee to check illegal entry and smuggling. The navy has bases in Trincomalee, Jaffna and Kalpitiya for this purpose. In addition the navy also maintains a base at Kochikade and a shore establishment at Welisara (both places are close to Colombo). It is further proposed to establish a new naval base in southern Sri Lanka. The navy received in February 1972 two of five gun boats, each a hundred tons, offered as an outright gift by the Chinese government. They are intended to strengthen the island's maritime defences and its capacity to maintain surveillance of its coasts.[14]

In normal times, however, the armed services are known to perform other functions too. They assist in tractor operations to clear jungle lands for purposes of the 'grow more food' campaign as well as in national development work where their technical skills come useful. The air force runs fortnightly charter flights between Sri Lanka and the Maldives and an air taxi service for foreign tourists from one location to another within the island.[15] It has in this way become a foreign exchange earner for the country.[16]

It will be realised from this account of Sri Lanka's meagre defences that the island is in no position to defend itself against an external aggressor. At best it could hold the aggressor at bay for a maximum of seventy-two hours until military assistance arrived from other sources.[17]

There have been two approaches to the question of the island's defences against a foreign invader. One was exemplified by D. S. Senanayake, and stretched to its utmost limits by Sir John Kotelawala, namely a leaning towards Britain and the United States. The other pursued by the Bandaranaikes prefers friendship and non-aggression pacts with the neighbouring states. The unexpressed premise of both parties is the danger that is India.

Fear of India stems from the presence of Indian Tamil workers in the heartland of Sri Lanka who are sometimes equated to the Sudeten Germans of Czechoslovakia and on other occasions viewed as a potential Fifth Column. These fears are aggravated by the statements of south Indian politicians and the activities of an embryonic local-based D.M.K. organisation among the Indian Tamil plantation workers. They are made still worse by the determination of the Ceylon Tamil minority which occupies the northern and some parts of the eastern coastal areas of the island – areas most vulnerable to an Indian attack – to maintain its separate cultural and ethnic identity. The recent pronouncements of Ceylon Tamil political leaders to launch a struggle for a separate Tamil state have only served to confirm these anxieties. Ironically, it was left to a Trotskyist minister reputed for his international outlook to articulate the fears of the Indian danger when he wrote:[18]

'Even though the Tamil people who inhabit Sri Lanka are a minority in Sri Lanka, if they are regarded together with the

Tamil people who live in south India near the northern boundary of Sri Lanka, the Tamil people appear as the majority and the Sinhalese people as the minority. Also, when one contemplates the history of Sri Lanka, that history is full of battles between these two sections.'

The threat posed is that from a possibly chauvinistic government in New Delhi which might seek to buttress a weak domestic position by engaging in foreign war. There are many among the Sinhalese who point to the examples of Kashmir, Hyderabad, Goa and in recent times Bangladesh to support this view. There is the parallel or alternative fear of a conjectural sovereign Dravidistan in south India, more specifically, Tamil Nadu.

It may be assumed that it was for this reason as well as for other equally cogent ones that D. S. Senanayake concluded in November 1947 his defence agreement with the British government.[19] Under the agreement, Sri Lanka was to provide military bases and facilities to Britain while Britain in return would ensure Sri Lanka's defence against external attack as well as assist in the training of local military personnel

D. S. Senanayake did not in any of his public utterances indicate that he anticipated Indian aggression. But there are grounds for concluding that this was a consideration, other than of course his willingness to grant facilities to Britain so as to speed up the process of independence for his country. There was also the fact that the British presence in Sri Lanka would relieve the local taxpayer of a considerable burden. In his speeches, Senanayake frequently referred to the possibilities of Soviet intervention in the affairs of Sri Lanka, but this possibility was remote at this time. It is quite probable that the Ceylonese statesman was, with his usual adroitness, introducing a red herring into the discussion. His successors Dudley Senanayake and Sir John Kotelawala were content to let the *status quo* remain.

Left-wing parties criticised the defence agreement as being a limitation on the island's sovereignty and the tying of the country to the Anglo-American power bloc. They did not, however, make any allegation of the agreement being directed against India. Their support of citizenship rights for Indian Tamil workers in Sri Lanka would have made them completely vulnerable had they chosen this line of attack as well. The left generally advocated friendship pacts with the neighbouring states of south and south-east Asia.

S. W. R. D. Bandaranaike himself took up the position that the defence agreement would result in Sri Lanka getting involved on the side of the west in the Cold War that was reaching crisis proportions at this time. He had expressed misgivings about the wisdom of entering into such an agreement when a member of the D. S. Senanayake government.[20] In opposition, he was more forthright in characterising the foreign policies of U.N.P. governments as being likely 'to deepen this country's dependence upon and subservience to the Anglo-American bloc' and 'to lead to the involvement of Sri Lanka in war'.[21] He was more specific than the left-wing parties in his advocacy of a policy for Sri Lanka.

Bandaranaike agreed with his U.N.P. adversaries that the island could ill afford to defend herself but held that alliance with a distant power like Britain would not make Sri Lanka less exposed to attack. On the contrary, he argued that in the event of a war between the two power blocs, Sri Lanka would be the only country in south-east Asia to be ranged on one particular side 'providing ourselves as . . . the only target . . . to hostile forces and hostile action from the other side which will be much closer to us than our presumed allies'.[22] The reference of course was to possible attack from China and the Soviet Union.

Bandaranaike's answer to the island's defence problem was the adoption of a policy of complete neutrality. He argued strongly in favour of Sri Lanka becoming a Switzerland of Asia.[23] Along with this, he advocated regional co-operation among the countries of south and south-east Asia, and more specifically, 'a mutual defence scheme' for south-east Asia involving India, Burma, Sri Lanka, Pakistan and Indonesia.[24]

It is obvious that Bandaranaike believed that friendship with India and closer identification with the neighbouring countries of south and south-east Asia were better insurances against exposure to war than a military alliance with a distant and aligned power. In office, as prime minister, he pursued his theme of dynamic neutralism with great vigour and obtained for Sri Lanka a position of importance and prominence in the councils of the Afro-Asian states. The measure of the respect he commanded in Nehru's India was evidenced by the fact that on the day he died, the Indian prime minister ordered all public offices in New Delhi to be closed for the half day to mark India's sympathy for the Ceylonese leader.

Mrs Bandaranaike followed the path laid down by her husband. In her first term of office, 1960–5, she maintained close and friendly relations with Nehru and Shastri. She follows a similar policy vis-à-vis Mrs Gandhi in her second term as well. Despite however the forging of closer links with India by both Bandaranaikes, there still continues to lurk in the minds of many among the Sinhalese intelligentsia a fear and suspicion of India.

It cannot be gainsaid that the island occupies a place of immense importance in the defence strategies of the Indian general staff, no doubt amply proved by the alacrity with which the government of India came to Sri Lanka's assistance when her armed forces were under severe strain from the attacks of the P.L.F.'s insurrectionary forces. Indian helicopters were readily provided, Indian frigates sealed off Sri Lanka's exposed coastline and Indian troops guarded installations at the Bandaranaike international airport.[25]

But notwithstanding the manifestations of goodwill and friendship on the part of India, the hope before India's successful Bangladesh action in 1972 was that a power balance as between India and Pakistan, with China on Pakistan's side, would keep in sufficient check any intended aggressive or expansionist designs being nurtured by Indian chauvinists. On 29 June 1970, the nationalistically inclined editor of the leading English newspaper in Sri Lanka gave expression to a hitherto vaguely articulated policy in local circles when he wrote that Sri Lanka could do with some advice from Kautilya (the Indian Machiavelli), adding that 'the wise man directs us towards Peking and Islamabad'.[26] The dismemberment of Pakistan, the creation of Bangladesh, the failure of China to go to the assistance of Pakistan and the signing of the Indo-Soviet Treaty of Friendship in August 1971 alters, from the point of view of these Ceylonese interests (and they are quite representative), the power structure in the south Asian region.

SRI LANKA AND THE COMMONWEALTH

Between the U.N.P. and the S.L.F.P. there is agreement on the uses that the Commonwealth has for Sri Lanka but the concept of utility varies substantially. Left-wing parties however have always been strongly in favour of Sri Lanka leaving the Commonwealth.

The U.N.P. of 1947–56 did not even give a thought to the idea of Sri Lanka obtaining republican status within the Commonwealth. Both D. S. Senanayake and Sir John Kotelawala were as good as any of the loyal prime ministers of Australia or New Zealand. The defence and external affairs agreements that the former concluded with H.M. government in November 1947 were indicative of the U.N.P.'s desire to maintain close ties with Britain.[27] In fact D. S. Senanayake proudly told a Commonwealth Conference he attended that he represented 'the oldest monarchy in the Commonwealth'[28] while Sir John Kotelawala referred to Queen Elizabeth as 'our chosen Queen' and hoped that Sri Lanka would always remain within the Commonwealth and would prefer to recognise its head as a queen or a king rather than become a republic.[29] The reticent statesman, Dudley Senanayake, did not display any keenness during the four terms he served as prime minister to declare Sri Lanka a republic. In opposition, in 1970, he advocated continuance of the Commonwealth connection on the plea that Sri Lanka's exit would adversely affect her tea trade with Britain to the advantage of other tea-producing countries which had retained their membership, such as India, Kenya, Tanzania and Uganda.[30]

The Bandaranaikes on the other hand preferred to follow the Indian pattern. Bandaranaike, in 1952, lauded India's independent foreign policy, which he said redounded to her benefit, without her having necessarily to defer to the Commonwealth relationship.[31] In 1951, when he inaugurated his S.L.F.P., he wished to take Sri Lanka out of the Commonwealth, but in office in 1956, as prime minister, he thought better of the relationship, and at the conference of Commonwealth prime ministers in 1956 sought and obtained permission for Sri Lanka to continue as a republic within the Commonwealth. He rejected the idea of 'sloppy sentimentality' over the Commonwealth and explained in his speech to the Commonwealth Press Association in London in July 1956 that Sri Lanka preferred a republican form of government and that for the Ceylonese 'the queen herself is too far away with too few personal contacts to stimulate that feeling of personal attachment which you have for her'.[32] But he felt that membership had certain obvious advantages such as belonging 'economically to the sterling bloc' and the usefulness of 'mutual consultations and discussions on a friendly basis on various problems'.[33] What however attracted him most, at that point of time (July 1956), was the common tradition that Commonwealth countries shared with Britain, which he proceeded to enumerate, namely a democratic parliamentary form of government, independence of the judiciary, an administration 'free from undue political influence, free from corruption' and 'the absence of discrimination between the state and the citizen'.[34]

Bandaranaike had the grant of military bases to Britain under the defence agreement of 1947 cancelled in 1957, but he preferred to go about it in a friendly and amicable manner without, as he himself said, 'causing dislocation, inconvenience or embarrassment to the British Government'.[35] It was indeed his hope that the end of these bases would help to further strengthen the 'bonds of friendship between the United Kingdom and ourselves'.[36] In fact the generous financial settlement made to the British Treasury for the takeover of the facilities that the British had installed in Trincomalee provided evidence of Bandaranaike's desire to maintain cordial relations with Britain. In this respect he was not very different from his adversary of yester year, D. S. Senanayake. The settlement, in the opinion of Sri Lanka's governor-general at the time, was more generous than was warranted, and when told so by Sir Oliver Goonetilleke, the prime minister replied: 'Never mind Sir, they have been very good friends of Sri Lanka and will continue to be so.'[37] D. S. Senanayake in his time was accused of similar extravagance. When at the end of the war, he agreed in 1946 to fix the island's sterling balances with the British government at Rs. 1,260 millions, the leftists argued that it should have been some twenty times more.[38]

Presumably Bandaranaike hoped to utilise the periodical meetings of Commonwealth statesmen and officials as a forum where Sri Lanka could make her presence felt. It was in keeping with his design for Sri Lanka, despite her smallness, to play a role in international affairs. His untimely death prevented him from articulating this role.

Bandaranaike's wife has made use of his ideas to draw attention to the policies that she has chosen to expound at Commonwealth conferences and international gatherings. At the meeting of Commonwealth prime ministers in 1960, she vehemently expressed Sri Lanka's opposition to South Africa being allowed to retain membership in the Commonwealth after assuming republican status. At the Commonwealth conference in Singapore in January 1971, Mr Bandaranaike was critical of Britain's arms deal with South Africa and the grant by Britain of a base at Diego Garcia to a superpower such as the United States. The views she expressed on these matters were directly relevant to the proposal she was canvassing both at this conference and at the United Nations to have the Indian Ocean declared a neutral, nuclear-free zone supported by guarantees from the big powers.[39] Mrs Bandaranaike's own views on the Commonwealth tie were expressed at the Singapore conference when she ascribed to it the complete frankness that is possible, the full and free consultation that must take place between its members, the total lack of bitterness that characterises their interrelationships, and the economic advantages that have accrued to Sri Lanka from continued membership.[40]

In the matter of wars in which neighbouring Commonwealth countries have been involved, Sri Lanka has offered her services as mediator and in fact functioned as intermediary. In the Sino-Indian conflict of 1962, Mrs Bandaranaike summoned a six-nation conference of nonaligned countries in Colombo which drew up proposals for a ceasefire. Mrs Bandaranaike was officially authorised by the conference to convey the proposals to India and China. Her views gained acceptance at this conference and the proposals were generally favourable to India, though in the end these did not work out satisfactorily. In the Indo-Pakistan War of 1971, Mrs Bandaranaike declared, in December 1971, Sri Lanka's strict neutrality and urged the secretary-general of the United Nations to use his good offices to end the conflict.[41] Sri Lanka was also prepared to be associated with initiatives accepted by the United Nations towards achieving a settlement.[42] Earlier in August 1971, Mrs Bandaranaike wrote to President Yahya Khan offering her services to ease the Bangladesh crisis.[43]

It is in the field of economic cooperation that Sri Lanka has stood most to gain from Commonwealth membership. Her relations in this sphere are particularly strong with Britain, her biggest trading partner, Australia, New Zealand, Canada, India and Pakistan. She has an 80 million rupee tea market in South Africa, but relations with that country have never been cordial.

It is through the Colombo Plan, sponsored at the Commonwealth conference in Colombo in 1950 by J. R. Jayawardene, Sri Lanka's minister of finance at the time in the D. S. Senanayake administration, and Percy Spender, the Australian minister of foreign affairs, that the island has benefited immensely from aid and technical assistance provided especially by Britain, Canada, Australia and New Zealand, in that order, as well as, to a lesser extent by India and Pakistan. The latter have mainly granted opportunities for studies to Ceylonese students. Sri Lanka in turn has also awarded scholarships for study in various fields to persons in these two countries.

Sri Lanka had up to 1970, under the Plan, received technical assistance from donor countries (which includes Japan) in the form of training facilities, experts and equipment to the value of Rs 146.6 million out of a total aid of Rs 191.8 million provided for the underdeveloped countries of the south and south-east Asian region as a whole.[44] In addition she received 3,693 trainee and student places and 671 Colombo Plan experts during this period.[45] Sri Lanka for her part provided ninety-six training places to students from neighbouring countries up to 1970.[46] During the six-year period up to 1972, Sri Lanka obtained Rs 1,318 million of project, commodity and food aid under the Plan.[47] This includes aid from the United States, in its role as a participant in the Colombo Plan.

Among the countries of the Commonwealth, Britain and Canada, in that order, have been the biggest aid-givers to Sri Lanka. Since November 1965 Britain has provided £20.21 million in aid through the six programmes organised by the Aid Sri Lanka Consortium of Powers. Except for £1 million given as a food aid grant, the balance of £19.21 million was in the form of interest-free loans payable over a period of twenty-five years, including an initial three-year grace period.[48] Canadian assistance has been in the form of food aid, dollar grants and development loans which together have totalled to Rs 314 million since 1951.[49]

Since 1965 and especially after 1970, Sri Lanka has sought to enter into closer economic cooperation with India. During 1965–1970 there were exploratory discussions about the possibilities of joint ventures between Indian business magnates and their Ceylonese counterparts, but for various reasons none of these reached fruition. After 1970, with the balance of payments situation becoming increasingly grave, Sri Lanka sought opportunities for reducing her trade imbalance with India. For instance in 1971 India imported only Rs 10 million worth of goods from Sri Lanka as against Rs 209 millions of Ceylonese imports from India. With a view to narrowing the gap and also promoting industrial development in Sri Lanka, Mrs Bandaranaike wrote to Mrs Gandhi in August 1971 inquiring about the possibilities of greater economic cooperation between their two countries and the prospects of re-activising the joint consultation machinery for promoting Indo–Sri Lanka industrial and business ventures that had been already set in motion during 1965–70.[50] Mrs Gandhi is reported to have responded favourably, and by February 1972 joint feasibility studies had been conducted on six major industrial ventures in respect of paper, graphite, silicate, mica, refractory and rubber-based industries.[51] These ventures will feed the domestic market, while any of the excess production will be bought by India or sold to other countries.

SRI LANKA IN THE UNITED NATIONS

Membership of the United Nations had been the constant ambition of governments up to 1956, more to prove the fact of the island's independent status than for any other reason, but repeated vetoing by the Soviet Union denied Sri Lanka entry until 1955 when a package deal between the superpowers let Sri Lanka in. The Soviet view until then was that Sri Lanka was not a sovereign state, presumably on the grounds that she had close defence ties with Britain. Sri Lanka's repeated applications for membership derived strength from the support received from Commonwealth countries in the U.N., but obviously the Soviet Union was not convinced. When membership came in 1955, the prime minister of the time, Sir John Kotelawala, naturally claimed the kudos for himself and the U.N.P. which he led.[52] But the general election that ensued (in 1956) did not provide evidence of the electors being impressed on this score, as there were more pressing issues on which they were determined to oust the Kotelawala government.

It is not evident that the Ceylonese governments in office prior to the country's admission to the U.N. were in any way over-anxious to secure admission to the world organisation. As a matter of formality, the application for entry was filed from time to time, but it did not become a major issue in domestic politics. The island had the advantage of membership of other international organisations despite her exclusion from the main body. In fact, at the first Colombo conference of the five south and south-east Asian prime ministers in April 1954, Nehru proposed that the four other participants (India, Burma, Pakistan and Indonesia) should recommend Sri Lanka's admission. But Sir John Kotelawala was reported to have replied that his cabinet had discussed the matter and that it preferred Sri Lanka's request to 'take its normal course', the reason being that it feared difficulties would arise in view of Sri Lanka's rubber-rice agreement of 1952 with China, rubber then being one of the strategic raw materials included in the U.S.'s embargo on trade with China.[53] Nehru had replied that no absolute ban had been enforced, but it is reported that Sir John was not willing to take any risks.[54]

There is little evidence of any of the U.N.P. prime ministers wishing to use the U.N. as a forum for enhancing their country's international status. The position the U.N.P. had taken in regard to the U.N. through the years was best expressed by its leader of the opposition (J. R. Jayawardene) in 1971 when he warned the prime minister (Mrs Bandaranaike) against being forced, evidently by her left-wing ministers, to 'lean heavily' on the Soviet bloc.[55] Jayawardene's view was that in the U.N. it was better for Sri Lanka to refrain from taking sides and to remain friendly with all nations because of the need to obtain aid from all quarters.[56] For these reasons, he emphasised that Sri Lanka should not play 'too dominant a role' in the U.N.[57]

The Bandaranaikes however had a different conception of the role that Sri Lanka should assume in the international organisation. S. W. R. D. Bandaranaike felt that the service that a country could render in the U.N. should not be measured only in terms of its size, population, power or strength. He thought that the world body could express itself 'most effectively by bringing to bear a certain moral force', an endeavour in which the weak and the strong would be able to render a useful service.[58] In other words, he was contemplating a position for his country similar to that of Switzerland, but a more positive one in the sense that the skills of its leadership could be made available to help solve the pressing problems of the hour. He was however not able to develop this theme owing to the serious domestic problems that engaged most of his attention during his tenure of the premiership.

Mrs Bandaranaike, during both her terms as prime minister (1960–5 and 1970–), has had better opportunities to give concrete expression to the ideas enunciated by her husband. Sri Lanka secured a place in the Security Council in 1960–1 and was one of the states in this phase involved in mediating between the big powers during the Congo crisis. Sri Lanka also contributed towards effecting a settlement between Turks and Greeks in Cyprus and in easing the crisis in relations between Malaysia and Indonesia in 1963. Mrs Bandaranaike further actively involved herself in promoting the candidature of Sri Lanka's permanent delegate to the U.N., H. S. Amerasinghe, for the post of secretary-general.[59]

In October 1971 Mrs Bandaranaike addressed the U.N. General Assembly and canvassed support for her proposal for making the Indian Ocean a nuclear free zone of peace.[60] Its details are best described in her own words:[61]

> In the Indian Ocean a defined area shall be declared to be a Zone of Peace and reserved exclusively for peaceful purposes under an appropriate regulatory system. Within the zone, no armaments of any kind, defensive or offensive, may be installed on or in the sea, on the subjacent sea bed or on the land areas. Ships of all nations may exercise the right of transit but warships carrying warlike equipment, including submarines, may not stop for other than emergency reasons of a technical, mechanical, or humanitarian nature. No maoeuvres by warships of any state shall be permitted. Naval intelligence operations shall be forbidden. No weapon tests of any kind may be conducted. The regulatory system to be established will be under effective international control.

The proposal was also in effect an expression of Sri Lanka's opposition to the Anglo-American communications centre in Diego

Garcia. Only China among the nuclear powers supported it. The others however did not vote against it but abstained. The proposal did achieve a kind of negative support when it obtained fifty votes as against forty-nine abstentions and none against.

Both U.N.P. and S.L.F.P. governments were strong in their support of the Arab cause in the dispute with Israel. Mrs Bandaranaike went further than Dudley Senanayake by breaking off diplomatic relations with Israel until such time as the latter conformed to the U.N. resolutions on the subject. Both prime ministers had their eye on the local Muslim vote in their espousal of the Arab cause. Mrs Bandaranaike's perspectives were nevertheless broader in that she sought greater identification for Sri Lanka with the Afro-Asia nonaligned nations by her positive expressions of solidarity with the United Arab Republic.

Generally speaking, Sri Lanka in the U.N. has consistently joined other states in condemning aggression from whichever quarter, as for example the Anglo-French Suez adventure of 1956 and the Soviet action in Hungary in 1956 and in Czechoslovakia in 1968. In June 1959, Bandaranaike expressed disapproval of the Chinese military action in Tibet. Sri Lanka also repeatedly called for a peaceful settlement of the war in Vietnam. But whereas U.N.P. government have preferred to function in low profile in the U.N., mainly with a view to not antagonising the western powers, the Bandaranaikes have been forthright in articulating their position on controversial international issues.

FOREIGN AID

From 1965, and in particular since 1969, there has been in progress a sharp political debate between the rival political parties as to the merits and disadvantages of Sri Lanka obtaining foreign assistance especially in the form of loans. While U.N.P. leaders, especially Dudley Senanayake, insist that an underdeveloped country like Sri Lanka cannot hope to progress without such assistance, Mrs Bandaranaike and other U.F. leaders aver that Sri Lanka should learn to be self-reliant and that trade not aid is the answer to the problem of development. For instance, Mrs Bandaranaike in her speech, during the discussion on the world economic situation and trends on 18 January 1971 at the

Commonwealth conference in Singapore, complained that foreign aid had meant external borrowings at relatively high interest rates which were also sometimes subject to rigorous conditions.[62] She indicated that her government would have preferred the outright benefits that would have accrued from better terms of trade. Actually Sri Lanka has given her active support towards achieving this objective by backing UNCTAD's scheme of generalised preferences for the manufactures of developing countries. In April 1972 the U.F. minister of internal and foreign trade expressed views similar to those of Mrs Bandaranaike at the UNCTAD III meeting in Santiago. In particular he urged remedial action to free Sri Lanka from the burdens imposed by frequent upward revision of freight rates and the substantial debt service burdens arising out of an external debt.[63]

In the decade 1960–9, Sri Lanka borrowed extensively from the I.B.R.D., I.M.F., I.D.A., foreign governments and foreign commercial banks.[64] In 1960, the external debt was a mere Rs 225.3 million but by 1969 it had multiplied more than ten times over to the tune of Rs 2,642.5 million. From 1967 to 1970 loans amounting to Rs 350 million were raised from financial institutions and banks in Europe and America as well. Between 1965–70 a total of Rs 723.4 million was raised in the form of short-term loans from the I.M.F. of which Rs 301.7 million was paid back by 20 May 1970, leaving a balance of Rs 421.7 million. The inevitable result has been an unbearable debt service burden on the country. In 1960 amortisation and interest payments took away a mere 2 per cent of export earnings (Rs 33.3 million) but by 1969 these rose to 22 per cent of export earnings (Rs 418.1 million).[65]

The unfortunate aspect of these borrowings is that they have been utilised for current domestic consumption and not for promoting economic growth. Moreover, most of the foreign aid obtained has been tied aid. Rarely has it been free of strings attached. Tying is with reference to particular projects as those organised by the I.B.R.D., or to projects and specific sources of supply, or in the form of commodity loans. The direct costs of tied aid according to the Pearson Report (1969) often exceed 20 per cent, in the context of the costs of goods supplied. Prices are much in excess of those that prevail in the open market.

Loans from the I.M.F. were also subjected to the Sri Lanka government agreeing to alter, among other things, its policies on social welfare, and to impose restrictions on the local credit market. This became standard practice during the term of office of the Dudley Senanayake 'national government'. Four Letters of Intent on these lines were addressed to the I.M.F. in 1965, 1966, 1968, and 1969 and a supplementary Letter of Intent in December 1969.[66] The implementation of these intentions was one of the prime causes for the electoral rout of the 'national government' at the general election of May 1970.

The 'national government's' electoral standing was made far worse when it fell in line with the conditions that the I.B.R.D. and the I.D.A. imposed for the grant of a loan to finance the first stage of the mammoth Mahaveli river diversion project. The project was no doubt going to provide many benefits for the island by way of opening up lands for development and absorbing excess population but the U.F., not without reason, alleged in its election manifesto of 1970 that the 'national government' had agreed to (1) allow the I.B.R.D. and I.D.A., which they identified with the United States, the right for thirty years 'to interfere in and determine the economic destinies of nearly two-thirds of Sri Lanka'; (2) the I.B.R.D. having veto powers over all appointments and dismissals to major posts in the river diversion scheme and in regard to all major tenders and purchases of machinery; (3) levy a water tax of not less than Rs 40 per acre from the farmers of the north central province, the province which was to gain most from the river diversion, where the existing tax was a mere fraction (between Rs 2 and Rs 5 per acre) of what was proposed; and (4) obtain the prior sanction of the I.B.R.D. if Parliament ever proposed varying these conditions. The U.F. exaggerated the position when it said that the last-mentioned term was an infringement of the country's sovereignty. Dudley Senanayake and other leaders of his 'national government' countered that these were reasonable conditions when viewed in the context of the advantages that the scheme would confer on the island.[67] U.F. spokesmen, however, insisted that they would re-negotiate the agreement and would repudiate it if the I.B.R.D. proved unwilling to concede more favourable terms. Some of them pointed to the example of Egypt's construction of the Aswan Dam with Soviet assistance when aid from the west was suspended. In the end the U.F. government itself was not able materially to alter the terms.

In office, the U.F. has complained bitterly about the heavy external debts it inherited from the 'national government'. But the economic situation is just as parlous with them as it was with their predecessors owing to the crushing welfare burdens imposed on the national budget. The Trotskyist minister of finance attempted to negotiate assistance from the international credit agencies, but found that their conditions would ruin the U.F. government. In March 1972 the minister stated that the I.B.R.D. had been proposing various forms of devaluation, including devaluation of the rupee by 55 per cent, but he had no intention of doing so. He accused the I.B.R.D. of wanting the U.F. government 'to fall down at its feet'.[68]

Despite these charges and accusations, it is significant that during the term of office of the 'national government' (1965–70), the I.B.R.D. did a great deal towards mobilising a fair amount of economic assistance from an Aid Sri Lanka Consortium of non-communist governments comprising Australia, Britain, Canada, Denmark, West Germany, France, India, Italy, Japan and the United States to help the island get on the road to economic recovery. Six meetings of the consortium were convened by the bank during 1965–70 for organising six programmes of project and commodity aid. The total pledged under the first five programmes amounted to Rs 1,568.4 million.[69] A sixth meeting of the consortium held in Paris in February 1970 promised a further Rs 630 million. The bank itself gave Sri Lanka loans to the value of Rs 226.5 million during 1965–9, while its affiliate, the I.D.A., provided Rs 41.1 million.[70] In 1970 the bank and the I.D.A. committed themselves to providing a loan of Rs 1,000 million for the Mahaveli river diversion project and they paid the first instalment of Rs 180 million towards stage one of this project. Another international credit agency, the Asia Development Bank, gave loans amounting to Rs 26.9 million during the same period. In contrast, during the entire period of M.E.P.–S.L.F.P. rule (1956–65), these credit agencies provided a mere Rs 107 million in loans (the Asian Development Bank had not come into existence then).[71]

The 'national government's' friendly disposition towards the west was no doubt an important consideration in influencing the donor countries and the credit agencies concerned. But just as pertinent was the fact that, as the Manfred G. Blobel I.B.R.D.–

I.D.A. mission to Sri Lanka remarked in its report of January 1968, the 'national government' had, 'despite the difficult political situation, established a creditable record of action on a number of important economic fronts'.[72] The same government had also, during its first year of office, taken the necessary steps adequately to compensate the foreign oil companies, mostly American and British, for those of their assets which the preceding S.L.F.P. government had nationalised.

The states of the communist bloc for their part are just as enthusiastic whenever S.L.F.P.-oriented governments take office. But it must also be said that these states did not deliberately seek to cut off aid during the term of office of the 'national government' (1965–70). Further, their loans are at lower rates of interest than those from the west, and in some instances free of interest.

During the phases of S.L.F.P. or S.L.F.P.-oriented rule, 1956 to 1965, and from 1970 to April 1972 Sri Lanka received a total of Rs 841.2 million in loans.[73] Of this, China contributed Rs 315 million free of interest, the German Democratic Republic Rs 200 million, the Soviet Union Rs 192.8 million and Yugoslavia Rs 73.3 million. In addition, the Chinese made outright grants totalling Rs 130 million. They have also provided in the form of gifts (1) machinery and equipment worth Rs 40 million for a textile mill they are setting up in Pugoda; (2) an international conference hall in memory of S. W. R. D. Bandaranaike at an estimated cost of Rs 35 million; and (3) five gunboats of about 100 tons each.

During 1965–70, relations with China became strained as a result of the 'national government's' seizure of Chinese communist literature and Mao badges and protests by U.N.P.-oriented Ceylonese Muslims about the alleged ill-treatment of Muslims in Sinkiang. But by February 1970 relations with the 'national government' had improved and the Chinese were willing to assist in the setting up of the textile mill referred to in the preceding paragraph. The Soviets for their part set up a steel rolling mill and a tyre and tube factory in 1967 under the terms of the loan agreement signed in 1958 and offered to assist in the expansion of a state flour mill. In September 1969 they entered into an agreement with the 'national government' to provide technical assistance to Sri Lanka.

In 1970, with drastic changes in foreign policy, oriented more in the direction of the communist bloc and the middle east countries, the U.F. government hoped there would be adequate appreciation from these quarters. But this was not to be. In October 1970, the minister of internal and external trade had occasion to complain about this when he wrote:[74]

> We are fighting neo-colonialism and imperialism. Our foreign policy is very clear and that policy has been effectively implemented. Consequently we are beginning to suffer from retaliatory measures particularly in trade and aid.

And he censured Sri Lanka's socialist friends for not coming to the island's assistance.

It was obvious from developments in the post-1970 phase that the west had begun to show concrete evidence of its disapproval of the new orientations in Sri Lanka's foreign policy. The closure of Asia Foundation and the winding up of Peace Corps activities in Sri Lanka irritated American opinion. The United States expressed regret that the government of Sri Lanka had decided to terminate the agreement signed in 1962 providing for Peace Corps services.[75] The agreement had in fact been signed during Mrs Bandaranaike's first tenure as prime minister. Nor was the granting of full diplomatic recognition to the German Democratic Republic any more helpful, especially as the West Germans had been Sri Lanka's second biggest aid-givers in the 1965–70 phase. Aid was stopped but was resumed in 1973. The suspension of diplomatic relations with Israel on 29 July 1970, according to Mrs Bandaranaike herself, had had some adverse repercussions on Sri Lanka's trade with certain firms in Britain with Israeli connections.[76]

Foreign Trade

Prior to 1956, Sri Lanka's trade followed the traditional colonial pattern of ties with the sterling and dollar areas. Britain was the principal trading partner and still continues to be. There was no effort made to diversify trade, and commerce with the communist bloc was negligible. Up to 1950, it was less than 1 per cent of Sri Lanka's total import and export trade.

From 1950 to the mid-1950s some diversification of trade took place, but except for the rubber–rice agreement with China in

1952, this trade diversion was not of any great significance. The U.N.P. governments in office up to 1956 were not too anxious to enter into trade relations with communist countries. The agreement with China was forced on the Dudley Senanayake government of the day because of the collapse of the short-lived Korean War rubber boom in that year. In fact, before negotiations began with the Chinese, the Sri Lanka government asked the United States to guarantee a reasonable price for rubber but this was refused and then when a request was made to the United States for rice to be supplied on a government-to-government basis, Sri Lanka was directed to make purchases in the open market.[77] The prospect however was held out of possible assistance for this transaction from the government of the United States. In 1955 another step in the direction of trade diversification was taken by the Kotelawala government when a trade and payments agreement was concluded with Poland.

Trade with the communist countries did not add up to very much. The annual average value of exports for 1951–5 was Rs 149 million or 8.5 per cent of the total, and imports Rs 97 million (6.2 per cent).

With the election of S. W. R. D. Bandaranaike's M.E.P. to office in 1956, there was an expansion of trade with the communist bloc, one of the immediate results of the new prime minister's policy of neutralism and friendship with all states, regardless of their alignments. Bilateral trade and payments agreements were concluded with the Soviet Union, Yugoslavia, and the communist states of eastern Europe.

Between 1956 and 1960, the annual average value of exports to communist countries, inclusive of China was Rs 149 million (8.5 per cent) and imports Rs 145 million (7.9 per cent). Under the successor government of Mrs Bandaranaike, 1960–5, there was further expansion, the average annual value of exports for 1961–5 being Rs 210 million (11.6 per cent) and imports Rs 224 million (13.4 per cent). There was in fact a trade imbalance.

The pattern of this multilateralised trade had been firmly established when the pro-west 'national government' took office in 1965. The new government not merely kept these trade outlets but had them considerably expanded. In 1966, 20 per cent of Sri Lanka's export trade of Rs 1,710 million was with the communist bloc. It was the same in 1969 (20 per cent), the last year of office of this government. There was continuing evidence of a trade imbalance with the communist countries during this phase. In 1966, Sri Lanka imported 20.7 per cent of her total requirements and in 1969, 20.9 from the communist states.

Sri Lanka's bilateral trade and payments agreements tend to work to her disadvantage when countries which buy her goods sell them, sometimes shipping them directly, with the relevant Commonwealth preference certificates, to her traditional buyers at discount rates for hard currency. The practice is pursued by some of the communist states of eastern Europe and it has resulted in some depression of prices of Sri Lanka's traditional exports. In August 1971, the minister of finance announced that countries which buy produce under bilateral agreements would hereafter have to give a guarantee that produce will be shipped directly to the purchasing country.[78]

Sri Lanka is burdened with two of the problems of most primary-producing countries – a low elasticity of demand for her exports and a rising import bill aggravated further by constant price rises in freight rates. Hence the adverse terms of trade and a perpetual balance of payments crisis. Table 6.1 gives the picture of Sri Lanka's desperate plight.

TABLE 6.1

FOREIGN TRADE, 1951–70

Annual Average (in Rs millions)

	Export f.o.b.	Imports c.i.f.	Trade Balance
1951–5 (U.N.P.)	1,745	1,545	200
1956–60 (M.E.P.-S.L.F.P.)	1,743	1,823	-80
1961–5 (S.L.F.P.)	1,819	1,660	159
1966–70 (U.N.P.-'National')	1,910	2,229	-319

Source. *Annual Reports* of the Central Bank.

It will be seen that the situation in terms of burdens on governments was worst for the U.N.P.-oriented 'national government' of 1965–70. But the deterioration began from 1956 and there was consequently very little foreign exchange available for serious developmental efforts.

Tea accounts for 60 to 65 per cent of export earnings but world demand, it is estimated, is rising at a mere 1.5 per cent per annum. Next to Britain, the United States, Austrialia, Iraq and South Africa, in that order, are the major buyers of Ceylon teas. The Soviet Union and the communist states of eastern Europe also purchase a fair quantity of Ceylon tea.

Though the middle east is an important patron of low grown Ceylon teas, trade with the countries of this area has to be balanced by imports from them, not all of which are of much use to the local consumer. Consequently there is a trade imbalance with some of these countries. In 1971, the United Arab Republic had an outstanding trade imbalance of £3.8 million and Syria Rs 10 million.[79]

The U.F. government's expression of solidarity with the Arab cause did have a favourable effect on the island's trade relations with the middle east countries. In February 1971, the U.F. minister of foreign and internal trade negotiated agreements that were quite advantageous to Sri Lanka with the United Arab Republic and the Republic of Iraq.[80] The former agreed to purchase Rs 42.9 million worth of tea for 1971 as against Rs 35.7 million in 1970, besides rubber, coconut products and cocoa to the value of Rs 11.4 million, while Sri Lanka in return would import cotton and textiles, phosphates, sugar and crude oil. The latter pledged to make a minimum annual purchase of 40 million pounds of tea valued at approximately Rs 72 million for the next five years and to supply Sri Lanka in turn with crude oil and dates. However Iraq's purchases of tea for 1970 amounted to 30 million pounds valued at Rs 53 million. Trade relations with Iraq were in fact first established in 1961 by the same minister during the S.L.F.P.'s tenure of office in 1960–5.

Rubber is the second most important of Ceylon's export produce, providing between 15 to 20 per cent of export earnings. Satisfactory prices depend on competition from synthetic rubber and American stockpile releases. Natural rubber has a competitive advantage over synthetic by way of cost reduction through better yields and improved production methods. A replanting programme is in operation and it is expected that the increased yields will offset the decline in prices. China is the island's principal customer, taking more than 50 per cent of exports while Poland, West Germany, the United States and the Soviet Union in that order are the other purchasers.

The rubber–rice agreement initially entered into with China in

1952 and renewed five times since then has worked to the distinct advantage of Sri Lanka.[81] The Chinese bought rubber up to 1959 at prices between 3 to 6 pence per pound above the world market prices prevailing in Singapore, and after 1959 at 5 Ceylon cents (after devaluation at $6\frac{1}{4}$ Ceylon cents) per pound above Singapore prices. In addition China has supplied the major part of Sri Lanka's rice requirements at prices below world market levels. The quantity of rice imported remained at 200,000 tons a year from 1961 to 1972. Since 1967 China has supplied more than 50 per cent of the island's rice imports. In 1969 it was as high as 71 per cent. The increased percentage was due to the continuing success of the 'grow more rice' camapaign organised by the 'national government', so that there was no need to have recourse to Sri Lanka's other markets in Burma and Thailand for her rice requirements.

In recent times there has been some unease because of excessive dependence on China for the import of rice and the sale of rubber. The minister of foreign and internal trade stated in April 1972 at a press conference in New Delhi that Sri Lanka might consider reviewing her rubber–rice agreement with China as soon as self-sufficiency in rice was achieved, which he expected would be in 1974.[82]

Coconut products are the third most important of Sri Lanka's exports. They comprise about 15 per cent of export earnings. As in the case of rubber, price declines in the long term are likely because of competition from other oils and fats, particularly soya bean, though not to the same extent. Production in recent times has also been affected owing to the widespread prevalence of the coconut pest, cummingi. The prospects of earnings rising lie mainly in the expansion of yields. Of the three coconut products, India and Pakistan are the largest buyers of copra, the Soviet Union and China of coconut oil, and Britain and West Germany of desiccated coconut.

ALIGNMENT AND NONALIGNMENT

Sri Lanka's political relationships with the outside world lend themselves to easy classification because of the well-known stances of her prime ministers, and the attitudes of the main political parties. In many respects it is the prime ministers who lend form and substance to matters of foreign concern, other ministers seldom evincing much interest in what goes beyond the confines of the island. Some of the prime ministers, for their part, showed an enthusiasm for involvement in international questions because they were quick to perceive the potentialities that lay in a small, non-committed nation playing the role of mediator, if not arbitrator, in the conflicts between bigger powers in the world around them. Depending on their skills, initiative and acceptability, they saw in such foreign feats the opportunity for boosting the island's image in the world at large and the dividends this could pay by way of enhanced political kudos for themselves in the domestic sphere.

The Senanayakes, D. S. and Dudley, preferred generally to avoid foreign entanglements. Both were, in this respect, retiring statesmen who concentrated most of their attention on local matters. But they both had an enduring interest in maintaining the Commonwealth connection, close ties with Britain, and friendship with the west generally.

The closest Sri Lanka came to complete alignment with the west, if not the United States, was when Sir John Kotelawala held the premiership. It is true that in all his public pronouncements he protested his country's neutrality but his autobiography, *An Asian Prime Minister's Story* and the account of his foreign missions, *Between Two Worlds*, leave no doubt that he would have steered Sri Lanka into the Anglo-American bloc but for the fact that he feared the political consequences on the home front. He used the veneer of neutralism to disguise his attachment to the west. His hatred of communism, which at times came near to an obsession, was international talk. In some ways, he was openly eclectic, borrowing the phraseology of S. W. R. D. Bandaranaike such as 'Ceylon being a Switzerland of the east', of 'functioning between two worlds' to convey attitudes which were the very negation of those of his distinguished opponent.

S. W. R. D. Bandaranaike was a trail-blazer who cut out a path for Sri Lanka in the international jungle of power conflicts. His concept of neutralism was not dissimilar to that of Nehru, with the difference that he adapted it to suit the needs of a smaller country which, in his view, had a message to convey. During his tenure of office, he sought to give meaning to his policies by making his government's views on the pressing international problems of the day internationally known. It was evidently his ambition to make his mark on the international stage, but the serious domestic problems that confronted him, and his unfortunate assassination, deprived him of the opportunity.

Mrs Bandaranaike has had ample scope to spell out the policies of her husband in all their detail. It is sometimes argued that she has deviated from the master's concepts of nonalignment. Her close identification with the Afro-Asian group, unqualified condemnation of colonialism and racism, support for the independence struggles of subject peoples, and diplomatic recognition of new states in the communist bloc, should not however be mistaken for alignment with an anti-western group of powers. Both Mrs Bandaranaike and her cabinets have been only too well aware that commitment to one side only could result in damaging the possibilities of Sri Lanka obtaining assistance from the states of both power blocs. This awareness was typified in the recent remark of her Trotskyist minister of finance when in his second budget speech he said that small countries like Sri Lanka could not afford to be big choosers.

The leaders of the traditional Marxist parties have, since 1956, fallen in line with the foreign policies of the Bandaranaikes, differing only on questions of detail. But between them, the L.S.S.P. and the C.P., there are differences in that the former's leaders, while supporting the Soviet Union as a workers' state, show no hesitation in condemning Soviet action in for example Hungary and Czechoslovakia, while the latter's leadership on such occasions play the role of apologists. Nor does the L.S.S.P. leadership conceal its admiration for the Yugoslavs.

The overriding principle in the foreign policies of both the U.N.P. and S.L.F.P. has been an unflinching pursuit of the national interest. The results no doubt give rise to a difference of opinion, but neither party has in its stances, especially in the post-1956 phase, attempted seriously to alienate either power bloc. In other words, Sri Lanka's post-1956 foreign policies in a sense reflect her domestic political position, a movement towards the centre.

In the 1947–52 phase, the prime minister (D. S. Senanayake) confined his interest to the subject of relations with Britain in particular and the Commonwealth in general. In other matters he allowed a free hand virtually to two of his ministers at the time,

S. W. R. D. Bandaranaike, a neutralist, and J. R. Jayawardene who was noted for his pro-American and pro-west leanings.

However on occasion Senanayake preferred to act independently of Britain. In 1952 his government extended diplomatic recognition to the People's Republic of China even before Britain or some of the other states in the Commonwealth. But his suspicions of communist attempts to interfere in local politics, not altogether unfounded, led him and his successors to refrain from exchanging diplomatic representatives with the Soviet Union and China and for that matter with other communist states.

Bandaranaike was D. S. Senanayake's representative at the conferences of Afro-Asian states summoned during this phase. He received no specific instructions from Senanayake on how he should express Sri Lanka's views on the questions of the hour. At the Asian Relations Conference convened in New Delhi in March 1947, Bandaranaike was the only spokesman at this conference who expressed the hope that it would lead to 'a federation of free and equal Asian countries'.[83] This was a recurring theme in many of his speeches on foreign policy. He could not, however, take concrete action on it, when he had the opportunity as prime minister, for reasons already stated. In January 1949, Bandaranaike was again Sri Lanka's representative at the conference held in New Delhi to condemn the Dutch action in Indonesia. Even before the conference, the D. S. Senanayake government closed the island's ports and air space to Dutch ships and planes transporting materials of war to Indonesia. Bandaranaike has remarked that at this conference attempts were made to influence him to get Sri Lanka to fall in line with a British proposal to save the face of the Dutch.[84] Bandaranaike stated that D. S. Senanayake left it to him to do as he wished.[85] In related international agencies, such as WHO, Bandaranaike (when he functioned as Senanayake's representative) stated that Cold War politics tended to intrude into what were purely technical discussions. On such occasions too he claims he adopted the attitude of 'not being unduly bound to the chariot wheels of anyone', treating each question on its merits and expressing views without fear or favour.[86]

Jayawardene expatiated against reprisals against Japan at the San Francisco Conference on the Japanese Peace Treaty. The position he took was that a Buddhist country like Sri Lanka would not be a party to vengeful action against another Buddhist country, Japan. His views on a friendly approach to Japan were in line with American policy and he won praise for his stand in sections of the American press. As stated elsewhere, Jayawardene was, with Australia's Percy Spender, co-author of the Colombo Plan. In October 1952, as minister of agriculture and food in the Dudley Senanayake government, Jayawardene expressed misgivings about the wisdom of the proposed rubber–rice agreement with China. His view was that the move would put Ceylon 'out of step' with her friends in the U.N. – an obvious reference to the United States among other friendly states.[87]

During Sir John Kotelawala's premiership (1953–6) Sri Lanka became in all but name a committed supporter of the west, despite Sir John's claims to nonalignment. In fact one of the reasons for the resignation from his cabinet of one of his leading ministers and his close kinsman, R. G. Senanayake, was his disapproval of what he felt was the prime minister's pro-American foreign policy.[88] During his visit to the United States in December 1954, the prime minister in his public utterances took pains to explain why his country could not join SEATO but he also maintained that 'he kept an open mind on the subject'.[89] It was his view that talk of American aid to Asian countries with strings was without foundation, that the United States had no intention of dictating to Asia and that there was 'hardly another example in history of aid on the scale envisaged by America'.[90] Earlier, in May 1954, Sir John permitted American *Globemasters* to make use of local airport facilities when transporting French troops in Indo-China. The prime minister boldly defended his position. His view was that as long as there was no ceasefire, it was not correct 'to deter one outside party from giving aid to the belligerents without any guarantee that the other party would not do the same' and he added that he 'saw no purpose in being neutral for the benefit of the wrong party'.[91]

At the conferences Sir John convened or attended, he openly and frankly expressed his opposition to communism at the local and international levels. From his point of view they were interlinked. This was expressed at the five-nation conference of south-east Asian prime ministers in Colombo over which Sir John himself presided in April 1954. It was more forcefully articulated at the Bogor Conference in December 1954, and at Bandung in

April 1955.[92] He had unorthodox views on Taiwan which did not appeal to either the K.M.T. nationalists or the People's Republic of China.[93]

Sir John's pronouncements drew strong criticism from the opposition in Ceylon's Paliament. His performance at the Bandung Conference was the subject of a motion of no-confidence on his government, on 27 April 1955. The opposition leader, S. W. R. D. Bandaranaike, in concluding his speech remarked that the prime minister had created 'a most unfortunate position, almost a position of isolation, for this country'.[94] At the general election a year later, the subject of Sir John's pro-west foreign policy loomed large, opposition spokesmen asserting that their continuance would result in the atom bomb being dropped in Ceylon.[95]

The M.E.P. government of S. W. R. D. Bandaranaike, effected drastic changes in foreign policy which put the country firmly on the nonaligned path. The new prime minister saw in this policy certain positive advantages that would accrue to Sri Lanka. In a statement to the House of Representatives on 24 July 1957 he set out his concept of nonalignment when he said:[96]

> We prefer what we call a neutral state which is nothing more than that we like to be friendly with all and like to obtain what is advantageous to our own new society – while following our own way of life – through whatever benefit we can get from east or west, north or south, from everyone, and, at the same time, prevent misunderstanding between two opposing camps which brings us close to another war in which all mankind will perish.

And he added:

> It [neutralism] certainly means this: that in the pursuit of that policy we reserve to ourselves the right of criticising our friends – and I hope all are our friends – when we feel they have not acted correctly. We shall not incur the charge of having double standards in dealing with questions of this kind.

The prime minister insisted, quite rightly, that in the pursuit of this policy his government had not sacrificed the friendships Sri Lanka had, but that instead a number of new friendships had been made. This was indeed borne out by the actions of his government. The grant of military bases to Britain under the defence agreement of 1947 was withdrawn, but Sri Lanka decided, and was permitted, to become a republic within the Commonwealth. In the same year (1956) diplomatic relations were established with China and the Soviet Union. This was followed by an exchange of diplomatic contact between Sri Lanka and some of the other communist states in eastern Europe.

In the opening of these diplomatic channels of communication Bandaranaike saw the possibility of economic and cultural benefits accruing to Sri Lanka. Her trade patterns changed for the better as a result of the bilateral trade agreements that were concluded with communist countries. At the same time economic assistance became available from them without there being any significant drop in aid from the west.

In 1958 Bandaranaike began campaigning for greater economic co-operation among the Asian countries. He repeated the call made earlier by other Asian statesmen for an economic Bandung.[97]

There is little doubt that these policies won for Sri Lanka a place of prominence and respect among the nations of the world, particularly in the councils of the nonaligned states. During the approximately three and a half years of his premiership, many of the leading personages of the communist and Afro-Asian world visited Ceylon and counselled with Bandaranaike and issued joint statements with him on the pressing international problems of the day[98] – Chou En-Lai, Nehru, Nobusuke Kishi, Soekarno, Viliam Siroky, and Tito, among others. Sri Lanka's foreign policy since 1956 has been more or less, depending on the political complexion of governments, variations of the central theme of nonalignment.

During 1960–5 (Mrs Bandaranaike) there was evidence of a shift towards an anti-western position within the existing framework of nonalignment, just as in 1965–70 (Dudley Senanayake) the shift was more in the direction of the west though again the operation did not go beyond the confines already agreed on from 1956.

Mrs Bandaranaike took an important part in the conferences of nonaligned nations at Belgrade in September 1961 and in Cairo in October 1964. She visited China in 1961 with a view to forging closer relationships. Her government's subsequent nationalisation of the major assets of American- and British-owned petroleum companies and the reluctance to pay adequate compensation to them coupled with the delays in the payment of what was offered brought about a suspension of American aid. It was resumed only after the succeeding 'national government' of Dudley Senanayake agreed on compensation acceptable to the oil companies. In December 1962, Mrs Bandaranaike convened a conference of six nonaligned nations (Sri Lanka, the United Arab Republic, Ghana, Cambodia, Indonesia and Burma) to formulate proposals to end the Sino-Indian War. Mrs Bandaranaike was authorised to convey these proposals to the contending powers, and they were generally regarded as favourable to India.[99] Nothing however came of these.

When she returned to office for the second time in 1970, Mrs Bandaranaike headed a front comprising Trotskyists, communists and her own S.L.F.P. To some extent the alliance with the Marxists had a bearing on the foreign policy her U.F. government chose to follow. Sri Lanka established full diplomatic relations with the German Democratic Republic despite requests by the Bonn Embassy in Colombo to have it delayed. The Democratic Republic of Korea and the Provisional Revolutionary Government of South Vietnam were also recognised. More far-reaching was the decision to sever diplomatic relations with Israel until such time as the latter conformed to the U.N. security council's decision in 1967 or came to an amicable settlement with the United Arab Republic. These actions on the whole were intended to moderate Sri Lanka's allegedly excessive dependence on the west and bring about her closer identification with the nonaligned states and anti-colonial movements. Mrs Bandaranaike made the position clear in her pronouncements at the Lusaka Conference in 1970. At the same time it was hoped that the west would not get completely alienated. Both calculations proved wrong.

As already stated, the communist and socialist-oriented nonaligned states failed to come readily to the U.F. government's assistance. Worse still the west cooled off. On 8 May 1972 for instance, the *Ceylon Daily News* reported that the World Bank had submitted an 'extremely critical report' on Sri Lanka's economic situation to the Aid Sri Lanka Group and advised action only after the U.F. government had taken 'meaningful steps to arrest the general deterioration of the economy'. The same issue of the *Ceylon Daily News* also spoke of a hardening of Bonn's attitude on aid matters because of the U.F. government's support of the German Democratic Republic's attempts to gain admission to the United Nations and its allied agencies.

During the P.L.F. insurrection of March–April 1971, when the island's armed forces and the police were under severe strain, Mrs Bandaranaike appealed for military assistance from the western and Soviet blocs and from the nonaligned nations. Britain, the United States and India provided, obviously in their own interests, adequate supplies of arms and ammunition. The Soviet Union, the United Arab Republic, Yugoslavia and Pakistan also gave some assistance. The Chinese were unable, for inadequately explained reasons, to respond with the same alacrity as the other states. Weeks after the crisis had passed its worst phase, the Chinese prime minister wrote, on 26 April 1971, to Mrs Bandaranaike denouncing the revolutionaries, and offering Sri Lanka an interest-free loan of Rs 150 million. The text of Chou En-Lai's communication was released to the public a month later, on 27 May.[100] Mrs Bandaranaike dismissed the rumours circulating in Ceylon and abroad of foreign support for the insurrection.[101] The North Korean Embassy staff in Colombo had nevertheless been implicated and they were asked to leave the country. Mrs Bandaranaike claimed that the aid Sri Lanka received from countries so vastly different in their outlook from each other, without any strings attached, was evidence of the success of her policy of neutralism.[102] But the bald fact is that they did so in their own self-interest, due to Sri Lanka's strategic situation in the Indian Ocean especially in the context of nuclear war. They have not been as willing to come to Ceylon's economic assistance. If an ultra-left government came into being in Ceylon, it would have confiscated all foreign assets in the country and aligned itself with any big communist power which was willing to be its patron. Since the revolutionaries were to some extent Maoist-inspired and their leader, Rohana Wijeweera, was an expelled student of the Patrice Lumumba University, Moscow, they would probably have sought Chinese assistance had they succeeded.

7 Conclusion

COMPARISONS

At least two of the new states of the post-Second World War phase besides Sri Lanka, namely India and Malaysia, may be considered in the category of nations in dangerous equilibrium, with the difference however that Sri Lanka's political experience indicates that she has survived this state over a longer period of time than the other two. Sri Lanka in this sense may therefore be regarded as being in a continuous state of dangerous equilibrium. India and Malaysia have still not produced the viable democratic alternative that Sri Lanka has. They still conform to the one-party dominance model.[1] We have yet to see whether power can or will be transferred to an opposition party and whether the government that results will be stable and conform to democratic practices as in Sri Lanka, or entrench itself permanently. Conversely, the government that must give way could refuse to do so. Malaysia in this respect appears to face a serious situation after the events of May 1969,[2] and her Sino-Malay problem, given the rival social, religious and cultural polarities begs a solution. Many of the other new nations of Asia and Africa have fallen victims to *coups d'état* and dictatorships or are showing distinct signs of veering away from democracy.

NATIONAL INTEGRATION

In an emergent state with a plural society and a colonial past such as Sri Lanka, nationalism and national integration has tended to take a tortuous course.

A select English educated elitist group, mostly deracinated urbanites conforming to Hans Kohn's concept of western-style nationalism[3] conceives of national integration in terms of a political ideal of constitutional government and a unity in diversity.

It speaks the language of sophistication and addresses its message to the westernised intelligentsia and/or the politically conscious working class. But it has failed to penetrate the layers beneath – the fragmented competitive subsocieties of the real Sri Lanka in the countryside, with its rural elites and peasant economy.

The other type is similar to the kind described by Karl Deutsch as being associated with the 'mass mobilisation of pre-commercial, pre-industrial peasant peoples'.[4] Attempts in this direction are made by indigenous-syle Sinhalese nationalists.[5] They emphasise the 'critical stigmata of nationalism' – the language, culture, traditions and heroes of the dominant nationality – the Sinhalese Buddhists. It is what Clifford Geertz calls the reassertion of primordial societies which becomes increasingly evident once the alien ruler departs.[6] The ethnic and religious minority groups do not get activated in the same way because they are apprehensive of majority domination. Some cower for protection under the majority umbrella, others organise protest movements.

However, though the primordial societies of Sri Lanka are in turmoil, their leadership continues to be invested in the English-educated elites who realise the dangers imminent in internecine strife to the accompaniment of economic retrogression. At one end of the political spectrum are conservative modernists represented by the U.N.P. while at the other are the traditional left-wing groups who disapprove of the drift to the primordial past. The centre, comprising S.L.F.P. elements, seeks a middle solution after having traversed the primordial path.

Out of the dialectics of the conflicting endeavours of these rival political groupings and the protest movements of majority and minority, Sri Lanka, it might be said, is in the process of moving to a higher stage of national evolution, what Geertz calls the 'integrative revolution', the situation where new states successfully contrive to weave the subnationalisms of their primordial societies into the fabric of modern politics.[7] The process is a delicate operation, because any attempt to focus attention on one group, supposedly at the expense of the others, or even the impression that such attention is being focused, can throw it out of balance. This was Sri Lanka's experience in the decade or so after independence. Consequently centrifugal tendencies – extreme Sinhalese Buddhist militancy and Tamil separatism – have to be contained. W. Howard Wriggins' *Ceylon: The Dilemmas of a*

New Nation,[8] B. H. Farmer's *Ceylon: A Divided Nation*[9] and R. N. Kearney's *Communalism and Language in the Politics of Ceylon*[10] illustrate with great clarity the problems involved.

POLITICAL STABILITY

In the twenty-five years since independence Sri Lanka has had nine prime ministers, one of whom held office on three different occasions and another on two. In effect therefore there have been to date six persons holding the office of prime minister and of them one held office for more than three and a half years while two served for a little more than four and a half years each and a third lasted the full term of five years. Further, in the span of twenty-five years only two major political parties (U.N.P. and S.L.F.P.) have dominated the political scene. In the first phase each of these parties had a nine-year run, the U.N.P. from 1947 to 1956 and the S.L.F.P. from 1956 to 1965. In the second phase, the U.N.P. with its allies had a five-year run, 1965–70, while the S.L.F.P. with its partners started its term in 1970 and they have so far maintained a stable government. Added to all this is the fact that the five changes in government have all been effected in a peaceful and constitutional manner. This record is unusual compared to what has happened in many of the new states of Asia and Africa.

Part of the success of Sri Lanka's political set-up must be attributed to the solidarity-makers and problem-solvers in the major political parties. They have to a large extent harmonised differing, competing and sometimes conflicting social and economic interests and in terms of Eldersveld's view managed to cope with 'widely varying local milieus of opinion, tradition and social structure'.[11] But in moments of crisis these parties have succumbed to the pressures of the dominant Sinhalese Buddhist group on the controversial problems of language, education and religion. However they have quickly righted themselves by moving back to a centrist position.

Further, a measure of stability is established by political parties moving in the direction of what Robert Michels has called an 'omnibus tendency'.[12] Parties seek to outbid their opponents and in the process sacrifice their 'political virginity by entering into promiscuous relationship with the most heterogeneous political elements'.[13] In this way parties which would have otherwise worked outside the political framework, such as the traditional Marxists and ethnic militants (Sinhalese and Tamil), have been accommodated by the major parties and in the process obtained at least partial satisfaction of their goals. Again the situation is delicately poised because the traditional Marxists and the ethnic militants could be forced to opt out by extreme elements in their ranks.

Still another source of stability is evidenced in the willingness of the major parties to broaden the basis of representative government by creating new elites or re-structuring existing ones. Maurice Duverger's view[14] that 'all government is by nature oligarchic but the origins and training of the oligarchs may be very different and these determine their actions' and that the formula 'government of the people by the people must be replaced by the formula government of the people by an elite sprung from the people' sums up adequately the attempts being made by the established political parties in Sri Lanka to democratise their leadership patterns in the context of newer parties tapping the neglected layers of society. But the equilibrium can at any time be upset if those outside the pale feel they will not be socialised into the body politic. The violent P.L.F. insurrection of March–April 1971 by neglected youth seeking upward social mobility points out to such a danger. And similar outbreaks can take place in the future as well.

INTERNAL CONSTRAINTS

A welfare state providing services beyond its capacity has numbed economic growth. These social services have to be largely provided from export earnings which are very much at the mercy of a fluctuating international market. An alternative is to borrow extensively from donor countries in the western and communist blocs and from the international credit agencies. Both sources will not provide assistance to feed and service a population merely to keep governments viable. To prune the social services is to court political disaster. The U.N.P. governments of the 1952–6 and 1965–70 phases paid this price.

The situation is made worse by the rapid growth of population in the last twenty-five years and an imbalance in the age composition. A majority of the population is under twenty-one years. This implies a greater burden on the welfare system. In addition, the fact that education is free but not geared to national needs makes the school-going population take the easy road of enrolling in the liberal arts. The inevitable result is a glut of employables in the white collar market. Governments have consequently not been able to provide the kind of jobs that are demanded. An explosive situation therefore exists, characterised by intense and sometimes violent inter-ethnic and inter-religious rivalries and an impatient youth which seeks to register its protest by open insurrection.

EXTERNAL CONSTRAINTS

Sri Lanka is mainly dependent on foreign shipping lines to carry her produce and bring her her domestic requirements. Freight charges influence prices of exports and imports. The conference lines since 1956 have from time to time increased their charges despite protests from governments in office.

The marked shortage of hard currency makes matters worse. Consequently credit accommodation has to be obtained mostly from western sources and the international credit agencies. Debt servicing has as a result become an intolerable burden and absorbs a fair percentage of the foreign exchange budget. The devaluation of sterling and dollar has aggravated an already near insoluble problem.

BALANCING FACTORS

Despite the political imbalances caused by these internal and external disturbances, there are important factors which rivet Sri Lanka to a centrist position in politics.

The balance of trade makes Sri Lanka dependent on Britain for the sale of the greater part of her tea, and on China for the major share of her rubber. Governments have therefore no option but to steer clear of controversy with either power. If a left of centre government nationalised British-owned tea plantations, the tea trade may face a crisis especially if British tea buyers decided to fall back on other sources for their supplies and boycotted Sri Lanka's tea. Similarly, a right of centre government will meet with catastrophe if it antagonised the People's Republic of China, which pays favourable prices for rubber and sells to Sri Lanka rice at competitive prices.

A left of centre government cannot afford to go too far to the left because this could dry up the most important sources of credit – the I.M.F. and the World Bank. It would also mean the end of aid from the western-oriented Aid Sri Lanka Consortium of foreign powers. On the other hand, the communist states are not willing to commit themselves to the hilt because there is no certainty that a sympathetic left of centre government will always be in office. The effort would be totally wasted if it is replaced by a right of centre government.

There is one other factor that prevents Sri Lanka from crossing to the communist camp altogether. That is the dominance of Trotskyism in the socialist movement of Sri Lanka to the detriment of pro-Moscow or pro-Peking communism. The Trotskyist leadership is unwilling to encourage Sri Lanka to traverse too far in these directions because this would spell the ruin of their kind of socialism.

Thus a combination of factors, internal and external, keeps Sri Lanka firmly on the democratic path. The political maturity of the electors makes democratic mechanisms viable. But economic and ethnic factors cause disturbances which can produce grave crises and endanger democratic foundations. Government has therefore become both an art and a method of containing and equitably managing the ethnic and economic tensions that pervade a society where the pace of economic growth is sometimes stagnant and most of the time slow if not sluggish.

Notes

CHAPTER 1

1. See S. Paranavitana, 'Aryan Settlements: The Sinhalese', in University of Ceylon, *History of Ceylon*, Vol. I, Part I (Colombo, 1959), p. 84.
2. See his 'Prince Vijaya and the Aryanization of Ceylon', *The Ceylon Historical Journal*, Vol. 1, No. 3 (January 1952), p. 67.
3. See G. C. Mendis, *The Early History of Ceylon* (Colombo, 1946), p. 3.
4. See C. W. Nicholas, 'Agriculture and Irrigation', in *History of Ceylon*, Vol. I, Part I, pp. 553–8.
5. For further details see Walpola Rahula, *History of Buddhism in Ceylon: The Anuradhapura Period, 3rd Century B.C.–10th Century A.D.* (Colombo, 1956).
6. See S. Paranavitana, 'Triumph of Dutthagamani', in *History of Ceylon*, Vol. I, Part I, pp. 151–61.
7. See C. W. Nicholas, 'Civil Wars and the Emergence of Parakramabahu the Great' and 'The Reign of Parakramabahu I', in *History of Ceylon*, Vol. I, Part II (Colombo, 1960), pp. 442–86.
8. See S. Natesan, 'The Northern Kingdom', in *History of Ceylon*, Vol. I, Part II, pp. 691–702, and S. Arasaratnam, *Ceylon* (Englewood Cliffs, N.J., 1964), pp. 98–116.
9. For further information and an excellent account of the negotiations see K. W. Goonewardena, *The Foundations of Dutch Power in Ceylon 1638–1658* (Amsterdam, 1958), especially pp. 12–22.
10. For further information see S. Arasaratnam, *Dutch Power in Ceylon (1658–1687)* (Amsterdam, 1958).
11. *Op. cit.* See also Arasaratnam, 'The Administrative Organisation of the Dutch East India Company in Ceylon', *The Ceylon Journal of Historical and Social Studies*, Vol. 8, Nos 1 and 2, pp. 1–13.
12. For additional information see T. Vimalananda (ed.), *Buddhism in Ceylon under the Christian Powers and the Educational and Religious Policy of the British Government in Ceylon 1797–1832* (Colombo, 1963).
13. See K. M. de Silva (ed.), *Letters on Ceylon 1846–50: The Administration of Viscount Torrington and the 'Rebellion' of 1848* (Colombo, 1965), especially the excellent account in pp. 5–31.
14. See G. C. Mendis (ed.), *The Colebrook–Cameron Papers: Documents on British Colonial Policy in Ceylon 1796–1833*, Vols. I and II (London, 1956), especially his Introduction, pp. ix–lxiv in Vol. I.
15. For complete information on the coffee industry in Ceylon during the British period, see I. H. Van Den Driesen's unpublished Ph.D. thesis, University of London, entitled 'Some Aspects of the History of the Coffee Industry in Ceylon'.
16. For further information see S. Rajaratnam, 'The Ceylon Tea Industry, 1886–1931', *The Ceylon Journal of Historical and Social Studies*, Vol.

4, no. 2 (July–December 1961), pp. 169–202, and S. Rajaratnam, 'Plantation Rubber Industry in Ceylon', *University of Ceylon Review*, Vol. XX, No. 1 (April 1962), pp. 96–124.

17. For further information see R. N. Kearney, *Communalism and Language in the Politics of Ceylon* (Durham, North Carolina, 1967).
18. See my 'The Crewe-McCallum Reforms 1912–1921', *The Ceylon Journal of Historical and Social Studies*, Vol. 2, No. 1 (January 1959), pp. 84–120, and my 'The Finance Committee under the Manning Constitution of 1924', *University of Ceylon Review*, Vol. XVIII, Nos 3 and 4 (July–October 1960), pp. 223–55.
19. *Ibid.*
20. For details see the *Report of the Special Commission on the Constitution of Ceylon* (Cmd 3131). Also referred to as the *Donoughmore Report.*
21. For an analysis of the Donoughmore constitution see I. D. S. Weerawardena, *Government and Politics in Ceylon* (*1931–1946*) (Colombo, 1951), and S. Namasivayam, *The Legislatures of Ceylon, 1928–1948* (London, 1950).
22. *Op. cit.*
23. Sir Andrew Caldecott's 'Reforms Despatch of 1938', also referred to as *Ceylon Sessional Paper XXVIII* of 1938.
24. See Sir Ivor Jennings, *The Constitution of Ceylon*, 3rd ed. (Bombay, 1953), p. x.
25. Also referred to as *Sessional Paper XIV* of 1944.
26. *Ceylon: Report of the Commission on Constitutional Reform* (London, reprinted 1955), (Cmd 6677). Also referred to as the *Soulbury Report.*
27. For the details of the agreement see *Jennings, Constitution of Ceylon*, pp. 252–79.

CHAPTER 2

1. Central Bank of Ceylon, *Survey of Ceylon's Finances 1953* (Colombo 1954), and Central Bank of Ceylon, *Survey of Ceylon's Consumer Finances 1963* (Colombo, 1964). See also Dr M. A. Fernando's 'Employment in the Rural Sector', *Ceylon Daily News*, 30 May 1971, and 'The Educated Unemployed', *Ceylon Daily News*, 2 June 1971. Both articles are extracts from a Central Bank Survey published in the *Central Bank Bulletin* (April 1971).
2. For detailed information, see D. L. Jayasuriya, 'Developments in University Education: The Growth of the University of Ceylon (1942–1965)', *University of Ceylon Review*, Vol. XXIII (April–October 1965) Nos 1 & 2, pp. 83–153. Also Sir Ivor Jennings, 'Race, Religion and Economic Opportunity in the University of Ceylon', *University of Ceylon Review*, Vol. II (November 1944), pp. 1–13, S. J. Tambiah, 'Ethnic Representation in Ceylon's Higher Administrative Service 1870–1946', *University of Ceylon Review*, Vol. XIII (April–July 1955), pp. 113–34, M. A. Strauss, 'Family Characteristics and Occupational Choices of University Entrants as Clues to the Social Structure of Ceylon', *University of Ceylon Review*, Vol. IX (April–July 1951), pp. 125–35 and Bryce Ryan, 'Status Achievement, and Education in Ceylon: An Historical Perspective', *Journal of Asian Studies*, Vol. XX, No. 4 (August 1961), pp. 463–76.
3. The figures are taken from *Survey of Ceylon's Consumer Finances 1963*, and from Dr M. A. Fernando's articles referred to in note 1 above.

4. The figures are from the first-ever collection of statistics of personnel in the public service released by the General Treasury on 22 August 1970. See *Ceylon Observer Magazine Edition*, 23 August 1970. Note, there were in August 1970, 7,508 administrative, professional and technical officers, 94,567 teachers, 35,167 minor employees and 77,275 in labour grades (*ibid.*).
5. *Survey of Ceylon's Finances 1963*, p. 61.
6. p. 67.
7. For a summary of the results of this survey, see *Ceylon Observer Magazine Edition*, 9 April 1972.
8. See table 40 (p. 65) for information on the percentages of income receivers and table 88 (p. 125) for information on dissavers.
9. See also Department of Census and Statistics, *Survey of Rural Indebtedness in Ceylon 1957* (Colombo, 1959). This survey estimated the total indebtedness in the rural areas at Rs 516 million or about Rs 424 per rural family, a figure which at that time constituted about 34 per cent of annual income or 9 per cent of the value of property owned by the family. Even in 1957 the greater percentage of loans was taken for consumption purposes. 44.1 per cent of the Rs 516 million borrowed was from friends and relatives. 39.03 per cent of loans in the 1963 Survey (p. 127) was from friends.
10. *The Betrayal of Buddhism* (Report of the Unofficial Buddhist Committee of Inquiry) (Balangoda, 1955), p. 27.
11. *Ibid.*
12. *Poya* days coincide with the waxing and waning of the moon and are of religious significance to the Buddhists.
13. *Parliamentary Debates* (House of Representatives), Vol. 23, column 684.
14. Leslie Goonewardene in a contribution in Sinhalese to the L.S.S.P. souvenir of 1970 entitled 'New Outlook of the L.S.S.P.' which was reproduced in English translation in the *Ceylon Daily News*, 21 December 1970.
15. Sections 8 to 11 of the constitution.
16. Section 7 of the constitution provides for Sinhalese as the official language of Sri Lanka and it is part of the constitution. Section 8(2) provides that regulations for the use of the Tamil language 'shall not in any manner be interpreted as being a provision of the constitution but shall be deemed to be subordinate legislation', etc.
17. See S. U. Kodikara, *Indo-Ceylon Relations since Independence* (Colombo, 1965), p. 111. Note, at its ninth annual sessions in April 1949, the C.I.C. condemned the provisions of the Ceylon Citizenship Act as 'humiliating, discriminatory and anti-social' and the qualifications required under the Indian and Pakistani Residents (Citizenship) Act as being 'complex and involved, and beyond the capacity of workers with little or no education' (*ibid.*). The latter assertion was, considering the educational and literacy standards of the Indian population, factually correct.
18. Kodikara, p. 114, footnote 26.
19. *Ibid.*, pp. 113–14.
20. *Ibid.*, pp. 124–5.
21. *Ibid.*, pp. 125–7.
22. Particularly, Sri Lanka failed to persuade the government of India to abandon the concept of 'statelessness'. Also, certain actions on the part of the government of Sri Lanka in the implementation of the agreement

of October 1954 gave rise to serious complaints from the government of India.

23. See statement by Bandaranaike in the S.L.F.P. organ, *Free Lanka*, 16 February 1955.
24. See press communique issued by Ministry of Defence and External Affairs, *Ceylon Daily News*, 23 July 1970. From May 1970 (after the U.F. government took office to February 1973, 86,687 Indians were granted Indian citizenship (till December 1972) of whom 58,276 were repatriated to India (till January 1973) while 36,740 were granted Sri Lanka citizenship (till January 1973). See text of press conference by the deputy minister of defence and foreign affairs in *Ceylon Daily News*, 22 February 1973. Note, the U.F. government and the *Ceylon Daily News* in its editorial of 19 February 1973 alleged that the Dudley Senanayake 'national government' had been lax in implementing the Indo-Ceylon Agreement of October 1964 in view of the U.N.P.'s alliances with the C.W.C. and the F.P. For a refutation of this charge see 'U.N.P. and Indo–Ceylon Pact' by Dudley Senanayake and the editor's reply to Senanayake in *Ceylon Daily News*, 23 February 1973.
25. For the details see *Ceylon Daily News*, 28 August 1970, 8 March 1972 and 14 March 1972.
26. *Report of the Special Commission on the Constitution of Ceylon* (Donoughmore Report). Cmd 3131, pp. 105–6.
27. See *Census of Ceylon 1946* (Colombo, 1950).
28. *Report of the Kandyan Peasantry Commission*, Sessional Paper XVIII of 1951, paragraph 296.
29. *Census of Ceylon, 1946.*
30. *Report of the Kandyan Peasantry Commission*, paragraph 309.
31. *Survey of Ceylon's Consumer Finances 1963*, p. 89.
32. *Ibid.*
33. *Ibid.*, table 16, p. 37.
34. See note 28.
35. See *Final Report of the National Education Commission*, 1961, Sessional Paper XVII of 1962, paragraph 38. See also paragraphs 39–42.
36. For a detailed account on Sinhalese caste structure, see Bryce Ryan, *Caste in Modern Ceylon: The Sinhalese System in Transition* (New Brunswick, N.J., 1953).
37. *Soulbury Report*, paragraph 273.
38. *Report of the First Delimination Commission*, Sessional Paper XII of 1946, paragraph 32.
39. *Ibid.*, paragraph 81.
40. *Ibid.*, paragraph 30.
41. *Ibid.*
42. See E. D. L. Siriwardena, *Education for Racial Integration in Ceylon*, unpublished M.A. thesis, University of Ceylon, p. 67.
43. *Ibid.*, p. 104.
44. See, for instance, the speeches of Sir P. Arunachalam, one of the foremost of the Ceylon Tamil leaders in the first quarter of the twentieth century, in S. W. R. D. Bandaranaike (ed.), *The Hand Book of the Ceylon National Congress 1919–1928* (Colombo, 1928), pp. 70–97 and 118–43.
45. See *Donoughmore Report*, pp. 90–1.
46. *Soulbury Report*, paragraph 259.
47. For a detailed account see Michael Banks, 'Caste in Jaffna', pp. 61–77

in E. R. Leach (ed.), *Aspects of Caste in South India, Ceylon and North-West Pakistan*, Vol. 2 (Cambridge, 1960).

48. *Report of the First Delimitation Commission*, paragraph 31.
49. Quoted by I. D. S. Weerawardena in his 'The General Elections in Ceylon, 1952', *Ceylon Historical Journal*, Vol. II, Nos 1 and 2, p. 128.
50. For the full text of the appeal, see *Ceylon Daily News*, 15 June 1970.
51. For further information see The Bauddha Jatika Balavegaya (the National Organisation for the Protection of Buddhism), *Catholic Action: A Reply to the Catholic Union of Ceylon* (Colombo, 1963). See also statement by L. H. Mettananda, President of the Balvegaya, denouncing Prime Minister S. W. R. D. Bandaranaike for appointing Roman Catholics to a number of important positions in the public services, in *Ceylon Daily News*, 30 July 1956.
52. See *Ceylon Daily News*, 22 July 1970.
53. *Ibid.*
54. See *ibid.*, 2 and 18 November 1970. See also comments by Badiuddin Mahmud in *ibid.*, 14 November 1970.
55. See the statement issued by the general secretary of the I.S.F. in *ibid.*, 18 November 1970.

Chapter 3

1. See *Ceylon Observer Magazine Edition*, 12 March 1972, for statistics compiled by the Ministry of Planning and Employment for its medium-term development plan.
2. See National Planning Council, *The Ten-Year Plan* (Colombo, 1959), p. 19, Table V (Workforce Projections, 1956–81). For further information see Central Bank of Ceylon, *Survey of Ceylon's Consumer Finances, 1963* (Colombo, 1964), 'Survey of Employment, Unemployment and Under-Employment in Ceylon 1959–60', *International Labour Review* (March 1963), *Report to the Government of Ceylon on Rural Employment Problems* (ILO: Geneva, 1965), R. K. Srivastava, S. Selvaratnam and V. Ambalavanar, *Unemploymen in Ceylon – A Possible Line of Action*, Ministry of Planning and Economic Affairs (November 1967) and R. K. Srivastava, S. Selvaratnam and A. T. P. L. Abeykoon, *Ceylon Labour Force Projections 1968–78*, Ministry of Planning and Economic Affairs (October 1968). For a recent retailed analysis refer to International Labour Office, The Report of an Inter-Agency Team, *Matching Employment Opportunities and Expectations: A Programme of Action for Ceylon* (Geneva, 1971), International Labour Office, The Technical Papers of an Inter-Agency Team, *Matching Employment Opportunities and Expectations: A Programme of Action for Ceylon* (Geneva, 1971) and Birge Möller, *Employment Approaches to Economic Planning in Developing Countries with Special Reference to the Development Planning of Ceylon* (Sri Lanka) (Scandinavian Institute of Asian Studies Monograph Series No. 9: Stockholm, 1972).
3. See *Human Resource Development and Utilisation: A Note on Technical Assistance, Needs and Possibilities in Ceylon*, Ministry of Planning and Economic Affairs, paragraph 2.8, nd.
4. *Ibid.*
5. *Ibid.*, paragraph 2.6.

6. For the details, see communique issued by the Ministry of Planning and Employment in *Ceylon Daily News*, 13 March 1972.
7. See the statement of the Minister of Education on his proposed educational reforms in *Ceylon Daily News*, 29 July 1971, and for additional information, *Ceylon Daily News*, 8 January 1972.
8. *Ceylon Daily News*, 29 July 1971.
9. *Ibid.*
10. *Ibid.*
11. *Ibid.* See also text of press interview by the minister of education in *Ceylon Observer Magazine Edition*, 28 November 1970.
12. *Report of the Planning Committee on Education, Health, Housing and Manpower* (Colombo, May 1967), p. 40. Note, health services in general put up per capita expenditure on health from Rs 15.40 in 1960–1 to Rs 16.00 in 1967–8; see Ministry of Planning and Economic Affairs, *Economic Development 1966–68: Review and Trends* (Colombo, August 1967), p. 69.
13. *The Ten-Year Plan*, p. 316.
14. I. R. Duben (U.N.D.P. Special Fund Social Planner), *Policy, Problems and Shortcomings, Priorities and Technical Assistance Available in Social Infrastructure* (cyclostyled) paragraph 4.1, n.d.
15. See report of proceedings of the House of Representatives on 17 February 1972 in *Ceylon Daily News*, 18 February 1972.
16. Note, the principal Act was the Rent Restriction Act No. 29 of 1948 which consolidated and improved earlier laws that existed from 1942. Amendments were made in 1953, 1961, 1964 and 1966. It was felt that a comprehensive and consolidated Act as that of 1972 would be preferable to a series of amendments to the existing Act of 1948 as amended on the occasions mentioned. The latter course would have made cross-references complicated and difficult.
17. The Department of National Planning, *The Short-Term Implementation Programme* (Colombo, 1962), p. 278.
18. *Ibid.*, p. 33.
19. *Report of the Transport Commission*, Sessional Paper XXIII, 1967, paragraph 78.
20. The Department of National Planning, *The Development Programme 1964–1965* (Colombo, 1964), p. 49.
21. *Ibid.*
22. See Report of I.B.R.D. team headed by Manfred G. Blobel in *Ceylon Daily News*, 11 May 1971.
23. *Report of the Land Utilisation Committee*, Sessional Paper XI, 1968, paragraphs 104–6.
24. *Ibid.*, paragraph 125.
25. *Ibid.*, paragraph 126.
26. *The Short-Term Implementation Programme*, pp. 68 (Table IIA) and 122.
27. *Ibid.*, p. 122.
28. *Ibid.*
29. *Ibid.*
30. *Ibid.*, p. 3, footnote 1.
31. *Ibid.*
32. *Ibid.*, paragraph 12.
33. *Report of the Land Utilisation Committee*, paragraph 73.
34. See L. De Silva, 'A Critical Evaluation of Agricultral Policy 1960–68',

p. 97 in *Staff Studies*, Central Bank of Ceylon, Vol. 1, No. 1 (April 1971). Note, a survey carried out by the Investigation Unit of the Water Resources Board reported that paddy lands 'are owned by peasants in several isloated parcels, varying in sizes, located not at one place but at several different places under the same scheme' and it recorded an instance where 2,176½ acres were owned and occupied by 815 owners in 3,641 different parcels, and of this, more than one-third (750 acres) remained uncultivated. See I. Collonege, 'Land Fragmentation: A Solution', in *Ceylon Daily News*, 11 April 1971. See also G. Obeyesekere, *Land Tenure in Village Ceylon* (Cambridge, 1967) for an account of the joint ownership of land prevalent in southern Sri Lanka.

35. *Report of the Land Utilisation Committee*, paragraph 52.
36. *Administration Report of the Commissioner of Agrarian Services 1966–1967*, paragraph 61.
37. See D. S. Senanayake, *Agriculture and Patriotism* (Colombo; Associated Newspapers of Ceylon Limited, 1935). C. P. de Silva made the remarks referred to in conversations with politicians and civil servants.
38. *Report of the First Delimitation Commission*, Sessional Paper XIII, 1946, p. 84 and *Report of the Delimitation Commission*, Sessional Paper XV, 1959, p. 123.
39. *Report of the Taxation Inquiry Commission*, Sessional Paper X, 1968, paragraph 101.
40. *Ibid.*, paragraph 305.
41. *Report on Development and Taxation in the Plantation Industries* (unpublished), p. 13.
42. Planning Secretariat, *Six Year Programme of Investment 1954/55–1959/1960* (Colombo, 1955), pp. 240–1. See also I.B.R.D., *The Economic Development of Ceylon* (Colombo, 1952), Vols I and II.
43. See his 'Observations on the Problem of Economic Development in Ceylon', in National Planning Council, *Papers by Visiting Economists* (Colombo, 1959), p. 28.
44. In 'The Tasks of Economic Planning in Ceylon', *ibid.*, p. 75.
45. In 'Industrial Organisation and Economic Development', *ibid.*, p. 95.
46. *Ibid.*
47. Note, as early as 1952 the I.B.R.D. mission to Ceylon observed the trend 'of calling for more industry as a means of providing employment' and it noted quite rightly that it would be better to utilise employable labour in a meaningful way in any programme of industrialisation than merely to consider it as a charge on the public revenues to be disposed of in whatever way possible. *The Economic Development of Ceylon*, pp. 265–7.
48. A survey of industrial production conducted by the Department of Census and Statistics in 1970 calculated Sri Lanka's average private sector labour productivity at 7.3 units as against 4.2 units average labour productivity in the public sector. Labour productivity is defined as 'the value added per employee in units of Rs 1,000'. See 'Survey of Industrial Production', completed by the Department of Census and Statistics in December 1970 in *Ceylon Observer Magazine Edition*, 20 December 1970.
49. *Budget Speech 1970–71* (Colombo, October 1970), p. 67.
50. *Ibid.*, p. 68.
51. The Department of National Planning, *The Development Programme 1964–1965* (Colombo, 1964), p. 46.

52. *Ibid.*
53. N. S. Karunatilake, 'Recent Developments in the Economy and their Impact on Ceylon's Industrialisation', in Industrial Development Board, *Research and Industry* (Colombo, 1970), p. 37.
54. *Ibid.*, p. 41.
55. The foreign exchange entitlement scheme provided for multiple rates of exchange for certain transactions. It involved the payment of premium rates of exchange for hard currency in respect of specified transactions stipulated by the government.
56. Ministry of Planning and Economic Affairs, *Government Policy on Private Foreign Investment* (Colombo, 1966).
57. Central Bank of Ceylon, *Annual Report of the Monetary Board to the Minister of Finance for the Year 1970*, p. 44.
58. *Ibid.*, p. 49.
59. N. S. Karunatilake, 'Recent Developments . . .', p. 54.
60. See N. M. Perera, *Budget Speech 1970–71*, p. 35. Also, N. M. Perera, *The Economy of Ceylon: Trends and Prospects* (Government of Ceylon, November 1971) (mimeographed), pp. 23–33.
61. *The Ten-Year Plan*, p. 104.
62. See I.B.R.D., *Report of the Prospects for Tourist Development in Ceylon* (Ministry of Planning and Economic Affairs; Colombo, March 1968) and Central Bank of Ceylon, *Annual Report for the Year 1970*, p. 199.
63. The statistical data in this section has been obtained from the annual Administrative Reports of Commissioners in charge of the co-operative movement, from budget speeches, as well as from other state documents relating to the movement.
64. T. B. Ilangaratna, *Economic and Social Progress 1956–62* (Supplement to the Budget Speech 1963) (Colombo, 1963), p. 57.
65. N. M. Perera, *Budget Speech 1970–71*, p. 11.
66. See *Foreign Aid*, Tables I and VI, pp. 35 and 42.
67. N. M. Perera, *Budget Speech*.
68. Central Bank of Ceylon, *Annual Report of the Monetary Board to the Minister of Finance for the Year 1969*, p. 13.
69. p. 3.
70. Donald R. Snodgrass, *Ceylon: An Export Economy in Transition* (Illinois, 1966), p. 110.
71. Felix Dias Bandaranaike (Minister of Finance), *The Budget and Economic Development* (Colombo, 1961), pp. 9 and 13.
72. p. 35.
73. *The Short-Term Implementation Programme*, p. 5.
74. V. Kanesalingam, 'Industrial Policy and Development in Ceylon', in *Research and Industry*, p. 68.
75. See I.B.R.D. and I.D.A., *The Problem of Foreign Exchange and Long-Term Growth of Ceylon* (Ministry of Planning and Economic Affairs; Colombo, January 1968), paragraph 11.
76. See I.B.R.D. and I.D.A., *Recent Economic Trends in Ceylon* (Ministry of Planning and Economic Affairs; Colombo, September 1966), paragraph 44. Also, *The Development Programme 1966–67* (Ministry of Planning and Economic Affairs; Colombo, July 1966), pp. 1–9.
77. Ministry of Planning and Employment, *The Five Year Plan 1972–1976* (Colombo, November 1971).
78. For the details see *Ceylon Daily News*, 10 November 1971.
79. For a summary of the report see *Ceylon Daily News*, 22 March 1972.

80. See Central Bank of Ceylon, *Annual Report of the Monetary Board to the Minister of Finance for the Year 1971.*

CHAPTER 4

1. For a diligent exposition by a westerner see Richard F. Gombrich, *Precept and Practice: Traditional Buddhism in the Rural Highlands of Ceylon* (Oxford, 1971). The chapters 'Total Responsibility in Theory and Practice' (pp. 214–43) and 'The Ethic of Intention' (pp. 244–68) are particularly useful.
2. Sir Frederick Rees, one of the members of the Soulbury Commission, makes an oblique reference to this (confirmed in a conversation with the writer) in 'The Soulbury Commission, 1944–45', *The Ceylon Historical Journal*, Vol. 5, Nos 1–4, pp. 23–48, when he wrote (p. 45) 'the rather subtle methods adopted by Sir Oliver Goonetilleke were much more obvious than he himself realised' (note, Sir Oliver Goonetilleke and D. S. Senanayake were the two persons, according to Sir Ivor Jennings, solely responsible for obtaining independence for Ceylon, see his *The Constitution of Ceylon*, 3rd ed. (Bombay, 1953), p. x). Sir Charles Jeffries, in his *Sir Oliver E. Goonetilleke* (Pall Mall; London, 1969), p. 76, refers to the remarks of Rees and reports 'I suspect that he [Goonetilleke] realised it well enough and could not care less'. J. L. Fernando in his column 'Then and Now' in the *Ceylon Observer* (Sunday edition), 1 February 1959, wrote revealingly: 'Later came even delicate hints that there would be under the set-up of independent Sri Lanka an attractive job of a governor-generalship. The suggestions were delicately expressed but freely made to more than one person – to Sir Henry Moore, even to the fire-eating Sir Geoffrey Layton and My Lord Soulbury himself. D. S. Senanayake was not much good at putting across these subtle magnetic appeals but he had a trained one-man brains trust to attend to such arrangements.' Note, the late J. L. Fernando was one of Sri Lanka's top journalists and a close confidant of D. S. Senanyake. The 'one-man brains trust' was none other than Goonetilleke. Sir Henry Moore was British governor of Ceylon immediately prior to independence and became Ceylon's first governor-general. Admiral Layton was wartime commander-in-chief of Ceylon.
3. See Cmd 3131 (*Donoughmore Report*) pp. 126–7.
4. *Ibid.*
5. For the report of an illuminating discussion between Dr N. M. Perera and Hector Abhayavardhana on this subject, see 'Radicalisation in Ceylon', *Maral*, Vol. III, No. 5 (February 1961), pp. 35–48.
6. See *Survey of Ceylon's Consumer Finances 1963*, pp. 61–106, for further information.
7. *Ibid.*
8. For the most thorough and analytical examination of parties in Ceylon see Calvin A. Woodward, *The Growth of a Party System in Ceylon* (Providence, 1969).
9. For a detailed account of D. S. Senanayake's pioneering zeal in this sphere see *The Ceylon Historical Journal*, Vol. 5, Nos 1–4.
10. For a detailed examination see my 'Oppositional Politics in Ceylon (1947–1968)', *Government and Opposition*, Vol. 4, No. 1, pp. 54–69.
11. See, for instance, speech by Sir John Kotelawala on 9 June 1950 in *Ceylon Daily News*, 12 June 1950.

12. D. S. Senanayake died a few weeks before the opening of the Exhibition.
13. For his speech on 'the middle path', see *The Ceylon Historical Journal*, Vol. 5, Nos 1–4, pp. 110–14.
14. For the account of the causes of the U.N.P.'s defeat, etc. see I. D. S. Weerawardena, *The Ceylon General Election 1956* (Colombo, 1960). Also W. Howard Wriggins, *Ceylon: Dilemmas of a New Nation* (Princeton, N.J., 1960), pp. 326–69.
15. See Wriggins, *Ceylon*, and Donald E. Smith, 'The Sinhalese Buddhist Revolution', in Donald E. Smith (ed.), *South Asian Politics and Religion* (Princeton, 1966).
16. For further details see Chapter 6.
17. *Ceylon Daily News: Parliaments of Ceylon 1960* (Colombo, n.d.), p. 195.
18. From the U.N.P. manifesto for the March 1960 general election.
19. See Central Bank of Ceylon, *Annual Report of the Monetary Board to the Minister of Finance for the year 1969*.
20. See text of letter addressed to Dudley Senanayake by Festus Perera in the *Daily Mirror*, 13 October 1970.
21. This memorandum was privately circulated to members of the U.N.P.'s working committee in February 1971. It was made available to the writer by a member of the working committee. The details were however also given wide publicity in the local press.
22. See report of J. R. Jayawardene's speech in the House of Representatives in *Ceylon Daily News*, 4 December 1971.
23. For the full text of the resolution see *ibid.*, 20 December 1971.
24. For details on the injunction see *ibid.*, 18 April 1972 and 3 June 1972, and for information on the resolution of the differences between Senanayake and Jayawardene, see *ibid.*, 1 June 1972.
25. See *ibid.*, 16 July 1951.
26. See *Tribune*, 22 September 1961.
27. See I. D. S. Weerawardena, 'The General Elections in Ceylon, 1952', *The Ceylon Historical Journal*, Vol. 2, Nos 1–2, pp. 109–78, for further information.
28. See *Ceylon Faces Crisis* (Federal Party Pamphlet: Colombo, 1957), for details of this pact.
29. For a vivid and authentic account of these riots, see T. Vittachi, *Emergency '58: the story of the Ceylon race riots* (London, 1958).
30. Paragraph 3 of the M.E.P. manifesto of 1956.
31. For further details see my 'The Role of the Governor-General in Ceylon', *Modern Asian Studies*, Vol. II, No. 3 (1968).
32. For the details see my 'The Governor-General and the Two Dissolutions of Parliament, December 5, 1959 and April 23, 1960', *The Ceylon Journal of Historical and Social Studies*, Vol. 3, No. 2 (July–December 1960).
33. S. Ponniah's, *Satyagaraha and the Freedom Movement of the Tamils in Ceylon* (Jaffna, Ceylon, 1963), provides the fullest account of the events of 1961.
34. For the full details see statement by Felix R. Dias Bandarnaike in *Parliamentary Debates* (House of Representatives), Vol. 46, cols 1490–529. See also S. U. Kodikara, 'Communalism and Political Modernisation in Ceylon', in *Modern Ceylon Studies*, Vol. 1, No. 1, pp. 94–114, especially pp. 108–9.
35. See *Sessional Paper* IX of 1964 – Interim Report of the Press Commission and *Sessional Paper* XI of 1964 – Final Report of the Press Commission.

36. See my 'Buddhism and Politics, 1960–65', in Smith (ed.), *South Asian Politics and Religion.*
37. See my 'Ceylon: A New Government Takes Office', *Asian Survey*, Vol. XI, No. 2, pp. 177–84.
38. See *Ceylon Daily News*, 5 June 1950.
39. The details are recounted in Leslie Goonewardene's *A Short History of the Lanka Sama Samaja Party* (Colombo, 1960).
40. These views were expressed in a pamphlet entitled *The Present Political Situation* which Gunnawardene presented to his party in January 1971. Parts of this were reproduced in *Ceylon Daily News*, 9 January 1971 and *The Times Weekender*, 11 January 1971.
41. See the statement issued by the Central Committee of the C.P. in *Ceylon Daily News*, 18 September 1970.
42. See Leslie Goonewardene, p. 42.
43. *Ceylon Daily News*, 14 August 1953.
44. Made available to the writer.
45. See political pamphlet by Dr Colvin R. de Silva, *Their Politics and Ours* (Colombo, 1954).
46. See text of the resolution adopted at a plenary meeting of the Central Committee of the C.P. on 31 May 1959, in *25 Years of the Ceylon Communist Party* (Colombo, 1968), pp. 74–5.
47. See text of resolution adopted at the meeting of the Central Committee of the C.P. on 22 June 1964 in *ibid.*, pp. 98–100.
48. See Leslie Goonewardene, *Short History*, pp. 34–9. Also Doric De Souza, 'Parliamentary Democracy in Ceylon', *Young Socialist*, No. 1, pp. 18–25, and No. 3, pp. 125–39.
49. See official statement issued by Leslie Goonewardene, secretary of the L.S.S.P. at the time, in *Ceylon Daily News*, 3 January 1952.
50. See Weerawardene, 'The General Elections in Ceylon 1952'.
51. From the secret circular of 27 January 1954 entitled *Report on the Political Situation.*
52. Dr Colvin R. de Silva, *Their Politics and Ours.*
53. See the test of the L.S.S.P. manifesto entitled *What We Stand For* (Colombo, 1959).
54. See *Ceylon Daily News*, 6 November 1947.
55. See *Ceylon Daily News*, 8 February 1951
56. See Leslie Goonewardene's statement in *Ceylon Daily News*, 3 January 1952.
57. See de Silva, *Their Politics and Ours.*
58. See note 40 above.
59. See report of press conference by Philip Gunawardene in *The Times of Ceylon*, 3 October 1970.
60. Best expressed in the pages of *25 Years of the Ceylon Communist Party.* Also refer Basil Perera, *Pieter Keuneman – A Profile* (Colombo, 1967), pp. 55–79.
61. See Dr N M. Perera, '35 Years After', in *Ceylon Daily News*, 22 December 1970.
62. See interview given by Dr Colvin R. de Silva to the *Ceylon Observer Magazine Edition* entitled '35 Years of the L.S.S.P.: Overthrowing Capitalism our New Challenge' in its issue of 20 December 1970. But for a critical view of the L.S.S.P.'s change of policy see George J. Lerski, 'The Twilight of Ceylonese Trotskyism', *Pacific Affairs*, Vol. 3 (Autumn 1970).

63. See note 41 above.
64. See Leslie Goonewardene, 'New Outlook of the L.S.S.P.', in *Ceylon Daily News*, 21 December 1970. See also V. Karalasingham, 'An L.S.S.P. Viewpoint: What Should be Today's Slogans', in *Ceylon Daily News*, 2 September 1970 and the full text of the resolution of the Central Committee of the L.S.S.P. in *Ceylon Daily News*, 2 September 1971.
65. See (Mrs) V. K. Jayawardene, *The Rise of the Labour Movement in Ceylon* (Durham, North Carolina, 1972), and R. N. Kearney, *Trade Unions and Politics in Ceylon* (Berkeley, 1971).
66. See text of letter to the editor by Sanmugathasan in *The Ceylon Daily Mirror*, 1 May 1970.
67. See *Ceylon Observer*, 12 August 1970.
68. For the full text see *Ceylon Daily News*, 8 August 1970. See also press statement issued by Sanmugathasan in *Ceylon Daily News*, 18 February 1971, in which he denounced 'U.S. imperialism' in Laos and the U.F. government for not condemning 'this brazen act of aggression'.
69. See news caption 'Tampoe on the Great Betrayal', in *Ceylon Daily News*, 22 August 1970.
70. For a fuller account see my 'Ceylon: The People's Liberation Front and the Revolution that Failed', *Pacific Community*, January 1972. Also Dr W. A. Wiswa Warnapala's, 'The April Revolt in Ceylon', *Asian Survey*, March 1971.
71. About 75 per cent of the P.L.F. regulars were from the 18–20 age group. See report of a press conference by the Sri Lanka army commander, General Attygalla, in *The New York Times*, 22 April 1971.
72. For the text of the minister's speech see *Ceylon Daily News*, 30 April 1971.
73. For the text of the P.L.F.'s blueprint for the seizure of power in this fashion see the *Ceylon Daily Mirror*, 31 July 1970.
74. See statement issued by the three T.C. M.P.s declaring their unanimous decision to support the U.F. government in *Ceylon Observer*, *Magazine Edition*, 2 April 1971. Note, one of the these M.P.s, V. Ananthasangari (Kilinochchi), withdrew from the U.F. later and joined the T.U.F.
75. For a complete account of the origins and activities up to 1966 of the F.P. see my 'The Tamil Federal Party in Ceylon Politics', *Journal of Commonwealth Political Studies*, Vol. IV, No. 2, pp. 117–37.
76. *Ibid.*
77. See S. Ponniah, pp. 54–77.
78. For the details of these talks see *ibid.*, pp. 137–44.
79. For the text of the memorandum see *The Times of Ceylon*, 18 September 1970. Also for Chelvanayakam's views see report of the proceedings of the Constituent Assembly in *Ceylon Daily News*, 21 May 1971.
80. See report in *Ceylon Daily News*, 24 March 1972.
81. Unlike the F.P., the C.W.C. did not insist on a written signed agreement. Instead they gave the prime minister a typed note containing the agreed conclusions and preferred to leave it to his good faith to implement these (based on interview with C.W.C. officials).
82. Refer V. K. Jayawardene, *The Rise of the Labour Movement in Ceylon*, and Kearney, *Trade Unions and Politics in Ceylon*.
83. See Central Bank of Ceylon, *Annual Report of the Monetary Board to the Minister of Finance for the year 1970*.
84. For the details see *Ceylon Daily News*, 1 August 1971.
85. See *Ceylon Observer Magazine Edition*, 5 December 1971.

86. See full text of statement in *Ceylon Daily News*, 29 November 1971.
87. The text of the statement condemning the Bill was made available to the writer by an office-bearer in the Civil Rights Movement. For the full text of the statement condemning the Criminal Justice Commissions Bill, see *Ceylon Observer Magazine Edition*, 2 April 1972.

CHAPTER 5

1. See his *The Constitution of Ceylon*, 3rd ed. (Bombay, 1953), p. 147.
2. In 'I Remember Ceylon', *Times of Ceylon Annual 1963*, Colombo.
3. In the last days of his governor-generalship the writer was present at a private function where Sir Oliver told some of the guests that he had tried his best to 'serve' five prime ministers who functioned during his term of office.
4. For further details see my 'The Role of the Governor-General in Ceylon', in *Modern Asian Studies*, Vol. II, No. 3 (1968), pp. 193–220.
5. *Ibid.* Also Sir Charles Jeffries, *Sir Oliver E. Goonetilleke* (London, 1969), pp. 155–6.
6. Jennings, *Constitution of Ceylon*, p. 171.
7. See J. L. Fernando, *Three Prime Ministers of Ceylon – An 'Inside Story'* (Colombo, 1963), pp. 39–40.
8. Private information. Also *ibid.*, pp. 52–3 and 68–9.
9. See B. P. Peiris, 'Memoirs', in the *Sunday Mirror*, 20 February 1966. B. P. Peiris was secretary to the cabinet at this time.
10. See my 'The Governor-General and the Two Dissolutions of Parliament, December 5, 1959 and April 23, 1960', *The Ceylon Journal of Historical and Social Studies*, Vol. 3, No. 2 (July–December 1960), pp. 187–207, for further information.
11. *Ibid.*
12. For a critical assessment of this action see S. A. de Smith, *The New Commonwealth and its Constitutions* (London, 1964), pp. 84–5.
13. (a) On 12 December 1959, the executive committee of the S.L.F.P. elected C. P. de Silva president of the party and authorised him to request the governor-general to remove the prime minister, W. Dahanayake, from office and to appoint him (C. P. de Silva) prime minister. A 'prayer' on these lines was submitted to the governor-general by C. P. de Silva, but Sir Oliver Goonetilleke declined to take any action on it (for the full text of the 'prayer', see *Ceylon Observer* (Sunday edition), 13 December 1959). (b) In March 1965 after Mrs Bandaranaike's ruling coalition had suffered losses at the general election and she delayed tendering her resignation owing to the fact that no party had secured an overall majority, it was suggested in local political circles that the governor-general should exercise his constitutional right of dismissal. His Excellency did not, however, have to consider the question, for Mrs Bandaranaike tendered her resignation shortly afterwards. *The Ceylon Daily News Parliament of Ceylon 1965*, Colombo, n.d. (p. 24) states that the governor-general consulted the crown's law officers and the latter advised that Mrs Bandaranaike be told that unless she resigned, she would be dismissed.
14. See Peiris, 'Memoirs', *Sunday Mirror*, 5 and 12 June 1966.
15. See my 'The Governor-General and the Two Dissolutions of Parliament'.

16. Private information, mentioned to the writer by a member of the Dudley Senanayake cabinet at the time.
17. See my 'Ceylonese Cabinet Ministers – Their Political, Economic and Social Background, 1947–1960', *Ceylon Economist*, Vol. 5, No. 1.
18. For the text of the 'prayer', see *Ceylon Observer* (Sunday edition), 13 December 1959.
19. For details see my 'The Cabinet System in Ceylon 1947–1959', in *The Indian Year Book of International Affairs 1959*, pp. 397–431.
20. For the text of the prime minister's letter to Mr Suntharalingam asking for an explanation as to why he left the Chamber while a division was being taken on the Bill and Mr Suntharalingam's statement on his resignation see *Parliamentary Debates* (House of Representatives) Vol. 5, columns 599–605.
21. The memorandum, dated 14 April, 1948, was made available to the writer by the courtesy of the private secretary to the minister of local government at the time.
22. For the documentation on these conflicts, see my 'The Cabinet System in Ceylon 1947–1959'.
23. See Sir John Kotelawala, *An Asian Prime Minister's Story* (London, 1956), p. 130.
24. The minister expressed disagreement with the 'language of the area' clause in the Indo-Ceylon Agreement of June 1954 agreed to between the prime ministers of both countries; see *Ceylon Daily News*, 19 January 1954, and opposition to the cabinet's decision of having Sinhalese as the only official language of Ceylon, see text of interview in *Ceylon Daily News*, 20 January 1956.
25. For the prime minister's explanation of the boycott, etc. see *Parliamentary Debates* (House of Representatives), Vol. 36, columns 12–13.
26. From a confidential memorandum by Bandaranaike to the Parliamentary Joint Select Committee on Constitutional Reform made available to the writer by S. J. V. Chelvanayakam M.P. who was a member of this committee.
27. For the details see my 'The Governor-General and the Two Dissolutions of Parliament'.
28. *Ibid.*
29. See Jennings' reference to this in his 'The House of Representatives', in *Ceylon Daily News* supplement of 27 November 1947.
30. Section 27(1) of the constitution.
31. See *Ceylon Daily News*, 4 October 1947, *Ceylon Observer*, 7 October 1947, and *Times of Ceylon*, 11 October 1947.
32. *Ceylon Daily News*, 13 October 1947.
33. Leslie Goonewardene, *A Short History . . .*, p. 42.
34. For an account of the complicated manoeuvres which preceded the election see *Ceylon Daily News*, 19 April 1956. These were checked with S. J. V. Chelvanayakam M.P. by the writer and are correct.
35. See *Ceylon Daily News*, 6 November 1947.
36. *Ibid.*
37. See Leslie Goonewardene, *op. cit.*, pp. 37–51.
38. See *25 Years of the Ceylon Communist Party*, p. 45, where it is stated that the C.P. 'made the right-opportunist mistake of wrongly assessing the nature of the newly-formed U.N.P. and thinking that it could also play a part in a united front against imperialism. This mistake was openly admitted and corrected by the C.P. within a few months.'

39. For further information see my 'Oppositional Politics in Ceylon (1947–1968)', *Government and Opposition*, Vol. 4, No. 1 (Winter 1969), pp. 54–69.
40. See for instance the press release issued by the opposition on 11 January 1949 and the statement of the leader of the opposition in the *Ceylon Daily News* of 24 November 1950.
41. For the full text of the directive issued by the chief government whip calling on members of the government parliamentary group to vote against motions brought forward by the opposition irrespective of their merits, see *Ceylon Daily News*, 3 June 1948.
42. See *Ceylon Daily News*, 12 June 1950.
43. *Parliamentary Debates* (House of Representatives), 11 June 1954, columns 1122–204.
44. See his press statement in *Ceylon Daily News*, 7 March 1971.
45. See *Ceylon Daily News*, Independence Supplement, 4 February 1953.
46. *Parliamentary Debates* (House of Representatives), 27 November 1953, column 1136.
47. For Bandaranaike's views on the part he should play in solving the Indian question and his role in these talks, see *Parliamentary Debates* (House of Representatives), 5 March 1954, column 1136, also column 3267.
48. *Parliamentary Debates* (House of Representatives), 21 June 1955, column 175.
49. *Ibid.*, columns 175–6.
50. *Parliamentary Debates* (House of Representatives), 4 May 1956, column 416.
51. Interview with F.P. M.P.s.
52. For the details of these campaigns, etc. see S. Ponniah.
53. *Ceylon: Report of the Commission on Constitutional Reform* (*Soulbury Report*), Cmd 6677, paragraph 278 (ii).
54. *Ibid.*, paragraph 278 (iii).
55. Section 40(1).
56. Section 40(2).
57. See *Report of the First Delimitation Commission*, Sessional Paper XIII of 1946.
58. See *Report of the Delimitation Commission*, Sessional Paper XV of 1959.
59. The Burgher returned was a leading C.P. man (Pieter Keuneman) who was returned on a party vote rather than because of the fact that he was a member of the Burgher community.
60. *The Constitution of Ceylon*, p. 214.
61. *Ibid.*, p. 52.
62. See my 'The Public Service Commission and Ministerial Responsibility: The Ceylonese Experience', *Public Administration*, Vol, 46 (Spring 1968), pp. 81–93.
63. *Ibid.*
64. For a detailed description see my 'Public Administration in Ceylon', in S. S. Hsueh (ed.), *Public Administration in South and Southeast Asia* (Brussels, 1962), pp. 199–240.
65. For the details of this circular, see *Ceylon Daily News*, 21 July 1971.
66. See report of the minister's speech in *ibid.*, 25 December 1971.
67. For the text of the address see *ibid.*, 24 December 1971.
68. See his speech in *ibid.*, 30 November 1970.

69. See communique issued by the Ministry of Housing and Construction in *ibid.*, 31 May 1971.
70. See statement by the permanent secretary, Ministry of Planning and Employment, in *ibid.*, 9 December 1971.
71. From the U.F. manifesto.
72. A hall in the capital city, Colombo.
73. For the full text, see *Ceylon Daily News*, 20 July 1970.
74. *Ibid.*
75. For further details, see *ibid.*, 14 December 1969.
76. For the full text of the broadcast, see *Ceylon Observer*, 11 September 1970.
77. For the full text, see *Ceylon Daily News*, 20 July 1970.
78. See the explanation of procedure by the minister of constitutional affairs in *ibid.*, 29 January 1971.
79. See the text of the letter written by the minister of constitutional affairs to the editor, *ibid.*, published in its issue of 29 January 1971.
80. *Ibid.*, 18 January 1971.
81. *Ibid.*
82. For the text of the resolution, see *ibid.*, 29 June 1971.
83. See statement issued by S. J. V. Chelvanayakam M.P. on behalf of the F.P. parliamentary group in *ibid.*, 29 June 1971.
84. For further details see text of letter written by C. X. Martyn M.P. for Jaffna to S. J. V. Chelvanayakam M.P. in *ibid.*, 25 May 1971.
85. See text of letter by S. J. V. Chelvanayakam M.P. to C. X. Martyn M.P. in *The Times Weekender*, 30 July 1971.
86. See *Ceylon Daily News*, 26 June 1971.
87. *Ibid.*, 7 December 1971.
88. See text of interview by the minister to the *Ceylon Observer* in *Ceylon Observer Magazine Edition*, 2 January 1971.
89. For the full text of the statement, see *Ceylon Daily News*, 22 May 1972.
90. See *ibid.*, 30 December 1971.
91. On a reading of the constitution and the views expressed by the president of the first panel of three judges of the Constitutional Court which examined the objections raised against the U.F. government's Press Council Bill, the National State Assembly presumably has the right to override an adverse opinion of the court by utilising the procedure required for amending the constitution. However, the president of the first panel stated that he hoped 'the Assembly will respect our views and will not pass the Bill with a two-thirds majority' if the court held that sections of the Bill were in conflict with the constitution. See report of the proceedings of the court in *Ceylon Daily News*, 24 November 1972. The first president (T. S. Fernando) is a man of considerable judicial eminence and integrity and is also the president of the highest court in Sri Lanka – the Court of Appeal.
92. Section 45(4) of the constitution authorises the president to act in such a manner as to ensure public security and the preservation of public order.
93. The first panel of three judges of the Constitutional Court comprising T. S. Fernando (president), J. A. L. Cooray and H. Deheragoda was selected on 16 November 1972 to hear petitions filed against the Press Council Bill by eight citizens of Sri Lanka and the leader of the opposition. In the course of the hearings, a constitutional crisis developed on the question whether the court should give its decision within the four-

teen-day time limit prescribed under Section 65 of the constitution for Bills not deemed urgent in the national interest. It was the view of a distinguished Queen's Council (S. Nadesan) appearing before the court on behalf of the Civil Rights Movement of Ceylon that the fourteen-day limit was not 'imperative'. The president of the court (T. S. Fernando) agreed with this submission (see *Ceylon Daily News*, 25 November 1972). The court accordingly continued to hear submissions beyond the fourteen-day limit. The matter was raised in the National State Assembly on 6 December 1972 and the minister of public administration, local government, home affairs and justice (Felix Dias Bandaranaike) expressed the personal opinion that the court should convey its opinion within the fourteen-day time limit, adding however that if the court asked for an extension to the time limit imposed, he hoped some arrangement could be worked out to grant such an extension (for the proceedings in the National State Assembly, see *Ceylon Daily News*, 7 December 1972). On 7 December, the Speaker of the National State Assembly informed the Assembly that the court had not given its decision as provided for under section 65 of the constitution and announced that the Assembly will proceed with the Press Council Bill under standing orders and provisions contained in Chapter IX of the constitution (see *Ceylon Daily News*, 8 December 1972). A debate on the Speaker's announcement and the constitutional issues arising therefrom followed on 12 and 13 December on a request made by the leader of the opposition. The latter argued that fundamental rights were involved. Government spokesmen criticised the judges of the court for their failure to give a decision within the time limit prescribed (for the proceedings see *Ceylon Daily News* of 13 and 14 December 1972). On 14 December (1972) the three judges of the Constitutional Court involved resigned.

On 4 January 1973, the government moved the second reading of the Press Council Bill. Leading opposition members raised objections to the procedure, especially as no decision on it had been given by the Constitutional Court, the judges concerned having resigned. The procedural objections were debated on 4, 5 and 19 January. R. Premadasa M.P. on behalf of the opposition went further and argued that the court which heard objections to the Bill had not been properly constituted since it had not gazetted its rules of procedure as constitutionally required (for the details see *Ceylon Daily News* of 5 and 6 January 1973). On 19 January the Speaker gave his ruling upholding the objection of R. Premadasa M.P. (for the text of the ruling see *Ceylon Daily News*, 20 January 1973). He therefore held that the Bill would have to go before a new court. The Speaker ruled that the court was obliged to give its ruling within the time limits prescribed by the constitution (*ibid.*).

On 2 February 1973 a new court of three judges sat to hear the objections to the Press Council Bill. The president of the court (Mr Justice Jaya Pathirana) announced that a decision would be given within the fourteen-day time limit. The court accordingly communicated their decision to the Speaker on 12 February. On 22 February the Speaker communicated the decision of the court to the National State Assembly. The court had pronounced that all the objections raised against the Bill were invalid (see *Ceylon Daily News*, 23 February 1973).

94. As provided for under section 94(3) of the constitution.
95. Most of the occasions prescribed have been taken by the framers from

the propositions cited by the writer in his 'The Governor-General and the Two Dissolutions of Parliament'.

96. See *ibid.* for the details.

CHAPTER 6

1. Sir John Kotelawala, *An Asian Prime Minister's Story* (London, 1956), p. 127.
2. See letter addressed by the minister of communications to the secretary for the Ceylon Committee for Human Rights in Bangladesh in *Ceylon Daily News,* 28 October 1971.
3. *Ibid.*
4. See note issued by the Ministry in *Ceylon Daily News,* 16 May 1971.
5. See two valuable articles which appeared in the *Ceylon Daily News,* both under the pseudonym 'Asoka': 'Ceylon and the Indian Ocean' (25 November 1970) and 'Ceylon in the Nuclear Area' (29 November 1970).
6. See *The New York Times,* 22 April 1971.
7. See *ibid.,* 14 April 1971.
8. See 'Advertising Supplement of the Ceylon Police Department', *Ceylon Daily News,* 10 April 1971.
9. *Ibid.*
10. See *ibid.,* 13 November 1971.
11. See statement of the prime minister in *ibid.,* 1 December 1971.
12. For the detailed figures of expenditure on the armed forces, see *ibid.,* 6 November 1971.
13. For further details see statement by the prime minister in *ibid.,* 15 March 1972.
14. See *ibid.,* 24 February 1972. These boats are fitted with anti-aircraft, anti-submarine, anti-surface armaments as well as sophisticated navigation, communication and detection equipment. They are capable of medium range sea operations at high speed.
15. An agreement to operate these fortnightly charter flights to the Maldives was signed between the commander of the Ceylon air force and the director of the Maldavian National Trading Corporation in December 1971. See *ibid.,* 2 December 1971.
16. For example during the three-month period September to November 1971, the air force through these operations earned 52,000 US dollars. See statement by the prime minister in *ibid.,* 15 March 1972.
17. One of the highest officers of the Indian army (then retired) told the author in 1971 that 'Operation Ceylon' would not take more than three days. A better equipped aggressor would of course take less time.
18. See Leslie Goonewardene (minister of communications), 'New Outlook of the L.S.S.P.', in *Ceylon Daily News,* 21 December 1970.
19. For the details of this agreement, see Jennings, *The Constitution of Ceylon* (3rd ed.), (Bombay, 1953), pp. 252–4. The agreement came into effect as from the date on which Sri Lanka obtained independence – 4 February 1948.
20. See speech of S. W. R. D. Bandaranaike on 17 June 1952, in *Towards a New Era: Selected Speeches of S. W. R. D. Bandaranaike made in the Legislature of Ceylon 1931–1959,* compiled by G. E. P. De S Wickremaratne (Colombo, 1961), p. 816.
21. *Ibid.,* p. 803.
22. *Ibid.,* p. 819.

23. *Ibid.*, p. 815.
24. See G. H. Jansen, *Afro-Asia and Non-Alignment* (London, 1966), p. 93.
25. See my 'The People's Liberation Front: The Revolution that Failed', in *Pacific Community*, January 1972. Also Saeed Naqvi, 'Ceylon's Long Night and After', in *The Statesman Weekly*, 22 May 1971.
26. See editorial entitled 'India and Ceylon', in *Ceylon Daily News*, 29 June 1970.
27. The external affairs agreement provides for mutual consultations between the governments of the Commonwealth, and for Sri Lanka if the need arises, to utilise British channels of diplomatic 'communication as well as the vast storehouse of information that the Foreign and Commonwealth Relations Offices have at their disposal'. For further information see Jennings, *The Constitution of Ceylon*, pp. 140–2, 254–276.
28. Sir John Kotelawala, *An Asian Prime Minister's Story* (London, 1956), p. 112.
29. *Ibid.*
30. See report of debate in the Constituent Assembly in *Ceylon Daily News*, 22 July 1970.
31. *Towards a New Era*, pp. 813–14.
32. See *The Foreign Policy of Ceylon: Extracts from Statements by the late Prime Minister, Mr. S. W. R. D. Bandaranaike and Texts of Joint Statements issued by him and Visiting Heads of State* (3rd ed., revised and enlarged) (Colombo, 1961), pp. 23–5.
33. *Ibid.*,
34. *Ibid.*
35. *Ibid.*, p. 18.
36. Speech delivered on the occasion of the handing over of the naval base at Trincomalee by Britain on 15 October 1957, *ibid.*, p. 20.
37. Sir Charles Jeffries, *A Biography of Sir Oliver E. Goonetilleke* (London, 1969), p. 125.
38. Even as late as in 1970, the Trotskyist minister of finance (Dr N. M. Perera) had occasion to repeat this charge. See *Ceylon Daily News*, 16 November 1970. These balances represented the moneys owing to Sri Lanka in respect of expenditure by H.M. forces in Sri Lanka during the war. Dr Perera argued that Sri Lanka had supplied export produce, in particular rubber, which was in short supply after the Japanese occupation of Malaysia and the Netherland East Indies at prices well below what they should have fetched on the basis of the laws of supply and demand.
39. For the full text of Mrs Bandaranaike's speech, see *Ceylon Daily News*, 22 January 1971.
40. For the full text of this speech, see *ibid.*, 16 November 1971.
41. For further details see *ibid.*, 16 December 1971.
42. *Ibid.*
43. *Ibid.*, 24 August 1971.
44. See Annual Report of the Colombo Plan Council for Technical Co-operation in South and South-East Asia, 1970–71, in *ibid.*, 16 February 1972.
45. *Ibid.*
46. *Ibid.*
47. See text of Mrs Bandaranaike's address on the occasion of the 20th anniversary celebrations of the Colombo Plan in *ibid.*, 2 July 1971.

48. See *Sun,* 29 August 1970, and Ministry of Planning and Economic Affairs, *Foreign Aid* (Colombo, 1969) for further details.
49. See *Foreign Aid*, pp. 16–17.
50. See *Ceylon Daily News,* 27 August 1971. See also the report of a press interview given by the permanent secretary, Ministry of Planning, in *ibid.*, 12 April 1972 and the report of the press conference by the minister of foreign and internal trade in *ibid.*, 4 April 1972.
51. *Ibid.*, 8 February 1972.
52. See 'Postscript' facing p. 196 in Kotelawala.
53. See Jansen, p. 161.
54. *Ibid.*
55. See report of the proceedings of the House of Representatives in *Ceylon Daily News,* 1 December 1971.
56. *Ibid.*
57. *Ibid.*
58. See the text of his address to the U.N. General Assembly, New York, on 22 November 1956 in *The Foreign Policy of Ceylon*, pp. 5–9.
59. Mrs Bandaranaike wrote to heads of government of all U.N. countries soliciting their support for Ceylon's candidate: see *Ceylon Daily News,* 3 June 1971.
60. For the full text of Mrs Bandaranaike's speech, see *ibid.*, 13 October 1971.
61. *Ibid.*
62. For the full text see *ibid.*, 20 January 1971.
63. See *ibid.*, 19 April 1972.
64. The figures in this paragraph are obtained from the *Annual Report of the Central Bank for 1970,* the *Budget Speech 1970–71* by Dr N. M. Perera, and B. A. D. Wijewardene's 'Official External Debt and the Debt Servicing Capacity of Ceylon', in *Staff Papers*, pp. 111–29.
65. Wijewardene, 'Official External Debt . . .' pp. 113–14.
66. For the full text of these Letters of Intent, see the *Budget Speech 1970–71*, pp. 6–10.
67. See *Ceylon Daily News,* 28 March, 1972.
68. *Ibid.*
69. See *Foreign Aid*, table 1, p. 35.
70. The figures have been obtained from *ibid.*, pp. 29–30 and table 7 facing p. 42.
71. *Ibid.*
72. See I.B.R.D.–I.D.A., *The Problem of Foreign Exchange and Long-Term Growth of Ceylon* (Colombo: Ministry of Planning and Economic Affairs, 1968), paragraph 10.
73. The data is collected from *Foreign Aid*, and newspaper reports.
74. Quoted in *Ceylon Daily News,* 26 October 1970.
75. See *ibid.*, 21 July 1970.
76. See text of press communique from the Ministry of Defence and External Affairs in *ibid.*, 30 July 1970.
77. See Kotelawala, p. 139.
78. See Dr N. M. Perera's statement in *Ceylon Daily News,* 14 August 1971.
79. See report of press interview given by the minister of foreign and internal trade to the *Ceylon Observer Magazine Edition,* 11 March 1971.
80. For the details see *Ceylon Daily News,* 2 March 1971.
81. For a very useful analysis on how beneficial to Ceylon trade has been

with the communist states, see the article entitled 'Our Trade with Socialist Countries' by T. Pathmanahan in *ibid.*, 7 April 1971.

82. See *ibid.*, 8 April 1971.
83. Jansen, p. 55. Ceylon was not an independent state nor had she progressed even towards the limited self government envisaged under the Soulbury Constitution which was to take effect in October 1947. D. S. Senanayake nevertheless was for all intents and purposes acknowledged as the Ceylonese leader and chief minister by the imperial authorities. Bandaranaike could therefore be regarded as his representative.
84. See speech on external affairs made on 17 June 1952 as leader of the opposition in *Towards a New Era*, p. 808.
85. *Ibid.*
86. *Ibid.*, p. 809.
87. See Jayawardene's speech at the U.N. Day dinner in *Ceylon Daily News*, 25 October 1952, and at the annual general meeting of the Ceylon Merchants' Chamber in *ibid.*, 30 October 1952.
88. See Kotelawala, p. 130.
89. *Ibid.*, pp. 139 and 140.
90. *Ibid.*, p. 172.
91. *Ibid.*, p. 127.
92. See *ibid.*, pp. 184–94.
93. *Ibid.*, p. 185. It was his view that the Taiwanese should be allowed to work out their own destinies without coercion from the nationalists or the communists.
94. See *Towards a New Era*, p. 834.
95. See, e.g. Weerawardena, *Ceylon General Election 1956*, pp. 74, 77 and 149.
96. See *The Foreign Policy of Ceylon*, pp. 14–15.
97. See Bandaranaike's address at the Chinese Commodity Exhibition in Colombo on 18 March 1958 and his address to the Ceylon Chamber of Commerce on 27 March 1958 in *ibid.*, pp. 65–9.
98. For the text of these statements, refer *ibid.*, pp. 101–22.
99. See J. P. Anand, 'Sino-Ceylonese Relations', *The Institute for Defence Studies and Analyses Journal*, vol. 3, no. 3 (January 1971), p. 329.
100. See *Ceylon Daily News*, 27 May 1971 for the full text of the letter.
101. See text of an exclusive interview Mrs Bandaranaike gave the editor of the *Ceylon Observer*, *The Ceylon Observer Magazine Edition*, 10 October 1971; also text of interview by Mrs Bandaranaike to Frank Giles (*The Sunday Times*, London) also published in *Ceylon Daily News*, 5 November 1971. Also refer text of a letter sent by Sri Lanka's ambassador in Peking to Mrs Bandaranaike on a conversation he is reported to have had with Chou En-lai which was read out by the minister of posts and telecommunications in the Senate in *Ceylon Daily News*, 18 June 1971. The ambassador is reported to have written that Chou En-lai was 'highly concerned about the developments in Sri Lanka, especially with regard to the suspicions that Chinese arms were being smuggled in crates that were delivered at the construction site of the Bandaranaike Memorial Hall' and had also 'expressed regret that China was unable to provide military aid to Sri Lanka as Chinese ships carrying arms to Tanzania had left Colombo before Sri Lanka's request was made'. The Chinese prime minister had further stated that China

disapproved of the theories of the Che Guevara and had denounced the insurrectionists as counter-revolutionaries.

102. See text of Mrs Bandaranaike's interview to the editor, *Ceylon Observer*, *The Ceylon Observer Magazine Edition*, 10 October 1971.

CHAPTER 7

1. See Rajni Kothari, 'The Congress "System" in India', *Asian Survey*, 4 (December 1964), pp. 1161–73, W. H. Morris-Jones, 'Dominance and Dissent: Their Inter-relations in the Indian Party System', *Government and Opposition*, 1 (August 1966), pp. 451–66, and his *Government and Politics of India* (London, 1964), chapter V.
2. See The National Operations Council, *The May 13 Tragedy: A Report* (Kuala Lumpur, 1969).
3. See his *The Idea of Nationalism: A Study in its Origins and Background* (New York, 1961).
4. See his *Nationalism and Social Communication* (Massachusetts, 1953), p. 164.
5. See Ananda Guruge's edition of the speeches, essays and letters of the foremost of Sinhalese Buddhist nationalists, Anagarika Dharmapala, in *Return to Righteousness* (Colombo, 1965) and D. C. Vijayavardhana's thought-provoking and seminal work on Sinhalese Buddhist nationalism, *The Revolt in the Temple: Composed to Commemorate 2500 Years of the Land, the Race and the Faith* (Colombo, 1953). R. Kearney's *Communalism and Language in the Politics of Ceylon* (Durham, North Carolina, 1968) gives a detailed and excellent analysis of Sinhalese nationalism from British times to developments in the post independence years.
6. See his chapter 'The integrative revolution: Primordial sentiments and civil politics in the new states', in Clifford Geertz (ed.), *Old Societies and New States: The Quest for Modernity in Asia and Africa* (New York, 1963), pp. 105–57.
7. *Ibid.*
8. Princeton, New Jersey, 1960.
9. London, 1963.
10. Durham, North Carolina, 1967.
11. See his *Political Parties: A Behavioural Analysis* (Chicago, 1964), pp. 1–13 for further details.
12. See his *Political Parties* (Glencoe: Illinois, 1949), pp. 374–6.
13. *Ibid.*
14. See his *Political Parties* (London and New York, 1954).

Bibliographical Note

H. A. I. Goonetilleke's monumental two-volume work, *A Bibliography of Ceylon: A systematic guide to the literature on the land, people, history and culture published in Western Languages from the sixteenth century to the present day* (Switzerland, 1970) makes any notes on the literature of politics superfluous. But some select references may be helpful to the discriminating reader in need of ready material.

No detailed information on the history of Sri Lanka is necessary, because it is not an integral part of this work other than the interest we have focused on the island's constitutional evolution from colonial status to independence under the British auspices. Parts I and II of Volume I of the University of Ceylon, *History of Ceylon* (Colombo, 1959 and 1960) are the most useful sources for information from earliest times to 1505; while general works such as Ludowyk's *The Story of Ceylon* (London, 1962) and Arasaratnam's *Ceylon* (Englewood Cliffs, N.J., 1964) provide a continuous account from earliest times to the present day.

Lennox Mills's *Ceylon under British Rule 1795–1832* (London, 1933) and G. C. Mendis's *Ceylon under the British* (Colombo, 1952) are useful for their sections on constitutional development, while Pakeman's *Ceylon* (London, 1964) and Ludowyk's *The Modern History of Ceylon* (London, 1966) are excellent for their sections on political developments in the British and post-independence phases up to the early sixties.

Namasivayam's *The Legislatures of Ceylon* (London, 1951) is particularly good on the analysis of constitutional progress from the 1920s up to and including the Donoughmore period, while Weerawardena's *Government and Politics in Ceylon (1931–1946)* is the best on the Donoughmore constitution. The two constitutional documents Command 3131, *Report of the Donoughmore Commission*, 1928, and Command 6677, *Report of the Soulbury*

Commission, are particularly useful, and Jeffries's *Ceylon: The Path to Independence* (London, 1962) provides inside information on the subject in question.

Kotelawala's *An Asian Prime Minister's Story* (London, 1956), Fernanado's *Three Prime Ministers of Ceylon: An 'Inside Story'* (Colombo, 1963) and Jeffries's *A Biography of Sir Oliver E. Goonetilleke* (London, 1969) are good biographical material containing relevant political information.

The best on the politics of Sri Lanka are Jennings's *The Constitution of Ceylon* (3rd edition, Bombay, 1953), Wriggins's *Ceylon: the Dilemmas of a New Nation* (Princeton, 1960), Farmer's *Ceylon: A Divided Nation* (London, 1963), Smith's chapters on political Buddhism in post-1956 Ceylon in his (editor) *South Asian Politics and Religion* (Princeton, 1966) pp. 453–509, Singer's *The Emerging Elite: A Study of Political Leadership in Ceylon* (Durham, North Carolina, 1968), Lerski's *Origins of Trotskyism in Ceylon* (Stanford, 1968), Woodward's *Growth of a Party System in Ceylon* (Providence, 1968), Kearney's *Trade Unions and Politics in Ceylon* (Berkeley, 1971) and Kumari Jayawardene's *The Rise of the Labour Movement in Ceylon* (Durham, North Carolina, 1972).

Studies on general elections, providing evidence and analyses of political events at the time and their results, are available in Jennings, 'The Ceylon General Election of 1947' in *University of Ceylon Review*, Vol. VI, No. 3 (July 1948), pp. 133–95, Weerawardena, 'The General Elections in Ceylon, 1952' in *Ceylon Historical Journal*, Vol. II, Nos 1 and 2 (July, October 1952), pp. 111–78, and Weerawardena, *Ceylon General Election 1956* (Colombo 1960). Party manifestos, the bio-data of winning candidates and election statistics are to be found in the Ceylon Daily News, *Parliament of Ceylon* for 1947, 1956 (none was produced for 1952), 1960, 1965 and 1970.

Useful additional bibliographical information can be obtained from Wriggins, pp. 471–83, and Woodward, pp. 323–32.

Index